HERE'S WHAT OTHERS SAY ABOUT THIS EXCITING BOOK:

Walt Brown's book is the rarest of species: It is the most complete reference work I have encountered on the scientific aspects of the multifaceted subject of origins and at the same time presents a comprehensive theoretical framework (his hydroplate theory) for reconciling the many seemingly unrelated, and sometimes apparently contradictory, facts that bear on these questions. This book is essential for any teacher or student who is serious about resolving these issues on the basis of the evidences rather than opinions or unsubstantiated or unverifiable hypotheses.

> Dr. C. Stuart Patterson
> Professor of Chemistry, Emeritus and former Academic Dean
> Furman University
> Greenville, South Carolina

Most high school students are inherently interested in origins. Until recently this topic has been difficult to teach because there have been many books that present the case for evolution, but very few resources that clearly explain the scientific case for creation. As a public high school biology teacher for more than 25 years, I find *In The Beginning: Compelling Evidence for Creation and the Flood* to be the most concise, scholarly treatment of the scientific evidence supporting a creation model of origins that I have ever read. This book is a must for every science teacher's reading list and I think it would be a valuable resource in every public school library. Dr. Brown has provided a clear, dispassionate view of science and the quest for answers relating to our origins. Educators should welcome his book as a breath of fresh air.

> Terrence R. Mondy
> Science Teacher
> Wheeling High School
> Wheeling, Illinois

"Classic uniformitarian geology has failed to solve a number of problems in geology. By contrast, using catastrophic basic assumptions, Dr. Brown has given scientists a mode of attacking many problems that is philosophically sound and scientifically acceptable to the objective thinker. Never before have I encountered a more intellectually satisfying and respectable attack on a broad spectrum of geologic and biologic problems that are laid bare in this work."

> Douglas A. Block, Ph.D.
> Geology Professor emeritus
> Rock Valley College
> Rockford, Illinois

"Having given the 5th edition of Walt Brown's *In the Beginning* to scores of people from literally every background, I cannot give too strong a recommendation of this next version. I have lectured on this subject to my students at Georgia Tech and peers in debates. In every setting this book bridges a chasm between concise simplicity and indepth scholarship; the organization of the material in bullet format with supporting documentation allows the reader to plunge into the material at whatever depth he or she chooses. It is impossible to get a grip on one's destiny without also having a firm grip on one's origin; *In the Beginning* is the tool to form a scientific foundation toward that end."

> Kent Davey, Ph.D.
> Technical Director, American MAGLEV Technology
> Edgewater, Florida

"*In the Beginning* is a great creation science book for teens and adults. It's easy to read, carefully researched, meticulously documented, and offers answers to the most important questions of the origins controversy. Besides the usual creation-science approach, . . . the book is unique in explaining for the first time how twenty-one major earth features — including mountains, volcanoes, the Grand Canyon, and ice ages — resulted from a worldwide flood. At the same time, it reveals serious yet little-known problems with many evolutionist ideas about earth history and the origin of life — including many ideas that evolutionists themselves have discarded, but are still taught as fact in children's textbooks. You owe it to yourself to get this book."

> Mary Pride's Big Book of Home Learning
> Volume Three, Science Reviews

Preface to the Special Edition

As the reader of this book, you may have several questions: Why was the book written? How is it organized and why? For whom is it intended?

Frequently people have requested that we publish a **special edition** of *In the Beginning*—one without biblical references. Such an edition would be appropriate for libraries, public schools, many colleges and universities, and people who want only a scientific approach. Powerful insights into our origins can easily be made without the Bible. Perhaps the best way to show this to simply publish this special edition.

This study of the creation/evolution issue began unexpectedly in June of 1970. I was an evolutionist and a new professor at the U.S. Air Force Academy. I heard some surprising claims that there was evidence for a global, mountain-covering flood. Such a flood was always hard for me to imagine. After all, where could so much water come from? Where did all the water go? Every attempt I had heard to answer the first question was inadequate at best. Few, if any, ever tried to answer the second.

However, if that much water sloshed around on the earth for a year, many dead animals and plants should be buried in vast amounts of mud and other sediments. This would nicely explain how most fossils formed, especially those on the highest mountains. But the fossil record was supposedly the best evidence for evolution, a theory I had passively accepted. If a global flood produced most fossils, where was the evidence for evolution?

The more I struggled with this question, the more amazed I became at the lack of evidence supporting evolution and the abundant evidence supporting creation. By 1972, I had become a creationist.

As I began to talk with friends and colleagues about origins, invitations to speak arose. Speaking publicly on the subject forced me to organize my thoughts. In this way, the early drafts of the first edition of this book began to "evolve."

By 1978, my wife and I decided that the subject was so broad and important that I needed to devote myself full-time to study, research, writing, and occasional speaking engagements. Therefore, I should leave a demanding, interesting, and successful military career at the first opportunity. That came in 1980. Since then, study, writing, debates, *In the Beginning* Seminars, and other speaking engagements have kept me busy.

Initially, those attending the *In the Beginning* Seminar, a 6-7 hour program, were given handout material summarizing the seminar and many frequently asked questions. The first three editions of this book served that purpose. Requests for the book grew to the point that it had to be modified for those who had not attended the seminar. However, the book's basic organization still follows the seminar format.

The seminar begins with a 90-minute summary of the scientific evidence dealing with origins. That evidence falls into nine areas, three in the life sciences, three in the astronomical and physical sciences, and three in the earth sciences. Part I of this book summaries these many evidences. The seminar audience then votes as a group for two of the nine areas about which they wish to hear more details, typically 60-90 minutes each. Part II of this book contains the most popular of those nine choices. The last speaking portion of the seminar is an hour of questions and answers. Having heard thousands of such queries, I have anticipated many of your questions in Part III.

This format allows the audience (reader) to go in the direction of greatest interest in the time (pages) available, and yet always see "the big picture." The intended reader is anyone interested in the subject of origins—high school students with little scientific interest to those with multiple Ph.D.'s in science. Some parents have even paraphrased bite-sized topics for their children at mealtime or bedtime.

I would like to make a special offer to students at all levels. This book contradicts what some schools teach about origins. Let me make a proposal. As you read this book, note questions to raise with your teachers. If they disagree with any scientific aspects of this book, I would be pleased to cordially discuss it with them, provided you are present. Doing this by telephone would be easiest for all. Simply send me a letter giving some specifics, and I will send you a telephone number and several times when I can be reached. If you and your teacher or professor wish, you may record our three-way conversation for the rest of your class to hear. If nothing else, the process will sharpen everyone's critical thinking skills, put more information "on the table," and move us all a little closer to the truth.

Many have helped with this book and offered constructive suggestions. To each person I am very grateful. The mistakes, of course, are mine alone. I especially appreciate the help of my assistant, Brad Anderson, who used his considerable talents in designing the book and preparing it for publication.

My hope is that *In the Beginning: Compelling Evidence for Creation and the Flood* will help you, the reader, as you explore the amazing events "in the beginning."

Walt Brown

In the Beginning

Compelling Evidence for Creation and the Flood

by

Walt Brown

CSC CENTER FOR SCIENTIFIC CREATION

5612 NORTH 20TH PLACE   PHOENIX, AZ 85016

HTTP://WWW.INDIRECT.COM/WWW/WBROWN

To my wife, Peggy, and my
parents, Dorothy and Walt,
Sr., with gratitude.

Cover and book design by Bradley W. Anderson

Front Cover: Earth from space, NASA; Saturn, NASA, apparent Plesiosaur, Michihimo Yano; mammoth, Zoological Museum of St. Petersburg; planet composite, NASA; Grand Canyon, copyright-LANDISCOR INC.

Back Cover: Steve Daniels

In the Beginning: Compelling Evidence for Creation and the Flood
First edition, 1980, Sixth Edition, © 1995, Special Edition, © 1996
Copyright © 1996 by Walter T. Brown, Jr. All rights reserved.

Center for Scientific Creation
5612 N. 20th Place
Phoenix, AZ 85016

http://www.indirect.com/www/wbrown

Library of Congress Catalog Card Number: 96-84303
Brown, Walter T., Jr. 1937 -
In the Beginning: Compelling Evidence for Creation and the Flood
Includes index
      1. Science. 2. Creation-evolution. 3. Evolution. 4. Life-origin. 5. Universe-origin
      I. Title II. Brown, Walt

ISBN 1-878026-05-4 (softcover)
ISBN 1-878026-06-2 (hardcover)

Printed in Hong Kong

Contents

Figure 1

Part I:

The Scientific Case for Creation

Part I is a brief summary, in outline form, of 118 categories of scientific evidence that supports a sudden creation and opposes gradual evolution. Usually these details are based on research done by evolutionists who are experts in that particular, narrow field. By choosing evolutionists rather than creationists, charges of bias will be avoided.

For many years, students, teachers, and professors have been unaware of most of this information, especially the broader conclusions that can be reached. Scientific infor-mation cannot be suppressed for long, and so it is not surprising that there is a growing awareness and excitement concerning these evidences. Some of this information has been largely unknown for over a century. Other evidence involves new discoveries. If all these evidences were openly presented in the science classroom, better education would result. Regardless of your age or education, you can learn and help others learn new information on a subject that holds great interest for most people—the subject of origins.

Figure 2: Dog Variability. By progressively breeding for certain traits, dogs can be different and distinctive. This is a common example of microevolution—differences in size, shape, color, and chemistry. It is not macroevolution—the upward progression in complexity from bacteria to man. Macroevolution has never been observed in any breeding experiment.

Life Sciences

Before considering how life began, we must first understand the term "organic evolution." Organic evolution, as theorized, is a naturally occurring, beneficial change that produces increasing and inheritable complexity. Increased complexity would be shown if the offspring of one form of life had a different and improved set of vital organs. This is sometimes called the molecules-to-man theory—or *macroevolution*. (See Figure 3 on page 4.) *Microevolution*, on the other hand, does not involve increasing complexity. It only involves minor chemical alterations or changes in size, shape, or color. Microevolution can be thought of as "horizontal" change, whereas macroevolution (if it were ever observed) would involve an "upward" and beneficial change in complexity. Notice that microevolution plus time will not produce macroevolution. [*micro + time ≠ macro*]

Both creationists and evolutionists agree that microevolution occurs. Minor change has been observed since history began. But notice how often evolutionists give evidence for microevolution to support macroevolution. It is macroevolution, which requires new abilities and increasing complexity, that is at the center of the creation-evolution controversy. In this book, *the term "organic evolution" will therefore mean macroevolution.*

(Most readers will want to read the accompanying references and notes that begin on page 32.)

The Theory of Organic Evolution Is Invalid.

Organic Evolution Has Never Been Observed.

1. The Law of Biogenesis
Spontaneous generation (the emergence of life from nonliving matter) has never been observed. All observations have shown that life comes only from life. This has been observed so consistently that it is called the law of biogenesis. The theory of evolution conflicts with this law by claiming that life came from nonliving matter through natural processes.[a]

2. Acquired Characteristics
Acquired characteristics cannot be inherited.[a] For example, the long necks of giraffes did not result from their ancestors stretching their necks to reach high leaves. Nor can the large muscles acquired by a man in a weight lifting program be inherited by his child.

3. Mendel's Laws
Mendel's laws of genetics and their modern-day refinements explain almost all physical variations observed in living things. Mendel discovered that genes (the units of heredity) are merely reshuffled from one generation to another.   Different **combinations** are formed, not different genes. The different combinations produce the many variations within each kind of life, such as in the dog family. (See Figure 2 on page 2.) A logical consequence of Mendel's laws is that there are **limits** to such variation.[a] Breeding experiments[b] and common observations[c] have also confirmed these boundaries.

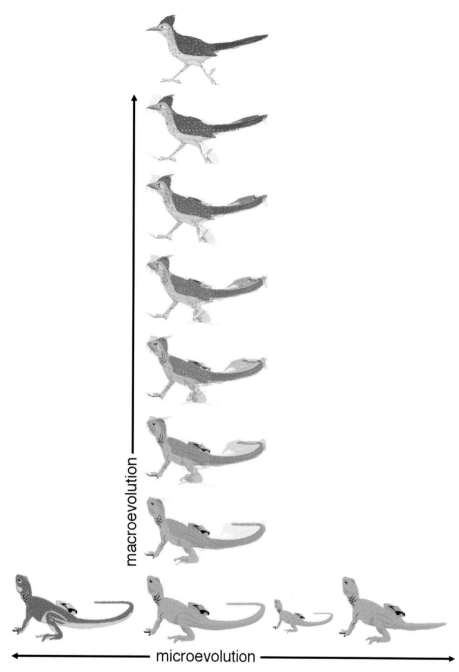

Figure 3: Microevolution vs. Macroevolution. Notice that macroevolution would require an upward change in the complexity of certain traits and organs. Microevolution only involves horizontal changes, or no increasing complexity.

Since science should always base its conclusions on what is seen and reproducible, what can be observed? We see variations in lizards, four of which are shown at the bottom. We also see birds, represented at the top. The inbetween forms (or intermediates), which should be vast in number if macroevolution occurred, are never seen—as fossils or living species.

Ever since Darwin, evolutionists have had to make excuses for why the world and our fossil museums are not overflowing with intermediates.

5. Natural Selection
Natural selection cannot produce **new** genes; it only **selects** among preexisting characteristics.[a] For example, many have mistakenly believed that resistances "evolved" in response to pesticides and antibiotics. Instead, a few resistant insects and bacteria were already present when the pesticides and antibiotics were first applied. The vulnerable insects and bacteria were killed, allowing resistant varieties, which then had less competition, to proliferate. While natural selection occurred, nothing evolved and, in fact, some biological diversity was lost.[b]

The variations Darwin observed among finches on different Galapagos islands is another example of natural selection producing micro- (**not** macro-) evolution. In other words, while natural selection sometimes explains the survival of the fittest, it does not explain the origin of the fittest.[c] Actually, natural selection prevents major evolutionary changes.[d]

4. Bounded Variations
While Mendel's laws give a **theoretical** explanation for why variations are limited, there is broad **experimental** verification as well. For example, if evolution happened, organisms (such as bacteria) that quickly produce the most offspring, should have the most variations and mutations. Natural selection would then select the more favorable changes, allowing them to survive, reproduce, and pass on their beneficial genes. Their offspring should tend to inherit short reproduction cycles and produce many "children." We see the opposite. In general, more complex organisms, such as humans, have fewer offspring and longer reproduction cycles.[a] Again, it appears that variations within existing kinds of organisms are bounded.

6. Mutations
Mutations are the only known means by which new genetic material becomes available for evolution.[a] Rarely, if ever, is a mutation beneficial to an organism in its natural environment. Almost all observable mutations are harmful; some are meaningless; many are lethal.[b] No

known mutation has ever produced a form of life having greater complexity and viability than its ancestors.[c]

7. Fruit Flies

More than ninety years[a] of fruit fly experiments, involving 3,000 consecutive generations, give absolutely no basis for believing that any natural or artificial process can cause an increase in complexity and viability. No clear genetic improvement has ever been observed in any form of life, despite the many unnatural efforts to increase mutation rates.[b]

8. Complex Organs

There is no reason to believe that mutations or any natural process could ever produce any new organs—especially those as complex as the eye,[a] the ear, or the brain.[b] For example, an adult human brain contains over 10^{14} (a hundred thousand billion) electrical connections[c], more than all the electrical connections in all the electrical appliances in the world. Just the human heart, a ten-ounce pump that will operate without maintenance or lubrication for about 75 years, is an engineering marvel.[d]

9. Fully-Developed Organs

All species appear completely developed, not partially developed. They show design.[a] There are no examples of half-developed feathers, eyes,[b] skin, tubes (arteries, veins, intestines, etc.), or any of thousands of other vital organs. Tubes that are not 100% complete are a liability; so are partially developed organs. For example, if a leg of a reptile were to evolve into a wing of a bird, it would become a bad leg long before it became a good wing.[c] (See Figure 3.)

10. Distinct Types

If evolution happened, one would expect to see gradual transitions among many living things. For example, variations of dogs might blend in with variations of cats. Actually, some animals, such as the duckbilled platypus, have organs completely unrelated to their alleged evolutionary ancestors. The platypus has fur, is warm-blooded, and suckles its young like mammals. It lays leathery eggs, has a single ventral opening (for elimination, mating, and birth), and has claws and a shoulder girdle like most reptiles. The platypus can detect electrical currents (a.c. and d.c.) like some fish, and has a bill like a duck (a bird). It has webbed forefeet like an otter, a flat tail like a beaver, and the male can inject poisonous venom like a pit viper. Such "patchwork" animals and plants, called mosaics, have no logical place on the evolutionary tree.

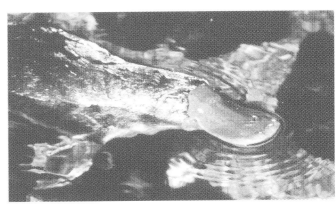

Figure 4: Duckbilled Platypus. The duckbilled platypus is only found in Tasmania and eastern Australia. European scientists who first studied platypus specimens thought some clever taxidermist had stitched together parts of different animals. Its "patchwork" appearance is only seen by those who believe each animal must have close similarities with other animals. Actually, the platypus is perfectly designed for its environment.

There is no direct evidence that any major group of animals or plants arose from any other major group.[a] Species are only observed going out of existence (extinctions), never coming into existence.[b]

11. Altruism

Many animals, including humans, will endanger or even sacrifice their lives to save another—sometimes the life of a member of a completely different species.[a] According to evolution theory, natural selection, which supposedly explains all individual characteristics, should eliminate such altruistic, or sacrificial, behavior. How could risky behavior that only benefits another ever be inherited, since its possession tends to prevent the altruistic individual from passing on its genes for altruism?[b] If evolution is correct, selfish behavior should have completely eliminated unselfish behavior. Furthermore, cheating and aggressiveness would have "weeded out" cooperation. Altruism contradicts evolution.[c]

12. Extraterrestrial Life?

No verified form of extraterrestrial life of any kind has ever been observed. If evolution had occurred on earth, one would expect that at least simple forms of life, such as microbes, would have been found by the elaborate experiments sent to the moon and Mars. (See **"Is There Life in Outer Space?"** on page 159.)

13. Languages

Nonhumans communicate, but not with language. True language requires both vocabulary and grammar. With great effort, human trainers have taught some chimpanzees to recognize a few hundred spoken words, to point

Figure 5: Mars Lander. Many people, including Carl Sagan, predicted that life would be found on Mars. Their rationale was that since life evolved on Earth, some form of life must have evolved on Mars. That prediction proved to be false. The arms of the Mars Lander, shown above, sampled the Martian soil. The sophisticated test performed on those samples did not even find a trace of a germ.

to up to 200 symbols, and to make limited hand signs. These impressive feats are sometimes exaggerated by capturing and editing the animals' successes on film. (Some early demonstrations were flawed by the trainer's hidden promptings.[a])

Chimpanzees have not demonstrated these skills in the wild and do not pass their skills on to other chimpanzees. When a trained chimp dies, so does the trainer's investment. Also, trained chimps have essentially no grammatical ability. Only with grammar can a few words express many ideas. No evidence exists that language evolves in nonhumans.

Did language evolve in humans? Charles Darwin claimed it did. If so, the earliest languages should be the simplest. On the contrary, language studies reveal that the more ancient the language (for example: Latin, 200 B.C.; Greek, 800 B.C.; and Vedic Sanskrit, 1500 B.C.), the more complex it is with respect to syntax, case, gender, mood, voice, tense, and verb form. The best evidence indicates that languages devolve; that is, they become simpler rather than more complex.[b] Most linguists reject the idea that simple languages evolve into complex languages.[c]

14. Speech
Speech is uniquely human.[a] Furthermore, studies of 36 documented cases of children raised without human contact (feral children) show that speech appears to be learned only from other humans. Apparently, humans do not automatically speak. If this is so, the first humans must have been endowed with a speaking ability. There is no evidence that speech has evolved.[b]

15. Codes and Programs
In our experience, codes are produced only by intelligence, not by natural processes or chance. A code is a set of rules for converting information from one useful form to another. Examples include the Morse Code and Braille. The genetic material that controls the physical processes of life is coded information. It also is accompanied by elaborate transmission, translation, and duplication systems, without which the genetic material would be useless, and life would cease. Therefore, it seems most reasonable to conclude that the genetic code, the accompanying transmission, translation, and duplication systems, and all living organisms were produced by an extremely high level of intelligence using nonnatural (or supernatural) processes.

Likewise, no natural process has ever been observed to produce a program. A program is a planned sequence of steps to accomplish some goal. Computer programs are common examples. The information stored in the genetic material of all life is a complex program. Since programs are not produced by chance or natural processes, the most probable conclusion is that some intelligent, supernatural source developed these programs.

16. Information
All isolated systems contain specific, but perishable, amounts of information.[a] No isolated, nontrivial system has ever been observed to spontaneously increase its information content. Natural processes, without exception, destroy information. Only outside intelligence can increase the information content of an otherwise isolated system. All scientific observations are consistent with this generalization, which has three corollaries or consequences:

- Macroevolution cannot occur.[b]

- Outside intelligence was involved in the creation of the universe and all forms of life.[c]

- A "big bang" did not and could not precede life.[d]

The Arguments for Evolution Are Outdated and Often Illogical.

17. A Common Designer
It is illogical to maintain that similarities between different forms of life always imply a common ancestor;[a] they may imply a common designer. In fact, in cases where experiments have shown that similar structures are controlled by different genes[b] or developed from different parts of embryos,[c] a common designer is the more likely explanation.

18. Vestigial Organs
The existence of human organs whose function is unknown does not imply that they are vestiges of organs inherited from our evolutionary ancestors.[a] As medical knowledge has increased, at least some functions of all organs have been discovered.[b] For example, the human appendix was once thought to be a useless remnant from our evolutionary past. Today it is known that the appendix plays a role in antibody production and protects part of the intestine from infections. Its removal also increases a person's susceptibility to leukemia, Hodgkin's disease, cancer of the colon, and cancer of the ovaries. Indeed, the absence of true vestigial organs implies that evolution never happened.

19. Two-Celled Life?
Many single-celled forms of life exist, but there are no known forms of animal life with 2, 3, 4, or 5 cells.[a] Even the forms of life with 6-20 cells are parasites. They must have a complex animal as a host to provide such functions as digestion and respiration. If macroevolution happened, one should find many forms of life with 2-20 cells as transitional forms between one-celled and many-celled organisms.

20. Embryology
As an embryo develops, it does not repeat an evolutionary sequence. Embryologists no longer consider the superficial similarities that exist between a few embryos and the adult forms of simpler animals as evidence for evolution.[a] It is now known that Ernst Haeckel, who popularized this incorrect but widespread belief, deliberately falsified his drawings.[b]

21. Rapid Burial
Fossils all over the world show evidences of rapid burial. Many fossils, such as fossilized jellyfish,[a] show by the details of their soft, fleshy portions[b] that they were buried rapidly, before they could decay. Many other animals,

Figure 6: Polystrate Fossil. Fossils that cross two or more sedimentary layers (strata) are called poly (many) strate (strata) fossils. Consider how quickly this tree trunk must have been buried. Had it been slowly, its top would have decayed. Obviously, the tree could not have grown up through the strata without sunlight and air. The only alternative is ***rapid burial***. Some polystrate trees are upside down, something that might occur in a large flood. Similar trees were observed in the process of being buried in the lake-bottom sediments of Spirit Lake soon after Mount St. Helens erupted in 1980. Polystrate tree trunks are found at many places. The above tree is in Germany.

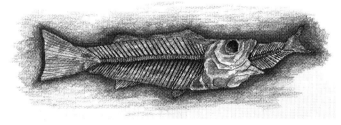

Figure 7: Fish Swallowing Another Fish. The fossilization process must have been quite rapid to have caught a fish in the act of swallowing another fish. Thousands of such fossils have been found.

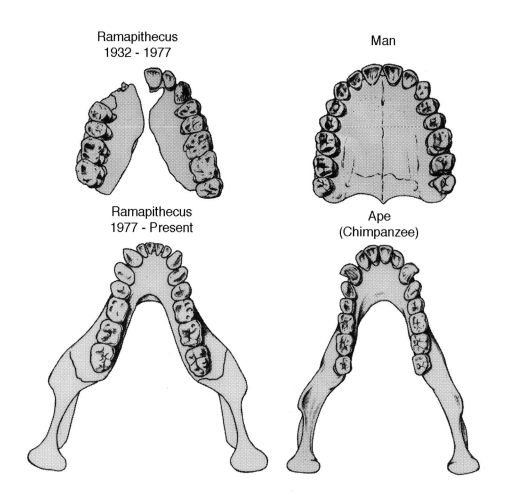

Ramapithecus
1932 - 1977

Man

Ramapithecus
1977 - Present

Ape
(Chimpanzee)

Figure 8: *Ramapithecus*. Some textbooks still claim *Ramapithecus* is man's ancestor, an intermediate between man and some apelike ancestor. This mistaken belief resulted from piecing together, in 1932, fragments of upper teeth and bones into the two large pieces shown in the upper left corner. This was done so the teeth resembled the parabolic arch of man, shown in the upper right. In 1977, the complete lower jaw of *Ramapithecus* was found. The true shape of the jaw was not parabolic, but rather U-shaped, a distinctive of apes.

buried in mass graves and in twisted and contorted positions, suggest violent and rapid burials over large areas.[c] These observations, together with the occurrence of compressed fossils and fossils that cut across two or more layers of sedimentary rock, are strong evidence that the sediments encasing these fossils were deposited rapidly—not over hundreds of millions of years. Furthermore, almost all sediments were sorted by water. The worldwide fossil record is, therefore, evidence of the rapid death and burial of animal and plant life by a worldwide, catastrophic flood. The fossil record is not evidence of slow change.[d]

22. Parallel Strata

The earth's sedimentary layers are typically parallel to adjacent layers. Such uniform layers are seen, for example, in the Grand Canyon and in road cuts in mountainous terrain. Had these parallel layers been deposited slowly over thousands of years, erosion would have cut many channels in the topmost layers. Their subsequent burial by other sediments would produce nonparallel patterns. Since parallel layers are the general rule, and the earth's surface erodes rapidly, one can conclude that almost all sedimentary layers were deposited rapidly relative to the local erosion rate—not over long periods of

time. (For an understanding of the mechanisms involved, see pages 135-145.)

23. Fossil Gaps

If evolution happened, the fossil record should show continuous and gradual changes from the bottom to the top layers. Actually, many gaps or discontinuities appear throughout the fossil record.[a] Fossil links are missing between numerous plants,[b] between single-celled forms of life and invertebrates, between invertebrates and vertebrates,[c] between fish and amphibians,[d] between amphibians and reptiles,[e] between reptiles and mammals,[f] between reptiles and birds,[g] between primates and other mammals,[h] and between apes and other primates.[i] The fossil record has been studied so thoroughly that it is safe to conclude that these gaps are real; they will never be filled.[j] (See **What Was Archaeopteryx?** on page 148.)

24. Missing Trunk

The evolutionary tree has no trunk. In the earliest part of the fossil record (generally the Cambrian sedimentary rock layers), life appears suddenly, full-blown, complex, diversified,[a] and dispersed—worldwide.[b] Complex species, such as fish,[c] worms, corals, trilobites, jellyfish,[d] sponges, mollusks, and brachiopods appear suddenly, with practically no known sign anywhere on earth of gradual development from simpler forms. These layers contain representatives of all plant and animal phyla, including flowering plants,[e] vascular plants,[f] and vertebrates (animals with backbones).[g] Insects, a class comprising four-fifths of all known animals (living and extinct), have no evolutionary ancestors.[h] The fossil record does not support evolution.[i]

25. Out-of-Place Fossils

The vertical sequencing of fossils is frequently not in the assumed evolutionary order.[a] For example, in Uzbekistan, 86 consecutive hoofprints of horses were found in rocks dating back to the dinosaurs.[b] Dinosaur and humanlike footprints have been found together in Turkmenia[c] and in Arizona.[d] Sometimes, land animals, flying animals, and marine animals are fossilized side-by-side in the same rock.[e] Dinosaur, whale, elephant, horse, and many other fossils, plus crude human tools, have reportedly been found in the phosphate beds of South Carolina.[f] In the Grand Canyon, in Venezuela, and in Guyana, spores of ferns and pollen from flowering plants are found in Cambrian[g] and Precambrian[h] rocks—rocks deposited before life supposedly evolved. Coal beds contain round, black lumps called coal balls, some of which contain flowering plants which allegedly evolved 100 million years after the coal bed was formed.[i] A leading authority on the Grand Canyon even published photographs of horselike hoofprints visible in rocks that, according to the theory of evolution, predate hoofed animals by more than a hundred million years.[j] Similar hoofprints are alongside 1000 dinosaur footprints in Virginia.[k]

Petrified trees in the petrified forest of Arizona contain fossilized nests of bees and cocoons of wasps. The petrified forests are supposedly 220 million years old, while bees (and flowering plants which bees require) supposedly evolved 140 million years later.[l] Most evolutionists and textbooks systematically ignore discoveries which conflict with the evolutionary time scale.

26. Ape-Men?

Stories claiming that fossils of primitive, apelike men have been found are overstated.[a]

- It is now universally acknowledged that Piltdown man was a hoax, and yet, it was in textbooks for more than forty years.[b]

- Prior to 1978, the evidence for *Ramapithecus* consisted of a mere handful of teeth and jaw fragments. It is now known that these fragments were pieced together incorrectly by Louis Leakey[c] and others in a form resembling part of the human jaw.[d] *Ramapithe-*

Figure 9: Nebraska Man. Artist's drawings, even those based on speculation, powerfully influence the public. Nebraska man (and presumably Nebraska woman) were mistakenly based on one tooth of an extinct pig. And yet in 1922, *The Illustrated London News* published this picture showing our supposed ancestors. Of course no fossil evidence could support the image conveyed here of a naked man carrying a club.

cus was just an ape.[e] (See Figure 8.)

- The only evidence for Nebraska man turned out to be a pig's tooth. (See Figure 9.)

- Eugene Dubois conceded forty years after he discovered Java "man" that it was just a large gibbon. Dubois also admitted that he had withheld parts of four other thigh bones of apes, found in the same area, which supported that conclusion.[f]

- The skulls of Peking man are considered by many experts to be the remains of apes that were systematically decapitated and exploited for food by true man.[g] The classification *Homo erectus* is considered by most experts to be a category that should never have been created.[h]

- The first confirmed limb bones of *Homo habilis* have recently been discovered. They show that this animal clearly had apelike proportions[i] and should never have been classified as manlike (*Homo*).

- The Australopithecines, which were made famous by Louis and Mary Leakey, are quite distinct from humans. Several detailed computer studies of the Australopithecines have shown that their bodily proportions were not intermediate between man and living apes.[j] Another study of their inner ear bones, that were used to maintain balance, showed a striking similarity with those of chimpanzees and gorillas, but great differences with those of humans. One Australopithecine fossil—a $3\frac{1}{2}$-foot-tall, long-armed, 60-pound adult called Lucy—was initially presented as evidence that all Australopithecines walked upright in a human manner. However, studies of Lucy's entire anatomy, not just a knee joint, now show that this is very unlikely.[k] She probably swung from the trees.[l] The Australopithecines are probably an extinct ape.[m]

- For about 100 years the world was led to believe that Neanderthal man was stooped and apelike. Recent studies show that this erroneous belief was based upon some Neanderthals who were crippled with bone diseases such as arthritis and rickets.[n] Neanderthal man, Heidelberg man, and Cro-Magnon man were completely human. Artists' depictions of them, especially of their fleshy portions, are often quite imaginative and are not supported by the evidence.[o]

Furthermore, the techniques used to date these fossils are highly questionable. (See pages 21-24.)

▲

27. Fossil Man
Bones of many modern-looking humans have been found deep in rocks that, according to evolution, were formed long before man began to evolve. Examples include the Calaveras skull,[a] the Castenedolo skeletons,[b] Reck's skeleton,[c] and many others.[d] Other remains, such as the Swanscombe skull, the Steinheim fossil, and the Vertesszöllos fossil, present similar problems.[e] These remains are almost always ignored by evolutionists.

Life Is So Complex That Chance Processes, Even With Billions of Years, Cannot Explain Its Origin.

▲

28. Chemical Elements of Life
The chemical evolution of life, as you will see in the next few pages, is ridiculously improbable. What could improve the odds? One should begin with an earth having high concentrations of the key elements comprising life, such as: carbon, oxygen, and nitrogen.[a] However, the closer one examines these elements, the more unlikely the evolution of life appears.

Carbon. The rocks that supposedly preceded life have very little carbon.[b] One must imagine a strange, almost unreasonably carbon-rich atmosphere to supply the needed carbon. For comparison, today's atmosphere only holds only 1/30,000th of the carbon that has been on the earth's surface since life first appeared.

Oxygen. Did the early earth have oxygen in its atmosphere? If it did, the compounds (called amino acids) needed for life to evolve would have been destroyed by oxidation. But if there had been no oxygen, there would have been no ozone in the upper atmosphere, since ozone is simply a form of oxygen. Without ozone to shield the earth, the sun's ultraviolet radiation would destroy life.[c] The only known way for both ozone and life to be here is for both to come into existence simultaneously.

Nitrogen. Nitrogen is easily absorbed by clay and various rocks. Had millions of years passed before life evolved, the sediments that preceded life should be filled with nitrogen. Searches have never located such sediments.[d]

Basic chemistry does not support the evolution of life.[e]

▲

29. Proteins
Living matter is composed largely of proteins—long chains of amino acids. Since 1930, it has been known that amino acids cannot join together if oxygen is present. In other words, proteins could not have evolved from chance chemical reactions if the atmosphere contained oxygen. However, the chemistry of the earth's rocks, both on land and below ancient seas, shows that the earth had oxygen before the earliest fossils formed.[a] Even earlier, oxygen would have been produced by solar radiation breaking water vapor apart into oxygen and hydrogen. Then some hydrogen, the lightest of all chemical elements, would have escaped into outer space, leaving behind oxygen.[b]

To form proteins, amino acids must also be highly concentrated. However, the early oceans or atmosphere would have diluted amino acids to the point where the required collisions between them would rarely occur. Besides, amino acids do not naturally link up to form proteins. Instead, proteins tend to break down into amino acids.[c] Furthermore, the proposed energy sources for forming proteins (the earth's heat, electrical discharges, or the sun's radiation) destroy the protein products thousands of times faster than they could have formed.[d] The many attempts to show how life might have arrived on earth have only demonstrated the futility of the effort, the immense complexity of even the simplest life,[e] and the need for a vast intelligence to precede life.

30. The First Cell

If, despite the virtually impossible odds, proteins arose by chance processes, there is not the remotest reason to believe that they could ever form a membrane-encased, self-reproducing, metabolizing, living cell.[a] There is no evidence that there are any stable states between the assumed naturalistic formation of proteins and the formation of the first living cells. No scientist has ever advanced a testable procedure by which this fantastic jump in complexity could have occurred—even if the entire universe had been filled with proteins.[b]

31. Barriers, Buffers, and Chemical Pathways

Living cells contain thousands of different chemicals, some acidic, others basic. Many chemicals would react with others were it not for an intricate system of chemical barriers and buffers. If living things evolved, these barriers and buffers must have also evolved—but at just the right time to prevent harmful chemical reactions. How could such precise, almost miraculous, events have happened for each of the many millions of species?[a]

All living organisms are maintained by thousands of chemical pathways, each involving a long series of complex chemical reactions. For example, the clotting of blood, which involves twenty to thirty steps, is absolutely vital to help heal a wound. However, clotting could be fatal, if it happened inside the body. Omitting one of the many steps, inserting an unwanted step, or altering the timing of a step would probably cause death. If one thing goes wrong, all the other marvelous steps that were performed flawlessly were in vain. Apparently, these complex pathways were created as an intricate, highly integrated unit.

32. Genetic Distances

Techniques now exist for measuring the degree of similarity between forms of life. These "genetic distances" are calculated by taking a specific protein and examining the sequence of its components. The fewer changes required to convert a protein of one organism into the corresponding protein of another organism, supposedly the closer their relationship. Similar comparisons can now be made between the genetic material (DNA and RNA) of different organisms. The results of these studies seriously contradict the theory of evolution.[a] There is not a trace of evidence at the molecular level for the traditional evolutionary series: simple sea life→fish→amphibians→reptiles→mammals.[b] Each category of organism appears to be almost equally isolated.[c] One computer-based study, using cytochrome c, a protein used in energy production, compared 47 different forms of life. If evolution happened, this study should have found that, for example, the rattlesnake was most closely related to other reptiles. Instead, based on this one protein, the rattlesnake was most similar to man.[d] Since this study, hundreds of similar contradictions have been discovered.

33. Genetic Information

The genetic information contained in each cell of the human body is roughly equivalent to a library of 4,000 books.[a] The probability that mutations and natural selection produced this vast amount of information, even if matter and life somehow arose, is essentially zero.[b] It would be analogous to continuing the following procedure until 4,000 books have been produced:[c]

   a. Start with a meaningful phrase.
   b. Retype the phrase, but make some errors and insert some additional letters.
   c. Examine the new phrase to see if it is meaningful.
   d. If it is, replace the original phrase with it.
   e. Return to step "b."

To accumulate 4,000 books of meaningful information, this procedure would have to produce the equivalent of far more than $10^{40,000}$ animal offspring. (Just to begin to understand how large $10^{40,000}$ is, realize that the visible universe has less than 10^{80} atoms in it.)

34. DNA Production

To produce DNA, a cell requires more than 75 different types of proteins.[a] But these proteins, in turn, are produced only at the direction of DNA.[b] Since each requires the other, a satisfactory explanation for the origin of one must also explain the origin of the other.[c] Apparently, this entire manufacturing system came into existence simultaneously. This implies creation.

35. Handedness: Left and Right

Genetic material, DNA and RNA, is composed of nucleotides. In living things, nucleotides are always "right-handed." (They were initially named "right-handed" because a beam of polarized light passing through them rotated like a right-handed screw.) Nucleotides rarely form outside of life, but when they do, half are left-handed, and half are right-handed. In other words, nucleotides that might have formed before life appeared on earth would be unsuitable for the evolution of life's genetic material.[a]

Each type of amino acid, when found in nonliving material or when synthesized in the laboratory, comes in two chemically equivalent forms. Half are right-handed and half are left-handed—mirror images of each other. However, the amino acids in life, including plants, animals, bacteria, molds, and even viruses, are essentially all left-handed. No known natural process can isolate either the left-handed or the right-handed variety. The mathematical probability that chance processes could produce merely one tiny protein molecule with only left-handed amino acids is virtually zero.[b]

A similar observation can be made concerning a special class of organic compounds called "sugars." In living systems, sugars are all right-handed. Based on our present understanding, natural processes produce equal proportions of left-handed and right-handed sugars. Since the sugars in living things are almost all right-handed, our present understanding leads to the conclusion that random natural processes did not produce life.

If any living thing took in (or ate) amino acids or sugars that had the wrong handedness, the organism's body could not process it. Such food would be useless. Since evolution favors slight variations that enhance survivability and produce more offspring, consider just how advantageous a mutation might be that switched (or inverted) a plant's handedness. "Inverted" (or wrong-handed) trees would proliferate rapidly since they would no longer provide nourishment to bacteria, mold, or termites. "Inverted" forests would fill the continents. Other "inverted" plants and animals would also benefit and would overwhelm the balance of nature. Why do we not see such species with right-handed amino acids and left-handed sugars? Similarly, why are there not more poisonous plants? Why doesn't any beneficial mutation permit its carriers to swamp most other species? Apparently, beneficial mutations are rarer than evolutionists believe. (See **Mutations** on page 4.)

36. Improbabilities

The simplest conceivable form of single-celled life should have at least 600 different protein molecules. The mathematical probability that only one molecule could form by the chance arrangement of the proper sequence of amino acids is far less than 1 in 10^{450}.[a] (The magnitude of the number 10^{450} can begin to be appreciated by realizing that the visible universe is about 10^{28} inches in diameter.)

37. Symbiotic Relationships

Many different forms of life are completely dependent upon each other. Examples include fig trees and the fig gall wasp,[a] the yucca plant and the yucca moth,[b] many parasites and their hosts, and pollen-bearing plants and the honeybee. Even the members of the honeybee family, consisting of the queen, workers, and drones, are interdependent. If one member of each interdependent group evolved first (such as the plant before the animal, or one member of the honeybee family before the others), it could not have survived. Since all members of the group obviously have survived, they must have come into existence at essentially the same time.

Figure 10: Male and Female Birds. Even evolutionists admit that evolution cannot explain sexual reproduction.

38. Sexual Reproduction

If sexual reproduction in plants, animals, and humans is a result of evolutionary sequences, an absolutely unbelievable series of chance events must have occurred at each stage.

a. The amazingly complex, radically different, yet complementary reproductive systems of the male and female must have **completely** and **independently** evolved at each stage at about the **same time** and **place**. Just a slight incompleteness in only one of the two would make both reproductive systems useless, and the organism would become extinct.

b. The physical, chemical, and emotional systems of the male and female would also need to be compatible.

c. The millions of complex products of the male reproductive system (pollen or sperm) must have an affinity for and a mechanical, chemical,[a] and electrical[b] compatibility with the eggs of the female reproductive system.

d. The many intricate processes occurring at the molecular level inside the fertilized egg would have to work with fantastic precision—processes that scientists can only describe in a general sense.

e. The environment of this fertilized egg, from conception through adulthood and until it also reproduced with another sexually capable adult (who also "accidentally" evolved), would have to be tightly controlled.

f. Millions of species must have had a similar string of remarkable "accidents."

Either this series of incredible and complementary events occurred by random, evolutionary processes, or else, an intelligent designer created sexual reproduction.

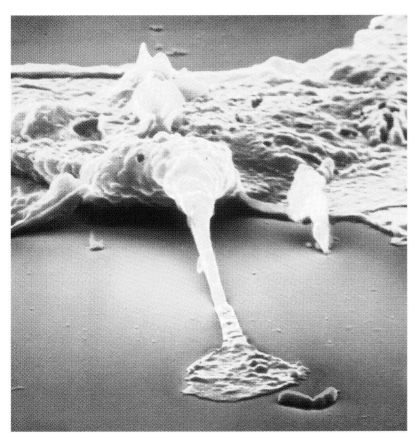

Figure 11: A white blood cell, called neutrophils, is stalking a bacterium, shown in green. Your health, and that of many animals, depends on the effectiveness of these "search and destroy missions." Consider the capabilities and associated equipment the white blood cell must have to do its job. It must identify friend and foe. Once a foe is identified, the white blood cell must rapidly seek and overtake the invader. Then the white blood cell must engulf the bacterium, destroy it, and have the endurance to repeat this many times. Miniaturization, fuel efficiency, and compatibility with other members of the body are also key requirements. The equipment for each function requires careful design. Unless all this worked well from the beginning of life, *a requirement that rules out evolution,* bacteria and other agents of disease would have won, and we would not be here to marvel at these hidden abilities in our bodies.

A few "stem cells" in your bone marrow produce more than 100 billion of these white blood cells a day, plus other types of blood cells. Each white blood cell moves at up to 30 microns (almost half the diameter of a human hair) each minute. So many white blood cells are in your body that their total distance traveled every day would circle the earth twice. © Boehringer Ingelheim International GmbH; photo by Lennart Nilsson.

Furthermore, if sexual reproduction evolved, the steps by which an embryo becomes either a male or a female should be similar for all animals. Actually, these steps vary among the different animals.[c] Finally, evolutionary theory predicts that nature would select asexual rather than sexual reproduction.[d] But if asexual reproduction (the splitting of an organism into two identical organisms) evolved before sexual reproduction, how did complex sexual diversity arise or survive? Evolution cannot explain it.

39. Immune Systems

How could immune systems of animals and plants have evolved? Each immune system can recognize invading bacteria, viruses, and toxins. Each system can quickly mobilize just the right type of defenders to search out and destroy these invaders. Each system has a memory and learns from every attack.

If the many instructions that direct an animal's or plant's immune system were not already programmed into the organism's genetic system when it first appeared on the earth, the first of thousands of potential infections would have destroyed the organism. This would have nullified any rare genetic improvements that might have accumulated. In other words, the large amount of genetic information governing the immune system could not have accumulated in a slow, evolutionary sense.[a] Obviously,

for the organism to have survived, this information must have all been there from the beginning.

40. Living Technology

Most complex phenomena known to science are found in living systems—including electrical, acoustical, mechanical, chemical, and optical phenomena. Detailed studies of various animals have also revealed certain physical equipment and capabilities that cannot even be copied by the world's best designers using the most sophisticated technologies. Examples of these designs include the miniature and reliable sonar systems of dolphins, porpoises, and whales; the frequency-modulated radar and discrimination system of the bat;[a] the aerodynamic capabilities and efficiency of the hummingbird; the control systems, internal ballistics, and combustion chamber of the bombardier beetle;[b] the precise and redundant navigational systems of many birds and fish; and especially the self-repair capabilities of practically all forms of life. Each component of these complex systems could not have evolved without placing the organism at a selective disadvantage. All evidence points to intelligent design.

Many bacteria, such as *Salmonella, Escherichia coli,* and some *Streptococci,* propel themselves with a miniature motor at up to 15 body-lengths per second.[c] These extremely efficient, reversible motors rotate up to 100,000 revolutions per minute.[d] Each shaft rotates a bundle of

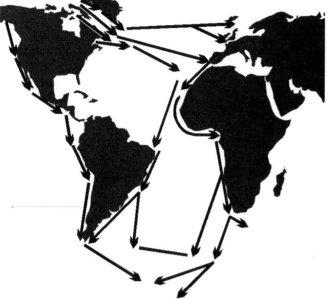

Figure 12: Arctic Tern Migration Route and Cockpit. The arctic tern, a bird of average size, navigates across oceans (as shown above) and returns with the skill normally associated with the navigational equipment in a modern intercontinental aircraft. A round trip for the tern might be 22,000 miles. Of course, the tern's "electronics" are highly miniaturized, extremely reliable, and maintenance free. Furthermore, the tern requires no training. If the equipment in the lower picture could not have evolved, how could the tern's more amazing, corresponding "equipment" have evolved?

whiplike flagella that act as a propeller. The motors, having rotors and stators, are similar in many respects to electrical motors.[e] The electrical charges come from a flow of protons, not electrons. Several million dollars per year are being spent, primarily in Japan, trying to learn how these motors work. Since the bacteria can stop, start, and change directions and speeds, they probably have sophisticated sensors, switches, and control mechanisms. All of this is highly miniaturized. ***Eight million*** of these bacterial motors would fit in the circular cross-section of an average human hair.[f] Evolutionary theory

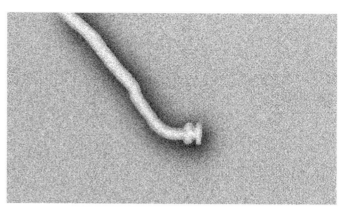

Figure 13: Bacterial Motor. Drawing based on a microphotograph of the flagellum of a salmonella bacterium.

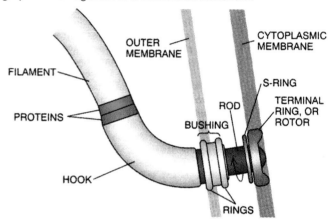

Figure 14: Schematic of a Bacterial Motor. Although there is no complete understanding of how these tiny motors work, the many studies of them have deduced the presence of the above components. From "Learning How Bacteria Swim Could Set New Gears in Motion," by Tom Koppel, figure by Johnny Johnson. Copyright © September 1991 by Scientific American, Inc. All rights reserved.

teaches that bacteria were one of the first forms of life to evolve, and therefore, they are simple. While bacteria are small, they are not simple.

---

41. The Validity of Thought

If life is ultimately the result of random processes or chance, then so is thought. Your thoughts—including what you are thinking now—would, in the final analysis, be a consequence of a long series of accidents. Therefore, your thoughts would have no validity, including the thought that life is a result of chance, or natural, processes.[a] By destroying the validity of ideas, evolution undercuts even the idea of evolution.

We have all heard it said that humans use only a small fraction of their mental abilities. If this is true, how could such unused abilities have evolved? Certainly not by natural selection, since those capabilities are not used.[b]

Life Science Conclusions

After Darwin published *The Origin of Species* in 1859, many came to believe that all forms of life had a common ancestor. Those who believed that over long periods of time molecules had turned into man thought there were only a few gaps in this "evolutionary tree"—gaps that would be filled as scientific knowledge increased. Just the opposite has happened. As science has progressed, the obvious "missing links" in this hypothetical tree have multiplied enormously, and the difficulties in "bridging" these gaps have become even more apparent. For example, in Darwin's day, all life fell into two categories (or kingdoms): animals and plants. Today we know that life falls into five radically different kingdoms, only two of which are animals and plants. This, of course, does not include viruses, which are complex and unique in their own way. In the 1800s, the animal kingdom was divided into four animal phyla; today there are about forty.

Darwin suggested that the first living creature evolved in a "warm little pond." Some recent writers have imagined that life arose in an "organic soup"—a more sophisticated but equally vague version of Darwin's warm pond. We now know that the chance formation of the first living cell is a leap of gigantic proportions, vastly more improbable than the evolution of bacteria into humans. In Darwin's day, a cell was thought to be about as simple as a ping-pong ball. Even today most evolutionists think of bacteria as simple. However, we know that they are marvelously integrated and complex manufacturing plants with many mysteries, such as bacterial motors, yet to be understood. Furthermore, cells come in two radically different types—those with a nucleus and those without. The evolutionary leap from one to the other is staggering to imagine.

The more evolutionists learn about life, the greater complexity they find. A century ago there were no sophisticated microscopes. Consequently, the leaps from single to multiple-cell organisms were also underestimated. The development of the computer has also given us a partial appreciation of the vast electronics, extreme miniaturization, and storage capabilities of the brain. The human eye, which Darwin admitted made him shudder, was only a single jump in complexity. Yet it is now known that there are at least a dozen radically different kinds of eyes, each requiring similar jumps if evolution happened. Likewise, the literal leap that we call flight must have evolved not once, but on at least four different occasions: for certain birds, insects, mammals, and reptiles. Until recently, it was thought that sunlight provided the energy for all life. We now know that at widely separated locations on the dark ocean floor there are complex organisms that use only chemical and thermal energy. For one energy conversion system to evolve into another is analogous to slowly changing a house's heating system from gas to electricity by thousands of rare accidents. Furthermore, these accidents changed only one minor component each year, without the occupants freezing in the winter. In addition, this strange, unexplained process must happen several times in two different oceans. Many other giant leaps must have also occurred if evolution happened: the first photosynthesis, cold-blooded to warm-blooded animals, floating marine plants to vascular plants, placental mammals to marsupials, egg-laying to viviparous animals, insect metamorphosis, the transition of mammals to the sea (whales, dolphins, porpoises, seals, sea lions, and sea cows), the transition of reptiles to the sea (plesiosaurs, ichthyosaurs), and on and on.

The gaps in the fossil record are well known. A century ago evolutionists argued that these gaps would be filled as knowledge increased. Most paleontologists now admit that this prediction failed. Of course, the most famous "missing link" is that between man and apes. However, the term is deceiving. There should be not one intermediate link, but thousands, if the evolutionary tree connects man and apes with their many linguistic, social, mental, and physical differences.

Scientific advancements have shown us that evolution is even more ridiculous than it appeared to people in Darwin's day. ***It is a theory without a mechanism***. Not even appeals to long periods of time will allow simple organisms to "jump gaps" and become more complex and viable. In fact, as will be seen in the next section, long periods of time make such leaps even less likely. All the breeding experiments, which many hoped would show macroevolution, have failed. The arguments used by Darwin and his followers are now discredited or, at best, in dispute, even among evolutionists. Finally, the research of the last several decades has shown that the requirements for life are incredibly complex. Just the design that thinking people can see around them obviously implies a designer. Nevertheless, evolutionists still argue against this design by, oddly enough, using arguments which they spent a great deal of time designing. ***The theory of organic evolution certainly appears to be invalid***.

As we leave the life sciences and examine the astronomical and physical sciences, we will see many other serious difficulties. If the earth, the solar system, our galaxy, or even the heavier chemical elements could not have evolved, as now appears to be the case, then organic evolution could never have even begun.

Figure 15: Unique Planets. This is a composite photograph (not-to-scale) of all the planets in the solar system, except Pluto. From the top, and furthest from your eye, are Mercury, Venus, Earth (and the Moon to the right), Mars, Jupiter, Saturn, Uranus, and Neptune. The photographs were taken by Mariner 10 (Mercury), Pioneer (Venus), Apollo (Earth), earth-based telescopes (Moon and Mars), and Voyager (the four giant planets).

Each planet is unique. Similarities, that one would expect if the planets evolved from the same swirling dust cloud, are seldom found. Yet most planetary studies began by assuming that the planets evolved and are therefore similar. Typical arguments went as follows: "By studying the magnetic field (or any other feature) of Planet X, we will better understand how Earth's magnetic field evolved." It turns out that each magnetic field is surprisingly different. "By studying Earth's sister planet, Venus, we will see how plate tectonics shaped its surface and better understand how plate tectonics works on Earth." It is now recognized that plate tectonics does not occur on Venus. (Part II of this book will explain why plate tectonics also does not occur on Earth.)

Astronomical and Physical Sciences

The Universe, the Solar System, the Earth, and Life Were Recently Created.

Naturalistic Explanations for the Evolution of the Solar System and Universe Are Unscientific and Hopelessly Inadequate.

42. Strange Planets

Many undisputed observations contradict the current theories on how the Solar System evolved.[a] One theory says planets formed when a star, passing near our sun, tore matter from the sun. More popular theories hold that the Solar System formed from a cloud of swirling gas, dust, or larger particles. If the planets and their 63 known moons evolved from the same material, they should have many similarities. After several decades of planetary exploration, this expectation is now recognized as false.[b] (See Figure 15.) According to these evolutionary theories:

Backward-Spinning Planets. All Planets should spin in the same direction, but Venus, Uranus, and Pluto rotate backwards.[c]

Backward Orbits. All 63 moons in our Solar System should orbit their planets in the same sense, but at least six have backward orbits.[d] Furthermore, Jupiter, Saturn, and Neptune have moons orbiting in both directions.

Inclined Orbits. The orbit of each of these 63 moons should lie in the equatorial plane of the planet it orbits, but many, including the earth's moon, are in highly inclined orbits.[e]

Figure 16: Saturn and Five of Its Moons. Saturn has 20 known moons, more than any other planet. One of them, named Phoebe, has an orbit that is almost perpendicular to Saturn's equator. This is difficult for evolutionists to explain.

Hydrogen and Helium. Since about 98% of the sun is hydrogen or helium, Earth, Mars, Venus, and Mercury should have similar compositions. Instead, much less than 1% of these planets is hydrogen or helium.[f]

Angular Momentum. The sun should have 700 times more angular momentum than all the planets combined. Instead, the planets have 50 times more angular momentum than the sun.[g]

43. Evolving Planets?

Contrary to popular opinion, planets should not form from the mutual gravitational attraction of particles orbiting the sun. Orbiting particles are much more likely to be scattered or expelled by their gravitational interactions than they are to be pulled together. Experiments have shown that colliding particles are much more likely to fragment than to stick together.[a] Similar comments can be made concerning the improbability that particles orbiting a planet will ever grow into a moon. This is why the particles in the rings of Saturn, Jupiter, and Uranus show no evidence of clumping into larger bodies.

Despite these problems, let us assume that pebble-size to moon-size particles somehow evolved. "Growing a planet" by many small collisions will produce an almost *nonspinning* planet, since the spins imparted by impacts will be largely self-cancelling.[b] All planets spin, some much more than others.

Growing a large, gaseous planet (such as Jupiter, Saturn, Uranus, or Neptune) far from the central star, is especially difficult for evolutionists to explain for several reasons.[c]

   a. Gases dissipate rapidly in the vacuum of outer space, especially the lightest two gases—hydrogen and helium, which comprise most of the giant planets.

   b. Because gas molecules orbiting a star do not gravitationally pull in other gas molecules, a rocky planet, several times larger than the earth, must first form to attract all the gas gravitationally. (The hydrogen and helium on Jupiter are more than 300 times as massive as the earth.) This must happen very quickly, before the gas dissipates.[d]

   c. Stars like our sun—even those which evolutionists say are young—do not have enough orbiting hydrogen or helium to form one Jupiter.[e]

Based on demonstratable science, gaseous planets and the rest of the solar system did not evolve.

44. Origin of the Moon

Naturalistic theories on the moon's origin are highly speculative and completely inadequate.[a] The moon did not spin off the earth, nor did it congeal from the same material as the earth since its orbital plane is too inclined. Furthermore, the relative abundances of its elements are too dissimilar from those of the earth.[b] The moon's nearly circular orbit is also strong evidence that it was never torn from, nor captured by, the earth.[c] If the moon formed from particles orbiting the earth, other particles should be easily visible inside the moon's orbit; none are. If the moon was not pulled or splashed from the earth, was not

built up from smaller particles near its present orbit, and was not captured from outside its present orbit, only one hypothesis remains; the moon was created in its present orbit. (See **Evolving Planets?** on page 18, **Moon Recession** on page 25, **Moon Dust and Debris** on page 25, **Crater Creep** on page 25, and **Hot Moon** on page 26.)

45. Evolution of the Solar System?

Evolutionists claim the solar system condensed out of a vast cloud of swirling dust about 4.6 billion years ago. Many particles that were not swept up as part of a planet would have then begun a gradual spiral in toward the sun. Colliding asteroids also would create dust particles that, over millions of years, would spiral in toward the sun. (For an explanation of this spiral effect, See **Poynting-Robertson Effect** on page 27.) Particles should still be falling into the sun's upper atmosphere, burning up, and giving off an easily measured, infrared glow. Measurements taken during the solar eclipse of 11 July 1991, showed no such glow.[a] Therefore, the assumed "millions of years" and this explanation for the origin of the solar system are probably wrong.

46. Mountains of Venus

Venus must have a strong crust to support its extremely high, dense[a] mountains. One mountain, Maat Mons, rises higher than Earth's Mount Everest does above sea level. Since Venus is relatively near the sun, its atmosphere is 900°F—so hot that its *surface* rocks must be weak or "tarlike." (Lead melts at 622°F and zinc at 787°F.) Only if the *subsurface* rocks are cold and strong can these mountains defy gravity. This allows us to draw two conclusions, both of which contradict major evolutionary assumptions.

First, evolutionists assume that planets grew (evolved) by rocky debris falling from outer space, a process called *gravitational accretion*. The heat generated by the impacts of a planet's worth of projectiles would have left the inner planets molten. However, Venus was never molten. Had it been, its hot atmosphere would have prevented its subsurface rocks from cooling enough to support its mountains. Therefore, Venus did not evolve by gravitational accretion.

Secondly, evolutionists believe the entire solar system is billions of years old. If Venus were billions of years old, its atmospheric heat would have soaked deeply enough into the planet to weaken its subsurface rocks. Not only could Venus' crust not support mountains, the hot mountains themselves could not maintain their steep slopes.

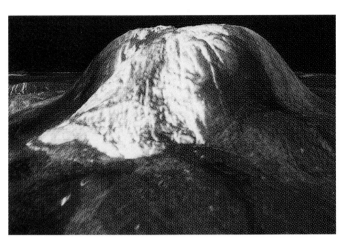

Figure 17: Maat Mons on Venus. If Venus' mountains were composed of lighter material, they would "float" in the denser rock below, just as an iceberg floats in denser liquid water. Mountains on earth are buoyed up, because they have a density of 2.7 gm/cm^3 and "float" in rock that is about 3.3 gm/cm^3. Recent studies, using the Magellan spacecraft that orbited and mapped Venus for several years, have shown that Venus' mountains are not composed of material lighter than the surrounding rock. So what supports them? It must be Venus' strong crust, despite the extremely high temperatures on Venus. This implies that Venus is not old and did not evolve.

47. Space, Time, and Matter

No scientific theory exists to explain the origin of space, time, or matter. Since each is intimately related to or even defined in terms of the other, a satisfactory explanation for the origin of one must also explain the origin of the others.[a] Naturalistic explanations have completely failed.

48. First Law of Thermodynamics

The first law of thermodynamics states that the total amount of energy in the universe, or in any isolated part of it, remains constant. It further states that although energy (or its mass equivalent) can change form, it is not now being created or destroyed. Countless experiments have verified this. A corollary of the first law is that natural processes cannot create energy. Consequently, energy must have been created in the past by some agency or power outside and independent of the natural universe. Furthermore, if natural processes cannot produce the relatively simple inorganic portion of the universe, then it is even less likely that natural processes can explain the much more complex organic (or living) portion of the universe.

49. Second Law of Thermodynamics

If the entire universe is an isolated system, then, according to the second law of thermodynamics, the energy in the universe that is available for useful work has always been decreasing. However, as one goes back in time, the amount of energy available for useful work would eventually exceed the total energy in the universe that, according to the first law of thermodynamics, remains constant. This is an impossible condition, thus implying that the universe had a beginning.[a]

50. A Beginning

Heat always flows from hot bodies to cold bodies. If the universe were infinitely old, the temperature throughout the universe should be uniform. Since the temperature of the universe is not uniform, the universe is not infinitely old. Therefore, the universe had a beginning.

51. Decay

A further consequence of the second law is that when the universe began, it was more organized and complex than it is today—not in a highly disorganized and random state as assumed by evolutionists and proponents of the big bang theory.[a]

52. Big Bang?

Three observations led to the general acceptance of the big bang theory: the cosmic background radiation (CBR), the amount of helium in the universe, and the redshift of distant starlight. All three have been poorly understood.

CBR. All matter radiates heat, regardless of its temperature. Everywhere astronomers look, they can detect an extremely uniform radiation, called the cosmic background radiation (CBR). It appears to come from perfectly radiating matter whose temperature is 2.73 K—nearly absolute zero. The CBR was initially thought to be left over from the big bang. Many incorrectly believe that the big bang theory predicted this radiation.[a]

Since the CBR is so uniform, the matter from which it originated must have been spread uniformly throughout the universe. But if matter was uniformly distributed, it would hardly gravitate in any direction; even after tens of billions of years, galaxies would not evolve. Since the matter in the universe is highly concentrated into galaxies, galaxy clusters, and superclusters, the CBR does not appear to be a remnant of a big bang.[b]

Helium. The amount of helium in the universe is not explained by the big bang theory; the theory was adjusted to fit the amount of helium.[c] Ironically, the lack of helium in certain types of stars (B type stars)[d] and the presence of beryllium in other stars[e] contradicts the theory.

Redshift. The redshift of distant starlight is usually interpreted as a Doppler effect; namely, stars and galaxies are moving away from the earth, stretching out (or reddening) the wave lengths of light we see. While this may be true, other possible explanations do not involve an expanding universe.[f] Besides, many objects with high redshifts seem connected, or associated, with other objects of low redshifts. They could not be traveling at such different velocities and be connected for long. For example, many quasars have very high redshifts, and yet they statistically cluster with galaxies having low redshifts. Sometimes, quasars appear to be connected to galaxies by threads of gas.[g] Finally, redshifted light from galaxies has some strange features that are inconsistent with the Doppler effect. If redshifts are from objects moving away from the earth, one would expect the amount of redshifting to take on continuous values. Instead, redshifts tend to cluster at specific, evenly-spaced values.[h] Much remains to be learned about redshifts.

A big bang should neither produce highly concentrated[i] nor rotating bodies. Galaxies are examples of both. A large volume of the universe should not be—but apparently is—moving sideways, almost perpendicular to the direction of expansion.[j]

A big bang would, for all practical purposes, only produce hydrogen and helium. Therefore, the first generation of stars to somehow form after a big bang should consist of only hydrogen and helium. Some of these stars should still exist, but none can be found.[k] These observations make it doubtful that a big bang occurred.[l]

If a big bang occurred, what caused the bang? Stars with enough mass become black holes, so not even light can escape their enormous gravity. How then could anything escape the trillions upon trillions of times greater gravity caused by concentrating all the mass in the universe in a "cosmic egg" that existed before a big bang?[m]

If the big bang theory is correct, one can calculate the age of the universe. This age turns out to be younger than objects in the universe whose ages were based on other evolutionary theories. Since this is logically impossible, one or both sets of theories must be incorrect.[n]

▲

53. Missing Mass
Imagine seeing several rocks in outer space, moving radially away from the earth. If the rocks were simultaneously blasted away from the earth, their masses, changing velocities, and distances from the earth would have a very precise relationship with each other. When a similar relationship is checked for billions of observable galaxies, an obvious conclusion is that these galaxies did not explode from a common point in a huge "big bang."[a] It is even more obvious that if such an explosion occurred, it must have been much, much less than billions of years ago. ·

Evolutionists try to fix this problem in two ways. They think the universe is filled with at least ten times as much matter as can be seen. This is maintained even though two decades of searching for this hidden mass has turned up nothing other than the conclusion that the needed "missing mass" does not exist.[b]

A second "fix attempt" assumes that the rocks (or in the real problem, all the particles in the universe) were briefly, almost magically, accelerated away from some point. Supposedly, this matter reached speeds trillions of billions of times *faster than the speed of light* by an unknown, untestable phenomenon—not by a blast. Then this matter became controlled by gravity after it reached just the right speed to give it an apparent age of 10-20 billion years.[c] Such flights of imagination and speculation are common in the field of cosmology.

▲

54. Interstellar Gas
Detailed analyses indicate that neither stars nor planets could form from interstellar gas clouds.[a] To do so, either by first forming dust particles[b] or by direct gravitational collapse of the gas,[c] would require vastly more time than the alleged age of the universe. An obvious alternative is that stars and planets were created.

▲

55. Fast Binaries
Perhaps half of all stars are grouped in closely spaced pairs called "binaries." Fortunately, our sun does not have a binary partner. If it did, the wide range of temperatures on earth would probably not permit life. The mutual gravitational attraction between a binary pair of stars causes them to orbit each other, just as the moon orbits the earth. The closer the paired stars are, the more rapidly they orbit. Distances between a binary pair should not change appreciably, even over long periods of time.

Two particular stars have been found so close together that they orbit each other every eleven minutes! This implies that their centers are about 80,000 miles apart.[a] By way of comparison, our sun, which is a typical star, is more than 800,000 miles in diameter. There are other close binaries.[b]

The theory of stellar evolution was developed by arranging (on paper) different types of stars in a sequence according to their brightness and color. Stellar evolutionists believe that stars slowly change from one type to another. However, scientists have never observed such changes, and some stars do not fit this pattern. According to stellar evolution, the volume of each star, late in its lifetime, expands to about a million times that of our sun. Finally, it supposedly collapses and becomes a small star about the size of the earth (a white dwarf) or even smaller (a neutron star).

Only such tiny stars could have their centers 80,000 miles apart and still orbit each other. Obviously, they did not evolve from larger stars, since larger stars orbiting so closely would collide. If two stars cannot evolve into a condition that has them orbiting each other every eleven minutes, one wonders whether stars evolve at all.

56. Star Births?
If stars evolve, star births should about equal star deaths. The deaths of many stars are bright and sudden events called "supernovas." Similarly, the birth of a star should be accompanied by the appearance of new star light when compared with the many photographic plates made decades earlier. Instruments, which could detect dust falling into and forming supposedly new stars, have not done so.[a] Actually, the stars that some astronomers believe are very new are expelling matter. We have never seen a star born, but we have seen hundreds of stars die. There is no evidence that stars evolve,[b] nor are there any sound scientific explanations for how they could evolve.[c]

57. Stellar Evolution?
Stellar evolution is assumed in estimating the age of stars. These age estimates are then used to establish a framework for stellar evolution. This is circular reasoning.[a]

58. O Stars
The most luminous stars in our galaxy (the so-called "O" stars) are "burning fuel" hundreds of thousands of times more rapidly than our sun. This is so rapid that they must be quite young on an evolutionary time scale. If these stars did evolve, they should show easily measurable characteristics such as extremely high rates of rotation and enormous magnetic fields.[a] Since these characteristics are not observed, it seems quite likely these stars did not evolve.

59. Galaxies
There are good reasons why natural processes cannot form galaxies[a] and why galaxies cannot evolve from one type to another.[b] Furthermore, if spiral galaxies were billions of years old, their arms or bars would be severely twisted.[c] (See Figure 88 on page 155.) Since they have maintained their shape, either galaxies are young, or unknown physical phenomena are occurring within galaxies.[d] Even structures composed of galaxies are now known to be so amazingly large, and yet relatively thin, that they could not have formed by slow gravitational attraction.[e] If **slow, natural** processes cannot form such huge galactic structures, then rapid, supernatural processes may have.

Figure 18: Spiral Galaxies.

Techniques That Argue for an Old Earth Are Either Illogical or Are Based on Unreasonable Assumptions.

60. Hidden Assumptions
To estimate a date prior to the beginning of written records, one must assume the dating clock has operated at a known rate, the initial setting of the clock is known, and the clock has not been disturbed. These three assumptions are almost always unstated, overlooked, or invalid.

Figure 19: "Stalagmites." Water from an underground spring was channeled to this spot on a river bank for only one year. In that time, limestone built up around sticks lying on the bank. Limestone deposits can be formed rapidly if the chemistry in the ground water is right. Just because stalagmites and stalactites are growing slowly today does not mean they must be millions of years old. As we will see in Part II, the conditions after the flood would have established ideal ground-water conditions for rapidly forming such features.

61. Corals and Caves

Estimated old ages for the earth are frequently based on "clocks" that today are ticking at very slow rates. For example, coral growth rates were for many years thought to be very slow, implying that some coral reefs must be hundreds of thousands of years old. More accurate measurements of these rates under favorable growth conditions now show us that no known coral formation need be older than 3,400 years.[a] A similar comment can be made for the growth rates of stalactites and stalagmites in caves.[b]

62. Constant Decay?

A major assumption that underlies all radioactive dating techniques is that the rates of decay, which have been essentially constant over the past 90 years, have also been constant over the past 4,600,000,000 years. This bold, critical, and untestable assumption is made, even though no one knows what causes radioactive decay.[a] Furthermore, two lines of evidence suggest radioactive decay was once much greater than it is today.[b]

63. Radiometric Contradictions

The public has been greatly misled concerning the consistency and trustworthiness of radiometric dating techniques (the potassium-argon method, the rubidium-strontium method, and the uranium-thorium-lead method). For example, geologists hardly ever subject their radiometric age measurements to "blind tests."[a] In science, such tests are a standard procedure for overcoming experimenter bias. Many published radiometric dates can be checked by comparisons with the assumed ages for the fossils that sometimes lie above, or below, radiometrically dated rock. In more than 400 of these published checks (about half of those sampled), the radiometrically determined ages were at least one geologic age in error—indicating major errors in methodology. One wonders how many other dating checks were not even published because they, too, were in error.[b]

64. Index Fossils

In the early 1800s, some observers in Western Europe noticed that certain fossils are usually preserved in sedimentary layers that, when traced laterally, typically lie above other types of fossils. Decades later, after the theory of evolution was proposed, it was concluded that the upper organism must have evolved after the lower organism. These early geologists did not realize that there were hydrodynamically sound reasons why, during the flood, the organisms were sorted in that order. (For an explanation, see pages 134-145.) Geologic ages were then associated with each of these "index fossils." Those ages were extended to similar animals and plants based on the faulty reasoning that they must have evolved at

about the same time since they were similar. Today, geologic formations are almost always dated by their fossil content—which, as stated above, assumes evolution. Yet, evolution is supposedly shown by the sequence of fossils. This reasoning is circular.[a] Furthermore, it has produced many contradictory results. (See **"Out-of-Place Fossils"** on page 9.)

65. Geologic Column

Practically nowhere on the earth can one find the so-called "geologic column."[a] At most places on the continents, over half the "geologic periods" are missing. Only 15-20% of the earth's land surface has even one-third of these periods in the correct consecutive order.[b] Even within the Grand Canyon, more than 150 million years of this imaginary column are missing. Using the assumed geologic column to date fossils and rocks is fallacious.

66. Old DNA

When an animal or plant dies, its DNA begins decomposing.[a] Before 1990, almost no one believed that DNA would remain intact much beyond 10,000 years.[b] This limit was based on measuring DNA disintegration rates in **well-preserved** specimens of known age such as Egyptian mummies. DNA has now been reported in magnolia leaves that evolutionists claim are 17 million years old.[c] Fragments of DNA are also claimed to be in alleged 80 million-year-old dinosaur bones buried in a coal bed[d] and in the scales of a 200 million-year-old fossilized fish.[e] DNA is frequently reported in amber encased insects and plants that are supposedly 25-120 million years old.[f] All this has forced evolutionists to reexamine the 10,000-year limit.[g]

They now claim that DNA can be preserved longer if conditions are dryer, colder, and freer of oxygen, bacteria, and background radiation. The measured disintegration rates of DNA, apparently under these more ideal conditions, do not support this.[h] Therefore, the previously measured rates were probably not **several thousand times** in error. If, as is likely, such a huge error is not found, then the method for arriving at those million-year ages needs reexamining.

Evolutionists have a similar problem with the protein preserved in dinosaur bones. As with DNA, no proteins should last 75-150 million years, as is claimed for those bones.[i] The best evidence suggests that these plant and animal remains are not as old as evolutionists believe.

67. Human Artifacts

At various times and places, man-made objects have been found encased in coal. Examples include a thimble,[a] a spoon,[b] an iron pot,[c] an iron instrument,[d] an 8-

Figure 20: Humanlike Footprints With Trilobite. In 1968, 43 miles northwest of Delta, Utah, William J. Meister found these apparent human shoe prints within a 2-inch-thick slab of rock. Also in that slab were obvious trilobite fossils, one of them was squashed under the "heel." The 10-inch-long shoe print is at the left, and the rock mold of it is at the right. According to evolutionists, trilobites became extinct 240 million years *before* humans evolved. Notice how the back of the heel is worn, just as most of our shoes wear today. The heel was indented in the rock about an eighth of an inch deeper than sole. Others have since made similar discoveries at this location, although this is the only fossil where a trilobite was *inside* one of the apparent shoe prints.

carat gold chain,[e] and a metallic vessel inlaid with silver.[f] Many other "out of place artifacts" have been found inside deeply buried rocks: nails,[g] a screw,[h] a strange coin,[i] a clay figurine,[j] a strange hammer,[k] and other objects of obvious human manufacture.[l] By evolutionary dating techniques, these objects would be hundreds of millions of years older than man. Again, something is wrong.

68. Humanlike Footprints
Humanlike footprints, supposedly 150-600 million years old, have been found in rock formations in Utah,[a] Kentucky,[b] Missouri,[c] and possibly Pennsylvania.[d] At Laetoli, in the east African country of Tanzania, a team headed by Mary Leakey found a sequence of apparently modern human footprints.[e] They were dated at 3.7 million years. If human feet made any of these prints, then evolutionary chronology is drastically wrong.

69. Parallel Layers
Since no worldwide or even continental unconformity exists in the earth's sedimentary layers, those layers must have been deposited rapidly. (An *unconformity* represents a time break of unknown duration—for example, an erosional surface between two adjacent strata.) Parallel layers (called conformities) imply that the deposition was continuous and rapid. Since unconformi-

ties are simply local phenomena,[a] one can trace continuous paths from the bottom to the top of the geologic record that avoid these time breaks. The sedimentary layers along those paths must have been deposited rapidly and continuously as a unit.

Frequently, two adjacent and parallel sedimentary layers contain such different index fossils that evolutionists conclude that they were deposited hundreds of millions of years apart. However, since the adjacent layers are conformable, the layers must have been deposited without interruption or erosion. (For an explanation of how conformable layers can have such different fossils, see pages 135-145.) Often, in an apparently undisturbed sequence, the layer considered older by evolutionists is on top! (See **"Out-of-Place Fossils"** on page 9.) The evolutionary dating rules are self-contradictory.[b]

Most Dating Techniques Indicate That the Earth, the Solar System, and the Universe Are Young.

For the last 130 years the age of the earth, as assumed by evolutionists, has been doubling at a rate of once every 20 years. In fact since 1900, their estimate of its age has multiplied by a factor of 100!

Evolution requires an old earth, an old solar system, and an old universe. Nearly all informed evolutionists will admit that without billions of years their theory is dead. Yet, by hiding the "origins question" behind a vast veil of time, the unsolvable problems of evolution become difficult for scientists to see and laymen to imagine. Our media and textbooks have implied for over a century that this almost unimaginable age is correct, but rarely do they examine the shaky assumptions and growing body of contrary evidence. Therefore, most people instinctively believe the earth and universe are old, and are disturbed (at least initially) to hear contrary evidence.

Actually, most dating techniques indicate that the earth and solar system are young—possibly less than 10,000 years old. Here are some of these points of evidence.

70. Helium
The radioactive decay of only uranium and thorium would produce all of the atmosphere's helium in only 40,000 years. No known means exists by which large amounts of helium can escape from the atmosphere, even when considering helium's low atomic weight. The atmosphere appears to be young.[a]

71. Lead and Helium Diffusion
Lead diffuses (or leaks) from zircon crystals at known rates that increase with temperature. Since these crystals are found at different depths in the earth, those at greater depths and temperatures should have less lead. Even if the earth's crust is just a fraction of the age claimed by evolutionists, measurable differences in the lead content of zircons should exist throughout the top 4,000 meters. Instead, no measurable difference is found.[a] Similar conclusions are reached from a study of the helium contained in these same zircon crystals.[b] In fact, these helium studies lead to a conclusion that the earth's crust is less than 10,000 years old.[c]

72. Excess Fluid Pressure
Abnormally high oil, gas, and water pressures exist within relatively permeable rock.[a] If these fluids had been trapped more than 10,000 to 100,000 years ago, leakage would have dropped the pressure far below what it is today. This oil, gas, and water must have been trapped suddenly and recently.[b]

73. Volcanic Debris
Volcanoes are ejecting almost a cubic mile of material into the atmosphere each year. This is so rapid that if the rate were constant, about 10 times the entire volume of the earth's sediments should be produced in 4.6 billion years. Actually, only about 25% of the earth's sediments are of volcanic origin, and many volcanic deposits show much greater volcanic activity in the past. No means have been proposed which can remove or transform all of this volcanic material. The earth's sediments, therefore, appear to be much younger than 4.6 billion years old.[a]

74. River Sediments
More than 27 billion tons of river sediments are entering the oceans each year. Probably, the rate of sediment transport was even greater in the past as the looser topsoil was removed and as erosion smoothed out the earth's terrain. Even if erosion has been constant, the sediments now on the ocean floor would have accumulated in only 30 million years. No process has been proposed which can remove 27 billion tons of ocean sediments each year. Therefore, the oceans cannot be hundreds of millions of years old.[a]

75. Continental Erosion
The continents are eroding at a rate that would level them in much less than 25 million years.[a] However, evolutionists believe that fossils of animals and plants at high elevations have somehow avoided this erosion for more than 300 million years. Something is wrong.

76. Dissolved Metals

The rate at which elements such as copper, gold, lead, mercury, nickel, silicon, sodium, tin, and uranium are entering the oceans is very rapid when compared with the small quantities of these elements already in the oceans. There is no known means by which large amounts of these elements can come out of solution. Therefore, the oceans must be much younger than a million years.

77. Shallow Meteorites

Meteorites are steadily falling onto the earth. This rate was much probably greater in the past since planets have swept much of the original meteoritic material from the solar system. Experts have, therefore, expressed surprise that meteorites are found only in young sediments very near the earth's surface.[a] Even meteoritic particles in ocean sediments are concentrated in the topmost layers.[b] If the earth's sediments, which average about a mile in thickness on the continents, were deposited over hundreds of millions of years, as evolutionists believe, many iron meteorites should be buried well below the earth's surface. Since this is not the case, the sediments appear to have been deposited rapidly. Furthermore, since no meteorites are found immediately above the basement rocks on which these sediments rest, these basement rocks could not have been exposed to meteoritic bombardment for any great length of time.

Similar observations can be made concerning ancient rock slides. Rock slides are frequently found on the earth's surface, but are generally absent from supposedly old rock.[c]

78. Meteoritic Dust

Meteoritic dust is accumulating on the earth so fast that, after four billion years, the equivalent of more than 16 feet of this dust should have accumulated. Because this dust is high in nickel, the earth's crust should have an abundance of nickel. No such concentration has been found on land or in the oceans. Consequently, the earth appears to be young.[a]

79. Magnetic Decay

Direct measurements of the earth's magnetic field over the past 140 years show a steady and rapid decline in its strength. This decay pattern is consistent with the theoretical view that there is an electrical current inside the earth which produces the magnetic field. If this is correct, then just 20,000 years ago the electrical current would have been so vast that the earth's structure could not have survived the heat produced. This implies that the earth could not be older than 20,000 years.[a]

80. Molten Earth?

If the earth was initially molten, it would have cooled to its present condition in much less than 4.6 billion years. This conclusion holds even if one makes liberal assumptions about the amount of heat generated by radioactive decay within the earth.[a] The known temperature pattern inside the earth is only consistent with a young earth.

81. Moon Recession

As tidal friction gradually slows the earth's spin, the laws of physics require the moon to recede from the earth. This recession has been observed since 1754. Even if the moon began orbiting near the earth's surface, the moon should have moved to its present distance in several billion years less time than the 4.6 billion-year age that evolutionists assume for the earth and moon. Consequently, the earth-moon system must be much younger than evolutionists assume. (For more details, see technical note on page 177.)

82. Moon Dust and Debris

If the moon were billions of years old, it should have accumulated a thick layer of dust and debris from meteoritic bombardment. Before instruments were placed on the moon, some scientists were very concerned that astronauts would sink into a sea of dust—possibly a mile in thickness.[a] This did not happen. Very little space dust and debris is on the moon. In fact, after examining the rocks and dust brought back from the moon, scientists learned that only about 1/67th of the dust and debris came from outer space. Recent measurements of the influx rate of meteoritic material on the moon also do not support an old moon. (For more details, see technical note on page 182.)

83. Crater Creep

A tall pile of tar will slowly flow downhill, ultimately spreading into a nearly horizontal sheet of tar. Most material, under pressure, "creeps" in this way, although rocks deform very, very slowly.

Calculations show that large, high-rimmed craters on the moon should flow downhill and level out in only tens of thousands of years.[a] Large, steep-walled craters exist even on Venus and Mercury, where gravity is greater, and temperatures are hot enough to melt lead. Most large craters on the moon, Venus, and Mercury are thought to have formed shortly after the solar system formed. These bodies appear to be quite young, since their craters show no sign of "creep."

Figure 21: Moon Dust and Debris from Meteoritic Bombardment. Concern that astronauts and equipment would sink into a sea of dust was so great that two experimental programs (Ranger and Surveyor) were sent to the moon to assess the problem. The problem turned out not to exist, but was a consequence of the belief by some that the moon is billions of years old.

84. Hot Moon

The moon has a hot interior.[a] Since it has not yet cooled off, the moon is probably much less than a billion years old.

85. Young Comets

As comets pass near the sun, some of their mass vaporizes, producing a long tail and other debris.[a] Comets also fragment frequently or fall onto the sun[b] or other planets. Typical comets should disintegrate or disappear after several hundred orbits. For many comets this is less than 10,000 years. There is no evidence for a distant shell of cometary material surrounding the solar system,[c] and

there is no known way to add comets to the solar system at rates that even remotely balance their destruction.[d] In fact, the gravitational attractions of the planets tend to expel comets from the solar system, rather than capture them.[e] Consequently, comets and the solar system appear to be less than 10,000 years old.

86. Small Comets

Photographs, taken from earth-orbiting satellites, show small, ice-filled comets striking the earth's upper atmosphere at an average rate of one every twenty seconds.[a] (See Figure 23.) As each comet vaporizes, about 100 tons of water are added to the earth's atmosphere. If this

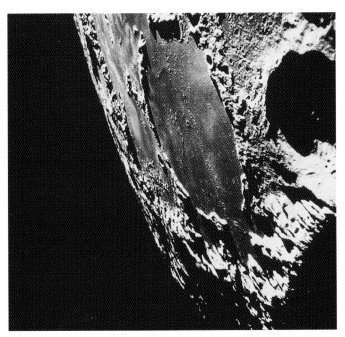

Figure 22: Young Craters. The craters on the Moon, Venus, and Mars have such high, steep walls that they should slowly slump over tens of thousands of years. This slumping is not observed, suggesting that these craters are younger than tens of thousands of years. (See **"Crater Creep"** on page 25.)

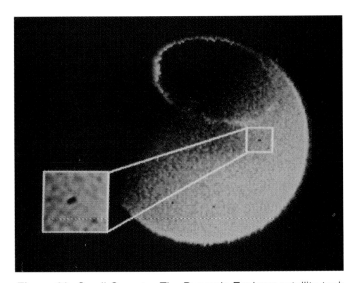

Figure 23: Small Comets. The Dynamic Explorer satellite took this picture in ultraviolet light showing small comets (the dark spots) colliding with the earth's upper atmosphere. The comets begin to break up 800 miles above the earth's surface, then frictional heating vaporizes the pieces and stops the descent at an elevation of about 35 miles. The water vapor blocks ultraviolet light from the earth, giving the dark spots. The northern lights are shown by the halo.

began when evolutionists say the earth started to evolve, the earth's oceans should have several times more water than they now have. Actually, the rate of impact was probably greater in the past since the planets have swept

many of these comets from the solar system. Therefore, the oceans and the earth look young.

87. Young Rings
The rings orbiting Saturn, Uranus, Jupiter, and Neptune are being rapidly bombarded by meteoroids. Saturn's rings, for example, should be pulverized and dispersed in about 10,000 years.[a] Since this has not happened, planetary rings are probably quite young. (See Figure 24.)

88. Hot Planets
Jupiter, Saturn, and Neptune each radiate away more than twice the heat energy they receive from the sun.[a] Uranus[b] and Venus[c] also radiate too much heat. Calculations show that it is very unlikely that this energy comes from nuclear fusion,[d] radioactive decay, gravitational contraction, or phase changes[e] within those planets. The only other conceivable explanation is that these planets have not existed long enough to cool off.[f]

89. Solar Wind
The sun's radiation applies an outward force on extremely small particles orbiting the sun. Particles less than 100,000th of a centimeter in diameter should have been "blown out" of the solar system if it were billions of years old. Yet these particles are still orbiting the sun.[a] Conclusion: the solar system is young.

90. Poynting-Robertson Effect
A large disk-shaped cloud of dust particles orbits the sun. The forces acting on these particles are so great that they should be destroyed or removed in less than 10,000 years. Since there appears to be no significant source of replenishment, the solar system is probably less than 10,000 years old. One of these forces is called the Poynting-Robertson effect. Here is how it works.

Rain falling on a speeding car tends to strike the front of the car and slow it down slightly. Similarly, the sun's rays that strike particles orbiting the sun tend to slow them down. For particles larger than those described in **Solar Wind** (above), this effect is strong enough to cause them to spiral into the sun. Thus, the sun's radiation and gravitational field act as a giant vacuum cleaner that pulls in about 100,000 tons of micrometeoroids per day. The best estimates are that less than half this dust is being continuously supplied by the disintegration of comets and asteroids.[a]

As a comet disintegrates, it becomes a cluster of particles called a meteor stream. The Poynting-Robertson effect causes the smaller particles in a meteor stream to spiral

Figure 24: Planetary Rings. The rings of Saturn, Uranus, and Jupiter (left to right) are rapidly breaking up, implying that they did not form too long ago.

into the sun more rapidly than the larger particles. After about 10,000 years, this segregation of orbits by particle size should be visible. Since this segregation is generally not visible, meteor streams must be a relatively recent phenomenon.[b]

Huge quantities of microscopic dust particles have also been recently discovered around some stars.[c] Yet, according to the theory of stellar evolution, those stars are many millions of years old and should have blown the dust away. Unless one can *demonstrate* that some vast process continually supplies that dust, one should consider whether the "millions of years" are imaginary.

91. Solar Fuel

If the sun, when it first began to radiate, had any nonnuclear sources of energy, they would have been depleted in much less than ten million years. Theory[a] and experiment[b] indicate that nuclear reactions are not the predominant energy source for the sun. Our star, the sun, must therefore be young (less than ten million years old). If the sun is young, then so is the earth.

92. Shrinking Sun

Since 1836, more than one hundred different observers at the Royal Greenwich Observatory and the U.S. Naval Observatory have made *direct*, visual measurements that suggest that the sun's diameter is shrinking at a rate of about 0.1% each century or about five feet per hour![a] Furthermore, records of solar eclipses indicate that this rapid shrinking has been going on for at least the past 400 years.[b] Several ***indirect*** techniques also confirm that the sun is shrinking, although these inferred collapse rates are only about 1/7th as much.[c] Using the most conservative data, one must conclude that had the sun existed several million years ago, it would have been so large that its heat would have destroyed life on earth. Yet, evolutionists say that a million years ago all the present forms of life were essentially as they are now, having completed their evolution that began a thousand million years ago.

During the last 30 years, one of the most perplexing problems in science has been the lack of solar neutrinos. Neutrinos are extremely light subatomic particles produced in nuclear reactions inside stars, including the sun. If all the sun's heat is produced by nuclear fusion, the earth should be bathed in three times as many neutrinos as scientists have consistently measured. However, if much of the sun's heat is due to its shrinking by gravitational collapse, then the lack of solar neutrinos would be explained.[d] But such a gravitational collapse could not have been going on very long.

93. Star Clusters
Stars moving in the same direction at significantly different speeds frequently travel in closely spaced clusters.[a] This would not be the case if they had been traveling for billions of years because just a slight difference in their velocities would disperse them after such great periods of time. Similar observations have been made of galaxy and galaxy-quasar combinations that apparently have vastly different velocities yet appear to be connected.[b]

94. Unstable Galaxies
Computer simulations of the motions of spiral galaxies show them to be highly unstable; they should completely change their shape in only a small fraction of the assumed evolutionary age of the universe.[a] The simplest explanation for so many spiral galaxies, including our Milky Way Galaxy, is that they and the universe are much younger than has been assumed.

95. Galaxy Clusters
Hundreds of rapidly moving galaxies often cluster tightly together. Their individual velocities, as measured by the redshift of their light, are so high that these clusters should be flying apart. In other words, the visible mass of the entire cluster, is much too small to hold the galaxies together gravitationally. However, since the galaxies within clusters are so close together, they could not have been flying apart for very long.

A similar statement can be made concerning many stars in spiral galaxies and gas clouds that surround some galaxies.[a] These stars and gas clouds are moving so rapidly that they should have broken their gravitational bonds long ago, if they were billions of years old. If the redshift of starlight always indicates a star's velocity, then a universe billions of years old is completely inconsistent with what is observed.[b] If redshifts can be caused by phenomena other than a star's velocity, then much of current astronomical thinking is wrong.

Conclusion

All dating techniques, especially the few that suggest vast ages, presume that a process observed today has always proceeded at its present rate. This assumption may be grossly inaccurate. Projecting presently known processes far back in time is more likely to be in error than extrapolation over a much shorter time. For the many dating "clocks" that show a young earth and a young universe, a much better understanding usually exists for how they work.

This contrary evidence understandably disturbs those who have always been told the earth is billions of years old. Can you imagine how disturbing this evidence is to the confirmed evolutionist?

Figure 25: Mountains of the World.

Earth Sciences

The Earth Has Experienced a Worldwide Flood.

Many of the Earth's Previously Unexplainable Features Can Be Explained by a Cataclysmic Flood.

The origin of each of the following features of the earth is a subject of controversy within the earth sciences. Each feature has many aspects that are inconsistent with standard explanations. Yet all appear to be consequences of a sudden and unrepeatable event—a cataclysmic flood whose waters erupted from worldwide, subterranean, and interconnected chambers with an energy release exceeding the explosion of ten billion hydrogen bombs. The many consequences of this event, which include the rapid formation of the features listed below, involved phenomena that are well understood.

96. **The Grand Canyon and Other Canyons**
97. **Mid-Oceanic Ridge**
98. **Continental Shelves and Slopes**
99. **Ocean Trenches**
100. **Seamounts and Tablemounts**
101. **Earthquakes**
102. **Magnetic Variations on the Ocean Floor**
103. **Submarine Canyons**
104. **Coal and Oil Formations**
105. **Glaciers and the Ice Ages**
106. **Frozen Mammoths**
107. **Major Mountain Ranges**
108. **Overthrusts**
109. **Volcanoes and Lava**
110. **Geothermal Heat**
111. **Metamorphic Rock**
112. **Strata**
113. **Plateaus**

114. **Salt Domes**
115. **Jigsaw Fit of the Continents**
116. **Fossil Graveyards**
For an amplification of the above, see pages 70-145.

The Seemingly Impossible Events of a Worldwide Flood Are Really Quite Plausible, If Examined Closely.

117. **Water Above Mountains?**
Is there enough water to cover all of the earth's preflood mountains in a global flood? Most people do not realize what a large volume of water there is on the earth. The oceans have ten times more water than there is land above sea level.

Most of the earth's mountains consist of tipped and buckled sedimentary layers. Since these sediments were initially laid down through water as nearly horizontal layers, the mountains must have been pushed up after the sediments were deposited. (See pages 70-100.)

If these mountains were again flattened out while the ocean basins rose in compensation for this downward flow of mass, the oceans would again flood the entire earth. Therefore, the earth has enough water to cover the smaller mountains that existed before the flood.

118. **Shells on Mountains**
Every major mountain range on the earth contains fossilized sea life—far above sea level.

References and Notes

1. The Law of Biogenesis

a. And yet, leading evolutionists are forced to accept some form of spontaneous generation. George Wald, formerly of Harvard University and a winner of the Nobel Prize in physiology and medicine, acknowledged the dilemma.

> *"The reasonable view was to believe in spontaneous generation; the only alternative, to believe in a single, primary act of supernatural creation. There is no third position."*

With no rationale given, Wald goes on to accept the impossible odds of spontaneous generation rather than creation.

> *"One has only to contemplate the magnitude of this task to concede that the spontaneous generation of a living organism is impossible. Yet here we are— as a result, I believe, of spontaneous generation."* George Wald, "The Origin of Life," *Scientific American*, Vol. 190, August 1954, p. 46.

● *"The beginning of the evolutionary process raises a question which is as yet unanswerable. What was the origin of life on this planet? Until fairly recent times there was a pretty general belief in the occurrence of 'spontaneous generation.' It was supposed that lowly forms of life developed spontaneously from, for example, putrefying meat. But careful experiments, notably those of Pasteur, showed that this conclusion was due to imperfect observation, and it became an accepted doctrine [the law of biogenesis] that life never arises except from life. So far as actual evidence goes, this is still the only possible conclusion. But since it is a conclusion that seems to lead back to some supernatural creative act, it is a conclusion that scientific men find very difficult of acceptance. It carries with it what are felt to be, in the present mental climate, undesirable philosophic implications, and it is opposed to the scientific desire for continuity. It introduces an unaccountable break in the chain of causation, and therefore cannot be admitted as part of science unless it is quite impossible to reject it. For that reason most scientific men prefer to believe that life arose, in some way not yet understood, from inorganic matter in accordance with the laws of physics and chemistry."* J. W. N. Sullivan, *The Limitations of Science* (New York: The Viking Press, Inc., 1933), p. 94.

2. Acquired Characteristics

a. While almost all biologists agree with this statement, many unconsciously slip into the belief, called Lamarckism, that the environment can directly and beneficially change egg and sperm cells. On occasions, Darwin did. This desire for a mechanism for macroevolutionary change reflects the insufficiency of presently claimed mechanisms. A few biologists are actively seeking ways to justify Lamarckism. The minor acquired characteristics they are claiming have no real significance for any present theory of organic evolution. For example, see "Lamarck, Dr. Steel and Plagiarism," *Nature*, Vol. 337, 12 January 1989, pp. 101-102.

3. Mendel's Laws

a. Monroe W. Strickberger, *Genetics*, 2nd edition (New York: Macmillan Publishing Co., 1976), p. 812.

● Alfred Russel Wallace, who independently proposed the theory of organic evolution slightly before Charles Darwin, was opposed to Mendel's laws of genetics. Wallace recognized that Mendel's experiments showed that the general characteristics of an organism remained within distinct boundaries. In a letter to Dr. Archdall Reid on 28 December 1909, Wallace wrote:

> *"But on the general relation of Mendelism to Evolution I have come to a very definite conclusion. This is, that it has no relation whatever to the evolution of species or higher groups, but is really antagonistic to such evolution! The essential basis of evolution, involving as it does the most minute and all-pervading adaptation to the whole environment, is extreme and ever-present plasticity, as a condition of survival and adaptation. But the essence of Mendelian characters is their rigidity. They are transmitted without variation, and therefore, except by the rarest of accidents, can never become adapted to ever varying conditions."* James Marchant, *Letters and Reminiscences* (New York: Harper & Brothers, 1916), p. 340.

b. Francis Hitching, *The Neck of the Giraffe: Where Darwin Went Wrong* (New Haven, Connecticut: Ticknor and Fields, 1982), p. 55.

● *"All competent biologists acknowledge the limited nature of the variation breeders can produce, although they do not like to discuss it much when grinding the evolutionary ax."* William R. Fix, *The Bone Peddlers: Selling Evolution* (New York: Macmillan Publishing Co., 1984), pp. 184-185.

● *"A rule that all breeders recognize, is that there are fixed limits to the amount of change that can be produced."* Lane P. Lester and Raymond G. Bohlin, *The Natural Limits to Biological Change* (Grand Rapids: Zondervan Publishing House, 1984), p. 96.

● Norman Macbeth, *Darwin Retried: An Appeal to Reason* (Ipswich, Massachusetts: Gambit, 1971), p. 36.

● William J. Tinkle, *Heredity* (Houston: St. Thomas Press, 1967), pp. 55-56.

c. *". . . the distinctions of specific forms and their not being blended together by innumerable transitional links, is a very obvious difficulty."* Charles Darwin, *The Origin of Species*, 6th edition (New York: Macmillan Publishing Co., 1927), p. 322.

● *"Indeed, the isolation and distinctness of different types of organisms and the existence of clear discontinuities in nature have been self-evident for centuries, even to non-*

biologists." Michael Denton, *Evolution: A Theory in Crisis* (London: Barnett Books, 1985), p. 105.

▲

4. Bounded Variations

a. *"The awesome morphological complexity of organisms such as vertebrates that have far fewer individuals on which selection can act therefore remains somewhat puzzling (for me at least), despite the geological time scales available and notwithstanding the insights provided by John Banner in his book* **The Evolution of Complexity** *and Richard Dawkins' demonstration of the power of selection in* **The Blind Watchmaker**.*"* Peter R. Sheldon, "Complexity Still Running," *Nature*, Vol. 350, 14 March 1991, p. 104.

▲

5. Natural Selection

a. '*[Natural selection] may have a stabilizing effect, but it does not promote speciation. It is not a creative force as many people have suggested.*" Daniel Brooks, as quoted by Roger Lewin, "A Downward Slope to Greater Diversity," *Science*, Vol. 217, 24 September 1982, p. 1240.

b. *"The genetic variants required for resistance to the most diverse kinds of pesticides were apparently present in every one of the populations exposed to these man-made compounds.*" Francisco J. Ayala, "The Mechanisms of Evolution," *Scientific American*, Vol. 239, September 1978, p. 65.

c. *"Darwin complained* [that] *his critics did not understand him, but he did not seem to realize that almost everybody, friends, supporters and critics, agreed on one point, his natural selection cannot account for the origin of the variations, only for their possible survival. And the reasons for rejecting Darwin's proposal were many, but first of all that many innovations cannot possibly come into existence through accumulation of many small steps, and even if they can, natural selection cannot accomplish it, because incipient and intermediate stages are not advantageous.*" Søren Løvtrup, *Darwinism: The Refutation of a Myth* (New York: Croom Helm, 1987), pp. 274-275.

d. In 1980, the "Macroevolution Conference" was held in Chicago. Roger Lewin, writing for *Science*, described it as a *"turning point in the history of evolutionary theory."* He went on to say:

> *"The central question of the Chicago conference was whether the mechanisms underlying microevolution can be extrapolated to explain the phenomena of macroevolution. At the risk of doing violence to the positions of some of the people at the meeting, the answer can be given as a clear, No."* Roger Lewin, "Evolution Theory under Fire," *Science*, Vol. 210, 21 November 1980, p. 883.

"In a generous admission Francisco Ayala, a major figure in propounding the Modern Synthesis [neo-Darwinism] *in the United States, said 'We would not have predicted stasis* [the stability of species over time] *from population genetics, but I am now convinced from what the paleontologists say that small changes do not accumulate.'"* Ibid., p. 884.

As stated earlier, micro + time ≠ macro.

● *"One could argue at this point that such 'minor' changes* [microevolution], *extrapolated over millions of years, could result in macroevolutionary change. But the observational evidence will not support this argument . . .* [examples given] *. . . Thus, the changes observed in the laboratory are not analogous to the sort of changes needed for macroevolution. Those who argue from microevolution to macroevolution may be guilty, then, of employing a false analogy—especially when one considers that microevolution may be a force of stasis* [produce stability], *not transformation . . . . For those who must describe the history of life as a purely natural phenomenon, the winnowing action of natural selection is truly a difficult problem to overcome. For scientists who are content to describe accurately those processes and phenomena which occur in nature (in particular, stasis), natural selection acts to prevent major evolutionary change.*" Michael Thomas, "Stasis Considered," *Origins Research*, Vol. 12, Fall/Winter 1989, p. 11.

▲

6. Mutations

a. *"Ultimately, all variation is, of course, due to mutation."* Ernst Mayr, "Evolutionary Challenges to the Mathematical Interpretation of Evolution," *Mathematical Challenges to the Neo-Darwinian Interpretation of Evolution*, editors Paul S. Moorhead and Martin M. Kaplan, proceedings of a symposium held at the Wistar Institute of Anatomy and Biology, 25 and 26 April, 1966 (Philadelphia: The Wistar Institute Press, 1967), p. 50.

● *"Although mutation is the ultimate source of all genetic variation, it is a relatively rare event, ..."* Ayala, p. 63.

b. *"The process of mutation is the only known source of the raw materials of genetic variability, and hence of evolution . . . . the mutants which arise are, with rare exceptions, deleterious to their carriers, at least in the environments which the species normally encounters."* Theodosius Dobzhansky, "On Methods of Evolutionary Biology and Anthropology," *American Scientist*, December 1957, p. 385.

● *"Accordingly, mutations are more than just sudden changes in heredity; they also affect viability, and, to the best of our knowledge, invariably affect it adversely."* C. P. Martin, "A Non-Geneticist Looks at Evolution," *American Scientist*, January 1953, p. 102.

"Mutation does produce hereditary changes, but the mass of evidence shows that all, or almost all, known mutations are unmistakably pathological and the few remaining ones are highly suspect." Ibid., p. 103.

"[Although mutations have produced some desirable breeds of animals and plants,] *all mutations seem to be in the nature of injuries that, to some extent, impair the fertility and viability of the affected organisms. I doubt if among the many thousands of known mutant types one can be found which is superior to the wild type in its normal environment, only very few can be named which are superior to the wild type in a strange environment.*" Ibid., p. 100.

- *"If we say that it is only by chance that they* [mutations] *are useful, we are still speaking too leniently. In general, they are useless, detrimental, or lethal."* W. R. Thompson, "Introduction to *The Origin of Species,*" Everyman Library No. 811 (New York: E. P. Dutton & Sons, 1956; reprint edition, Sussex, England: J. M. Dent and Sons, Ltd., 1967), p. 10.

- Visible mutations are those genetic changes that are easily detectable such as albinism, dwarfism, and hemophilia. Winchester quantifies the relative frequency of several types of mutations.

    "Lethal mutations outnumber visibles by about 20 to 1. Mutations that have small harmful effects, the detrimental mutations, are even more frequent than the lethal ones." A. M. Winchester, *Genetics,* 5th edition (Boston: Houghton Mifflin Co., 1977), p. 356.

- John W. Klotz, *Genes, Genesis, and Evolution,* 2nd edition, revised (St. Louis: Concordia Publishing House, 1972), pp. 262-265.

- *". . . I took a little trouble to find whether a single amino acid change in a hemoglobin mutation is known that doesn't affect seriously the function of that hemoglobin. One is hard put to find such an instance."* George Wald, *Mathematical Challenges to the Darwinian Interpretation of Evolution,* editors Paul S. Moorhead and Martin M. Kaplan, pp. 18-19.

Yet, evolutionists have taught for years that alpha hemoglobin A changed through mutations into beta hemoglobin A. This would require, at a minimum, 120 point mutations. In other words, the improbability Wald refers to above must be raised to the 120th power to produce just this one protein!

- *"Even if we didn't have a great deal of data on this point, we could still be quite sure on theoretical grounds that mutants would usually be detrimental. For a mutation is a random change of a highly organized, reasonably smoothly functioning living body. A random change in the highly integrated system of chemical processes which constitute life is almost certain to impair it—just as a random interchange of connections in a television set is not likely to improve the picture."* James F. Crow (Professor of Genetics, University of Wisconsin), "Genetic Effects of Radiation," *Bulletin of the Atomic Scientists,* Vol. 14, January 1958, pp. 19-20.

- *"The one* **systematic** *effect of mutation seems to be a tendency towards degeneration."* [emphasis in original] Sewall Wright, "The Statistical Consequences of Mendelian Heredity in Relation to Speciation," *The New Systematics,* editor Julian Huxley (London: Oxford University Press, 1949), p. 174.

- In discussing the many mutations needed to produce a new organ, Koestler says that:

    "Each mutation occurring alone would be wiped out before it could be combined with the others. They are all interdependent. The doctrine that their coming together was due to a series of blind coinci-

dences is an affront not only to common sense but to the basic principles of scientific explanation." Arthur Koestler, *The Ghost in the Machine* (New York: Macmillan Publishing Co., 1968), p. 129.

c. *"There is no single instance where it can be maintained that any of the mutants studied has a higher vitality than the mother species."* N. Heribert Nilsson, *Synthetische Artbildung* (Lund, Sweden: Verlag CWK Gleerup, 1953), p. 1157.

   "It is, therefore, absolutely impossible to build a current evolution on mutations or on recombinations." [emphasis in original] Ibid., p. 1186.

- *"No matter how numerous they may be, mutations do not produce any kind of evolution."* Pierre-Paul Grassé, *Evolution of Living Organisms* (New York: Academic Press, 1977), p. 88.

- *"I have seen no evidence whatsoever that these* [evolutionary] *changes can occur through the accumulation of gradual mutations."* Lynn Margulis, as quoted by Charles Mann, "Lynn Margulis: Science's Unruly Earth Mother," *Science,* Vol. 252, 19 April 1991, p. 379.

- *"It is true that nobody thus far has produced a new species or genus, etc., by macromutation. It is equally true that nobody has produced even a species by the selection of micromutations."* Richard B. Goldschmidt, "Evolution, As Viewed by One Geneticist," *American Scientist,* Vol. 40, January 1952, p. 94.

- *"If life really depends on each gene being as unique as it appears to be, then it is too unique to come into being by chance mutations."* Frank B. Salisbury (Plant Science Department, Utah State University), "Natural Selection and the Complexity of the Gene," *Nature,* Vol. 224, 25 October 1969, p. 342.

- *"Do we, therefore, ever see mutations going about the business of producing new structures for selection to work on? No nascent organ has ever been observed emerging, though their origin in pre-functional form is basic to evolutionary theory. Some should be visible today, occurring in organisms at various stages up to integration of a functional new system, but we don't see them: there is no sign at all of this kind of radical novelty. Neither observation nor controlled experiment has shown natural selection manipulating mutations so as to produce a new gene, hormone, enzyme system or organ."* Michael Pitman, *Adam and Evolution* (London: Rider, 1984), pp. 67-68.

7. Fruit Flies
a. Strickberger, p. 44.

b. *"Most mutants which arise in any organism are more or less disadvantageous to their possessors. The classical mutants obtained in Drosophila* [the fruit fly] *usually show deterioration, breakdown, or disappearance of some organs. Mutants are known which diminish the quantity or destroy the pigment in the eyes, and in the body reduce the wings, eyes, bristles, legs. Many mutants are, in fact, lethal to their possessors. Mutants which equal the normal fly in vigor are a minority, and mutants that would make a major improvement of the normal organization in the normal environments are unknown."* Theodosius Dobzhansky, *Evolution, Genetics, and Man* (New York: John Wiley & Sons, 1955), p. 105.

- *"A review of known facts about their* [mutated fruit flies] *ability to survive has led to no other conclusion than that they are always constitutionally weaker than their parent form or species, and in a population with free competition they are eliminated.   Therefore they are never found in nature (e.g. not a single one of the several hundreds of Drosophila mutations), and therefore they are able to appear only in the favourable environment of the experimental field or laboratory . . . ."* Nilsson, p. 1186.

- *"In the best-known organisms, like Drosophila, innumerable mutants are known. If we were able to combine a thousand or more of such mutants in a single individual, this still would have no resemblance whatsoever to any type known as a* [new] *species in nature."* Goldschmidt, p. 94.

- *"It is a striking, but not much mentioned fact that, though geneticists have been breeding fruit-flies for sixty years or more in labs all round the world—flies which produce a new generation every eleven days—they have never yet seen the emergence of a new species or even a new enzyme."* Gordon Rattray Taylor (former Chief Science Advisor, BBC Television), *The Great Evolution Mystery* (New York: Harper & Row, 1983), p. 48.

- *"Fruit flies refuse to become anything but fruit flies under any circumstances yet devised."* Hitching, p. 61.

- *"The fruitfly (Drosophila melanogaster), the favorite pet insect of the geneticists, whose geographical, biotopical, urban, and rural genotypes are now known inside out, seems not to have changed since the remotest times."* Grassé, p. 130.

▲

8. Complex Organs
a. *"While today's digital hardware is extremely impressive, it is clear that the human retina's real-time performance goes unchallenged. Actually, to simulate 10 milliseconds (ms) of the complete processing of even a single nerve cell from the retina would require the solution of about 500 simultaneous nonlinear differential equations 100 times and would take at least several minutes of processing time on a Cray supercomputer. Keeping in mind that there are 10 million or more such cells interacting with each other in complex ways, it would take a minimum of 100 years of Cray time to simulate what takes place in your eye many times every second."*   John K. Stevens, "Reverse Engineering the Brain," *Byte*, April 1985, p. 287.

- *"Was the eye contrived without skill in optics* [optics], *and the ear without knowledge of sounds?"*   Isaac Newton, *Opticks* (New York: McGraw-Hill, 1931), pp. 369-370.

- *"Certainly there are those who argue that the universe evolved out of a random process, but what random process could produce the brain of a man or the system of the human eye?"* Wernher von Braun (probably the one rocket scientist most responsible for the United States' success in placing men on the moon) from a letter written by Dr. Wernher von Braun and read to the California State Board of Education by Dr. John Ford on 14 September 1972.

- *"The probability of dust carried by the wind reproducing Dürer's 'Melancholia' is less infinitesimal than the probability of copy errors in the DNA molecule leading to the formation of the eye; besides, these errors had **no relationship whatsoever** with the function that the eye would have to perform or was starting to perform. There is no law against daydreaming, but science must not indulge in it."* [emphasis in original] Grassé, p. 104.

- *"It must be admitted, however, that it is a considerable strain on one's credulity to assume that finely balanced systems such as certain sense organs (the eye of vertebrates, or the bird's feather) could be improved by random mutations. This is even more true for some of the ecological chain relationships (the famous yucca moth case, and so forth). However, the objectors to random mutations have so far been unable to advance any alternative explanation that was supported by substantial evidence."* Ernst Mayr, *Systematics and the Origin of Species* (New York: Dover Publications, 1942), p. 296.

- Although Robert Jastrow generally accepts Darwinian evolution, he acknowledges that:

  > *"It is hard to accept the evolution of the human eye as a product of chance; it is even harder to accept the evolution of human intelligence as the product of random disruptions in the brain cells of our ancestors."*   Robert Jastrow, "Evolution: Selection for Perfection," *Science Digest*, December 1981, p. 87.

- Many leading scientists have commented on the staggering complexity of the human eye. What some do not appreciate is how many diverse types of eyes there are, each of which adds to the problem for evolution.

  ◆ One of the strangest is a multiple-lensed, compound eye found in fossilized worms! [See Donald G. Mikulic et al., "A Silurian Soft-Bodied Biota," *Science*, Vol. 228, 10 May 1985, pp. 715-717.]

  ◆ Another type of eye belongs to some trilobites, which evolutionists claim are very early forms of life. These trilobite eyes had **compound lenses**, sophisticated designs for eliminating image distortion (spherical aberration). Only the best cameras and telescopes contain compound lenses. Trilobite eyes *"represent an all-time feat of function optimization."* Riccardo Levi-Setti, *Trilobites*, 2nd edition (Chicago: The University of Chicago Press, 1993), pp. 29-74.   Shawver described trilobite eyes as having *"the most sophisticated eye lenses ever produced by nature."* Lisa J. Shawver, "Trilobite Eyes: An Impressive Feat of Early Evolution," *Science News*, Vol. 105, 2 February 1974, p. 72. Gould admits that *"The eyes of early trilobites, for example, have never been exceeded for complexity or acuity by later arthropods . . . . I regard the failure to find a clear 'vector of progress' in life's history as the most puzzling fact of the fossil* *record."* Stephen Jay Gould, "The Ediacaran Experiment," *Natural History*, February 1984, pp. 22-23.

b. *"To my mind the human brain is the most marvelous and mysterious object in the whole universe and no geologic period seems too long to allow for its natural evolution."* Henry Fairfield Osborn, an influential evolutionist speaking to the American Association for the Advancement of Science in December 1929, as told by Roger Lewin, *Bones of Contention* (New York: Simon and Schuster, Inc., 1987), p. 57.

● *"And in Man is a three-pound brain which, as far as we know, is the most complex and orderly arrangement of matter in the universe."* Isaac Asimov, "In the Game of Energy and Thermodynamics You Can't Even Break Even," *Smithsonian*, August 1970, p. 10.

Asimov forgot that the brain, and presumably most of its details, is coded by only a fraction of the individual's DNA. Therefore, it is more accurate to say that DNA is the most complex arrangement of matter known in the universe.

● The human brain is frequently likened to a supercomputer. In most respects the brain greatly exceeds any computer's capabilities. Speed in some operations is one area where the computer beats the brain—at least in some ways. For example, few of us can quickly multiply .0239 times 854.95. This task is called a floating point operation, because the decimal point "floats" until we (or a computer) decide where to place it. The number of floating point operations per second (FLOPS) is a measure of a computer's speed. The Cray T90 supercomputer can perform 60 thousand million FLOPS (60 gigaFLOPS). As of this writing, the fastest computers can achieve almost 300 gigaFLOPS. Within the next ten years, petaFLOPS machines, capable of more than a million million FLOPS, will probably be commonplace. However, some way must be found to prevent these superfast computers from melting.   Their electricity will generate too much heat.

Overall, the human brain seems to operate at petaFLOPS speeds—without overheating.   One knowledgeable observer on these ultrafast computers commented,

> *"The human brain itself serves, in some sense, a proof of concept* [that petaFLOPS machines are possible]. *Its dense network of neurons apparently operates at a petaFLOPS or higher level. Yet the whole device fits in a 1 liter box and uses only about 10 watts of power.*
>
> *"That's a hard act to follow."*   Ivars Peterson, "PetaCrunchers: Setting a Course toward Ultrafast Supercomputing," *Science News*, Vol. 147, 15 April 1995, p. 235.

How, then, could the brain have evolved?

c. *"The human brain consists of about ten thousand million nerve cells. Each nerve cell puts out somewhere in the region of between ten thousand and one hundred thousand connecting fibres by which it makes contact with other nerve cells in the brain. Altogether the total number of*

connections in the human brain approaches 10^{15} or a thousand million million . . . . a much greater number of specific connections than in the entire communications network on Earth." Denton, pp. 330-331.

● *". . . the human brain probably contains more than 10^{14} synapses . . ."* Deborah M. Barnes, "Brain Architecture: Beyond Genes," *Science*, Vol. 233, 11 July 1986, p. 155.

d. Marlyn E. Clark, *Our Amazing Circulatory System*, Technical Monograph No. 5 (San Diego: Creation-Life Publishers, 1976).

9. Fully-Developed Organs

a. William Paley, *Natural Theology* (England: 1802; reprint edition Houston, Texas: St. Thomas Press, 1972).

This work by Paley, which contains many powerful arguments for a designer or creator, is a classic in scientific literature. Some people might feel that its date of original publication (1802) makes it completely out of date. Not so. Hoyle and Wickramasinghe compared Darwin's ideas with those of Paley as follows:

> *"The speculations of **The Origin of Species** turned out to be wrong, as we have seen in this chapter. It is ironic that the scientific facts throw Darwin out, but leave William Paley, a figure of fun to the scientific world for more than a century, still in the tournament with a chance of being the ultimate winner."* Fred Hoyle and N. Chandra Wickramasinghe, *Evolution from Space: A Theory of Cosmic Creationism* (New York: Simon and Schuster, 1981), pp. 96-97.

b. *"To suppose that the eye with all its inimitable contrivances for adjusting the focus to different distances, for admitting different amounts of light, and for the correction of spherical and chromatic aberration, could have been formed by natural selection, seems, I freely confess, absurd in the highest degree."* Charles Darwin, *The Origin of Species*, p. 75.

Darwin then proceeded to speculate on how the eye might nevertheless have evolved. However, no evidence was given.

● Charles Darwin, in a personal letter to Asa Gray in February 1860, expressed concern about how the eye could have evolved.   Gray, a famous Harvard botany professor, who was to become a leading advocate of theistic evolution, had written Darwin expressing doubt that natural processes could explain the formation of organs such as the eye. [See Francis Darwin, *The Life and Letters of Charles Darwin*, Vol. 2 (New York: D. Appleton and Co., 1899), pp. 66-67.]

● *"The eye, as one of the most complex organs, has been the symbol and archetype of his* [Darwin's] *dilemma. Since the eye is obviously of no use at all except in its final, complete form, how could natural selection have functioned in those initial stages of its evolution when the variations had no possible survival value? No single variation, indeed no single part, being of any use without every other, and natural selection presuming no knowledge of the ultimate end or purpose of the organ, the criterion of utility, or survival, would seem to be irrelevant. And there are other equally provoking examples of organs and processes which seem to defy natural selection. Biochemistry provides the case of chemical synthesis built up in several stages, of which the intermediate substance formed at any one stage is of no value at all, and only the end product, the final elaborate and delicate machinery, is useful—and not only useful but vital to life. How can selection, knowing nothing of the end or final purpose of this process, function when the only test is precisely that end or final purpose?"* Gertrude Himmelfarb, *Darwin and the Darwinian Revolution* (Garden City, New York: Doubleday, 1959), pp. 320-321.

c. *"Of what possible use are the imperfect incipient stages of useful structures? What good is half a jaw or half a wing?"* Stephen Jay Gould, "The Return of Hopeful Monsters," *Natural History*, Vol. 86, June-July 1977, p. 23.

10. Distinct Types

a. *"And let us dispose of a common misconception. The complete transmutation of even one animal species into a different species has never been directly observed either in the laboratory or in the field."* Dean H. Kenyon (Professor of Biology, San Francisco State University), affidavit presented to the U.S. Supreme Court, No. 85-1513, *Brief of Appellants*, prepared under the direction of William J. Guste, Jr., Attorney General of the State of Louisiana, October 1985, p. A-16.

● *"Thus so far as concerns the major groups of animals, the creationists seem to have the better of the argument. There is not the slightest evidence that any one of the major groups arose from any other. Each is a special animal complex related, more or less closely, to all the rest, and appearing, therefore, as a special and distinct creation."* Austin H. Clark, "Animal Evolution," *Quarterly Review of Biology*, Vol. 3, No. 4, December 1928, p. 539.

● *"When we descend to details, we can prove that no one species has changed; nor can we prove that the supposed changes are beneficial, which is the groundwork of the theory* [of evolution].*"* Charles Darwin, *The Life and Letters of Charles Darwin*, Vol. 2, editor Francis Darwin (New York: D. Appleton and Co., 1898), p. 210.

● *"The fact that all the individual species must be stationed at the extreme periphery of such logic* [evolutionary] *trees merely emphasized the fact that the order of nature betrays no hint of natural evolutionary sequential arrangements, revealing species to be related as sisters or cousins but **never** as ancestors and descendants as is required by evolution."* [emphasis in original] Denton, p. 132.

b. *". . . no human has ever seen a new species form in nature."* Steven M. Stanley, *The New Evolutionary Timetable* (New York: Basic Books, Inc., 1981), p. 73.

11. Altruism

a. *". . . the existence of altruism between different species—which is not uncommon—remains an obstinate enigma."* Taylor, p. 225.

b. From an evolutionist's point of view, a very costly form of altruism occurs when an animal forgoes reproduction while caring for another individual's young. This occurs in some human societies where a man has multiple wives who share the child-raising duties, even though only one wife bears children. More well-known examples include celibate individuals (such as nuns and many missionaries) who devote themselves to helping others. Such traits should never have evolved, or if they accidentally arose, they should quickly die out.

Some inherited behavior is lethal to the animal but beneficial to unrelated species. For example, many animals, such as goats, lambs, rabbits, horses, frogs, and toads, scream from fear and thus increase their exposure to predators while warning other species. Since frogs and toads grow up without parental contact, this behavior is not simply intended to seek the help of parents.

c. Some evolutionists try to explain this long-standing and widely recognized problem for evolution as follows: *"Altruistic behavior may prevent the altruistic individual from passing on his or her genes, but it benefits the individual's clan that carries some of those genes."* This hypothesis has three problems—two of them fatal.

◆ If individual X's altruistic trait was inherited, that trait should be carried recessively in only half the individual's brothers and sisters, one-fourth of the first cousins, etc. The key question then is: Does this "fractional altruism" benefit these relatives enough that they sire children they would not have otherwise, **and** is that additional number of children enough to cause, on the average, one or more in the next generation to have the trait? If not, the trait will become extinct, since altruistic X, by definition, cannot pass on his trait.

◆ If X did not inherit the altruistic trait but got it from a rare mutation, then no brothers, sisters, or cousins have the trait. No matter how much the individual's clan benefits, the trait will become extinct. From an evolutionist's perspective, all altruistic traits had to originate this way. Therefore, altruistic traits cannot survive the first generation.

◆ The hypothesis fails to explain altruism between different species. Without discussing examples that require a knowledge of the life patterns of such species, consider a simple but well-known example: humans who forgo having children in order to care for animals.

13. Languages

a. *"Projects devoted to teaching chimpanzees and gorillas to use language have shown that these apes can learn vocabularies of visual symbols. There is no evidence, however, that apes can combine such symbols in order to create new meanings. The function of the symbols of an ape's vocabulary appears to be not so much to identify things or to convey information as it is to satisfy a demand that it use that symbol in order to obtain some reward.*" H. S. Terrance et al., "Can an Ape Create a Sentence?", *Science*, Vol. 206, 23 November 1979, p. 900.

b. David C. C. Watson, *The Great Brain Robbery* (Chicago: Moody Press, 1976), pp. 83-89.

● "*Many other attempts have been made to determine the evolutionary origin of language, and all have failed . . . . Even the peoples with least complex cultures have highly sophisticated languages, with complex grammar and large vocabularies, capable of naming and discussing anything that occurs in the sphere occupied by their speakers . . . . The oldest language that can reasonably be reconstructed is already modern, sophisticated, complete from an evolutionary point of view.*" George Gaylord Simpson (former Professor of Vertebrate Paleontology at Harvard University), "The Biological Nature of Man," *Science*, Vol. 152, 22 April 1966, p. 477.

● George Gaylord Simpson acknowledges the vast gulf that separates animal communication and human languages. Although he recognizes the apparent pattern of language development from complex to simple, he cannot digest it. He simply says, "*Yet it is incredible that the first language could have been the most complex.*" He then shifts to a new subject. George Gaylord Simpson, *Biology and Man* (New York: Harcourt, Brace & World, Inc., 1969), p. 116.

● "*. . . human language appears to be a unique phenomenon, without significant analogue in the animal world.*" Noam Chomsky, *Language and Mind* (Chicago: Harcourt, Brace & World, Inc., 1968), p. 59.

● "*The evolution of language, at least within the historical period, is a story of progressive simplification.*" Albert C. Baugh, *A History of the English Language*, 2nd edition (New York: Appleton-Century-Crofts, Inc., 1957), p. 10.

● "*The so-called primitive languages can throw no light on language origins, since most of them are actually more complicated in grammar than the tongues spoken by civilized peoples.*" Ralph Linton, *The Tree of Culture* (New York: Alfred A. Knopf, 1957), p. 9.

c. "*It was Charles Darwin who first linked the evolution of languages to biology. In* **The Descent of Man** *(1871), he wrote, 'the formation of different languages and of distinct species, and the proofs that both have been developed through a gradual process, are curiously parallel.' But linguists cringe at the idea that evolution might transform simple languages into complex ones. Today it is believed that no language is, in any basic way, 'prior' to any other, living or dead. Language alters even as we speak it, but it neither improves nor degenerates.*" Philip E. Ross, "Hard Words," *Scientific American*, Vol. 264, April 1991, p. 144.

14. Speech
a. Mark P. Cosgrove, *The Amazing Body Human* (Grand Rapids: Baker Book House, 1987), pp. 106-109.

"*If we are honest, we will face the facts and admit that we can find no evolutionary development to explain our* [the human brain's] *unique speech center.*" Ibid., p. 164.

b. Arthur Custance, *Genesis and Early Man* (Grand Rapids: Zondervan Publishing House, 1975), pp. 250-271.

16. Information
a. For example, each living system can be uniquely described by its age and the information stored in its DNA. Each basic unit of DNA, called a nucleotide, can be one of four types. Therefore, each nucleotide represents two ($2^2 = 4$) bits of information. Likewise, a mechanical system can be described by a set of mechanical drawings which, in turn, could be converted to digital information as is done in a fax machine. Conceptual systems, such as a filing system, or a system for betting on race horses, can be explained in books. Several bits of information can define each symbol in these books. The minimum number of bits of information needed to completely describe a system will be defined as its information content.

b. Since macroevolution requires increasing complexity through natural processes, the organism's information content must spontaneously increase at each stage. But since natural processes cannot increase the information content of a system such as a reproductive cell, macroevolution cannot occur.

c. Based on modern advances in the field of information theory, the only known way to decrease the entropy of an isolated system is by having intelligence *in* that system. [See for example Charles H. Bennett, "Demons, Engines and the Second Law," *Scientific American*, Vol. 257, November 1987, pp. 108-116.] Since the universe is far from its maximum entropy level, a vast intelligence is the only known means by which the universe could have been brought into being. See also **Second Law of Thermodynamics** on page 19 and **Decay** on page 19.

d. If the "big bang" occurred, all the matter in the universe was at one time a hot gas. A gas is one of the most random systems known to science. There is virtually no information content in the chaotic, random movements of gas molecules. Since an isolated, non-trivial system, such as the universe, cannot increase its information content, the "big bang" could not have preceded the complex, living universe we have today which contains immense amounts of information.

17. A Common Designer
a. "*By this we have also proved that a morphological similarity between organisms cannot be used as proof of a phylogenetic* [evolutionary] *relationship . . . it is unscientific to maintain that the morphology may be used to prove relationships and evolution of the higher categories of units, ...*" Nilsson, p. 1143.

b. Fix, pp. 189-191.

● Denton, pp. 142-155.

- *"Therefore, **homologous structures need not be controlled by identical genes, and homology of phenotypes does not imply similarity of genotypes**. It is now clear that the pride with which it was assumed that the inheritance of homologous structures from a common ancestor explained homology was misplaced; for such inheritance cannot be ascribed to identity of genes . . . . But if it is true that through the genetic code, genes code for enzymes that synthesize proteins which are responsible (in a manner still unknown in embryology) for the differentiation of the various parts in their normal manner, what mechanism can it be that results in the production of homologous organs, the same 'patterns', in spite of their **not** being controlled by the same genes? I asked this question in 1938, and it has not been answered."* [Nor has it been answered today.—W.B.; emphasis in original] Gavin R. deBeer (formerly Professor of Embryology in the University of London and Director of the British Museum, Natural History), *Homology, An Unsolved Problem* (London: Oxford University Press, 1971), p. 16.

c. *"Structures as obviously homologous as the alimentary canal in all vertebrates can be formed from the roof of the embryonic gut cavity (sharks), floor (lampreys, newts), roof and floor (frogs), or from the lower layer of the embryonic disc, the blastoderm, that floats on the top of heavily yolked eggs (reptiles, birds). It does not seem to matter where in the egg or the embryo the living substance out of which homologous organs are formed comes from. Therefore, **correspondence between homologous structures cannot be pressed back to similarity of position of the cells of the embryo or the parts of the egg out of which these structures are ultimately differentiated.**"* [emphasis in original] Ibid., p. 13.

18. Vestigial Organs

a. *"The existence of functionless 'vestigial organs' was presented by Darwin, and is often cited by current biology textbooks, as part of the evidence for evolution . . . . An analysis of the difficulties in unambiguously identifying functionless structures and an analysis of the nature of the argument, leads to the conclusion that 'vestigial organs' provide no evidence for evolutionary theory."* S. R. Scadding, "Do 'Vestigial Organs' Provide Evidence for Evolution?", *Evolutionary Theory*, Vol. 5, No. 3, May 1981, p. 173.

b. Jerry Bergman and George Howe, *"Vestigial Organs" Are Fully Functional* (Terre Haute, Indiana: Creation Research Society Books, 1990).

19. Two-Celled Life?

a. E. Lendell Cockrum and William J. McCauley, *Zoology* (Philadelphia: W. B. Saunders Co., 1965), p. 163.

- Lynn Margulis and Karlene V. Schwartz, *Five Kingdoms: An Illustrated Guide to the Phyla of Life on Earth* (San Francisco: W. H. Freeman and Co., 1982), pp. 178-179.

- Perhaps the simplest forms of multicellular life are the Myxozoans, which have 6-12 cells. While they are quite distinct from other multicellular life, they are even more distinct from single-celled life (kingdom Protista). [See James F. Smothers et al., "Molecular Evidence That the Myxozoan Protists are Metazoans," *Science*, Vol. 265, 16 September 1994, pp. 1719-1721.] So, if they evolved from anywhere, it would most likely have been from higher, not lower, forms of life. Such a feat should be called devolution, not evolution.

Colonial forms of life are an unlikely bridge between single-celled life and multicelled life. The degree of cellular differentiation between colonial forms of life and the simplest multicellular forms of life is vast. For a further discussion, see Libbie Henrietta Hyman, *The Invertebrates: Protozoa through Ctenophora*, Vol. 1 (New York: McGraw-Hill, 1940) pp. 248-255.

20. Embryology

a. *"This generalization was originally called the biogenetic law by Haeckel and is often stated as 'ontogeny recapitulates phylogeny.' This crude interpretation of embryological sequences will not stand close examination, however. Its shortcomings have been almost universally pointed out by modern authors, but the idea still has a prominent place in biological mythology."* Paul R. Ehrlich and Richard W. Holm, *The Process of Evolution* (New York: McGraw-Hill, 1963), p. 66.

- *"It is now firmly established that ontogeny does **not** repeat phylogeny."* [emphasis in original] George Gaylord Simpson and William S. Beck, *Life: An Introduction to Biology* (New York: Harcourt, Brace & World, Inc., 1965), p. 241.

- Hitching, pp. 202-205.

- *"The enthusiasm of the German zoologist, Ernst Haeckel, however, led to an erroneous and unfortunate exaggeration of the information which embryology could provide. This was known as the 'biogenetic law' and claimed that embryology was a recapitulation of evolution, or that during its embryonic development an animal recapitulated the evolutionary history of its species."* Gavin R. deBeer, *An Atlas of Evolution* (New York: Nelson, 1964), p. 38.

- *". . . the theory of recapitulation has had a great and, while it lasted, regrettable influence on the progress of embryology."* Gavin R. deBeer, *Embryos and Ancestors*, revised edition (London: Oxford University Press, 1951), p. 10.

- *"Moreover, the biogenetic law has become so deeply rooted in biological thought that it cannot be weeded out in spite of its having been demonstrated to be wrong by numerous subsequent scholars."* Walter J. Bock (Department of Biological Sciences, Columbia University), "Evolution by Orderly Law," *Science*, Vol. 164, 9 May 1969, pp. 684-685.

- *". . . we no longer believe we can simply read in the embryonic development of a species its exact evolutionary history."* Hubert Frings and Marie Frings, *Concepts of Zoology* (Toronto: Macmillan Publishing Co., 1970), p. 267.

- *"The type of analogical thinking which leads to theories that development is based on the recapitulation of ancestral stages or the like no longer seems at all convincing or even interesting to biologists."* Conrad Hal Waddington, *Principles of Embryology* (London: George Allen and Unwin Ltd., 1956), p. 10.

- *"The biogenetic law—embryologic recapitulation—I think, was debunked back in the 1920s by embryologists."* David Raup, as taken from page 16 of an approved and verified transcript of a taped interview conducted by Luther D. Sunderland on 27 July 1979. See also Luther D. Sunderland, *Darwin's Enigma* (San Diego: Master Book Publishers, 1984), p. 119.

- *"Surely the biogenetic law is as dead as a doornail."* Keith Stewart Thomson, "Ontogeny and Phylogeny Recapitulated," *American Scientist*, Vol. 76, May-June 1988, p. 273.

- *"The theory of recapitulation was destroyed in 1922 by Professor Walter Gasbang in a famous paper. Since then no respectable biologist has ever used the theory of recapitulation, because it was utterly unsound, created by a Nazi-like preacher named Haeckel."* Ashley Montagu, as quoted in Sunderland, p. 119.

b. Haeckel, who in 1868 advanced this "biogenetic law" that was quickly adopted in textbooks and encyclopedias throughout the world, distorted his data. Thompson explains:

> *"A natural law can only be established as an induction from facts. Haeckel was of course unable to do this. What he did was to arrange existing forms of animal life in a series proceeding from the simple to the complex, intercalating [inserting] imaginary entities where discontinuity existed and then giving the embryonic phases names corresponding to the stages in his so-called evolutionary series. Cases in which this parallelism did not exist were dealt with by the simple expedient of saying that the embryological development had been falsified. When the 'convergence' of embryos was not entirely satisfactory, Haeckel altered the illustrations of them to fit his theory. The alterations were slight but significant. The 'biogenetic law' as a proof of evolution is valueless."* W. R. Thompson, p. 12.

- M. Bowden, *Ape-Men: Fact or Fallacy?*, 2nd edition (Bromley, England: Sovereign Publications, 1981), pp. 142-143.

- Wilbert H. Rusch, Sr., "Ontogeny Recapitulates Phylogeny," *Creation Research Society Quarterly*, Vol. 6, June 1969, pp. 27-34.

- *"To support his case he [Haeckel] began to fake evidence. Charged with fraud by five professors and convicted by a university court at Jena, he agreed that a small percentage of his embryonic drawings were forgeries; he was merely filling in and reconstructing the missing links when the evidence was thin, and he claimed unblushingly that 'hundreds of the best observers and biologists lie under the same charge'."* Pitman, p. 120.

- *". . . ontogeny recapitulates phylogeny, meaning that in the course of its development [ontogeny] an embryo recapitulates [repeats] the evolutionary history of its species. This idea was fathered by Ernst Haeckel, a German biologist who was so convinced that he had solved the riddle of life's unfolding that he doctored and faked his drawings of embryonic stages to prove his point."* Fix, p. 285.

- *"[The German scientist Wilhelm His] accused Haeckel of shocking dishonesty in repeating the same picture several times to show the similarity among vertebrates at early embryonic stages in several plates of [Haeckel's book]."* Stephen Jay Gould, *Ontogeny and Phylogeny* (Cambridge, Massachusetts: The Belknap Press of Harvard University Press, 1977), p. 430.

▲

21. Rapid Burial
a. Preston Cloud and Martin F. Glaessner, "The Ediacarian Period and System: Metazoa Inherit the Earth," *Science*, Vol. 217, 27 August 1982, pp. 783-792. See also the cover of that issue.

- Martin F. Glaessner, "Pre-Cambrian Animals," *Scientific American*, Vol. 204, No. 3, March 1961, pp. 72-78.

b. Donald G. Mikulic et al., "A Silurian Soft-Bodied Biota," *Science*, Vol. 228, 10 May 1985, pp. 715-717.

c. Presse Grayloise, "Very Like a Whale," *The Illustrated London News*, 1856, p. 116.

- Sunderland, pp. 111-114.

- David Starr Jordan, "A Miocene Catastrophe," *Natural History*, Vol. 20, January-February 1920, pp. 18-22.

- Hugh Miller, *The Old Red Sandstone, or New Walks in an Old Field* (Boston: Gould and Lincoln, 1858), pp. 221-225.

d. Harold G. Coffin, *Origin By Design* (Washington, D.C.: Review and Herald Publishing Assn., 1983), pp. 30-40.

▲

23. Fossil Gaps
a. *"But, as by this theory innumerable transitional forms must have existed, why do we not find them imbedded in countless numbers in the crust of the earth?"* Darwin, *The Origin of Species*, p. 163.

". . . the number of intermediate varieties, which have formerly existed [must] truly be enormous. Why then is not every geological formation and every stratum full of such intermediate links? Geology assuredly does not reveal any such finely-graduated organic chain; and this, perhaps, is the most obvious and serious objection which can be urged against the theory [of evolution]." Ibid., p. 323.

Darwin then explained that he thought these gaps existed because of the "imperfection of the geologic record." Early Darwinians expected the gaps would be filled as exploration for fossils continued. Most paleontologists now agree that this expectation has not been fulfilled.

• The Field Museum of Natural History in Chicago has one of the largest collections of fossils in the world. Consequently, its Dean, Dr. David Raup, was highly qualified to summarize the situation regarding the transitions that should be observed in the fossil record.

> *"Well, we are now about 120 years after Darwin and the knowledge of the fossil record has been greatly expanded. We now have a quarter of a million fossil species but the situation hasn't changed much. The record of evolution is still surprisingly jerky and, ironically, we have even fewer examples of evolutionary transition than we had in Darwin's time. By this I mean that some of the classic cases of darwinian change in the fossil record, such as the evolution of the horse in North America, have had to be discarded or modified as a result of more detailed information—what appeared to be a nice simple progression when relatively few data were available now appears to be much more complex and much less gradualistic. So Darwin's problem has not been alleviated in the last 120 years and we still have a record which does show change but one that can hardly be looked upon as the most reasonable consequence of natural selection."* David M. Raup, "Conflicts Between Darwin and Paleontology," *Field Museum of Natural History Bulletin*, Vol. 50, No. 1, January 1979, p. 25.

• *"In fact, the fossil record does not convincingly document a single transition from one species to another."* Stanley, p. 95.

• Dr. Colin Patterson, a senior paleontologist at the British Museum (Natural History), was asked by Luther D. Sunderland why no evolutionary transitions were included in Dr. Patterson's recent book entitled *Evolution*. In a personal letter, Patterson said:

> *"I fully agree with your comments on the lack of direct illustration of evolutionary transitions in my book. If I knew of any, fossil or living, I would certainly have included them. You suggest that an artist should be asked to visualise such transformations, but where would he get the information from? I could not, honestly, provide it, and if I were to leave it to artistic licence, would that not mislead the reader? . . . Yet Gould and the American Museum people are hard to contradict when they say that there are no transitional fossils. As a palaeontologist myself, I am much occupied with the philosophical problems of identifying ancestral forms in the fossil record. You say that I should at least 'show a photo of the fossil from which each type organism was derived.' I will lay it on the line—there is not one such fossil for which one could make a watertight argument."* Copy of letter, dated 10 April 1979, from Patterson to Sunderland.

• *"But the curious thing is that there is a consistency about the fossil gaps: **the fossils go missing in all the important places**. When you look for links between major groups of animals, they simply aren't there; at least, not in enough numbers to put their status beyond doubt. Either they don't exist at all, or they are so rare that endless argument goes on about whether a particular fossil is, or isn't, or might be, transitional between this group or that."* [emphasis in original] Hitching, p. 19.

• *"There is no more conclusive refutation of Darwinism than that furnished by palaeontology. Simple probability indicates that fossil hoards can only be test samples. Each sample, then, should represent a different stage of evolution, and there ought to be merely 'transitional' types, no definition and no species. Instead of this we find perfectly stable and unaltered forms persevering through long ages, forms that have not developed themselves on the fitness principle, but **appear suddenly and at once in their definitive shape**; that do not thereafter evolve towards better adaptation, but become rarer and finally disappear, while quite different forms crop up again. What unfolds itself, in ever-increasing richness of form, is the great classes and kinds of living beings which **exist aboriginally and exist still, without transition types**, in the grouping of today."* [emphasis in original] Oswald Spengler, *The Decline of the West*, Vol. 2 (New York: Alfred A. Knopf, 1966), p. 32.

• *"This regular absence of transitional forms is not confined to mammals, but is an almost universal phenomenon, as has long been noted by paleontologists. It is true of almost all orders of all classes of animals, both vertebrate and invertebrate. A fortiori, it is also true of the classes, themselves, and of the major animal phyla, and it is apparently also true of analogous categories of plants."* George Gaylord Simpson, *Tempo and Mode in Evolution* (New York: Columbia University Press, 1944), p. 107.

> *". . . the geologic record did not then and still does not yield a finely graduated chain of slow and progressive evolution. In other words, there are not enough intermediates. There are very few cases where one can find a gradual transition from one species to another and very few cases where one can look at a part of the fossil record and actually see that organisms were improving in the sense of becoming better adapted."* Ibid., p. 23.

• *"Surely the lack of gradualism—the lack of intermediates—is a major problem."* Dr. David Raup, as taken from page 16 of an approved and verified transcript of a taped interview conducted by Luther D. Sunderland on 27 July 1979.

• *". . . there are about 25 major living subdivisions (phyla) of the animal kingdom alone, all with gaps between them that are not bridged by known intermediates."* Francisco J. Ayala and James W. Valentine, *Evolving, The Theory and Processes of Organic Evolution* (Menlo Park, California: The Benjamin Cummings Publishing Co., 1979), p. 258.

> *"Most orders, classes, and phyla appear abruptly, and commonly have already acquired all the characters that distinguish them."* Ibid., p. 266.

• *"All paleontologists know that the fossil record contains precious little in the way of intermediate forms; transitions between major groups are characteristically abrupt."* Gould, "The Return of Hopeful Monsters," p. 23.

- *"The extreme rarity of transitional forms in the fossil record persists as the trade secret of paleontology. The evolutionary trees that adorn our textbooks have data only at the tips and nodes of their branches; the rest is inference, however reasonable, not the evidence of fossils . . . . We fancy ourselves as the only true students of life's history, yet to preserve our favored account of evolution by natural selection we view our data as so bad that we never see the very process we profess to study."* Stephen Jay Gould, "Evolution's Erratic Pace," *Natural History*, Vol. 5, May 1977, p. 14.

  "New species almost always appeared suddenly in the fossil record with no intermediate links to ancestors in older rocks of the same region." Ibid., p. 12.

- The following was based on an interview with Dr. Niles Eldredge, an invertebrate paleontologist at the American Museum of Natural History.

  "But the smooth transition from one form of life to another which is implied in the theory is . . . not borne out by the facts. The search for 'missing links' between various living creatures, like humans and apes, is probably fruitless . . . because they probably never existed as distinct transitional types . . . But no one has yet found any evidence of such transitional creatures. This oddity has been attributed to gaps in the fossil record which gradualists expected to fill when rock strata of the proper age had been found. In the last decade, however, geologists have found rock layers of all divisions of the last 500 million years and no transitional forms were contained in them. If it is not the fossil record which is incomplete then it must be the theory." "Missing, Believed Nonexistent," *Manchester Guardian* (The Washington Post Weekly), Vol. 119, No. 22, 26 November 1978, p. 1.

Gould and Eldredge believe that transitional fossils are missing because relatively rapid evolutionary jumps occurred over these gaps. They call their theory "punctuated equilibria." They do not explain how this could happen.

Many geneticists are shocked by the proposal of Gould and Eldredge. Since both are intelligent men, one should not conclude they do not understand genetics. Instead, one must realize just how contradictory the fossil record is to gradual evolution. To some, the desperation of Gould and Eldredge is justified.

- *". . . the gradual morphological transitions between presumed ancestors and descendants, anticipated by most biologists, are missing."* David E. Schindel (Curator of Invertebrate Fossils, Peabody Museum of Natural History), "The Gaps in the Fossil Record," *Nature*, Vol. 297, 27 May 1982, p. 282.

- *"Despite the bright promise that paleontology provides a means of 'seeing' evolution, it has presented some nasty difficulties for evolutionists the most notorious of which is the presence of 'gaps' in the fossil record. Evolution requires intermediate forms between species and paleon-* tology does not provide them."* David B. Kitts (School of Geology and Geophysics, University of Oklahoma), "Paleontology and Evolutionary Theory," *Evolution*, Vol. 28, September 1974, p. 467.

- *"In spite of the immense amount of the paleontological material and the existence of long series of intact stratigraphic sequences with perfect records for the lower categories, transitions between the higher categories are missing."* Goldschmidt, p. 98.

  "When a new phylum, class, or order appears, there follows a quick, explosive (in terms of geological time) diversification so that practically all orders or families known appear suddenly and without any apparent transitions." Ibid., p. 97.

- *"There is no fossil record establishing historical continuity of structure for most characters that might be used to assess relationships among phyla."* Katherine G. Field et al., "Molecular Phylogeny of the Animal Kingdom," *Science*, Vol. 239, 12 February 1988, p. 748.

b. *"It has long been hoped that extinct plants will ultimately reveal some of the stages through which existing groups have passed during the course of their development, but it must be freely admitted that this aspiration has been fulfilled to a very slight extent, even though paleobotanical research has been in progress for more than one hundred years. As yet we have not been able to trace the phylogenetic history of a single group of modern plants from its beginning to the present."* Chester A. Arnold, *An Introduction to Paleobotany* (New York: McGraw-Hill, 1947), p. 7.

- *". . . to the unprejudiced, the fossil record of plants is in favour of special creation. If, however, another explanation could be found for this hierarchy of classification, it would be the knell [the death signal] of the theory of evolution. Can you imagine how an orchid, a duckweed, and a palm have come from the same ancestry, and have we any evidence for this assumption? The evolutionist must be prepared with an answer, but I think that most would break down before an inquisition. Textbooks hoodwink."* E. J. H. Corner, "Evolution," *Contemporary Botanical Thought*, editors Anna M. MacLeod and L. S. Cobley (Chicago: Quadrangle Books, 1961), p. 97.

- *"The absence of any known series of such intermediates imposes severe restrictions on morphologists interested in the ancestral source of angiosperms and leads to speculation and interpretation of homologies and relationships on the basis of the most meager circumstantial evidence."* Charles B. Beck, *Origin and Early Evolution of Angiosperms* (New York: Columbia University Press, 1976), p. 5.

c. Speaking of the lack of transitional fossils between the invertebrates and vertebrates, Smith admits:

  "As our present information stands, however, the gap remains unbridged, and the best place to start the evolution of the vertebrates is in the imagination." Homer W. Smith, *From Fish to Philosopher* (Boston: Little, Brown, and Co., 1953), p. 26.

• *"How this earliest chordate stock evolved, what stages of development it went through to eventually give rise to truly fishlike creatures we do not know. Between the Cambrian when it probably originated, and the Ordovician when the first fossils of animals with really fishlike characteristics appeared, there is a gap of perhaps 100 million years which we will probably never be able to fill."* Francis Downes Ommanney, *The Fishes*, Life Nature Library (New York: Time Incorporated, 1963), p. 60.

d. *". . . there are no intermediate forms between finned and limbed creatures in the fossil collections of the world."* Taylor, p. 60.

e. Evolutionists believe that amphibians evolved into reptiles, with either *Diadectes* or *Seymouria* as the claimed transition. Actually, by the evolutionist's own time scale, this "transition" occurs 35 million years (m.y.) **after** the earliest reptile, *Hylonomus* (a cotylosaur). A parent cannot appear 35 million years after its child! The scattered locations of these fossils also present problems for the evolutionist.

Table 1: Reptile Transition?

What	Who	When	Where

[See Steven M. Stanley, *Earth and Life Through Time* (New York: W. H. Freeman and Co., 1986), pp. 411-415. See also Robert H. Dott, Jr. and Roger L. Batten, *Evolution of the Earth*, 2nd edition (New York: McGraw-Hill, 1976), p. 311.]

It is true that the skeletal features of some amphibians and some reptiles are similar. However, huge differences exist in their soft internal organs, such as their circulatory and reproductive systems. For example, no evolutionary scheme has ever been given for the development of the many unique innovations of the reptile's egg. [See Denton, pp. 218-219 and Pitman, pp. 199-200.]

f. *"Gaps at a lower taxonomic level, species and genera, are practically universal in the fossil record of the mammal-like reptiles. In no single adequately documented case is it possible to trace a transition, species by species, from one genus to another."* Thomas S. Kemp, *Mammal-like Reptiles and the Origin of Mammals* (New York: Academic Press, 1982), p. 319.

g. *"The* [evolutionary] *origin of birds is largely a matter of deduction. There is no fossil evidence of the stages through which the remarkable change from reptile to bird was achieved."* W. E. Swinton, "The Origin of Birds," *Biology and Comparative Physiology of Birds*, editor A. J. Marshall (New York: Academic Press, 1960), Vol. 1, Chapter 1, p. 1.

• See "**What Was Archaeopteryx?**" on page 148.

h. *"When and where the first Primates made their appearance is also conjectural. . . . It is clear, therefore, that the earliest Primates are not yet known. . . ."* William Charles Osman Hill, *Primates* (New York: Interscience Publishers, Inc., 1953), Vol. 1, pp. 25-26.

• *"The transition from insectivore to primate is not clearly documented in the fossil record."* A. J. Kelso, *Physical Anthropology*, 2nd edition (New York: J. B. Lippincott Company, 1974), p. 141.

• *"Modern apes, for instance, seem to have sprung out of nowhere. They have no yesterday, no fossil record. And the true origin of modern humans—of upright, naked, tool-making, big-brained beings—is, if we are to be honest with ourselves, an equally mysterious matter."* Lyall Watson, "The Water People," *Science Digest*, May 1982, p. 44.

i. *"At any rate, modern gorillas, orangs and chimpanzees spring out of nowhere, as it were. They are here today; they have no yesterday, unless one is able to find faint foreshadowings of it in the dryopithecids."* Donald Johanson and Maitland Edey, *Lucy: The Beginnings of Humankind* (New York: Simon and Schuster, 1981; reprint edition, New York: Warner Books, 1982), p. 363

j. *"It may, therefore, be firmly maintained that it is not even possible to make a caricature of an evolution out of palaeobiological facts. The fossil material is now so complete that it has been possible to construct new classes and the lack of transitional series cannot be explained as due to the scarcity of the material. The deficiencies are real, they will never be filled."* Nilsson, p. 1212.

• *". . . experience shows that the gaps which separate the highest categories may never be bridged in the fossil record. Many of the discontinuities tend to be more and more emphasized with increased collecting."* Norman D. Newell (former Curator of Historical Geology at the American Museum of Natural History), "The Nature of the Fossil Record," *Adventures in Earth History*, editor Preston Cloud (San Francisco: W. H. Freeman and Co., 1970), pp. 644-645.

• *"A person may choose any group of animals or plants, large or small, or pick one at random. He may then go to a library and with some patience he will be able to find a qualified author who says that the evolutionary origin of that form is not known."* Bolton Davidheiser, *Evolution and Christian Faith* (Phillipsburg, New Jersey: The Presbyterian and Reformed Publishing Company, 1969), p. 302.

Davidheiser, a Ph.D. zoologist and a creationist, goes on to list over 75 additional examples to illustrate the above point.

24. Missing Trunk

a. *"There is another and allied difficulty, which is much more serious. I allude to the manner in which species belonging to several of the main divisions of the animal kingdom suddenly appear in the lowest known fossiliferous rocks."* Darwin, *The Origin of Species*, p. 348.

"The abrupt manner in which whole groups of species suddenly appear in certain formations, has been urged by several palaeontologists—for instance, by Agassiz, Pictet, and Sedgwick—as a fatal objection to the belief in the

transmutation of species. If numerous species, belonging to the same genera or families, have really started into life at once, the fact would be fatal to the theory of evolution through natural selection." Ibid., p. 344.

"To the question why we do not find rich fossiliferous deposits belonging to these assumed earliest periods prior to the Cambrian system, I can give no satisfactory answer." Ibid., p. 350.

"The case at present must remain inexplicable, and may be truly urged as a valid argument against the views here entertained." Ibid., p. 351.

- *"The most famous such burst, the Cambrian explosion, marks the inception of modern multicellular life. Within just a few million years, nearly every major kind of animal anatomy appears in the fossil record for the first time . . . . The Precambrian record is now sufficiently good that the old rationale about undiscovered sequences of smoothly transitional forms will no longer wash."* Stephen Jay Gould, "An Asteroid to Die For," *Discover*, October 1989, p. 65.

- Richard Monastersky, "Mysteries of the Orient," *Discover*, April 1993, pp. 38-48.

- *"One of the major unsolved problems of geology and evolution is the occurrence of diversified, multicellular marine invertebrates in Lower Cambrian rocks on all the continents and their absence in rocks of greater age."* Daniel I. Axelrod, "Early Cambrian Marine Fauna," *Science*, Vol. 128, 4 July 1958, p. 7.

- *"Evolutionary biology's deepest paradox concerns this strange discontinuity. Why haven't new animal body plans continued to crawl out of the evolutionary cauldron during the past hundreds of millions of years? Why are the ancient body plans so stable?"* Jeffrey S. Levinton, "The Big Bang of Animal Evolution," *Scientific American*, Vol. 267, November 1992, p. 84.

- *"Granted an evolutionary origin of the main groups of animals, and not an act of special creation, the absence of any record whatsoever of a single member of any of the phyla in the Pre-Cambrian rocks remains as inexplicable on orthodox grounds as it was to Darwin."* T. Neville George (Professor of Geology at the University of Glasgow), "Fossils in Evolutionary Perspective," *Science Progress*, Vol. 48, No. 189, January 1960, p. 5.

b. Strange Cambrian fossils that were known to exist only in the Burgess Shale of western Canada have recently been discovered in southern China. See:

♦ L. Ramsköld and Hou Xianguang, "New Early Cambrian Animal and Onychophoran Affinities of Enigmatic Metazoans," *Nature*, Vol. 351, 16 May 1991, pp. 225-228.

♦ Jun-yuan Chen et al., "Evidence for Monophyly and Arthropod Affinity of Cambrian Giant Predators," *Science*, Vol. 264, 27 May 1994, pp. 1304-1308.

Evolving so many unusual animals during a geologic period is mind-boggling. But doing it twice in widely separated locations stretches credulity to the breaking point. According to the theory of plate tectonics, China and Canada were even farther apart during the Cambrian.

c. *"But whatever ideas authorities may have on the subject, the lung-fishes, like every other major group of fishes that I know, have their origins firmly based in **nothing**, a matter of hot dispute among the experts, each of whom is firmly convinced that everyone else is wrong . . . . I have often thought of how little I should like to have to prove organic evolution in a court of law."* [emphasis in original] Errol White, "A Little on Lung-Fishes," *Proceedings of the Linnean Society of London*, Vol. 177, Presidential Address, January 1966, p. 8.

- *"The geological record has so far provided no evidence as to the origin of the fishes . . . ."* J. R. Norman, *A History of Fishes*, 3rd edition (New York: John Wiley & Sons, 1975), p. 343.

- *"All three subdivisions of the bony fishes first appear in the fossil record at approximately the same time. They are already widely divergent morphologically, and they are heavily armored. How did they originate? What allowed them to diverge so widely? How did they all come to have heavy armor? And why is there no trace of earlier, intermediate forms?"* Gerald T. Todd, "Evolution of the Lung and the Origin of Bony Fishes—A Causal Relationship?", *American Zoologist*, Vol. 20, No. 4, p. 757.

d. Cloud and Glaessner, pp. 783-792.

e. A. K. Ghosh and A. Bose, "Occurrence of Microflora in the Salt Pseudomorph Beds, Salt Range, Punjab," *Nature*, Vol. 160, 6 December 1947, pp. 796-797.

- A. K. Ghosh, J. Sen, and A. Bose, "Evidence Bearing on the Age of the Saline Series in the Salt Range of the Punjab," *Geological Magazine*, Vol. 88, March-April 1951, pp. 129-133.

- J. Coates et al., "Age of the Saline Series in the Punjab Salt Range," *Nature*, Vol. 155, 3 March 1945, pp. 266-267.

- *". . . it is well known that the fossil record tells us nothing about the evolution of flowering plants."* Corner, p. 100.

- Clifford Burdick, in his doctoral research at the University of Arizona in 1964, made discoveries similar to those cited in the four preceding references. However, since Burdick was a creationist, and his discoveries conflicted with the accepted evolutionary doctrine, the University of Arizona refused to give him his doctor's degree. [See Clifford Burdick, "Microflora of the Grand Canyon," *Creation Research Society Quarterly*, Vol. 3, No. 1, May 1966, pp. 38-50.]

f. S. Leclercq, "Evidence of Vascular Plants in the Cambrian," *Evolution*, Vol. 10, No. 2, June 1956, pp. 109-114.

g. John E. Repetski, "A Fish from the Upper Cambrian of North America," *Science*, Vol. 200, 5 May 1978, pp. 529-531.

• *"Vertebrates and their progenitors, according to the new studies, evolved in the Cambrian, earlier than paleontologists have traditionally assumed."* Richard Monastersky, "Vertebrate Origins: The Fossils Speak Up," *Science News*, Vol. 149, 3 February 1996, p. 75.

h. *"There are no fossils known that show what the primitive ancestral insects looked like, ... Until fossils of these ancestors are discovered, however, the early history of the insects can only be inferred."* Peter Farb, *The Insects*, Life Nature Library (New York: Time Incorporated, 1962), pp. 14-15.

• *"There is, however, no fossil evidence bearing on the question of insect origin; the oldest insects known show no transition to other arthropods."* Frank M. Carpenter, "Fossil Insects," *Insects* (Washington, D.C.: U.S. Government Printing Office, 1952), p. 18.

i. *"If there has been evolution of life, the absence of the requisite fossils in the rocks older than the Cambrian is puzzling."* Marshall Kay and Edwin H. Colbert, *Stratigraphy and Life History* (New York: John Wiley & Sons, 1965), p. 103.

25. Out-of-Place Fossils
a. Walter E. Lammerts has published eight lists totaling almost 200 wrong-order formations in the United States alone. See "Recorded Instances of Wrong-Order Formations or Presumed Overthrusts in the United States: Parts I-VIII," *Creation Research Society Quarterly*, September 1984, p. 88; December 1984, p. 150; March 1985, p. 200; December 1985, p. 127; March 1986, p. 188; June 1986, p. 38; December 1986, p. 133; and June 1987, p. 46.

b. Y. Kruzhilin and V. Ovcharov, "A Horse from the Dinosaur Epoch?", *Moskovskaya Pravda* [*Moscow Truth*], 5 February 1984.

c. Alexander Romashko, "Tracking Dinosaurs," *Moscow News*, No. 24, 1983, p. 10. (For an alternate but equivalent translation, see Frank Zindler, "Man—A Contemporary of the Dinosaurs?", *Creation/Evolution*, Vol. 6, No. 1, 1986, pp. 28-29.)

d. Paul O. Rosnau et al., "Are Human and Mammal Tracks Found Together with the Tracks of Dinosaurs in the Kayenta of Arizona?", Parts I and II, *Creation Research Society Quarterly*; Vol. 26, September 1989, pp. 41-48 and December 1989, pp. 77-98.

e. Andrew Snelling, "Fossil Bluff," *Ex Nihilo*, Vol. 7, No. 3, March 1985, p. 8.

• Carol Armstrong, "Florida Fossils Puzzle the Experts," *Creation Research Society Quarterly*, Vol. 21, March 1985, pp. 198-199.

• Pat Shipman, "Dumping on Science," *Discover*, December 1987, p. 64.

f. Francis S. Holmes, *Phosphate Rocks of South Carolina and the "Great Carolina Marl Bed"* (Charleston, South Carolina: Holmes' Book House, 1870).

• Edward J. Nolan, "Remarks on Fossils from the Ashley Phosphate Beds," *Proceedings of the Academy of Natural Sciences of Philadelphia*, pp. 80-81.

• John Watson (8302 Daleview Drive, Austin, Texas 78758) has done extensive library research on the relatively unknown fossil discoveries in these beds. Their vast content of bones provides the rich phosphate content. Personal communications, 1992.

g. R. M. Stainforth, "Occurrence of Pollen and Spores in the Roraima Formation of Venezuela and British Guiana," *Nature*, Vol. 210, 16 April 1966, pp. 292-294.

• A. K. Ghosh and A. Bose, pp. 796-797.

• A. K. Ghosh and A. Bose, "Spores and Tracheids from the Cambrian of Kashmir," *Nature*, Vol. 169, 21 June 1952, pp. 1056-1057.

• J. Coates et al., pp. 266-267.

h. George F. Howe et al., "A Pollen Analysis of Hakatai Shale and Other Grand Canyon Rocks," *Creation Research Society Quarterly*, Vol. 24, March 1988, pp. 173-182.

i. A. C. Noé, "A Paleozoic Angiosperm," *The Journal of Geology*, Vol. 31, May-June 1923, pp. 344-347.

j. Edwin D. McKee, *The Supai Group of Grand Canyon*, Geological Survey Professional Paper 1173 (Washington D.C.: U.S. Government Printing Office, 1982), pp. 93-96, 100.

k. Richard Monastersky, "A Walk along the Lakeshore, Dinosaur-Style," *Science News*, Vol. 136, 8 July 1989, p. 21.

l. Stephen T. Hasiotis, "Fossilized Combs Have Scientists Abuzz," *The Arizona Republic*, 26 May 1995, p. B7.

• Stephen T. Hasiotis (paleobiologist, U.S. Geological Survey, Denver), personal communication, 27 May 1995.

26. Ape-Men?
a. Lord Zuckerman candidly stated that if special creation did not occur, then no scientist could deny that man evolved from some apelike creature, *"without leaving any fossil traces of the steps of the transformation."* Solly Zuckerman (former Chief Scientific Advisor to the British Government and Honorary Secretary of the Zoological Society of London), *Beyond the Ivory Tower* (New York: Taplinger Publishing Co., 1970), p. 64.

• Bowden, pp. 56-246.

- Duane T. Gish, *Battle for Creation,* Vol. 2, editor Henry M. Morris (San Diego: Creation-Life Publishers, 1976), pp. 298-305.

- Ibid., pp. 193-200.

b. Speaking of Piltdown man, Lewin admits a common human problem that even scientists have:

> "How is it that trained men, the greatest experts of their day, could look at a set of modern human bones—the cranial fragments—and 'see' a clear simian signature in them; and 'see' in an ape's jaw the unmistakable signs of humanity? The answers, inevitably, have to do with the scientists' expectations and their effects on the interpretation of data." Lewin, *Bones of Contention,* p. 61.

c. Allen L. Hammond, "Tales of an Elusive Ancestor," *Science 83,* November 1983, pp. 37, 43.

d. Adrienne L. Zihlman and J. Lowenstein, "False Start of the Human Parade," *Natural History,* August/September 1979, pp. 86-91.

e. Hammond, p. 43.

- *"The dethroning of Ramapithecus—from putative [supposed] first human in 1961 to extinct relative of the orangutan in 1982—is one of the most fascinating, and bitter, sagas in the search for human origins."* Roger Lewin, *Bones of Contention,* p. 86.

f. Java man consisted of two bones that were found about 39 feet apart: a skull cap and femur (thighbone). Rudolf Virchow, the famous German pathologist, believed the femur was from a gibbon. By concurring, Dubois supported his own non-Darwinian theory of evolution—a theory too complex and strange to discuss here. [See Stephen Jay Gould, "Men of the Thirty-third Division," *Natural History,* April 1990, pp. 12-22.]

Whether or not the bones were from a large-brained gibbon, a hominid, another animal, or two completely different animals is not important. This episode shows how easily the person who knew the bones best could shift his interpretation from Java "man" to Java "gibbon." Even after other fragmentary finds were made at other sites in Java, the total evidence was so fragmentary that a wide range of interpretations was possible.

- *"Pithecanthropus [Java man] was not a man, but a gigantic genus allied to the Gibbons . . . ."* Eugene Dubois, "On the Fossil Human Skulls Recently Discovered in Java and Pithecanthropus Erectus," *Man,* Vol. 37, January 1937, p. 4.

> *"Thus the evidence given by those five new thigh bones of the morphological and functional distinctness of Pithecanthropus erectus furnishes proof, at the same time, of its close affinity with the gibbon group of anthropoid apes."* Ibid., p. 5.

- C. L. Brace and Ashley Montagu, *Human Evolution,* 2nd edition (New York: Macmillan Publishing Co., 1977), p. 204.

- Bowden, pp. 138-142, 144-148.

- Hitching, pp. 208-209.

- *"The success of Darwinism was accompanied by a decline in scientific integrity . . . . A striking example, which has only recently come to light, is the alteration of the Piltdown skull so that it could be used as evidence for the descent of man from the apes; but even before this a similar instance of tinkering with evidence was finally revealed by the discoverer of Pithecanthropus [Java man], who admitted, many years after his sensational report, that he had found in the same deposits bones that are definitely human."* W. R. Thompson, p. 17.

W. R. Thompson refers to Dubois' discovery in November 1890 of part of a lower jaw containing the stump of a tooth. This was found at Kedung-Brubus (also spelled Kedeong Broboes), 25 miles east of his find of Java "man" at Trinil, eleven months later. Dubois was confident that it was a human jaw of Tertiary age. [See Herbert Wendt, *In Search of Adam* (Westport, Connecticut: Greenwood Publishers, 1955), pp. 293-294.] Dubois' claims of finding "the missing link" would probably have been ignored if he had mentioned this jaw. Similar, but less convincing, charges have been made against Dubois concerning his finding of obvious human skulls at Wadjak, 60 miles from Trinil.

- Patrick O'Connell, *Science of Today and the Problems of Genesis,* 2nd edition (Roseburg, Oregon: self-published, 1969), pp. 139-142.

g. Ibid., pp. 108-138.

- Bowden, pp. 90-137.

- Marcellin Boule and Henri V. Vallois, *Fossil Men* (New York: The Dryden Press, 1957), p. 145.

h. "[The reanalysis of Narmada Man] *puts another nail in the coffin of Homo erectus as a viable taxon."* Kenneth A. R. Kennedy, as quoted in *"Homo Erectus* Never Existed?", *Geotimes,* October 1992, p. 11.

i. Donald C. Johanson et al., "New Partial Skeleton of *Homo Habilis* from Olduvai Gorge, Tanzania," *Nature,* Vol. 327, 21 May 1987, pp. 205-209.

j. Dr. Charles Oxnard and Sir Solly Zuckerman, referred to below, were leaders in the development of a powerful multivariate analysis procedure. This computerized technique simultaneously performs millions of comparisons on hundreds of corresponding dimensions of the bones of living apes, humans, and the Australopithecines. Their verdict, that the Australopithecines are not intermediate between man and living apes, is quite different from the more subjective and less analytical visual techniques of most anthropologists. This technique, however, has not yet been applied to the most famous Australopithecine, commonly known as "Lucy."

- *". . . the only positive fact we have about the Australopithecine brain is that it was no bigger than the brain of a gorilla. The claims that are made about the human character of the*

Australopithecine face and jaws are no more convincing than those made about the size of its brain. The Australopithecine skull is in fact so overwhelmingly simian as opposed to human that the contrary proposition could be equated to an assertion that black is white." Zuckerman, p. 78.

- *"Let us now return to our original problem: the Australopithecine fossils. I shall not burden you with details of each and every study that we have made, but table 1 summarizes the information and shows that whereas the conventional wisdom is that the Australopithecine fragments are generally rather similar to humans and when different deviate somewhat towards the condition in the African apes, the new studies point to different conclusions. The new investigations suggest that the fossil fragments are usually uniquely different from any living form . . . ."* Charles E. Oxnard (Dean of the Graduate School, University of Southern California, Los Angeles, and from 1973-1978 a Dean at the University of Chicago), "Human Fossils: New Views of Old Bones," *The American Biology Teacher*, Vol. 41, May 1979, p. 273.

- Charles E. Oxnard, "The Place of the Australopithecines in Human Evolution: Grounds for Doubt?", *Nature*, Vol. 258, 4 December 1975, pp. 389-395.

- *"For my own part, the anatomical basis for the claim that the Australopithecines walked and ran upright like man is so much more flimsy than the evidence which points to the conclusion that their gait was some variant of what one sees in subhuman Primates, that it remains unacceptable."* Zuckerman, p. 93.

- *"This Australopithecine material suggests a form of locomotion that was not entirely upright nor bipedal. The Rudolf Australopithecines, in fact, may have been close to the 'knuckle-walker' condition, not unlike the extant African apes."* Richard E. F. Leakey, "Further Evidence of Lower Pleistocene Hominids from East Rudolf, North Kenya," *Nature*, Vol. 231, 28 May 1971, p. 245.

k. Fred Spoor et al., "Implications of Early Hominid Labyrinthine Morphology for Evolution of Human Bipedal Locomotion," *Nature*, Vol. 369, 23 June 1994, pp. 645-648.

l. William L. Jungers, "Lucy's Limbs: Skeletal Allometry and Locomotion in *Australopithecus Afarensis*," *Nature*, Vol. 297, 24 June 1982, pp. 676-678.

- Jeremy Cherfas, "Trees Have Made Man Upright", *New Scientist*, Vol. 93, 20 January 1983, pp. 172-178.

- Jack T. Stern, Jr. and Randall L. Susman, "The Locomotor Anatomy of *Australopithecus Afarensis*," *American Journal of Physical Anthropology*, Vol. 60, March 1983, pp. 279-317.

m. *"There is indeed, no question which the Australopithecine skull resembles when placed side by side with specimens of human and living ape skulls. It is the ape—so much so that only detailed and close scrutiny can reveal any differences between them."* Solly Zuckerman, "Correlation of Change in the Evolution of Higher Primates," *Evolution as a*

Process, editors Julian Huxley, A. C. Hardy, and E. B. Ford (London: George Allen and Unwin Ltd., 1954), p. 307.

"We can safely conclude from the fossil hominoid material now available that in the history of the globe there have been many more species of great ape than just the three which exist today." Ibid., pp. 348-349.

n. Francis Ivanhoe, "Was Virchow Right About Neanderthal?", *Nature*, Vol. 227, 8 August 1970, pp. 577-578.

- William L. Straus, Jr. and A. J. E. Cave, "Pathology and the Posture of Neanderthal Man," *The Quarterly Review of Biology*, December, 1957, pp. 348-363.

- Bruce M. Rothschild and Pierre L. Thillaud, "Oldest Bone Disease," *Nature*, Vol. 349, 24 January 1991, p. 288.

o. Boyce Rensberger, "Facing the Past," *Science* 81, October 1981, p. 49.

▲

27. Fossil Man
a. J. D. Whitney, "The Auriferous Gravels of the Sierra Nevada of California," *Memoirs of the Museum of Comparative Zoology of Harvard College*, Vol. 6, 1880, pp. 258-288.

- Bowden, pp. 76-78.

- Frank W. Cousins, *Fossil Man* (Emsworth, England: A. E. Norris & Sons Ltd., 1971), pp. 50-52, 82, 83.

- W. H. B., "Alleged Discovery of An Ancient Human Skull in California," *American Journal of Science*, Vol. 2, 1866, p. 424.

- For many years, stories have circulated that the Calaveras skull, buried 130 feet below ground, was a practical joke. These claims can be traced back to such reports as:

  ♦ William H. Holmes, "Review of the Evidence Relating to Auriferous Gravel Man in California," *Smithsonian Institutional Annual Report*, 1899, pp. 419-472.

  ♦ Felix J. Kock, "The Calaveras Skull," *American Antiquarian*, Vol. 33, No. 4, Oct-Dec 1911, pp. 199-201.

  ♦ Waldemar Lindgren, *The Tertiary Gravels of the Sierra Nevada of California*, Geological Survey Professional Paper 73, (Washington, D.C.: U.S. Government Printing Office, 1911), pp. 54-57.

This tidy explanation conveniently overlooks the hundreds of human artifacts and bones found throughout that part of California, such as spearheads, mortars and pestles, and dozens of bowls made of stone. These artifacts have been found over the years under apparently undisturbed strata and a layer of basaltic lava. See for example:

  ♦ Whitney, pp. 262-264, 266, 274-276.

  ♦ G. Frederick Wright, *Man and the Glacial Period* (New York: D. Appleton and Co.,1897), pp. 294-301.

  ♦ George F. Becker, "Antiquities from under Tuolumne Table Mountain in California," *Bulletin of the Geological*

Society of America, Vol. 2, 20 February 1891, pp. 189-200.

b. Bowden, pp. 78-79.

• Cousins, pp. 48-50, 81.

• Sir Arthur Keith correctly stated the dilemma evolutionists face with the Castenedolo skeletons.

> *"As the student of prehistoric man reads and studies the records of the 'Castenedolo' find, a feeling of incredulity rises within him. He cannot reject the discovery as false without doing an injury to his sense of truth, and he cannot accept it as a fact without shattering his accepted beliefs."* Arthur Keith, *The Antiquity of Man* (London: Williams and Norgate, Ltd., 1925), p. 334.

However, after examining the strata above and below the Castenedolo skeletons, and after finding no indication that they were intrusively buried, Keith surprisingly concluded that the enigma must be resolved by an intrusive burial. He justified this by citing the unfossilized condition of the bones. However, these bones were encased in a clay layer. This would prevent water from transporting large amounts of dissolved minerals into the bone cells and explain the lack of fossilization. Fossilization depends much more on chemistry than age.

c. Bowden, pp. 183-193.

d. Ibid., pp. 79-88.

e. Fix, pp. 98-105.

• J. B. Birdsell, *Human Evolution* (Chicago: Rand McNally, 1972), pp. 316-318.

28. Chemical Elements of Life
a. The four most abundant chemical elements (by weight) in the human body are oxygen (65%), carbon (18%), hydrogen (10%), and nitrogen (3%).

b. Carbon is only the 18th most abundant element in the earth's crust by mass. Furthermore, almost all carbon is tied up in organic matter, such as coal and oil, or in sediments deposited after life began, such as limestone or dolomite.

c. Hitching, p. 65.

d. *"If there ever was a primitive soup* [to provide the chemical compounds for evolving life]*, then we would expect to find at least somewhere on this planet either massive sediments containing enormous amounts of the various nitrogenous organic compounds, amino acids, purines, pyrimidines and the like, or alternatively in much metamorphosed sediments we should find vast amounts of nitrogenous cokes. In fact no such materials have been found anywhere on earth. Indeed to the contrary, the very oldest of sediments . . . are extremely short of nitrogen."* J. Brooks and G. Shaw, *Origin and Development of Living Systems* (New York: Academic Press, 1973), p. 359.

e. *"The acceptance of this theory* [of the evolution of life on earth] *and its promulgation by many workers* [scientists and researchers] *who have certainly not always considered all the facts in great detail has in our opinion reached proportions which could be regarded as dangerous."* Ibid., p. 355.

Dangerous? Ignoring indisputable, basic evidence in most scientific fields is expensive and wasteful. Failure to explain the evidence to students betrays a trust and misleads those who will be the next generation's teachers and decision makers.

Readers should consider why, despite the improbabilities and lack of proper chemistry, many educators and the media have taught for a century that life evolved on earth. Abandoning or questioning that belief leaves only one strong contender—creation. Questioning evolution in some circles invites ostracism, much like commenting on the proverbial emperor's nakedness.

29. Proteins
a. A recent and authoritative study, using evolutionary dating techniques, concluded that the early biosphere contained oxygen 300 million years before the earliest known fossils (bacteria) were formed. Iron oxides were found that *"imply a source of oxygen enough to convert into insoluble ferric material the ferrous solutions that must have first formed the flat, continuous horizontal layers that can in some sites be traced over hundreds of kilometers."* Philip Morrison, "Earth's Earliest Biosphere," *Scientific American*, Vol. 250, April 1984, pp. 30-31.

• Charles F. Davidson, "Geochemical Aspects of Atmospheric Evolution," *Proceedings of the National Academy of Sciences*, Vol. 53, 15 June 1965, pp. 1194-1205.

• Steven A. Austin, "Did the Early Earth Have a Reducing Atmosphere?", *ICR Impact*, No. 109, July 1982.

• *"In general, we find no evidence in the sedimentary distributions of carbon, sulfur, uranium, or iron, that an oxygen-free atmosphere has existed at any time during the span of geological history recorded in well preserved sedimentary rocks."* Erich Dimroth and Michael M. Kimberley, "Precambrian Atmospheric Oxygen: Evidence in the Sedimentary Distributions of Carbon, Sulfur, Uranium, and Iron," *Canadian Journal of Earth Sciences*, Vol. 13, No. 9, September 1976, p. 1161.

• *"What is the evidence for a primitive methane-ammonia atmosphere on earth? The answer is that there is **no** evidence for it, but much against it."* [emphasis in original] Philip H. Abelson, "Chemical Events on the Primitive Earth," *Proceedings of the National Academy of Sciences*, Vol. 55, June 1966, p. 1365.

b. R. T. Brinkmann, "Dissociation of Water Vapor and Evolution of Oxygen in the Terrestrial Atmosphere," *Journal of Geophysical Research*, Vol. 74, No. 23, 20 October 1969, pp. 5355-5368.

c. *"I believe this* [the overwhelming tendency for chemical reactions to move in the direction opposite to that required for the evolution of life] *to be the most stubborn problem that confronts us—the weakest link at present in our argument* [for the origin of life]*."* Wald, p. 50.

d. *"The conclusion from these arguments presents the most serious obstacle, if indeed it is not fatal, to the theory of spontaneous generation. First, thermodynamic calculations predict vanishingly small concentrations of even the simplest organic compounds. Secondly, the reactions that are invoked to synthesize such compounds are seen to be much more effective in decomposing them."* D. E. Hull, "Thermodynamics and Kinetics of Spontaneous Generation," *Nature*, Vol. 186, 28 May 1960, p. 694.

● Pitman, p. 140.

● Duane T. Gish, *Speculations and Experiments Related to Theories on the Origin of Life*, ICR Technical Monograph, No. 1 (El Cajon, California: Institute for Creation Research, 1972).

e. Robert Shapiro, *Origins* (New York: Bantam Books, 1986).

● The experiments by Harold Urey and Stanley Miller are often mentioned as showing that the "building blocks of life" can be produced in the laboratory. Not mentioned in these misleading claims are:

◆ These "building blocks" are merely the simpler amino acids. The most complex amino acids have never been produced in the laboratory.

◆ Most of the other products of these chemical reactions are poisonous to life.

◆ Amino acids are as far from a living cell as bricks are from the Empire State Building.

◆ Half the amino acids produced have the wrong handedness. (See **"Handedness: Left and Right"** on page 11.)

◆ Urey and Miller's experimental apparatus contained components, such as a trap, that do not exist in nature. (A *trap* quickly removes chemical products from the destructive energy sources that make the products.)

All of the above show how necessary intelligence and design are for producing even the simplest components of life.

30. The First Cell
a. *"The complexity of the simplest known type of cell is so great that it is impossible to accept that such an object could have been thrown together suddenly by some kind of freakish, vastly improbable, event. Such an occurrence would be indistinguishable from a miracle."* Denton, p. 264.

"Is it really credible that random processes could have constructed a reality, the smallest element of which—a functional protein or gene—is complex beyond our own creative capacities, a reality which is the very antithesis of chance, which excels in every sense anything produced by the intelligence of man? Alongside the level of ingenuity

and complexity exhibited by the molecular machinery of life, even our most advanced artefacts appear clumsy. We feel humbled, as neolithic man would in the presence of twentieth-century technology. It would be an illusion to think that what we are aware of at present is any more than a fraction of the full extent of biological design. In practically every field of fundamental biological research ever-increasing levels of design and complexity are being revealed at an ever-accelerating rate." Ibid., p. 342.

● *"We have seen that self-replicating systems capable of Darwinian evolution appear too complex to have arisen suddenly from a prebiotic soup. This conclusion applies both to nucleic acid systems and to hypothetical protein-based genetic systems."* Shapiro, p. 207.

"We do not understand how this gap in organization was closed, and this remains the most crucial unsolved problem concerning the origin of life." Ibid., p. 299.

● *"More than 30 years of experimentation on the origin of life in the fields of chemical and molecular evolution have led to a better perception of the immensity of the problem of the origin of life on Earth rather than to its solution. At present all discussions on principal theories and experiments in the field either end in stalemate or in a confession of ignorance."* Klaus Dose, "The Origin of Life: More Questions Than Answers," *Interdisciplinary Science Reviews*, Vol. 13, No. 4, 1988, p. 348.

b. *"The events that gave rise to that first primordial cell are totally unknown, matters for guesswork and a standing challenge to scientific imagination."* Lewis Thomas, foreword to *The Incredible Machine*, editor Robert M. Pool (Washington, D.C.: National Geographic Book Service, 1986) p. 7.

● *"No experimental system yet devised has provided the slightest clue as to how biologically meaningful sequences of subunits might have originated in prebiotic polynucleotides or polypeptides."* Kenyon, p. A-20.

● Experts in this field hardly ever discuss publicly how the first cell could have evolved. However, the leading evolutionists in the world know that this problem exists. For example, on 27 July 1979, Luther D. Sunderland taped an interview with Dr. David Raup of the Field Museum of Natural History in Chicago. This interview was later transcribed and authenticated by both parties. Sunderland commented to Dr. Raup that *"Neither Dr. Patterson* [of the British Museum (Natural History)] *nor Dr. Eldredge* [of the American Museum of Natural History] *could give me any explanation of the origination of the first cell."* Dr. Raup replied, *"I can't either."*

● *"However, the macromolecule-to-cell transition is a jump of fantastic dimensions, which lies beyond the range of testable hypothesis. In this area all is conjecture. The available facts do not provide a basis for postulating that cells arose on this planet."* David E. Green and Robert F. Goldberger, *Molecular Insights Into the Living Process* (New York: Academic Press, 1967), pp. 406-407.

31. Barriers, Buffers, and Chemical Pathways
a. This delicate chemical balance, upon which life depends, was brought to this author's attention by biologist Terry Mondy.

32. Genetic Distances
a. Dr. Colin Patterson is the Senior Principal Scientific Officer in the Palaeontology Department at the British Museum (Natural History). In a talk he gave on 5 November 1981, to leading evolutionists at the American Museum of Natural History, he compared the amino acid sequences in several proteins of different animals. The relationships of these animals, according to evolutionary theory, have been taught in classrooms for decades. Patterson pointed out to a stunned audience that this new information contradicts the theory of evolution. In his words, *"The theory makes a prediction; we've tested it, and the prediction is falsified precisely."* Although he acknowledged that scientific falsification is never absolute, the thrust of his entire talk was that he now realized *"evolution was a faith,"* he had *"been duped into taking evolutionism as revealed truth in some way,"* and *"evolution not only conveys no knowledge but seems somehow to convey anti-knowledge, apparent knowledge which is harmful to systematics* [the science of classifying different forms of life].*"* "Prominent British Scientist Challenges Evolution Theory," Audio Tape Transcription and Summary by Luther D. Sunderland, personal communication. For other statements from Patterson's presentation see: Tom Bethell, "Agnostic Evolutionists," *Harper's Magazine*, February 1985, pp. 49-61.

• Field, pp. 748-753.

• *". . . it seems disconcerting that many exceptions exist to the orderly progression of species as determined by molecular homologies . . . ."* Christian Schwabe, "On the Validity of Molecular Evolution," *Trends in Biochemical Sciences*, July 1986, p. 280.

"It appears that the neo-darwinian hypothesis is insufficient to explain some of the observations that were not available at the time the paradigm took shape. . . . One might ask why the neo-darwinian paradigm does not weaken or disappear if it is at odds with critical factual information. The reasons are not necessarily scientific ones but rather may be rooted in human nature." Ibid., p. 282.

b. Denton, p. 285.

c. *"The really significant finding that comes to light from comparing the proteins' amino acid sequences is that it is impossible to arrange them in any sort of evolutionary series."* Ibid., p. 289.

"Thousands of different sequences, protein and nucleic acid, have now been compared in hundreds of different species but never has any sequence been found to be in any sense the lineal descendant or ancestor of any other sequence." Ibid., pp. 289-290.

"Each class at a molecular level is unique, isolated and unlinked by intermediates. Thus molecules, like fossils, have failed to provide the elusive intermediates so long sought by evolutionary biology." Ibid., p. 290.

"There is little doubt that if this molecular evidence had been available one century ago it would have been seized upon with devastating effect by the opponents of evolution theory like Agassiz and Owen, and the idea of organic evolution might never have been accepted." Ibid., pp. 290-291.

"In terms of their biochemistry, none of the species deemed 'intermediate', 'ancestral' or 'primitive' by generations of evolutionary biologists, and alluded to as evidence of sequence in nature, show any sign of their supposed intermediate status." Ibid., p. 293.

d. Ginny Gray, "Student Project 'Rattles' Science Fair Judges," *Issues and Answers*, December 1980, p. 3.

• Robert Bayne Brown, *Abstracts: 31st International Science and Engineering Fair* (Washington D.C.: Science Service, 1980), p. 113.

33. Genetic Information
a. Carl Sagan, *The Dragons of Eden* (New York: Random House, 1977), p. 25. (Each of Sagan's 4000 books contained 500 pages of 300 words per page.)

b. *"Biochemical systems are exceedingly complex, so much so that the chance of their being formed through random shufflings of simple organic molecules is exceedingly minute, to a point indeed where it is insensibly different from zero."* Hoyle and Wickramasinghe, p. 3.

"No matter how large the environment one considers, life cannot have had a random beginning. Troops of monkeys thundering away at random on typewriters could not produce the works of Shakespeare, for the practical reason that the whole observable universe is not large enough to contain the necessary monkey hordes, the necessary typewriters, and certainly the waste paper baskets required for the deposition of wrong attempts. The same is true for living material." Ibid., p. 148.

"The trouble is that there are about two thousand enzymes, and the chance of obtaining them all in a random trial is only one part in $(10^{20})^{2000} = 10^{40,000}$, an outrageously small probability that could not be faced even if the whole universe consisted of organic soup. If one is not prejudiced either by social beliefs or by a scientific training into the conviction that life originated on the Earth, this simple calculation wipes the idea entirely out of court." Ibid., p. 24.

"Any theory with a probability of being correct that is larger than one part in $10^{40,000}$ must be judged superior to random shuffling [of evolution]. The theory that life was assembled by an intelligence has, we believe, a probability vastly higher than one part in $10^{40,000}$ of being the correct explanation of the many curious facts discussed in preceding chapters. Indeed, such a theory is so obvious that one

wonders why it is not widely accepted as being self-evident. The reasons are psychological rather than scientific." Ibid., p. 130.

"From the beginning of this book we have emphasized the enormous information content of even the simplest living systems. The information cannot in our view be generated by what are often called 'natural' processes, as for instance through meteorological and chemical processes occurring at the surface of a lifeless planet. As well as a suitable physical and chemical environment, a large initial store of information was also needed. We have argued that the requisite information came from an 'intelligence', the beckoning spectre." Ibid., p. 150.

"Once we see, however, that the probability of life originating at random is so utterly minuscule as to make the random concept absurd, it becomes sensible to think that the favourable properties of physics on which life depends are in every respect deliberate." Ibid., p. 141.

Hoyle and Wickramasinghe go on to say that our own intelligences must reflect some sort of vastly superior intelligence, *"even to the extreme idealized limit of **God**."* They believe that life was created by some intelligence somewhere in outer space and later was transported to earth. [emphasis in original] Ibid., p. 144.

c. Murray Eden, as reported in "Heresy in the Halls of Biology: Mathematicians Question Darwinism," *Scientific Research*, November 1967, p. 64.

● *"It is our contention that if 'random' is given a serious and crucial interpretation from a probabilistic point of view, the randomness postulate is highly implausible and that an adequate scientific theory of evolution must await the discovery and elucidation of new natural laws—physical, physico-chemical, and biological."* Murray Eden, "Inadequacies of Neo-Darwinian Evolution as a Scientific Theory," *Mathematical Challenges to the Neo-Darwinian Interpretation of Evolution*, editors Paul S. Moorhead and Martin M. Kaplan, June 1967, p. 109.

▲───────────────

34. DNA Production

a. A ribosome, a complex structure that assembles the protein, is made up of about 55 different proteins. Twenty additional proteins are required to attach the 20 different types of amino acids to transfer RNA. Other enzymes also participate in the process.

b. Richard E. Dickerson, "Chemical Evolution and the Origin of Life," *Scientific American*, Vol. 239, September 1978, p. 73.

● *"The amino acids must link together to form proteins, and the other chemicals must join up to make nucleic acids, including the vital DNA. The seemingly insurmountable obstacle is the way the two reactions are inseparably linked—one can't happen without the other. Proteins depend on DNA for their formation. But DNA cannot form without pre-existing protein."* Hitching, p. 66.

c. *"The origin of the genetic code presents formidable unsolved problems. The coded information in the nucleotide sequence is meaningless without the translation machinery, but the specification for this machinery is itself coded in the DNA. Thus without the machinery the information is meaningless, but without the coded information the machinery cannot be produced! This presents a paradox of the 'chicken and egg' variety, and attempts to solve it have so far been sterile."* John C. Walton, (Lecturer in Chemistry, University of St. Andrews, Fife, Scotland), "Organization and the Origin of Life," *Origins*, Vol. 4, No. 1, 1977, pp. 30-31.

● *"Genes and enzymes are linked together in a living cell—two interlocked systems, each supporting the other. It is difficult to see how either could manage alone. Yet if we are to avoid invoking either a Creator or a very large improbability, we must accept that one occurred before the other in the origin of life. But which one was it? We are left with the ancient riddle: Which came first, the chicken or the egg?"* Shapiro, p. 135.

▲───────────────

35. Handedness: Left and Right

a. *"All nucleotides synthesized biologically today are right-handed. Yet on the primitive earth, equal numbers of right- and left-handed nucleotides would have been present. When we put equal numbers of both kinds of nucleotides in our reaction mixtures, copying was inhibited."* Leslie E. Orgel, "The Origin of Life on the Earth," *Scientific American*, Vol. 271, October 1994, p. 82.

● *"There is no explanation why cells use L [left handed] amino acids to synthesize their proteins but D [right handed] ribose or D-deoxyribose to synthesize their nucleotides or nucleic acids. In particular, the incorporation of even a single L-ribose or L-deoxyribose residue into a nucleic acid, if it should ever occur in the course of cellular syntheses, could seriously interfere with vital structure-function relationships. The well-known double helical DNA structure does not allow the presence of L-deoxyribose; the replication and transcription mechanisms generally require that any wrong sugar such as L-deoxyribose has to be eliminated, that is, the optical purity of the D-sugars units has to be 100%."* Dose, p. 352.

b. *"Many researchers have attempted to find plausible natural conditions under which [left-handed] L-amino acids would preferentially accumulate over their [right-handed] D-counterparts, but all such attempts have failed. Until this crucial problem is solved, no one can say that we have found a naturalistic explanation for the origin of life. Instead, these isomer preferences point to biochemical creation."* Kenyon, p. A-23.

● This is such a problem to those who believe life evolved that they are continually seeking a solution. From time to time someone claims that it has been solved, but only after checking the details does one find that the problem remains. Recently (1994) in Germany, a doctoral candidate, Guido Zadel, claimed he had solved the problem. Supposedly, a strong magnetic field will bias a reaction toward either the left-handed or right-handed form. Origin-of-life researchers were excited. Zadel's doctorate was awarded. At least 20 groups then tried to duplicate the results, always unsuccessfully. Zadel has now admitted that he dishonestly manipulated his data. [See Daniel Clery and David Bradley, "Underhanded 'Breakthrough' Revealed," *Science*, Vol. 265, 1 July 1994, p. 21.]

- James F. Coppedge, *Evolution: Possible or Impossible?* (Grand Rapids: Zondervan Publishing House, 1973), pp. 71-79.

- A. E. Wilder-Smith, *The Natural Sciences Know Nothing of Evolution* (San Diego: Master Book Publishers, 1981), pp. 15-32, 154-160.

- Dickerson, p. 76.

36. Improbabilities
a. Coppedge, pp. 71-72.

- *"Whether one looks to mutations or gene flow for the source of the variations needed to fuel evolution, there is an enormous probability problem at the core of Darwinist and neo-Darwinist theory, which has been cited by hundreds of scientists and professionals. Engineers, physicists, astronomers, and biologists who have looked without prejudice at the notion of such variations producing ever more complex organisms have come to the same conclusion: The evolutionists are assuming the impossible. Even if we take the simplest large protein molecule that can reproduce itself if immersed in a bath of nutrients, the odds against this developing by chance range from one in 10^{450} (engineer Marcel Goulay in Analytical Chemistry) to one in 10^{600} (Frank Salisbury in American Biology Teacher)."* Fix, p. 196.

- *"I don't know how long it is going to be before astronomers generally recognize that the combinatorial arrangement of not even one among the many thousands of biopolymers on which life depends could have been arrived at by natural processes here on the Earth. Astronomers will have a little difficulty at understanding this because they will be assured by biologists that is not so, the biologists having been assured in their turn by others that it is not so. The 'others' are a group of persons who believe, quite openly, in mathematical miracles. They advocate the belief that tucked away in nature, outside of normal physics, there is a law which performs miracles (provided the miracles are in the aid of biology). This curious situation sits oddly on a profession that for long has been dedicated to coming up with logical explanations of biblical miracles."* Fred Hoyle, "The Big Bang in Astronomy," *New Scientist*, Vol. 92, 19 November 1981, p. 526.

37. Symbiotic Relationships
a. Oscar L. Brauer, "The Smyrna Fig Requires God for Its Production," *Creation Research Society Quarterly*, Vol. 9, No. 2, September 1972, pp. 129-131.

- Bob Devine, *Mr. Baggy-Skin Lizard* (Chicago: Moody Press, 1977), pp. 29-32.

b. Jerry A. Powell and Richard A. Mackie, *Biological Interrelationships of Moths and Yucca Whipplei* (Los Angeles: University of California Press, 1966).

38. Sexual Reproduction
a. N. W. Pixie, "Boring Sperm," *Nature*, Vol. 351, 27 June 1991, p. 704.

b. Meredith Gould and Jose Luis Stephano, "Electrical Responses of Eggs to Acrosomal Protein Similar to Those Induced by Sperm," *Science*, Vol. 235, 27 March 1987, pp. 1654-1656.

c. *"But the sex-determination genes in the fruit fly and the nematode are completely unrelated to each other, let alone to those in mammals."* Jean Marx, "Tracing How the Sexes Develop," *Science*, Vol. 269, 29 September 1955, p. 1822.

d. *"This book is written from a conviction that the prevalence of sexual reproduction in higher plants and animals is inconsistent with current evolutionary theory."* George C. Williams, *Sex and Evolution* (Princeton, New Jersey: Princeton University Press, 1975), p. v.

- *"The evolution of sex is one of the major unsolved problems of biology. Even those with enough hubris to publish on the topic often freely admit that they have little idea of how sex originated or is maintained. It is enough to give heart to creationists."* Michael Rose, "Slap and Tickle in the Primeval Soup," *New Scientist*, Vol. 112, 30 October 1986, p. 55.

- *"Indeed, the persistence of sex is one of the fundamental mysteries in evolutionary biology today."* Gina Maranto and Shannon Brownlee, "Why Sex?", *Discover*, February 1984, p. 24.

- *"Sex is something of an embarrassment to evolutionary biologists. Textbooks understandably skirt the issue, keeping it a closely guarded secret."* Kathleen McAuliffe, "Why We have Sex," *Omni*, December 1983, p. 18.

- *"So why is there sex? We do not have a compelling answer to the question. Despite some ingenious suggestions by orthodox Darwinians (notably G. C. Williams 1975; John Maynard Smith 1978), there is no convincing Darwinian history for the emergence of sexual reproduction. However, evolutionary theorists believe that the problem will be solved without abandoning the main Darwinian insights— just as early nineteenth-century astronomers believed that the problem of the motion of Uranus could be overcome without major modification of Newton's celestial mechanics."* Philip Kitcher, *Abusing Science: The Case Against Creationism* (Cambridge, Massachusetts: The MIT Press, 1982), p. 54.

- *"From an evolutionary viewpoint the sex differentiation is impossible to understand, as well as the structural sexual differences between the systematic categories which are sometimes immense. We know that intersexes within a species must be sterile. How is it, then, possible to imagine bridges between two amazingly different structural types?"* Nilsson, p. 1225.

- *"One idea those attending the sex symposium seemed to agree on is that no one knows why sex persists."* [According to evolution, it should not.—W.B.] Gardiner Morse, "Why Is Sex?", *Science News*, Vol. 126, 8 September 1984, p. 155.

39. Immune Systems

a. *"Unfortunately, we cannot trace most of the evolutionary steps that the immune system took. Virtually all the crucial developments seem to have happened at an early stage of vertebrate evolution, which is poorly represented in the fossil record and from which few species survive. Even the most primitive extant vertebrates seem to rearrange their antigen receptor genes and possess separate T and B cells, as well as MHC molecules. Thus has the immune system sprung up fully armed."* Avrion Mitchison, "Will We Survive?", *Scientific American*, Vol. 269, September 1993, p. 138.

40. Living Technology

a. *"Ounce for ounce, watt for watt, it [the bat] is millions of times more efficient and more sensitive than the radars and sonars contrived by man."* Pitman, p. 219.

b. Robert E. Kofahl and Kelly L. Segraves, *The Creation Explanation* (Wheaton, Illinois: Harold Shaw Publishers, 1975), pp. 2-9.

- Thomas Eisner and Daniel J. Aneshansley, "Spray Aiming in Bombardier Beetles: Jet Deflection by the Coanda Effect," *Science*, Vol. 215, 1 January 1982, pp. 83-85.

c. David H. Freedman, "Exploiting the Nanotechnology of Life," *Science*, Vol. 254, 29 November 1991, pp. 1308-1310.

- Tom Koppel, "Learning How Bacteria Swim Could Set New Gears in Motion," *Scientific American*, Vol. 265, September 1991, pp. 168-169.

d. Y. Magariyama et al., "Very Fast Flagellar Rotation," *Nature*, Vol. 371, 27 October 1994, p. 752.

e. If one could scale down a conventional electrical motor to propel a bacterium through a liquid, friction would overcome almost all movement. This is because the ratio of inertial-to-viscous forces is proportional to scale. In effect, the liquid appears to become stickier the smaller you get. Therefore, the efficiency of the bacterial motor itself, which approaches 100% at slow speeds, is remarkable and currently unexplainable.

f. Yes, you read this correctly. The molecular motors are 25 nanometers in diameter while an average human hair is about 75 microns in diameter.

41. The Validity of Thought

a. *"But then arises the doubt, can the mind of man, which has, as I fully believe, been developed from a mind as low as that possessed by the lowest animals, be trusted when it draws such grand conclusions? I cannot pretend to throw*

the least light on such abstruse problems." Charles Darwin, *The Life and Letters*, Vol. 1, p. 313.

- *"For if my mental processes are determined wholly by the motions of atoms in my brain, I have no reason to suppose that my beliefs are true. They may be sound chemically, but that does not make them sound logically. And hence I have no reason for supposing my brain to be composed of atoms."* J. B. S. Haldane, *Possible Worlds* (London: Chatto & Windus, 1927), p. 209.

- *"If the solar system was brought about by an accidental collision, then the appearance of organic life on this planet was also an accident, and the whole evolution of Man was an accident too. If so, then all our present thoughts are mere accidents—the accidental by-product of the movement of atoms. And this holds for the thoughts of the materialists and astronomers as well as for anyone else's. But if their thoughts—i.e. of Materialism and Astronomy— are merely accidental by-products, why should we believe them to be true? I see no reason for believing that one accident should be able to give me a correct account of all the other accidents."* C. S. Lewis, *God In the Dock* (Grand Rapids: Eerdmans Publishing Co., 1970), pp. 52-53.

- *"Each particular thought is valueless if it is the result of irrational causes. Obviously, then, the whole process of human thought, what we call Reason, is equally valueless if it is the result of irrational causes. Hence every theory of the universe which makes the human mind a result of irrational causes is inadmissible, for it would be a proof that there are no such things as proofs. Which is nonsense. But Naturalism [evolution], as commonly held, is precisely a theory of this sort."* C. S. Lewis, *Miracles* (New York: Macmillan Publishing Co., 1947), p. 21.

- C. S. Lewis, "The Funeral of a Great Myth," *Christian Reflections* (Grand Rapids: Eerdmans Publishing Co., 1968), p. 89.

- *"If the universe is a universe of thought, then its creation must have been an act of thought."* James H. Jeans, *The Mysterious Universe*, new revised edition (New York: Macmillan Publishing Co., 1932), p. 181.

- *"A theory that is the product of a mind can never adequately explain the mind that produced the theory. The story of the great scientific mind that discovers absolute truth is satisfying only so long as we accept the mind itself as a given. Once we try to explain the mind as a product of its own discoveries, we are in a hall of mirrors with no exit."* Phillip E. Johnson, *Reason in the Balance: The Case Against Naturalism in Science, Law & Education* (Downers Grove, Illinois: InterVarsity Press, 1995), p. 62.

b. Darwin recognized this problem.

"Behind Darwin's discomfiture [on how the human brain evolved] was the dawning realization that the evolution of the brain vastly exceeded the needs of prehistoric man. This is, in fact, the only example in existence where a species was provided with an organ that it still has not learned how to use." Richard M. Restak, *The Brain: The*

Last Frontier (Garden City, New York: Doubleday & Company, Inc., 1979), p. 59.

42 . Strange Planets

a. *"To sum up, I think that all suggested accounts of the origin of the Solar System are subject to serious objections. The conclusion in the present state of the subject would be that the system cannot exist."* Harold Jeffreys, *The Earth: Its Origin, History, and Physical Constitution*, 6th edition (Cambridge, England: Cambridge University Press, 1976), p. 387.

● *"But if we had a reliable theory of the origin of planets, if we knew of some mechanism consistent with the laws of physics so that we understood how planets form, then clearly we could make use of it to estimate the probability that other stars have attendant planets. However, no such theory exists yet, despite the large number of hypotheses suggested."* R. A. Lyttleton, *Mysteries of the Solar System* (Oxford, England: Clarendon Press, 1968), p. 4.

● *"A great array of observational facts must be explained by a satisfactory theory [on the evolution of the solar system], and the theory must be consistent with the principles of dynamics and modern physics. All of the hypotheses so far presented have failed, or remain unproved, when physical theory is properly applied."* Fred L. Whipple, *Earth, Moon, and Planets*, 3rd edition (Cambridge, Massachusetts: Harvard University Press, 1968), p. 243.

b. *"The most striking outcome of planetary exploration is the diversity of the planets."* David Stevenson, as quoted by Richard A. Kerr, "The Solar System's New Diversity," *Science*, Vol. 265, 2 September 1994, p. 1360.

"I wish it were not so, but I'm somewhat skeptical that we're going to learn an awful lot about Earth by looking at other planetary bodies. The more that we look at the different planets, the more each one seems to be unique." Ibid.

● *"Stevenson and others are puzzling out how subtle differences in starting conditions such as distance from the sun, along with chance events like giant impacts early in the solar system history, can send planets down vastly different evolutionary paths."* Kerr, "The Solar System's New Diversity," p. 1360.

● *"You put together the same basic materials and get startlingly different results. No two are alike; it's like a zoo."* Alexander Dessler, as quoted by Richard A. Kerr, Ibid, p. 1361.

● *"The profound question, of course, is why doesn't Venus have plate tectonics?"* Stevenson, p. 1362.

c. *The Astronomical Almanac for the Year 1989* (Washington D.C.: U.S. Government Printing Office, 1989), p. E88.

d. Ibid., F2. (Six additional moons of Neptune were discovered by Voyager II after *The Astronomical Almanac for the Year 1989* was published.)

e. Ibid., F2.

f. *Van Nostrand's Scientific Encyclopedia*, 5th edition (New York: Van Nostrand Reinhold Co., 1976), pp. 493-494.

● *"First, we see that material torn from the Sun would not be at all suitable for the formation of the planets as we know them. Its composition would be hopelessly wrong. And our second point in this contrast is that it is the Sun that is normal and the Earth that is the freak. The interstellar gas and most of the stars are composed of material like the Sun, not like the Earth. You must understand that, cosmically speaking, the room you are now sitting in is made of the wrong stuff. You, yourself, are a rarity. You are a cosmic collector's piece."* Fred Hoyle, "The Nature of the Universe," Part IV, *Harper's Magazine*, March 1951, p. 65.

g. Lyttleton, p. 16.

● Fred Hoyle, *The Cosmology of the Solar System* (Hillside, New Jersey: Enslow Publishers, 1979), pp. 11-12.

● *"One of the detailed problems is then to explain how the Sun itself acquires nearly 99.9% of the mass of the solar system but only 2% of its angular momentum."* Frank D. Stacey, *Physics of the Earth* (New York: John Wiley & Sons, 1969), p. 4.

● Some have proposed transferring angular momentum from the sun to the planets by "magnetic linking." McCrea states:

"However, I scarcely think it has yet been established that the postulated processes would inevitably occur, or that if they did they would operate with the extreme efficiency needed in order to achieve the required distribution of angular momentum." William Hunter McCrea, "Origin of the Solar System," *Symposium on the Origin of the Solar System* (Paris, France: Centre National de la Recherche Scientifique, 1972), p. 8.

43. Evolving Planets?

a. John F. Kerridge and James F. Vedder, "An Experimental Approach to Circumsolar Accretion," *Symposium on the Origin of the Solar System* (Paris, France: Centre National de la Recherche Scientifique, 1972), pp. 282-283.

b. Tim Folger, "This Battered Earth," *Discover*, January 1994, p. 33.

● *"'We came to the conclusion,' says Lissauer, 'that if you accrete planets from a uniform disk of planetesimals, [the observed] prograde rotation just can't be explained,' The simulated bombardment leaves a growing planet spinning once a week at most, not once a day."* Richard A. Kerr, "Theoreticians Are Putting a New Spin on the Planets," *Science*, Vol. 258, 23 October 1992, p. 548.

● Luke Dones and Scott Tremaine, "Why Does the Earth Spin Forward?", *Science*, Vol. 259, 15 January 1993, pp. 350-354.

● Some believe the inner planets (Mercury, Venus, Earth, and Mars) gained their spins through a few very large and improbable impacts. However, this appeal to large or improbable impacts will not work for the giant outer planets

(Jupiter, Saturn, Uranus, and Neptune) which have the most spin energy. Such impacts on these gaseous planets would be even more improbable, because they move more slowly and are so far from the center of the solar system. Besides, impacts from large rocks would not account for the composition of the giant planets—basically hydrogen and helium.

c. *"Building Jupiter has long been a problem to theorists."* George W. Wetherill, "How Special is Jupiter?", *Nature*, Vol. 373, 9 February 1995, p. 470.

d. There is a further difficulty with this idea. If, as the solar system began to form, a large, rocky planet quickly formed near Jupiter's orbit, one would expect to see a large planet in the asteroid belt, just inside Jupiter's orbit. Of course, none exists.

o. B. Zuckerman et al., "Inhibition of Giant-Planet Formation by Rapid Gas Depletion around Young Stars," *Nature*, Vol. 373, 9 February 1995, pp. 494-496.

44. Origin of the Moon

a. *"The whole subject of the origin of the moon must be regarded as highly speculative."* Robert C. Haymes, *Introduction to Space Science* (New York: John Wiley & Sons, 1971), p. 209.

• On 10 November 1971, Dr. Harold Urey, a Nobel prize-winning chemist and lunar scientist, stated *"I do not know the origin of the moon, I'm not sure of my own or any other's models, I'd lay odds against any of the models proposed being correct."* Robert Treash, "Magnetic Remanence in Lunar Rocks," *Pensee*, Vol. 2, No. 2, May 1972, p. 22.

• *"In astronomical terms, therefore, the Moon must be classed as a well-known object, but astronomers still have to admit shamefacedly that they have little idea as to where it came from. This is particularly embarrassing, because the solution of the mystery was billed as one of the main goals of the US lunar exploration programme."* David W. Hughes, "The Open Question in Selenology," *Nature*, Vol. 327, 28 May 1987, p. 291.

b. Haymes, p. 209.

c. Paul M. Steidl, *The Earth, the Stars, and the Bible* (Grand Rapids: Baker Book House, 1979), pp. 77-79.

• M. Mitchell Waldrop, "The Origin of the Moon," *Science*, Vol. 216, 7 May 1982, pp. 606-607.

• Stacey, pp. 38-39.

45. Evolution of the Solar System?

a. Charles Petit, "A Mountain Cliffhanger of an Eclipse," *Science*, Vol. 253, 26 July 1991, pp. 386-387.

• Klaus-Werner Hodapp et al., "A Search During the 1991 Solar Eclipse for the Infrared Signature of Circumsolar Dust," *Nature*, Vol. 355, 20 February 1992, pp. 707-710.

46. Mountains of Venus

a. Richard A. Kerr, "A New Portrait of Venus: Thick-Skinned and Decrepit," *Science*, Vol. 263, 11 February 1994, pp. 759-760.

47. Space, Time, and Matter

a. Nathan R. Wood, *The Secret of the Universe*, 10th edition (Grand Rapids: Eerdmans Publishing Co., 1936).

49. Second Law of Thermodynamics

a. *"The more orthodox scientific view is that the entropy of the universe must forever increase to its final maximum value. It has not yet reached this: we should not be thinking about it if it had. It is still increasing rapidly, and so must have had a beginning; there must have been what we may describe as a 'creation' at a time not infinitely remote."* Jeans, p. 181.

51. Decay

a. *"A final point to be made is that the second law of thermodynamics and the principle of increase in entropy have great philosophical implications. The question that arises is how did the universe get into the state of reduced entropy in the first place, since all natural processes known to us tend to increase entropy? ... The author has found that the second law tends to increase his conviction that there is a Creator who has the answer for the future destiny of man and the universe."* Gordon J. Van Wylen, *Thermodynamics* (New York: John Wiley & Sons, 1959), p. 169.

• *"The time asymmetry of the Universe is expressed by the second law of thermodynamics, that entropy increases with time as order is transformed into disorder. The mystery is not that an ordered state should become disordered but that the early Universe apparently was in a highly ordered state."* Don N. Page, "Inflation Does Not Explain Time Asymmetry," *Nature*, Vol. 304, 7 July 1983, p. 39.

"There is no mechanism known as yet that would allow the Universe to begin in an arbitrary state and then evolve to its present highly-ordered state." Ibid., p. 40.

• *"The real puzzle is why there is an arrow of time at all; that is, why the Universe is not simply a thermodynamic equilibrium at all times (except during the inevitable local fluctuations). The theory of nonequilibrium systems [such as those described by Ilya Prigogine] may tell us how such systems behave, given that there are some; but it does not explain how they come to be so common in the first place (and all oriented in the same temporal direction). This is 'time's greatest mystery', and for all its merits, the theory of nonequilibrium systems does not touch it. What would touch it would be a cosmological demonstration that the Universe was bound to be in a low-entropy state after the Big Bang."* Huw Price, "Past and Future," *Nature*, Vol. 348, 22 November 1990, p. 356.

52. Big Bang?

a. *"The big bang made no quantitative prediction that the 'background' radiation would have a temperature of 3 degrees Kelvin (in fact its initial prediction was 30 degrees*

Kelvin); whereas Eddington in 1926 had already calculated that the 'temperature of space' produced by the radiation of starlight would be found to be 3 degrees Kelvin." Tom Van Flandern, "Did the Universe Have a Beginning?," *Meta Research Bulletin*, Vol. 3, No. 3, 15 September 1994, p. 33.

b. Margaret J. Geller and John P. Huchra, "Mapping the Universe," *Science*, Vol. 246, 17 November 1989, pp. 897-903. See also M. Mitchell Waldrop, "Astronomers Go Up Against the Great Wall," *Science*, Vol. 246, 17 November 1989, p. 885.

● John Travis, "Cosmic Structures Fill Southern Sky," *Science*, Vol. 263, 25 March 1994, p. 1684.

● Will Saunders et al., "The Density Field of the Local Universe," *Nature*, Vol. 349, 3 January 1991, pp. 32-38.

● *"But this uniformity* [in the cosmic background radiation, CBR] *is difficult to reconcile with the obvious clumping of matter into galaxies, clusters of galaxies and even larger features extending across vast regions of the universe, such as 'walls' and 'bubbles'."* Ivars Peterson, "Seeding the Universe," *Science News*, Vol. 137, 24 March 1990, p. 184.

● *"The theorists know of no way such a monster could have condensed in the time available since the Big Bang, especially considering that the 2.7 K background radiation reveals a universe that was very homogeneous in the beginning."* M. Mitchell Waldrop, "The Large-Scale Structure of the Universe Gets Larger—Maybe," *Science*, Vol. 238, 13 November 1987, p. 894.

● For many years, big bang theorists searched in vain with increasingly precise instruments for temperature concentrations in the practically uniform CBR. Without concentrations, matter could never gravitationally contract to form galaxies and galaxy clusters. Finally, in 1992, with great fanfare, an announcement was made in the popular media that slight concentrations were discovered. Two major shortcomings were not mentioned:

♦ The concentrations were less than one part in 10,000—not much more than the errors in the instruments. Such slight concentrations could not be expected to initiate much clustering. As Margaret Geller stated, *"Gravity can't, over the age of the universe, amplify these irregularities enough* [to form huge clusters of galaxies]." Travis, p. 1684.

♦ Typical variations in the CBR spanned areas of the sky that were too broad by factors of 100 or 1000.

Whatever caused these slight temperature variations (.00003°C) probably had nothing to do with a big bang.

c. *"And no element abundance prediction of the big bang was successful without some ad hoc parameterization to 'adjust' predictions that otherwise would have been judged as failures."* Van Flandern, p. 33.

d. Steidl, pp. 207-208.

● D. W. Sciama, *Modern Cosmology* (London: Cambridge University Press, 1971), pp. 149-155.

e. *"Examining the faint light from an elderly Milky Way star, astronomers have detected a far greater abundance of beryllium atoms than the standard Big Bang model predicts."* Ron Cowen, "Starlight Casts Doubt on Big Bang Details," *Science News*, Vol. 140, 7 September 1991, p. 151.

● Gerard Gilmore et al., "First Detection of Beryllium in a Very Metal Poor Star: A Test of the Standard Big Bang Model," *The Astrophysical Journal*, Vol. 378, 1 September 1991, pp. 17-21.

f. Jayant V. Narlikar, "Noncosmological Redshifts," *Space Science Reviews*, Vol. 50, August 1989, pp. 523-614.

g. Halton M. Arp, *Quasars, Redshifts, and Controversies* (Berkeley, California: Interstellar Media, 1987).

h. William G. Tifft, "Properties of the Redshift," *The Astrophysical Journal*, Vol. 382, 1 December 1991, pp. 396-415.

i. Geoffrey R. Burbidge, "Was There Really a Big Bang?" *Nature*, Vol. 233, 3 September 1971, pp. 36-40.

● Ben Patrusky, "Why Is the Cosmos 'Lumpy'?" *Science 81*, June 1981, p. 96.

● Stephen A. Gregory and Laird A. Thompson, "Superclusters and Voids in the Distribution of Galaxies," *Scientific American*, Vol. 246, March 1982, pp. 106-114.

j. Alan Dressler, "The Large-Scale Streaming of Galaxies," *Scientific American*, Vol. 257, September 1987, pp. 46-54.

k. *"One might expect Population III stars* [stars with only hydrogen and helium and no heavy metals] *to have the same sort of distribution of masses as stars forming today, in which case some should be small enough (smaller than 0.8 $M_\odot$, where $M_\odot$ is the mass of the Sun) still to be burning their nuclear fuel. The problem is that, despite extensive searches, nobody has ever found a zero-metallicity star."* Bernard Carr, "Where Is Population III?", *Nature*, Vol. 326, 30 April 1987, p. 829.

● *"Are there any stars older than Population II* [i.e., Population III stars]*? There should be, if our ideas about the early history of the universe are correct."* Leif J. Robinson, "Where Is Population III?", *Sky and Telescope*, July 1982, p. 20.

"There is no statistically significant evidence for Population III objects [stars]." Ibid.

● Stephen P. Maran, "Stellar Old-Timers: Where Are the Oldest Stars in Our Galaxy?", *Natural History*, February 1987, pp. 80-85.

l. *"I have little hesitation in saying that a sickly pall now hangs over the big-bang theory. When a pattern of facts becomes set against a theory, experience shows that the theory rarely recovers."* Fred Hoyle, "The Big Bang Under Attack," *Science Digest*, May 1984, p. 84.

m. One might also ask where the "cosmic egg" came from if there was a big bang. Of course, the question is unanswerable. Pushing any origin's explanation back far enough raises similar questions—all scientifically undemonstrable. Thus, the question of **ultimate** origins is not a purely scientific matter. What science can do is test possible explanations once the starting assumptions are well defined. For example, if a tiny "cosmic egg" existed, consisting of all the mass in the universe, it should not explode, based on present understanding. Saying that some strange, new phenomenon caused an explosion (or inflation) is philosophical speculation. While such speculation may or may not be correct, it is not science.

n. "Big Bang Gone Quiet," *Nature*, Vol. 372, 24 November 1994, p. 304.

● Michael J. Pierce et al., "The Hubble Constant and Virgo Cluster Distance from Observations of Cepheid Variables," *Nature*, Vol. 371, 29 September 1994, pp. 385-389.

● Wendy L. Freedman et al., "Distance to the Virgo Cluster Galaxy M100 from Hubble Space Telescope Observations of Cepheids," *Nature*, Vol. 371, 27 October 1994, pp. 757-762.

● N. R. Tanvir et al.,"Determination of the Hubble Constant from Observations of Cepheid Variables in the Galaxy M96," *Nature*, Vol. 377, 7 September 1995, pp. 27-31.

53. Missing Mass

a. This problem was first explained by R. H. Dicke, "Gravitation and the Universe: The Jayne Lectures for 1969," *American Philosophical Society of Philadelphia*, 1970, p. 62. Alan Guth's attempt to solve it (see "c" below) led to a variation of the big bang theory called the "inflationary big bang."

b. This missing mass is usually called "dark matter," since it cannot be seen. Candidates for this "missing mass" include neutrinos, black holes, dead stars, low-mass stars, and various subatomic particles and objects dreamed up by cosmologists simply to solve this problem. Each candidate has many scientific problems. One study of two adjacent galaxies shows that they have relatively little dark matter. [See Ron Cowen "Ringing In a New Estimate for Dark Matter," *Science News*, Vol. 136, 5 August 1989, p. 84.] Another study found no missing mass within 150 million light years from the earth. [See Eric J. Lerner, "COBE Confounds the Cosmologists," *Aerospace America*, March 1990, pp. 40-41.] A third study found no dark matter in a large elliptical galaxy, M105. [See "Dark Matter Isn't Everywhere," *Astronomy*, September 1993, pp. 19-20.]

● *"Even the most enthusiastic cosmologist will admit that current theories of the nature of the universe have some big holes. One such gap is that the universe seems to be younger than some of the objects contained within it.* [See **How Old Do Evolutionists Say the Universe Is?** on page 158.] *Another problem is that the observed universe just doesn't appear to have enough matter in it to explain the way it behaves now, nor the way theorists predict it will evolve."* Robert Matthews, "Spoiling a Universal 'Fudge Factor'," *Science*, Vol. 265, 5 August 1994, pp. 740-741.

c. This is called the "Inflationary Big Bang." It was proposed by Alan H. Guth in a paper entitled "A Possible Solution to the Horizon and Flatness Problem" in *Physical Review, D*, Vol. 23, 15 January 1981, pp. 348-356.

● The "missing mass problem" can be stated more directly. If the big bang occurred, the total mass of the expanding universe should have a very precise relationship with the outward velocities and distances of all galaxies and other matter. This mass must not deviate from this amount by even one part in 10^{55} (ten thousand million billion trillion trillion trillion).

If the mass were slightly greater than this critical value (the closed condition):

i. gravitational forces would have caused all the matter in the universe to collapse suddenly, perhaps within seconds,

ii. all the universe's mass would be crunched into a big ball, and

iii. we would not be here to wonder how everything began.

If the mass were slightly less than this critical value (the open condition):

i. particles would have expanded indefinitely,

ii. stars and galaxies would not have formed, and

iii. we would not be here to think about it.

The estimated mass of the visible universe is less than 1/10th of this critical value. Stars and galaxies exist. Therefore, the big bang probably did not occur. Only by believing that a vast amount of invisible, unmeasurable mass is hidden somewhere, can one maintain a faith in the big bang theory.

This problem can be viewed in another way. If the universe were billions of years old, it should:

i. have collapsed on itself (closed), or

ii. have expanded so much that stars and galaxies could never have formed (open), or

iii. have had its initial kinetic energy balance the gravitational energy within one part in 10^{55} for most particles we see in the universe! (flat)

Two decades of persistent measurements have repeatedly not supported "iii." Therefore, it seems most likely that the universe is not billions of years old.

54. Interstellar Gas

a. *"The process by which an interstellar cloud is concentrated until it is held together gravitationally to become a protostar is not known. In quantitative work, it has simply been assumed that the number of atoms per cm^3 has somehow increased about a thousand-fold over that in a dense nebula. The two principal factors inhibiting the formation of a protostar are that the gas has a tendency to disperse before the density becomes high enough for self-gravitation to be effective, and that any initial angular momentum would cause excessively rapid rotation as the material* contracts. *Some mechanism must therefore be provided for gathering the material into a sufficiently small volume that self-gravitation may become effective, and the angular momentum must in some way be removed."* Eva Novotny, *Introduction to Stellar Atmospheres and Interiors* (New York: Oxford University Press, 1973), pp. 279-280.

b. Martin Harwit, *Astrophysical Concepts* (New York: John Wiley & Sons, 1973), p. 394.

• *". . . there is no reasonable astronomical scenario in which mineral grains can condense."* Fred Hoyle and Chandra Wickramasinghe, "Where Microbes Boldly Went," *New Scientist*, Vol. 91, 13 August 1981, pp. 413.

c. *"Contemporary opinion on star formation holds that objects called protostars are formed as condensations from the interstellar gas. This condensation process is very difficult theoretically, and no essential theoretical understanding can be claimed; in fact, some theoretical evidence argues strongly against the possibility of star formation. However, we know that the stars exist, and we must do our best to account for them."* John C. Brandt, *The Physics and Astronomy of the Sun and Stars* (New York: McGraw-Hill, 1966), p. 111.

55. Fast Binaries
a. A. R. King and M. G. Watson, "The Shortest Period Binary Star?", *Nature*, Vol. 323, 4 September 1986, p. 105.

• Dietrick E. Thomsen, "A Dizzying Orbit for a Binary Star," *Science News*, Vol. 130, 11 October 1986, p. 231.

• "Ultrafast Binary Star," *Sky & Telescope*, February 1987, p. 154.

b. "Now You See It, Now You Don't," *Science News*, Vol. 135, 7 January 1989, p. 13.

• Patrick Moore, *The New Atlas of the Universe* (New York: Arch Cape Press, 1988), p. 176.

56. Star Births?
a. *". . . no one has unambiguously observed material falling onto an embryonic star, which should be happening if the star is truly still forming. And no one has caught a molecular cloud in the act of collapsing."* Ivars Peterson, "The Winds of Starbirth," *Science News*, Vol. 137, 30 June 1990, p. 409.

b. Steidl, pp. 143-145.

c. *"The origin of stars represents one of the most fundamental unsolved problems of contemporary astrophysics."* Charles J. Lada and Frank H. Shu, "The Formation of Sunlike Stars," *Science*, Vol. 248, 4 May 1990, p. 564.

• *"Nobody really understands how star formation proceeds. It's really remarkable."* Rogier A. Windhorst, as quoted by Corey S. Powell, "A Matter of Timing," *Scientific American*, Vol. 267, October 1992, p. 30.

• *"If stars did not exist, it would be easy to prove that this is what we expect."* Geoffrey R. Burbidge, as quoted by R. L. Sears and Robert R. Brownlee in *Stellar Structure*, editors Lawrence H. Aller and Dean McLaughlin (Chicago: University of Chicago Press, 1965), p. 577.

57. Stellar Evolution?
a. Steidl, pp. 134-136.

58. O Stars
a. *"The universe we see when we look out to its furthest horizons contains a hundred billion galaxies. Each of these galaxies contains another hundred billion stars. That's 10^{22} stars all told. The silent embarrassment of modern astrophysics is that we do not know how even a single one of these stars managed to form."* Martin Harwit, Book Reviews, *Science*, Vol. 231, 7 March 1986, pp. 1201-1202.

Harwit also lists three formidable objections to all modern theories of star formation:

"i. The contracting gas clouds must radiate energy in order to continue their contraction; the potential energy that is liberated in this pre-stellar phase must be observable somehow, but we have yet to detect and identify it.

"ii. The angular momentum that resides in typical interstellar clouds is many orders of magnitude higher than the angular momentum we compute for the relatively slowly spinning young stars; where and how has the protostar shed that angular momentum during contraction?

"iii. Interstellar clouds are permeated by magnetic fields that we believe to be effectively frozen to the contracting gas; as the gas cloud collapses to form a star, the magnetic field lines should be compressed ever closer together, giving rise to enormous magnetic fields, long before the collapse is completed. These fields would resist further collapse, preventing the formation of the expected star; yet we observe no evidence of strong fields, and the stars do form, apparently unaware of our theoretical difficulties."

59. Galaxies
a. *"The problem of explaining the existence of galaxies has proved to be one of the thorniest in cosmology. By all rights, they just shouldn't be there, yet there they sit. It's hard to convey the depth of frustration that this simple fact induces among scientists."* James Trefil, *The Dark Side of the Universe* (New York: Charles Scribner's Sons, 1988), p. 55.

Trefil amplifies the well-founded basis for this frustration in his fourth chapter entitled, "Five Reasons Why Galaxies Can't Exist."

- *"A completely satisfactory theory of galaxy formation remains to be formulated."* Joseph Silk, *The Big Bang* (San Francisco: W. H. Freeman and Co., 1980), pp. 22.

- *"The theory of the formation of galaxies is one of the great outstanding problems of astrophysics, a problem that today seems far from solution."* Steven Weinberg, *The First Three Minutes* (New York: Bantom books, Inc., 1977), p. 68.

- Fifty cosmologists attended a conference on galaxy formation. After summarizing much observational data, two of the most respected authorities optimistically estimated the probability that any existing theory on galaxy formation is correct is about 1 out of 100. [See P. J. E. Peebles and Joseph Silk, "A Cosmic Book," *Nature*, Vol. 335, 13 October 1988, pp. 601-606.]

b. *"We cannot even show convincingly how galaxies, stars, planets, and life arose in the present universe."* Michael Rowan-Robinson, "Review of the Accidental Universe," *New Scientist*, Vol. 97, 20 January 1983, p. 186.

- *"There is much doubt, however, that galaxies evolve from one type to another at all."* George Abell, *Exploration of the Universe*, 2nd edition (New York: Holt, Rinehart, and Winston, 1969), p. 629.

- *"Our conclusions, then, are that the sequence of the classification of galaxies is not an evolutionary sequence . . . ."* Paul W. Hodge, *The Physics and Astronomy of Galaxies and Cosmology* (New York: McGraw-Hill, 1966), p. 122.

c. Ibid., p. 123.

d. Harold S. Slusher, "Clues Regarding the Age of the Universe," *ICR Impact*, No. 19, January 1975, pp. 2-3.

- Steidl, pp. 161-187.

e. *"In its simplest form, the Big Bang scenario doesn't look like a good way to make galaxies. It allows too little time for the force of gravity by itself to gather ordinary matter— neutrons, protons and electrons—into the patterns of galaxies seen today. Yet the theory survives for want of a better idea."* Peterson, "Seeding the Universe," p. 184.

- The largest structure seen in the universe, "The Great Wall," has recently been discovered. It is composed of tens of thousands of galaxies lined up in a wall-like structure. It is so large that none of its edges have been found.

- *"It [the wall] is far too large and too massive to have formed by the mutual gravitational attraction of its member galaxies."* M. Mitchell Waldrop, "Astronomers Go Up Against the Great Wall," *Science*, Vol. 246, 17 November 1989, p. 885. See also Margaret J. Geller and John P. Huchra, "Mapping the Universe," *Science*, Vol. 246, 17 November 1989, pp. 897-903.

61. Corals and Caves
a. Ariel A. Roth, "Coral Reef Growth," *Origins*, Vol. 6, No. 2, 1979, pp. 88-95.

- J. Th. Verstelle, "The Growth Rate at Various Depths of Coral Reefs in the Dutch East Indian Archipelago," *Treubia*, Vol. 14, 1932, pp. 117-126.

b. Ian T. Taylor, *In the Minds of Men* (Toronto: TFE Publishing, 1984), pp. 335-336.

- Larry S. Helmick, Joseph Rohde, and Amy Ross, "Rapid Growth of Dripstone Observed," *Creation Research Society Quarterly*, Vol. 14, June 1977, pp. 13-17.

62. Constant Decay?
a. *"For some inexplicable reason, the nuclei of certain elements become unstable and spontaneously release energy and/or particles."* William D. Stansfield, *Science of Evolution* (New York: Macmillan Publishing Co., 1977), p. 82.

b. The first line of evidence concerns "blasting halos." See:

- Robert V. Gentry, "Variance of the Decay Constant over Geological Time," *Creation Research Society Quarterly*, Vol. 5, September 1968, pp. 83-84.

- Robert V. Gentry, *Creation's Tiny Mystery*, 2nd edition (Knoxville, Tennessee: Earth Sciences Associates, 1988), p. 282.

- Paul Ramdohr, "New Observations on Radioactive Halos and Radioactive Fracturing," *Oak Ridge National Laboratory Translation* (ORNL-tr-755), 26 August 1965, pp. 16-25.

- The second line of evidence concerns the apparent decrease in the vibrational rates of atoms. See pages 153-158 in this book.

63. Radiometric Contradictions
a. A blind test requires that the person making the measurements not know (or be "blind" to) which of several specimens is the one of interest. For example, to measure a rock's age by some radiometric technique, similar rocks— but of different ages—must accompany the rock. Only after the measurements are announced, can the technicians making the measurements be told the history of any specimen. To allow persons with vested interests in the outcome of the measurement—persons who know which sample they hope will produce a given measurement—to make the measurement, or in any way influence those who do, opens the experimental procedure to subtle biases. Blind tests insure objectivity.

A special type of blind test commonly used in medicine, is a "double-blind test." Neither doctor nor patients know who has received the special treatment being tested. A random selection determines which test patients receive the special treatment and which receive a placebo—something obviously ineffective, such as a sugar pill.

Experienced medical researchers give little credibility to any medicine or treatment that has not passed a well-designed and rigorously executed double-blind test. If "medicines" and "health foods" which have not demonstrated any significant effectiveness in double-blind tests were removed from the market, consumers would save billions of dollars each year. In the field of education, those proposals for enhancing learning that have been subjected to blind tests have usually been shown to be ineffective or so marginal that the effectiveness cannot be measured. Astrological forecasts that have undergone blind tests have also been shown to be worthless.

The Shroud of Turin, claimed to be the burial cloth of Christ, was supposedly dated by a blind test. Actually, the control specimens were so dissimilar that the technicians at the three laboratories making the measurements could tell which specimen was from the Shroud. [Personal communication with one scientist who participated in the measurement.] The test would have been blind if the specimens had been reduced to carbon powder before they were given to the testing laboratories.

Radiometric dates that do not fit a desired theory are often thrown out by alleging contamination. Few ever hear about such tests. If those who are unhappy with the results of a blind radiometric dating have not previously identified the contamination, their charges should carry little weight. If contamination is alleged before the test, the test may not be needed. Therefore, careful researchers should first objectively evaluate the possibility of contamination.

Humans are naturally biased. We tend to see what we want to see and explain away unwanted data. This applies especially to those proposing theories. Scientists (and this author) are not immune to this human shortcoming. Many popular ideas within geology would probably never have survived had a critical age measurement been subjected to a blind test.

b. John Woodmorappe, "Radiometric Geochronology Reappraised," *Creation Research Society Quarterly*, Vol. 16, September 1979, pp. 102-129.

- Robert H. Brown, "Graveyard Clocks: Do They Tell Real Time?", *Signs of the Times*, June 1982, pp. 8-9.

- *"It is obvious that radiometric techniques may not be the absolute dating methods that they are claimed to be. Age estimates on a given geological stratum by different radiometric methods are often quite different (sometimes by hundreds of millions of years). There is no absolutely reliable long-term radiological 'clock'."* Stansfield, p. 84.

64. Index Fossils

a. *"It cannot be denied that from a strictly philosophical standpoint geologists are here arguing in a circle. The succession of organisms has been determined by a study of their remains embedded in the rocks, and the relative ages of the rocks are determined by the remains of organisms that they contain."* R. H. Rastall, "Geology," *Encyclopaedia Britannica*, Vol. 10, 1954, p. 168.

- *"Are the authorities maintaining, on the one hand, that evolution is documented by geology and, on the other hand, that geology is documented by evolution? Isn't this a circular argument?"* Larry Azar, "Biologists, Help!" *BioScience*, Vol. 28, November 1978, p. 714.

- *"The intelligent layman has long suspected circular reasoning in the use of rocks to date fossils and fossils to date rocks. The geologist has never bothered to think of a good reply, feeling that explanations are not worth the trouble as long as the work brings results. This is supposed to be hard-headed pragmatism."* J. E. O'Rourke, "Pragmatism Versus Materialism in Stratigraphy," *American Journal of Science*, Vol. 276, January 1976, p. 47.

"The rocks do date the fossils, but the fossils date the rocks more accurately. Stratigraphy cannot avoid this kind of reasoning, if it insists on using only temporal concepts, because circularity is inherent in the derivation of time scales." Ibid., p. 53.

Although O'Rourke attempts to justify current practices of stratigraphers, he recognizes the inherent problems associated with such circular reasoning.

- *"But the danger of circularity is still present. For most biologists the strongest reason for accepting the evolutionary hypothesis is their acceptance of some theory that entails it. There is another difficulty. The temporal ordering of biological events beyond the local section may critically involve paleontological correlation, which necessarily presupposes the non-repeatability of organic events in geologic history. There are various justifications for this assumption but for almost all contemporary paleontologists it rests upon the acceptance of the evolutionary hypothesis."* Kitts, p. 466.

- *"It is a problem not easily solved by the classic methods of stratigraphical paleontology, as obviously we will land ourselves immediately in an impossible circular argument if we say, firstly that a particular lithology is synchronous on the evidence of its fossils, and secondly that the fossils are synchronous on the evidence of the lithology."* Derek V. Ager, *The Nature of the Stratigraphical Record*, 2nd edition (New York: John Wiley & Sons, 1981), p. 68.

- *"The charge that the construction of the geologic scale involves circularity has a certain amount of validity."* David M. Raup, "Geology and Creationism," *Field Museum of Natural History Bulletin*, Vol. 54, March 1983, p. 21.

- In a taped, transcribed, and approved 1979 interview with Dr. Donald Fisher, the state paleontologist for New York, Luther Sunderland asked Fisher how he dated certain fossils. Answer: *"By the Cambrian rocks in which they were found."* When Sunderland asked if this was not circular reasoning, Fisher replied, *"Of course; how else are you going to do it?"* "The Geologic Column: Its Basis and Who Constructed It," *Bible-Science News Letter*, December 1986, p. 6.

- *"The prime difficulty with the use of presumed ancestral-descendant sequences to express phylogeny is that biostratigraphic data are often used in conjunction with morphology in the initial evaluation of relationships, which leads to obvious circularity."* Bobb Schaeffer, Max K. Hecht, and Niles Eldredge, "Phylogeny and Paleontology," *Evolu-*

tionary Biology, Vol. 6 (New York: Appleton-Century-Crofts, Inc., 1972), p. 39.

65. Geologic Column
a. *"We are only kidding ourselves if we think that we have anything like a complete succession for any part of the stratigraphical column in any one place."* Ager, p. 32.

b. John Woodmorappe, "The Essential Nonexistence of the Evolutionary-Uniformitarian Geologic Column: A Quantitative Assessment," *Creation Research Society Quarterly*, Vol. 18, No. 1, June 1981, pp. 46-71.

66. Old DNA
a. This natural process is driven by the continual vibration of atoms in DNA. Just as marbles in a vibrating container always try to find lower positions, vibrating atoms tend to reorganize into arrangements that have a lower energy. Thus, DNA tends to form less energetic compounds such as water and carbon dioxide.

b. Bryan Sykes, "The Past Comes Alive," *Nature*, Vol. 352, 1 August 1991, pp. 381-382.

● *"Many scientists still consider this idea* [that DNA could last longer than 10,000 years] *far fetched, but Poinar points out that not long ago few people believed **any** ancient DNA could be sequenced. 'When we started, we were told that we were crazy,' he says."* Kathryn Hoppe, "Brushing the Dust off Ancient DNA," *Science News*, Vol. 142, 24 October 1992, p. 281.

c. Edward M. Golenberg et al., "Chloroplast DNA Sequence from a Miocene Magnolia Species," *Nature*, Vol. 344, 12 April 1990, pp. 656-658.

DNA disintegrates more rapidly when it is in contact with water. In commenting on the remarkably old DNA in a supposedly 17-million-year-old magnolia leaf, Pääbo remarked, *"The clay* [in which the leaf was found] *was wet, however, and one wonders how DNA could have survived the damaging influence of water for so long."* [See Svante Pääbo, "Ancient DNA," *Scientific American*, Vol. 269, November 1993, p. 92.] Maybe those magnolia leaves are not 17 million years old.

"That DNA could survive for such a staggering length of time was totally unexpected—almost unbelievable." Jeremy Cherfas, "Ancient DNA: Still Busy after Death," *Science*, Vol. 253, 20 September 1991, p. 1354.

d. *"Under physiological conditions, it would be extremely rare to find preserved DNA that was tens of thousands of years old."* Scott R. Woodward et al., "DNA Sequence from Cretaceous Period Bone Fragments," *Science*, Vol. 266, 18 November 1994, pp. 1229-1232.

e. Hoppe, p. 281.

● Virginia Morell, "30-Million-Year-Old DNA Boosts an Emerging Field," *Science*, Vol. 257, 25 September 1992, p. 1862.

f. Hendrick N. Poinar et al., "DNA from an Extinct Plant," *Nature*, Vol. 363, 24 June 1993, p. 677.

● Rob DeSalle et al., "DNA Sequences from a Fossil Termite in Oligo-Miocene Amber and Their Phylogenetic Implications," *Science*, Vol. 257, 25 September 1992, pp. 1933-1936.

● Raúl J. Cano et al., "Amplification and Sequencing of DNA from a 120–135-Million-Year-Old Weevil," *Nature*, Vol. 363, 10 June 1993, pp. 536-538.

g. Tomas Lindahl is a recognized expert on DNA and its rapid disintegration. He tried to solve this problem of DNA being too old by arguing that all the claimed discoveries of multi-million-year-old DNA resulted from contamination and poor measurement techniques. He wrote, *"The apparent observation that fully hydrated plant DNA might be retained in high-molecular mass form for 20 million years is incompatible with the known properties of the chemical structure of DNA."* [See Tomas Lindahl, "Instability and Decay of the Primary Structure of DNA," *Nature*, Vol. 362, 22 April 1993, p. 714.] His claims of contamination are effectively rebutted in many of the papers listed above and by:

♦ George O. Poinar, Jr., in "Recovery of Antediluvian DNA," *Nature*, Vol. 365, 21 October 1993, p. 700. (The work of George Poinar and others was a major inspiration for the book and film, *Jurassic Park*.)

♦ Edward M. Golenberg, "Antediluvian DNA Research," *Nature*, Vol. 367, 24 February 1994, p. 692.

The measurement procedures of Poinar and others were far better controlled than Lindahl realized. That is, modern DNA did not contaminate the fossil. However, Lindahl is probably correct in saying that DNA cannot last much longer than 10,000 years.

h. *"We know from chemical experiments that it* [DNA] *degrades and how fast it degrades. After 25 million years, there shouldn't be any DNA left at all."* Rebecca Cann, as quoted by Morell, p. 1862.

i. Richard Monastersky, "Protein Identified in Dinosaur Fossils," *Science News*, Vol. 142, 3 October 1992, p. 213.

● Gerard Muyzer et al., "Preservation of the Bone Protein Osteocalcin in Dinosaurs," *Geology*, Vol. 20, October 1992, pp. 871-874.

67. Human Artifacts
a. J. Q. Adams, "Eve's Thimble," *American Antiquarian*, Vol. 5, October 1883, pp. 331-332.

b. Harry V. Wiant, Jr., "A Curiosity from Coal," *Creation Research Society Quarterly*, Vol. 13, No. 1, June 1976, p. 74.

c. Wilbert H. Rusch, Sr., "Human Footprints in Rocks," *Creation Research Society Quarterly*, Vol. 7, March 1971, pp. 201-202.

d. John Buchanan, "Discovery of an Iron Instrument Lately Found Imbedded in a Natural Seam of Coal in the Neighbourhood of Glasgow," *Proceedings of the Society of Antiquarians of Scotland*, Vol. 1, Part 2, Section IV, 1853.

e. "A Necklace of a Prehistoric God," *Morrisonville Times* (Morrisonville, Illinois), 11 June 1891, p. 1.

f. "A Relic of a By-Gone Age," *Scientific American*, Vol. 7, 5 June 1852, p. 298.

g. David Brewster, "Queries and Statements Concerning a Nail Found Imbedded in a Block of Sandstone Obtained from Kingoodie (Mylnfield) Quarry, North Britain," reported to the British Association for the Advancement of Science, 1844.

● Rene Noorbergen, *Secrets of the Lost Races* (New York: The Bobbs-Merrill Co., Inc., 1977), p. 42.

h. Ibid.

i. J. R. Jochmans, "Strange Relics from the Depths of the Earth," *Bible-Science Newsletter*, January 1979, p. 1.

j. G. Frederick Wright, *Man and the Glacial Period* (New York: D. Appleton and Co., 1887), pp. 297-300.

● G. Frederick Wright, "The Idaho Find," *American Antiquarian*, Vol. 2, 1889, pp. 379-381.

k. Carl Baugh, "Ordovician Hammer Report," *Ex Nihilo*, February 1984, pp. 16-17.

● Carl Baugh, "Pre-Flood(?) Hammer Update," *Creation Ex Nihilo*, Vol. 8, No. 1, November 1985, pp. 14-16.

l. Frank Calvert, "On the Probable Existence of Man during the Miocene Period," *Anthropological Institute Journal*, Vol. 3, 1873, pp. 127-129.

● J. B. Browne, "Singular Impression in Marble," *The American Journal of Science and Arts*, January 1831, p. 361.

68. Humanlike Footprints

a. Melvin A. Cook, "William J. Meister Discovery of Human Footprints with Trilobites in a Cambrian Formation of Western Utah," *Why Not Creation?*, editor Walter E. Lammerts (Phillipsburg, New Jersey: Presbyterian and Reformed Publishing Co., 1970), pp. 185-193.

b. "Geology and Ethnology Disagree about Rock Prints," *Science News Letter*, 10 December 1938, p. 372.

c. Henry R. Schoolcraft and Thomas H. Benton, "Remarks on the Prints of Human Feet, Observed in the Secondary Limestone of the Mississippi Valley," *The American Journal of Science and Arts*, Vol. 5, 1822, pp. 223-231.

d. "Human-Like Tracks in Stone are Riddle to Scientists," *Science News Letter*, 29 October 1938, pp. 278-279.

e. "'Make no mistake about it,' says Tim [White, who is probably recognized as the leading authority on the Laetoli footprints]. 'They are like modern human footprints. If one were left in the sand of a California beach today, and a four-year-old were asked what it was, he would instantly say that someone had walked there. He wouldn't be able to tell it from a hundred other prints on the beach, nor would you. The external morphology is the same. There is a well-shaped modern heel with a strong arch and a good ball of the foot in front of it. The big toe is straight in line. It doesn't stick out to the side like an ape toe, or like the big toe in so many drawings you see of Australopithecines in books.'" Johanson and Edey, p. 250.

● Therefore, evolutionists conclude that the feet and stride of an apelike creature became humanlike several million years before the rest of their body. Most evolutionists credit Australopithecus afarensis (such as "Lucy") with this accomplishment. However, Lucy's fingers and toes were down-curved as are those of tree-swinging monkeys and apes. (See **Ape-Men?** on page 9.) The toes on the Laetoli footprints were straight. [See Russell H. Tuttle, "The Pitted Pattern of Laetoli Feet," *Natural History*, March 1990, pp. 61-64.]

69. Parallel Layers

a. Archibald Geikie, *Text-book of Geology* (London: Macmillan Publishing Co., 1882), p. 602.

b. *"Potentially more important to geological thinking are those unconformities that signal large chunks of geological history are missing, even though the strata on either side of the unconformity are perfectly parallel and show no evidence of erosion. Did millions of years fly by with no discernible effect? A possible though controversial inference is that our geological clocks and stratigraphic concepts need working on."* William R. Corliss, *Unknown Earth* (Glen Arm, Maryland: The Sourcebook Project, 1980), p. 219.

● George McCready Price, *The New Geology*, 2nd edition (Mountain View, California: Pacific Press Publishing Assn., 1923), pp. 486, 500, 504, 506, 543, 620-627.

● George McCready Price, *Evolutionary Geology and the New Catastrophism* (Mountain View, California: Pacific Press Publishing Assn., 1926), pp. 90-104.

70. Helium

a. "What Happened to the Earth's Helium?", *New Scientist*, Vol. 24, 3 December 1964, pp. 631-632.

● Melvin A. Cook, *Prehistory and Earth Models* (London: Max Parrish, 1966), pp. 10-14.

● Melvin A. Cook, "Where is the Earth's Radiogenic Helium?", *Nature*, Vol. 179, 26 January 1957, p. 213.

● Joseph W. Chamberlain, *Theory of Planetary Atmospheres* (New York: Academic Press, 1987), pp. 371-372.

71. *Lead and Helium Diffusion*

a. Robert V. Gentry et al., "Differential Lead Retention in Zircons: Implications for Nuclear Waste Containment," *Science*, 16 April 1982, pp. 296-298.

● Robert V. Gentry, "Letters," *Physics Today*, October 1982, pp. 13-14.

b. Robert V. Gentry, "Letters," *Physics Today*, April 1983, p. 13.

● Robert V. Gentry, Gary L. Glish, and Eddy H. McBay, "Differential Helium Retention in Zircons," *Geophysical Research Letters*, Vol. 9, No. 10, October 1982, pp. 1129-1130.

c. Robert V. Gentry, personal communication, 24 February 1984.

72. *Excess Fluid Pressure*

a. Parke A. Dickey, Calcutta R. Shriram, and William R. Paine, "Abnormal Pressures in Deep Wells of Southwestern Louisiana," *Science*, Vol. 160, No. 3828, 10 May 1968, pp. 609-615.

b. *"Some geologists find it difficult to understand how the great pressures found in some oil wells could be retained over millions of years. Creationists also use this currently puzzling situation as evidence that oil was formed less than 10,000 years ago."* Stansfield, p. 82.

Stansfield had no alternative explanation.

● Cook, *Prehistory and Earth Models*, p. 341.

73. *Volcanic Debris*

a. Ariel A. Roth, "Some Questions about Geochronology," *Origins*, Vol. 13, No. 2, 1986, pp. 75-76.

● *"It has been estimated that just four volcanoes spewing lava at the rate observed for Paricutín [a Mexican volcano that erupted in 1943] and continuing for five billion years could almost account for the volume of the continental crusts."* Stansfield, p. 81.

74. *River Sediments*

a. Stuart E. Nevins, "Evolution: The Ocean Says No!" *Symposium on Creation V* (Grand Rapids: Baker Book House, 1975), pp. 77-83.

● Roth, "Some Questions about Geochronology," pp. 69-71.

75. *Continental Erosion*

a. Nevins, pp. 80-81.

● George C. Kennedy, "The Origin of Continents, Mountain Ranges, and Ocean Basins," *American Scientist*, Vol. 47, December 1959, pp. 491-504.

● Roth, "Some Questions about Geochronology," pp. 65-67.

77. *Shallow Meteorites*

a. Fritz Heide, *Meteorites* (Chicago: University of Chicago Press, 1964), p. 119.

● Peter A. Steveson, "Meteoritic Evidence for a Young Earth," *Creation Research Society Quarterly*, Vol. 12, June 1975, pp. 23-25.

● *". . . neither tektites nor other meteorites have been found in any of the ancient geologic formations . . . ."* Ralph Stair, "Tektites and the Lost Planet," *The Scientific Monthly*, July 1956, p. 11.

● *"No meteorites have ever been found in the geologic column."* William Henry Twenhofel, *Principles of Sedimentation*, 2nd edition (New York: McGraw-Hill, 1950), p. 144.

● *". . . the astronomer Olbers had noticed: that there are no 'fossil' meteorites known, from any period older than the middle of the Quaternary. The quantity of coal mined during the last century amounted to many billions of tons, and with it about a thousand meteorites should have been dug out, if during the time the coal deposits were formed the meteorite frequency had been the same as it is today. Equally complete is the absence of meteorites in any other geologically old material that has been excavated in the course of technical operations."* F. A. Paneth, "The Frequency of Meteorite Falls throughout the Ages," *Vistas in Astronomy*, Vol. 2, editor Arthur Beer (New York: Pergamon Press, 1956), p. 1681.

● *"I have interviewed the late Dr. G. P. Merrill, of the U.S. National Museum, and Dr. G. T. Prior, of the British Natural History Museum, both well-known students of meteorites, and neither man knew of a single occurrence of a meteorite in sedimentary rocks."* W. A. Tarr, "Meteorites in Sedimentary Rocks?", *Science*, Vol. 75, 1 January 1932, pp. 17-18.

● *"No meteorites have been found in the geological column."* Stansfield, p. 81.

b. Hans Pettersson, "Cosmic Spherules and Meteoritic Dust," *Scientific American*, Vol. 202, February 1960, pp. 123-129.

c. *"Examples of ancient rock slides have been identified from the geologic column in few instances."* William Henry Twenhofel, *Treatise on Sedimentation*, Vol. 1, 2nd edition (New York: Dover Publications, 1961), p. 102.

78. *Meteoritic Dust*

a. Steveson, pp. 23-25.

79. *Magnetic Decay*

a. Thomas G. Barnes, *Origin and Destiny of the Earth's Magnetic Field*, 2nd edition (El Cajon, California: Institute for Creation Research, 1983).

80. *Molten Earth?*

a. Harold S. Slusher and Thomas P. Gamwell, *Age of the Earth,* ICR Technical Monograph No. 7 (El Cajon, California: Institute for Creation Research, 1978).

- Leonard R. Ingersoll et al., *Heat Conduction: With Engineering, Geological and Other Applications*, revised edition (Madison, Wisconsin: University of Wisconsin Press, 1954), pp. 99-107.

82. Moon Dust and Debris

a. Before instruments were sent to the moon, Isaac Asimov made some interesting (but false) predictions. After estimating the great depths of dust that should be on the moon, Asimov dramatically ended his article by stating:

> *"I get a picture, therefore, of the first spaceship, picking out a nice level place for landing purposes, coming in slowly downward tail-first and sinking majestically out of sight."* Isaac Asimov, "14 Million Tons of Dust Per Year," *Science Digest*, January 1959, p. 36.

- Lyttleton felt that the dust formed by only the erosion of exposed moon rocks by ultraviolet light and x-rays *"could during the age of the moon be sufficient to form a layer over it several miles deep."* Raymond A. Lyttleton, *The Modern Universe* (New York: Harper & Brothers, 1956), p. 72.

- Thomas Gold proposed that thick layers of dust accumulated in the lunar maria. [See Thomas Gold, "The Lunar Surface," *Monthly Notices of the Royal Astronomical Society of London*, Vol. 115, 1955, pp. 585-604.]

- Fears about the dust thickness were reduced when instruments were sent to the moon from 1964-1968. However, some concern still remained, at least in Neil Armstrong's mind, as he stepped on the moon. [See transcript of conversations from the moon, Chicago Tribune, 21 July 1969, Section 1, p. 1, and Paul D. Ackerman, *It's a Young World After All* (Grand Rapids, Michigan: Baker Book House, 1986), p. 19.]

83. Crater Creep

a. Glenn R. Morton, Harold S. Slusher, and Richard E. Mandock, "The Age of Lunar Craters," *Creation Research Society Quarterly*, Vol. 20, September 1983, pp. 105-108.

84. Hot Moon

a. Nicholas M. Short, *Planetary Geology* (Englewood Cliffs, New Jersey: Prentice-Hall, 1975), pp. 175-184.

85. Young Comets

a. Ron Cowen, "Comets: Mudballs of the Solar System," *Science News*, Vol. 141, 14 March 1992, pp. 170-171.

b. Ray Jayawardhana, "Keeping Tabs on Cometary Breakups," *Science*, Vol. 264, 13 May 1994, p. 907.

c. Mathematical errors led to the belief that a cloud of cometary material, called the Oort Cloud, surrounds the solar system. [See Raymond A. Lyttleton, "The Non-existence of the Oort Cometary Shell," *Astrophysics and Space Science*, Vol. 31, December 1974, pp. 385-401.]

Assuming the Oort Cloud exists preserves the multibillion year age of the solar system.

- *". . . many people would be happier if there were more objective evidence for the reality of the Oort Cloud."* John Maddox, "Halley's Comet Is Quite Young," *Nature*, Vol. 339, 11 May 1989, p. 95.

d. Hannes Alfven and Gustaf Arrhenius, *Evolution of the Solar System* (Washington D.C.: NASA, 1976), p. 234.

- Thomas D. Nicholson, "Comets, Studied for Many Years, Remain an Enigma to Scientists," *Natural History*, March 1966, pp. 44-46.

- Harold Armstrong, "Comets and a Young Solar System," *Speak to the Earth*, editor George F. Howe (Phillipsburg, New Jersey: Presbyterian and Reformed Publishing Co., 1975), pp. 327-330.

- Lyttleton, *Mysteries*, p. 110.

- *"A flaw in our understanding of the orbital evolution of comets is that the number of short-period comets—those with orbital periods less than 200 years, such as comet Halley—is much greater than theory predicts. The discrepancy is enormous; the observed number is two orders of magnitude larger than expected."* Julia Heisler, "Orbital Evolution of Comets," *Nature*, Vol. 324, 27 November 1986, p. 306.

e. Lyttleton, p. 393.

- If comet formation naturally accompanies star formation, as evolutionists claim, then many comets should have been expelled from other stars. Some expelled comets should have passed through our solar system in recent years. No comet with the distinctive interstellar orbit has ever been observed. [See Wetherill, p. 470.]

86. Small Comets

a. Louis A. Franks with Patrick Huyghe, *The Big Splash* (New York: Carol Publishing Group, 1990).

- Richard Monastersky, "Comet Controversy Caught on Film," *Science News*, Vol. 133, 28 May 1988, p. 340.

- Timothy M. Beardsley, "Ice Storm," *Scientific American*, Vol. 258, June 1988, p. 24.

- Jonathan Eberhart, "A Bunch of Little Comets—But Just a Little Bunch," *Science News*, Vol. 132, 29 August 1987, p. 132.

- Richard A. Kerr, "In Search of Elusive Little Comets," *Science*, Vol. 240, 10 June 1988, pp. 1403-1404.

- Richard A. Kerr, "Double Exposures Reveal Mini-Comets?", *Science*, Vol. 243, 13 January 1989, pp. 170-171.

- Richard Monastersky, "Small Comet Controversy Flares Again," *Science News*, Vol. 137, 9 June 1990, p. 365.

87. Young Rings

a. *"Yet nonstop erosion poses a difficult problem for the very existence of Saturn's opaque rings—the expected bombardment rate would pulverize the entire system in only 10,000 years! Most of this material is merely redeposited elsewhere in the rings, but even if only a tiny fraction is truly lost (as ionized vapor, for example), it becomes a real trick to maintain the rings since the formation of the solar system [as imagined by evolutionists]."* Jeffrey N. Cuzzi, "Ringed Planets: Still Mysterious—II" *Sky & Telescope*, Vol. 69, January 1985, p. 22.

"Furthermore, the narrow, sharp-edged rings don't fit the idea of a dispersed parent population battered to smithereens by interplanetary projectiles." Ibid., p. 23.

● Jeffrey N. Cuzzi, "Saturn: Jewel of the Solar System," *The Planetary Report*, July/August 1989, pp. 12-15.

● Richard A. Simpson and Ellis D. Miner, "Uranus: Beneath That Bland Exterior," *The Planetary Report*, July/August 1989, pp. 16-18.

88. Hot Planets

a. H. H. Aumann and C. M. Gillespie, Jr., "The Internal Powers and Effective Temperatures of Jupiter and Saturn," *The Astrophysical Journal*, Vol. 157, July 1969, pp. L69-L72.

● M. Mitchell Waldrop, "The Puzzle That Is Saturn," *Science*, 18 September 1981, p. 1351.

● Jonathan Eberhart, "Neptune's Inner Warmth," *Science News*, Vol. 112, 12 November 1977, p. 316.

b. Ibid.

c. "The Mystery of Venus's Internal Heat," *New Scientist*, Vol. 88, 13 November 1980, p. 437.

d. Andrew P. Ingersoll, "Jupiter and Saturn," *Scientific American*, Vol. 245, December 1981, p. 92.

e. Ingersoll and others have proposed that Saturn and Jupiter could generate internal heat if their helium gas liquefied or their liquid hydrogen solidified. Neither possibility could occur, since each planet's temperature greatly exceeds the critical temperature of helium and hydrogen. (The critical temperature of a particular gas is that temperature above which no amount of pressure can squeeze it into a liquid.) Even if the temperature were cold enough to permit gases to liquefy, how could nucleation be initiated? In December 1981, Ingersoll personally acknowledged his error to this author.

f. Paul M. Steidl, "The Solar System: An Assessment of Recent Evidence—Planets, Comets, and Asteroids," *Design and Origins in Astronomy*, editor George Mulfinger, Jr. (Norcross, Georgia: Creation Research Society Books, 1983), pp. 87, 91, 100.

● Jupiter would have rapidly cooled to its present temperature, even if it had been an unreasonably hot 20,000 Kelvin when it formed. Evolutionary models cannot be fit into such a short time. [See Edwin V. Bishop and Wendell C. DeMarcus, "Thermal Histories of Jupiter Models," *Icarus*, Vol. 12, 1970, pp. 317-330.]

89. Solar Wind

a. *"It has been thought previously that radiation pressure would have swept less massive particles out of the inner solar system, but there is a finite flux below $10^{14}g$."* Stuart Ross Taylor, p. 90.

90. Poynting-Robertson Effect

a. Steidl, *The Earth, the Stars, and the Bible*, pp. 60-61.

● Harold S. Slusher and Stephen J. Robertson, *The Age of the Solar System: A Study of the Poynting-Robertson Effect and Extinction of Interplanetary Dust*, ICR Technical Monograph No. 6, revised edition (El Cajon, California: Institute for Creation Research, 1978).

b. Stanley P. Wyatt, Jr. and Fred L. Whipple, "The Poynting-Robertson Effect on Meteor Orbits," *The Astrophysical Journal*, Vol. 3, January 1950, pp. 134-141.

● Ron Cowen, "Meteorites: To Stream or Not to Stream," *Science News*, Vol. 142, 1 August 1992, p. 71.

c. David A. Weintraub, "Comets in Collision," *Nature*, Vol. 351, 6 June 1991, pp. 440-441.

91. Solar Fuel

a. A. B. Severny, V. A. Kotov, and T. T. Tsap, "Observations of Solar Pulsations," *Nature*, Vol. 259, 15 January 1976, pp. 87-89.

b. Paul M. Steidl, "Solar Neutrinos and a Young Sun," *Design and Origins in Astronomy*, editor George Mulfinger, Jr. (Norcross, Georgia: Creation Research Society Books, 1983), pp. 113-125.

92. Shrinking Sun

a. John A. Eddy and Aram A. Boornazian, "Secular Decrease in the Solar Diameter, 1863-1953," *Bulletin of the American Astronomical Society*, Vol. 11, No. 2, 1979, p. 437.

b. G. B. Lubkin, "Analyses of Historical Data Suggest Sun Is Shrinking," *Physics Today*, September 1979, pp. 17-19.

c. David W. Dunham et al., "Observations of a Probable Change in the Solar Radius between 1715 and 1979," *Science*, Vol. 210, 12 December 1980, pp. 1243-1245.

● John Gribbin and Omar Sattaur, "The Schoolchildren's Eclipse," *Science 84*, April 1984, pp. 51-56.

d. Carl A. Rouse, "Gravitational Energy Release Induced by the Nuclear Energy Generation Process: The Resolution of the Solar Neutrino Dilemma," *Astronomy and Astrophysics*, Vol. 102, No. 1, September 1981, pp. 8-11.

93. *Star Clusters*

a. Arp, *Quasars, Redshifts, and Controversies*.

b. Fred Hoyle and Jayant V. Narlikar, "On the Nature of Mass," *Nature*, Vol. 233, 3 September 1971, pp. 41-44.

● William Kaufmann III, "The Most Feared Astronomer on Earth," *Science Digest*, July 1981, pp. 76-81, 117.

● Geoffrey Burbidge, "Redshift Rift," *Science 81*, December 1981, p. 18.

94. *Unstable Galaxies*

a. David Fleischer, "The Galaxy Maker," *Science Digest*, October 1981, Vol. 89, pp. 12, 116.

95. *Galaxy Clusters*

a. A huge dust ring has been observed orbiting two galaxies. The measured orbital velocity of this ring allows the calculation of the mass of the two galaxies and any hidden mass. There was no appreciable amount of hidden mass. [See Stephen E. Schneider, "Neutral Hydrogen in the M96 Group: The Galaxies and the Intergalactic Ring," *The Astrophysical Journal*, Vol. 343, 1 August 1989, pp. 94-106.] Statistical analyses of 155 other small galactic groups also suggest that there is not enough hidden mass to hold galaxies and galaxy clusters together.

● Faye Flam, "NASA PR: Hype or Public Education?," *Science*, Vol. 260, 4 June 1993, p. 1418.

b. Some try to explain away this problem by saying that galaxies and galaxy clusters contain hidden mass whose gravitational pull prevents them from flying apart. For this to work, the hidden mass (sometimes called dark matter) would have to be at least ten times greater than visible masses, such as stars. No direct evidence exists for so much hidden matter. It is simply assumed in order to preserve an old universe. (See **Missing Mass** *on page 20*.)

● *"It turns out that in almost every case the velocities of the individual galaxies are high enough to allow them to escape from the cluster. In effect, the clusters are 'boiling.' This statement is certainly true if we assume that the only gravitational force present is that exerted by visible matter, but it is true even if we assume that every galaxy in the cluster, like the Milky Way, is surrounded by a halo of dark matter that contains 90 percent of the mass of the galaxy."* Trefil, p. 93.

● Gerardus D. Bouw, "Galaxy Clusters and the Mass Anomaly," *Creation Research Society Quarterly*, Vol. 14, September 1977, pp. 108-112.

● Steidl, *The Earth, the Stars, and the Bible*, pp. 179-185.

● Silk, pp. 188-191.

● M. Mitchell Waldrop, "The Large-Scale Structure of the Universe," *Science*, Vol. 219, 4 March 1983, pp. 1050-1052.

● Arp, *Quasars, Redshifts, and Controversies*.

● Halton M. Arp, "NGC-1199," *Astronomy*, Vol. 6, September 1978, p. 15.

● Halton M. Arp, "Three New Cases of Galaxies with Large Discrepant Redshifts," *Astrophysical Journal*, 15 July 1980, pp. 469-474.

Figure 26: Fountains of the Great Deep. Notice the bulge of western Africa beginning to form.

Part II:

Fountains of the Great Deep

copyright—LANDISCOR INC.

Figure 27: The Grand Canyon, awesome and inspiring when viewed from its rim, is even more so from the air. From above, new insights become obvious. For example, have you ever wondered how the Grand Canyon formed? The standard answer for over a century is that the Colorado River and side streams carved out the Grand Canyon over millions of years. If you look carefully at the picture above (top center), you can see four segments of this river. Compare the relatively thin river with the canyon's vast expanse. Is it possible for this small amount of water to carve out such a huge canyon—one of the seven wonders of the natural world? If so, why did it not happen on the dozens of faster and larger rivers of the earth? After studying far broader issues in this section, you will see a huge water source and a surprisingly simple, but complete, explanation for the Grand Canyon's rapid formation.

The Hydroplate Theory — An Overview

There are many new reasons for concluding that the earth has experienced a devastating, worldwide flood, whose waters violently burst forth from under the earth's crust. Standard "textbook" explanations for many of the earth's major features are scientifically flawed. We can now explain, using well-understood phenomena, how this cataclysmic event rapidly formed all these features. Many other mysteries are better explained in terms of this literally earth-shaking event, an event far more catastrophic than most people have imagined.

The origin of the following geological features are subjects of controversy within the earth sciences.

- **The Grand Canyon and Other Canyons**
- **Mid-Oceanic Ridge**
- **Continental Shelves and Slopes**
- **Ocean Trenches**
- **Seamounts and Tablemounts**
- **Earthquakes**
- **Magnetic Variations on the Ocean Floor**
- **Submarine Canyons**
- **Coal and Oil Formations**
- **Glaciers and the Ice Ages**
- **Frozen Mammoths**
- **Major Mountain Ranges**
- **Overthrusts**
- **Volcanoes and Lava**
- **Geothermal Heat**
- **Metamorphic Rock**
- **Strata**
- **Plateaus**
- **Salt Domes**
- **Jigsaw Fit of the Continents**
- **Fossil Graveyards**

Each feature has many aspects that are inconsistent with standard explanations. Yet all appear to be consequences of a sudden and unrepeatable event—a cataclysmic flood whose waters erupted from worldwide, subterranean, and interconnected chambers with an energy release exceeding the explosion of ten billion hydrogen bombs. When **the hydroplate theory** is explained later in this chapter, it will resolve the parade of mysteries explored in the following paragraphs.

A Few of the Mysteries

Mid-Oceanic Ridge. One of our planet's most dramatic features was discovered in the 1950s. It is a mountain range, called the **Mid-Oceanic Ridge**, that is 46,000 miles long and wraps around the earth. (See Figure 28 on page 72.) Since most of it lies on the ocean floor, relatively few people even know it exists. How did it get there? Why is it primarily on the ocean floor? Why does it intersect itself in a Y-shaped junction beneath the Indian Ocean? Why is it composed of a type of rock, called **basalt**, that is so different from the rocks of most other mountains? We will soon consider the segment of the Mid-Oceanic Ridge that runs down the center of the Atlantic Ocean. It is called the **Mid-Atlantic Ridge**. Why is the Mid-Atlantic Ridge centered between Europe, Africa, and the Americas? If these continents were once connected, how did they break apart?

A popular theory called **plate tectonics** offers some possible answers to a few of these questions. According to the standard version of this theory, the earth's crust is composed of a dozen or so plates,[1] each approximately 30 miles thick. These plates supposedly move with respect to each other, at about an inch per year—the rate a fingernail grows. Continents and oceans ride on top of these plates. Sometimes a continent, such as North America, is on more than one plate. For example, different parts of North America, separated by the San Andreas Fault running up through California, are sliding

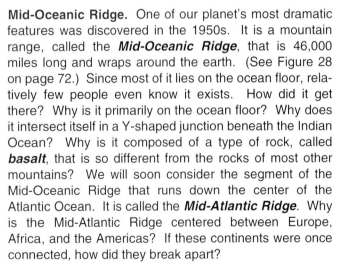

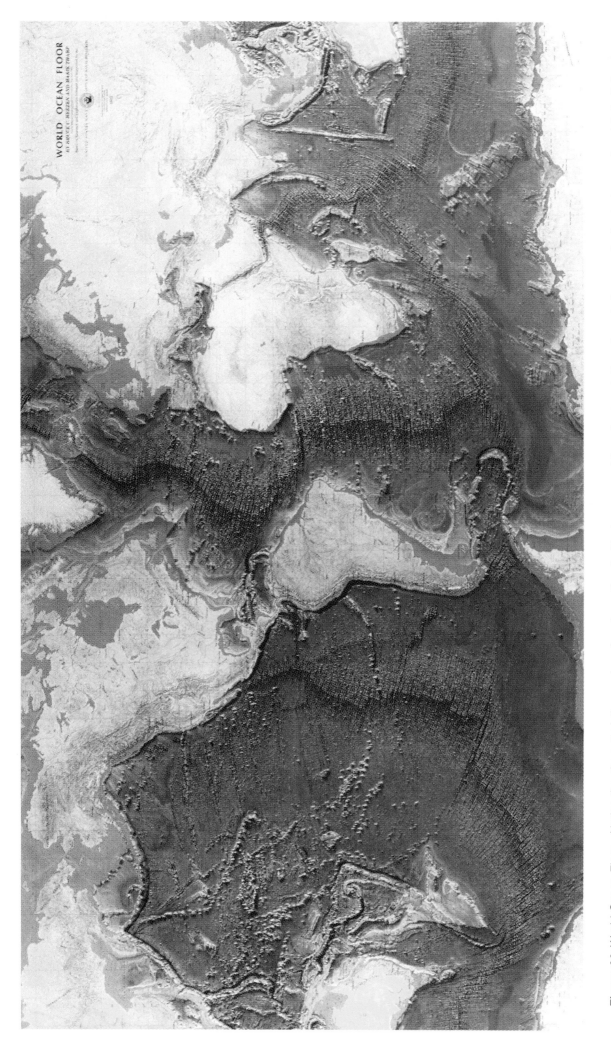

Figure 28: World Ocean Floor. Notice the characteristic margins of each continent. Moving seaward from the beach there is a shallow, gradually sloping continental shelf, then a relatively steep drop to the ocean floor called the continental slope. This strange pattern is worldwide. Why? For a better look at the typical shape of this margin, see Figure 30 on page 74. Notice also the different characteristics of (1) the continents and ocean basins, and (2) the Atlantic and Pacific basins. As one moves toward the polar regions on this type of map projection, the east-west distances are stretched and do not reflect their true distances.

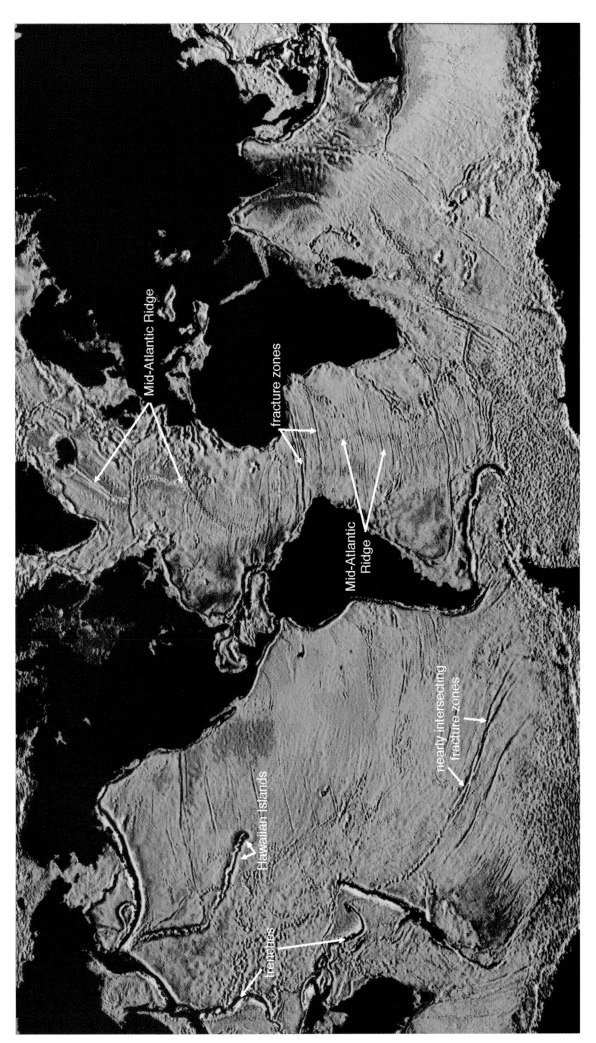

Figure 29: "Unlevel" Sea Level. A new technological development allows us to "see" the ocean floor. The U.S. Navy's SEASAT satellite measured with a radar altimeter the satellite's distance above the ocean's surface with an accuracy of several inches! It was thereby discovered that "sea level" is not level. Instead, the ocean's surface "humps up" over mountains on the ocean floor and depresses over trenches. The gravitational attraction of the Hawaiian Islands, for example, pulls the surrounding water toward it. This raises sea level there about 80 feet higher than it would otherwise be. The satellite's data have been color coded to make this amazing picture of the ocean's surface. Darker areas show depressions in sea level. Notice that the ocean surface is depressed over the long scars, called fracture zones, running generally perpendicular to the Mid-Oceanic Ridge. What theory explains this: the plate tectonic theory or the hydroplate theory? Note the nearly intersecting fracture zones in the South Pacific. Which theory explains them?

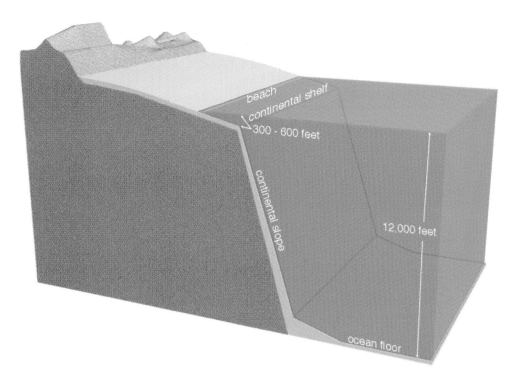

Figure 30: Continental Margin. The typical shape of ocean/continent boundaries is shown at the left. (Vertical scale exaggerated.) The actual continental boundary is generally considered to be halfway down the continental slope. By comparing this figure with Figure 28 on page 72, notice that Asia and North America would become connected if sea level were lowered about 300 feet. Two other pairs of continents (Australia-Asia and Europe-North America) would also be connected, except for a stream between them. Sediments and sedimentary rock are shown in yellow.

past each other. Supposedly, material from deep inside the earth is rising toward the crest of the entire Mid-Oceanic Ridge. Once it reaches the crest, it moves laterally away from the ridge. This claimed motion is similar to that of a conveyor belt arising from under a floor and then moving horizontally along the floor. However, many little-known problems, discussed below, accompany plate tectonics.

Cutting across the Mid-Oceanic Ridge at almost right angles are hundreds of long **fracture zones**. Whenever the axis of the Mid-Oceanic Ridge is offset, it is always along a fracture zone. (See Figure 28 on page 72.) Why? According to plate tectonics, plates move parallel to fracture zones. But fracture zones are not always parallel. Sometimes they are many degrees "out of parallel."[2] Several fracture zones practically intersect! How then can solid plates be bounded by and move in the direction of these fracture zones? Can a train move on tracks that aren't parallel?

In many places on the Atlantic and Pacific floor, segments of the Mid-Oceanic Ridge overlap for about 10 miles. These are called Overlapping Spreading Centers.[3] (Figure 31.) If plates are moving away from the Mid-Oceanic Ridge, then the distance between overlapping segments must be increasing. However, overlapping regions are always close to each other.

Perhaps the most perplexing question in the earth sciences today is barely verbalized in classrooms and textbooks: "What force moved plates over the globe and by what mechanism?" What was the energy source?

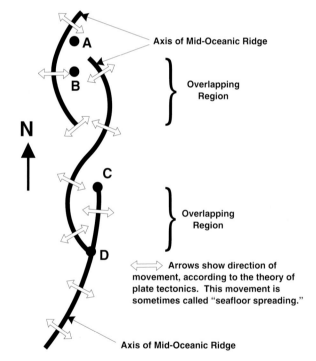

Figure 31: Overlapping Spreading Centers. Bold lines represent the axes of the Mid-Ocean Ridge. According to plate tectonics, the ocean floor is moving in the direction of the hollow arrows—away from the Mid-Oceanic Ridge. If so, in which direction is point B moving? If B is stationary, and A is moving east, why is there no fault between them? What could possibly be happening at C and D if the plate tectonic theory is correct?

The hydroplate theory gives a surprisingly simple answer. It involves gravity, the Mid-Atlantic Ridge, and water—lots of it.

Continental Shelves and Slopes. See Figures 28 and 30.

Ocean Trenches. Ocean trenches are long, narrow depressions on the ocean floor, sometimes deeper than seven Grand Canyons. They can be seen in the western Pacific in Figures 28 and 29. Advocates of the plate tectonic theory say a trench forms when a plate dives down into the mantle, a process they call **subduction**. How this dive begins is never fully explained. This would be similar to pushing a 30-mile-thick shovel into the ground. What pushes a continental-sized plate down at such a steep angle? Worse yet, when the plate reaches a depth of only several miles, the pressure is so great that frictional forces exceed the strength of rock. Therefore, this movement should be impossible. (See technical note on page 185.) This is similar to trying to push our shovel, now squeezed in the jaws of a vise, down further. It simply will not move.

Seamounts and Tablemounts. Notice how many submarine volcanoes, called seamounts, litter the Pacific floor. Some are almost as tall as Mount Everest. Surprisingly, few seamounts are in the Atlantic. If one plate dives (subducts) beneath another, why aren't seamounts and soft sediments scraped off the top of the descending plate? Why do seismic reflection profiles show almost no distortions of the horizontal sedimentary layers in trenches?

Hundreds of flat-topped seamounts, called tablemounts, are 3,000-6,000 feet below sea level. Apparently, as these volcanoes tried to grow above sea level, wave action planed off their tops. Therefore, (1) sea level was once much lower, (2) ocean floors were higher, or (3) both. Each possibility raises new and difficult questions.

Earthquakes. A major (but perhaps elusive) goal of earthquake research is to predict earthquakes. Normally, the best way to predict something is to understand how it works. However, earthquakes are not understood. Therefore, much effort is spent trying to find things that often occur before an earthquake. Two apparent precursors are the sudden change in the water depth in wells and the swelling of the ground.

The plate tectonic theory claims that earthquakes occur when plates rub against each other, temporarily lock, and then periodically jerk loose. Then why are some earthquakes, many quite powerful, far from plate boundaries? Why do such earthquakes occur when water is forced into the ground, after large water reservoirs are built and filled?[4]

Earthquakes sometimes displace the ground horizontally along a fault, as occurred along the San Andreas Fault during the great San Francisco earthquake of 1906.

Western California slid northward relative to the rest of North America. Since the San Andreas Fault has several prominent bends, how could movement have been going on for millions of years, as proponents of plate tectonics claim? Just as two interlocking pieces of a jigsaw puzzle cannot slip very far relative to each other, neither can both sides of a curved fault. Furthermore, if movement has occurred along the San Andreas Fault for millions of years, the adjacent rock should be hot due to frictional heating. Drilling into the fault did not locate this heat.[5] Apparently, movement has not occurred for that length of time and/or the walls of the fault were lubricated.

Magnetic Variations on the Ocean Floor. In the 1960s, an important discovery was misinterpreted. This, in turn, led to a general acceptance of the plate tectonic theory. People were told that paralleling the Mid-Oceanic Ridge are bands of ocean floor that have a reversed magnetic orientation. These "magnetic reversals" alternated with bands of rock having the normal (north pointing) polarity. At a few places, the pattern of reversals on one side of the ridge is almost a mirror image of those on the other side. All of this suggested that periodically the earth's magnetic field reversed, although there is no theoretical understanding of how this could have happened. Molten material supposedly rose at the ridge, solidified, took on the earth's current magnetic orientation, and then moved away from the ridge like a conveyer belt.

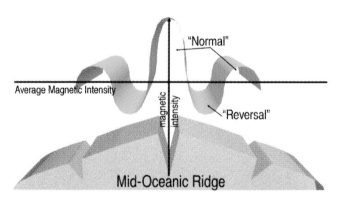

Figure 32: Magnetic Anomalies. Notice the wide fluctuations in magnetic intensity as one moves across the Mid-Oceanic Ridge. The so-called "reversals" are simply regions of lower magnetic intensity. Why should the intensity usually be greatest along the crest of the ridge?

This story is inaccurate. First, **there are no magnetic reversals on the ocean floor.** Nowhere on the ocean floor will the north-seeking arrow on a compass point to the south magnetic pole. However, as one moves across the Mid-Oceanic Ridge, the magnetic intensity fluctuates widely, as shown in Figure 32. Someone merely drew a line through these fluctuations and labeled everything below this average intensity as a "reversal." The false, but widespread, impression exists that these deviations from the average represent the magnetic field millions of years ago. Calling these fluctuations "reversals" causes one to completely miss a more likely explanation for these magnetic anomalies.

Although textbooks show these so-called "reversals" as smooth bands paralleling the Mid-Oceanic Ridge, there is nothing smooth about them. Many "bands" run perpendicular to the ridge axis—quite the opposite of what plate tectonics predicts. Furthermore, the perpendicular "bands" correspond to fracture zones.[6] The hydroplate theory will explain these magnetic anomalies.

Submarine Canyons. The ocean floor has several hundred canyons, some of which exceed the Grand Canyon in both length and depth. One of these submarine canyons is three times deeper than the Grand Canyon. Another is ten times longer (2,300 miles), so long that it would stretch nearly across the United States. Many of these V-shaped canyons are extensions of major rivers. Examples include the Amazon Canyon, the Hudson Canyon, the Ganges Canyon, the Congo Canyon, and the Indus Canyon. How did they form? What force could gouge out canyons 15,000 feet below sea level? Perhaps the ocean floor rose or the ocean surface dropped by this amount so ancient rivers could cut these canyons. If so, how? Most continental canyons were supposedly cut by swift rivers. However, currents measured in submarine canyons are much too slow, generally less than one mile per hour. Frequently the flow is in the wrong direction. Submarine landslides or currents of dense, muddy water sometimes occur. However, they would not form long, branching (or dendritic) patterns that characterize river systems and submarine canyons. Besides, experiments with thick, muddy water in submarine canyons have not demonstrated any canyon-cutting ability.

Coal and Oil Formations. There are surprisingly large amounts of coal in Antarctica. Various expeditions found thick seams of coal and fossilized tree trunks near the South Pole.[7] Some tree trunks were 24 feet long and 2 feet thick! At another location, there were 30 layers of anthracite (or high grade) coal, each 3-4 feet thick.[8] Was it once warm enough for trees to grow in Antarctica? If it was, how could so much vegetation grow where it is nighttime 6 months of the year? Was Antarctica once at a more tropical latitude? Not according to plate tectonics, which places the South Pole well inside Antarctica ever since the coal formed.[9] Perhaps vegetation floated there in a large flood.

Glaciers and the Ice Ages. How does an ice age begin? More importantly, how does an ice age end? As glaciers expand, they reflect more of the sun's radiation away from the earth. This lowers the earth's temperature, causing glaciers to grow even more. This cycle should continue. In other words, once an ice age begins, the

earth's temperature should continue to drop until the entire globe is frozen. Conversely, if glaciers diminish, as they have in recent years, the earth should reflect less heat, warm up, and melt all glaciers forever.

Frozen Mammoths. Some fleshy remains of about 50 elephantlike animals called mammoths, and a few rhinoceroses, have been found frozen and buried in Alaska and Siberia. One mammoth still had identifiable food in its mouth and stomach. To approximate this today, one would have to suddenly push a well-fed elephant (dead or alive) into a very large freezer and turn the thermostat to -150°F. Anything less severe would result in the animal's residual heat and stomach acids destroying the stomach's food. If the animal remained alive for more than a few minutes, one would not expect to find food in its mouth. What could cause such a large and sudden temperature drop in nature? Even if the sun suddenly stopped shining, the earth's temperature would not drop rapidly enough to produce these effects. Finally, these giant animals must be buried in what was presumably frozen ground—quite a trick.

Consider, also, how large herds of elephantlike animals, each requiring much food, could live so abundantly in the Arctic. Today the average January temperature in those parts of Siberia is -30°F. If your nose gets unbearably cold after a few minutes in +32°F weather, consider how you would feel if your nose were a six-foot-long trunk and the ***average*** temperature were 60°F colder for many weeks. In addition, where would you, or a mammoth, get drinking water?

Major Mountain Ranges. How did mountains form? Major mountains are usually crumpled like an accordion. (See Figure 33.) Satellite photos of mountain ranges show that some resemble rugs that have been pushed up against walls. But what force could push a long, thick slab of rock and cause it to buckle and sometimes fold back on itself? Even if a large enough force could be found to overcome the friction at the base of the slab, the force would crush the end being pushed before movement could even begin. Consequently, a mountain would not form. (See the technical note on page 186.)

Many of us have seen, especially in mountains and road cuts, thinly layered rocks that have been folded like a doubled-over phone book. How could brittle rock, showing little evidence of heating or cracking, fold? Sometimes these "bent" rocks are small enough to hold in one's hand. Rocks are strong in compression but weak in tension. Consequently, their stretched outer surfaces should easily fracture. Bent rocks, which are found all over the earth, often look as if they had the consistency of putty when they were squeezed. They must have been squeezed and folded soon after the sediments were laid

Figure 33: Folded Mountains. Textbooks and museums frequently refer to some uplifting force that formed mountains. Can you see that an uplifting force could not cause this pattern? The force had to be a horizontal compression. These buckled sedimentary layers are near the Sullivan River in southern British Columbia, Canada.

down, but before they hardened chemically. But what squeezed and folded them?

Overthrusts. A similar problem exists for large blocks of rock called overthrusts that appear to have slid horizontally over other rock for many miles. If this happened, these blocks should have lots of rubble under them. Many do not.

Why overthrusts occur has never been adequately explained. Anything pushing a large slab of rock with enough force to overcome frictional resistance would crush the slab before it would move. (See the technical note on page 186.) Those who appreciate this problem simply say that the pore pressure of water in the rocks lubricated the sliding, and maybe the slab slid downhill. Not enough water resides in rocks today to make this possible, and overthrusted blocks are not on slopes.

Volcanoes and Lava. Erupting lava usually exceeds 1800°F. Where does it come from, and why is it so hot? The earth's mantle and inner core are essentially solid. Only the outer core, which lies 1800-3200 miles below the earth's surface, is a liquid. The standard explanation is that magma originates in hot pockets, called **magma chambers**, at depths of about 60 miles. But how could magma escape to the surface? A key fact to remember is that at depths greater than 4 or 5 miles, the pressure is so great that all empty channels through which magma might rise should be squeezed shut. Even if a crack could open, the magma must rise through colder rock. Magma would then tend to solidify and plug up the crack. A second fact to keep in mind is that heat diffuses. So what concentrated enough heat to create the "hot pockets" and melt the vast volumes of rock that erupted in the past? On the Columbia Plateau in the northwestern United States, more than 50,000 square miles of **flood basalts** spilled out to an average depth of about $\frac{1}{2}$ mile. On the Deccan Plateau in western India, 200,000 square miles have been flooded with liquid basalt to an average depth of $\frac{3}{4}$ mile. The ocean floor, especially in the Pacific, has more and larger examples of flood basalts. Escaping magma at the Ontong-Java Plateau in the western Pacific was 25 times more extensive than on the Deccan Plateau. How then does magma form, and how does it get out?

The two deepest holes in the world are on the Kola Peninsula in northern Russia and in Germany's north-eastern Bavaria.[10] They were recently drilled to depths of 7.5 miles and 5.6 miles, respectively. (When holes are drilled below 5 miles and are immediately filled with water or dense mud, they will stay open.) Neither hole reached the basalt that underlies the granite continents. Deep in the Russian hole, to everyone's surprise, was hot, flowing, mineralized water (including salt water) encased in **crushed** granite.[11] Why was the granite crushed? In the German hole, the drill encountered salt-water-filled cracks throughout the lower few miles. The salt concentration was about **twice that of sea water**. Remember, surface waters cannot migrate below about 5 miles, because the weight of the overlying rock squeezes shut even microscopic flow channels. While scientists at these projects are mystified by the presence of deep salt water, the hydroplate theory provides a simple answer for these and other mysteries.

Another surprise at these drill sites was the greater-than-expected increase in the granite's temperature with increased depth. This raises the question of why the earth's crust is so hot.

Geothermal Heat. Outward flowing heat from inside the earth is called geothermal heat. In general, the deeper man has gone into the earth, first in caves and mines and later with drills, the hotter the rock gets. What is the origin of geothermal heat? As children, most of us were taught that the early earth was molten. Another scenario that has been widely taught is that the molten earth was caused by infalling, meteoritelike bodies, as the earth slowly grew and evolved. If either were true, it must have taken millions of years for the earth to cool enough to support life, and even longer for the earth to cool to its present temperature.

This popular story has several problems. First, the increase in temperature with depth, called the temperature gradient, varies at different locations by more than 600%.[12] This is true even when considering only continental rock far from volcanoes. The deep drilling in Russia and Germany encountered rock so much hotter than expected that each project was terminated early. If the earth has been cooling for billions of years, one would expect great uniformity in the temperature increase with depth. Unusually hot or cold regions should not exist since heat diffuses from hotter to colder regions.

Had the earth ever been molten, denser materials would have sunk toward the center of the earth, and lighter materials would have floated to the surface. One should not find dense, fairly nonreactive metals, such as gold, at the earth's surface. (One cannot appeal to volcanoes to lift gold to the earth's surface, since gold is not concentrated around volcanoes.) Even granite, the basic continental rock, is a mixture of many minerals with varying densities. If one melted granite and slowly cooled the liquid, the granite would not reform. Instead, it would be a "layer cake" of minerals sorted vertically by density. In other words, the earth's crust appears to have never been molten.

Complex mathematical solutions of heat conduction in spheres, such as the earth, are well known. These solutions can incorporate many facts, such as the earth's thermal properties, radioactive heat generation, the range of temperature gradients at the earth's surface, and many other details. Such analyses are hopelessly inconsistent with the "molten-earth" story and "billions of years of cooling." (See **Molten Earth?** on page 25.) What then is the source of geothermal heat, and why do temperature gradients vary so widely?

Strata. In many places the earth's crust has a layered, or stratified, appearance. The layers, or strata, have many puzzling characteristics. For example, most layers and particles within those layers are firmly and uniformly cemented. What accounts for their great uniformity in hardness? If truckloads of sand and other dry sediments were dumped on your driveway and bags of cement were placed in another pile, anyone would have difficulty mixing them uniformly. Without the right mixture throughout, the concrete would quickly crumble.

A typical cementing agent in sedimentary rock is limestone, or calcium carbonate ($CaCO_3$). Any geologist or mineralogist who stops to think about it will realize that the earth has too much limestone, at least based on present processes. Sediments and sedimentary rock on the continents alone average about a mile in thickness. Somewhere between 10-15% of this is limestone ($CaCO_3$).[13] How did so much limestone form—much of it quite pure? Most limestone is in extensive layers, tens of thousands of square miles in area and hundreds of feet thick. Under the Bahamas, it is more than 3 miles thick! The presence of pure limestone, without the impurities that normally drift in, argues for its rapid burial. Today, limestone forms either by precipitating out of sea water or by organisms taking it out of sea water to produce shells and other hard parts. In either case, oceans supply limestone sediments. The oceans already have about as much limestone dissolved in them as they can possibly hold. Therefore, where did all the limestone come from, especially its calcium and carbon, which are relatively rare outside of limestone?

Metamorphic Rock. When the temperature and/or pressure of certain rocks increase and exceed certain high values without melting, structural and chemical changes occur. The new rock is called a metamorphic rock. For example, limestone becomes marble (a metamorphic rock) when its temperature exceeds 1600°F and the confining pressure corresponds to the weight of a 23-mile-high column of rock. Most metamorphic rocks were formed in the presence of water—often flowing water.[14] What could have accounted for the extreme temperature, pressure, and abundance of water?

The standard answer is that the original rock (such as limestone) was heated and compressed under a tall mountain or deep in the earth. Later, either the mountain eroded away or the deep rock rose to the earth's surface. All of this would, of course, take millions of years. Since Mount Everest, the world's tallest mountain, is only $5\frac{1}{2}$ miles high, it is difficult to imagine mountains 23 miles high. Raising buried layers of rock 23 miles to the earth's surface is even more difficult to explain, but with millions of years available to do it, few consider it a problem. Not addressed in this standard explanation is the abundant, sometimes *flowing*, water. Surface water, remember, cannot seep deeper than about 5 miles, and even at 5 miles, it hardly flows. Metamorphic rock is a giant enigma.

Plateaus. Plateaus are relatively flat regions of large geographical extent that have been uplifted more than 500 feet relative to the surrounding regions. Professor George C. Kennedy explains the problems associated with plateaus quite well.

The problem of the uplift of large plateau areas is one which has puzzled students of the Earth's crust for a very long time . . . . Given an Earth with sialic [granitic] continents floating in denser simatic [basaltic] substratum, what mechanism would cause a large volume of low standing continents to rise rapidly a mile in the air? Furthermore, evidence from gravity surveys suggests that the rocks underlying the Colorado plateau are in isostatic balance, that is, this large area is floating at its correct elevation in view of its mass and density. Recent seismic evidence confirms this, in that the depth to the M discontinuity [the Moho, which will be explained later] under the Colorado plateau is approximately 10 kilometers [6 miles] greater than over most of continental North America. Thus, appropriate roots of light rock extend into the dense substratum to account for the higher elevation of the Colorado plateau. We have then a double-ended mystery, for the Colorado plateau seems to have grown downward at the same time that its emerged part rose upward. This is just as startling as it would be to

see a floating cork suddenly rise and float a half inch higher in a pan of water. To date, the only hypothesis to explain the upward motion of large regions like the Colorado plateau is that of convection currents. Slowly moving convection currents in the solid rock, some 40 to 50 kilometers [about 30 miles] below the surface of the Earth, are presumed to have swept a great volume of light rock from some unidentified place and to have deposited it underneath the Colorado plateau. A total volume of approximately 2,500,000 cubic miles of sialic rock is necessary to account for the uplift of the Colorado plateau. While it is not hard to visualize rocks as having no great strength at the high pressures and temperatures existing at depths of 40 to 50 kilometers, it is quite another matter to visualize currents in solid rock of sufficient magnitude to bring in and deposit this quantity of light material in a relatively uniform layer underneath the entire Colorado plateau region

The Tibetan plateaus present a similar problem, but on a vastly larger scale. There, an area of 750,000 square miles has been uplifted from approximately sea level to a mean elevation of roughly three miles, and the Himalayan mountain chain bordering this region has floated upward some five miles, and rather late in geologic time, probably within the last 20,000,000 years. The quantity of light rock which would need to be swept underneath these plateaus by convection currents to produce the effects noted would be an order of magnitude greater than that needed to uplift the Colorado plateau, that is approximately 25,000,000 cubic miles. Even more troublesome than the method of transporting all this light rock at shallow depths below the surface of the Earth is the problem of its source. The region from which the light rock was moved should have experienced spectacular subsidence, but no giant neighboring depressions are known. A lesser but large problem is how such enormous quantities of light rock can be dispersed so uniformly over so large an area.[15]

Salt Domes. At many locations, large, thick layers of salt are buried up to several miles below the earth's surface. These salt deposits are sometimes 100,000 square miles in area and a mile in thickness. Large salt deposits are not being laid down today, even in the Great Salt Lake. What concentrated this much salt? Sometimes a salt layer bulges up several miles, like a big underground bubble, to form a salt dome. Surprisingly large salt deposits lie under the Mediterranean Sea. A discoverer of this huge deposit claims that the Mediterranean must have evaporated 8-10 times to deposit so much salt.[16] His estimate is probably low, but even so, why didn't each

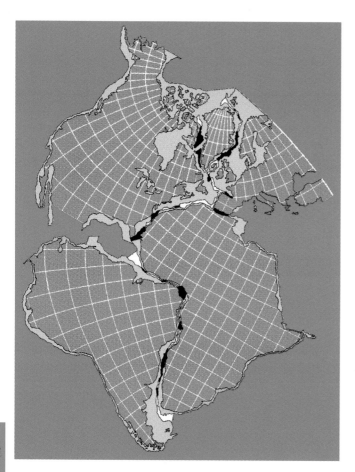

Figure 34: Continental Fit Proposed by Edward Bullard. Can you identify four distortions in this popular explanation of how the continents may have once fit together? First, the area of Africa has been shrunk by 35%. (You may need to look at a globe and compare Africa's length and width with those of South America.) Second, Central America, southern Mexico, and the Caribbean islands have been removed. Third, an east-west slice was made through the Mediterranean and Europe was rotated counter-clockwise and Africa was rotated clockwise. Finally, the continents were rotated relative to each other. (Notice the rotation of the north-south and east-west lines.) Overlapping areas are shown in black. From "The Confirmation of Continental Drift," by Patrick M. Hurley. Figure by Allen Beechel. Copyright © April 1968 by Scientific American, Inc. All rights reserved.

refilling of the Mediterranean basin dissolve the salt residue left from prior evaporations?

Jigsaw Fit of the Continents. Do continents drift? Do plates, composed of large pieces of continents and ocean floor, move over the earth's surface at slow but measurable rates? For centuries, beginning possibly with Francis Bacon in 1620, many have marveled at the apparent jigsaw fit of the continents bordering the Atlantic. It is only natural that bold thinkers, such as Alfred Wegener in 1912, would propose that the continents were once connected as shown in Figure 34, and somehow they moved to their present positions. But would continents, which often extend offshore hundreds

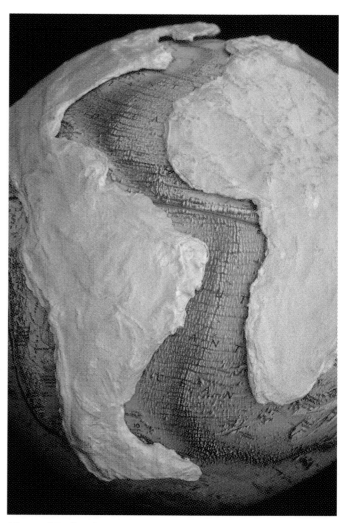

Figure 35: Continental Plates on a Globe. By far the best fit of the continents is with the base of the Mid-Atlantic Ridge.

of miles to the edge of the continental shelf, really fit together as shown in textbooks? Since the distortion produced by flattening a globe onto a two-dimensional map makes it difficult to answer this question, two plates, matching the shape and curvature of the continents, were formed on a globe. (Figure 36.)

The classical fit (Figure 34), proposed by Sir Edward Bullard, appears at first glance to be a better fit of the continents than that shown in Figure 36. Why? First, notice that Bullard removed Central America, southern Mexico, and continental material in the Caribbean. Where did it go? Also, a slice was made through the Mediterranean, and Europe was rotated counterclockwise and Africa clockwise. Furthermore, the area of Africa was shrunk by about 35%. Finally, North America and South America were rotated. None of this has any sound geological justification. Apparently, the sole motivation was to show a tight fit. Bullard certainly took great "latitude" in juggling continents. Few, if any, teachers or textbooks inform us of these distortions.

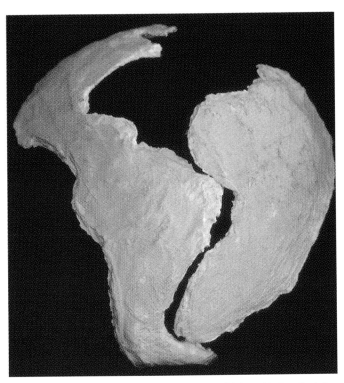

Figure 36: Continental Plates Made on a Globe. Notice that the fit of the actual continents is not as good as Bullard proposed.

Instead of fitting the continents to each other, notice in Figure 35 how well they each fit the base of the Mid-Atlantic Ridge. The hydroplate theory proposes that:

> a. ***These continents were once in the position shown in Figure 35.***
>
> b. ***They were connected by rock that was rapidly eroded and transported worldwide by erupting subterranean water.***
>
> c. ***Most of the earth's sediments were formed from this eroded rock.***
>
> d. ***The continents quickly slid (rapid continental drift) east and west from what is now the Mid-Atlantic Ridge and came to rest in their present positions.***[17]

Fossil Graveyards. Fossils rarely form today, because dead plants and animals decay before they are buried in enough sediments to preserve their shapes. We certainly do not observe fossils forming in layered strata that can be traced over thousands of square miles. So how did the fossils form? You will soon see that ***the volume of this eroded material (point "c" above) corresponds closely to the volume of the earth's sedimentary rocks which encase all fossils***. It will become apparent why animals and plants were trapped and buried in sediments that were quickly cemented to form the fossil

record and why fossils of sea life are on every major mountain range.

Summary. These are a few of the many mysteries associated with each of the 21 features. The hydroplate theory will explain these mysteries and tie together the causes and effects of this dramatic, global catastrophe.

Criteria for Evaluating Theories

To explain scientifically an unobserved event that cannot be repeated, we must begin by assuming the conditions that existed before the event. From these assumed starting conditions, we then try to determine what the laws of physics would produce. Three criteria are then used to evaluate a proposed explanation.

Criterion 1: Process. If we can uniquely explain many diverse observations, then our confidence in that explanation increases. However, if these starting conditions and the operation of physical laws (or known processes) would cause things that we should observe but do not, then our confidence in this explanation decreases. For example, a frequent and intriguing question is, "What caused the sudden extinction of the dinosaurs?" This was an unobserved and unrepeatable event. Therefore, Criterion 1 should first be applied.

We shall not attempt to solve the dinosaur extinction problem here, but will use the extinction question to demonstrate how such scientific theories should be addressed. Some explanations for the extinction of dinosaurs call for large climatic changes. While many types of climate variation might kill all dinosaurs, we must also (by Criterion 1) see if other consequences of such climatic changes are observed. Flowering plants and many small animals are even more vulnerable to large climatic changes. Since according to evolutionists, most of them did not become extinct with the dinosaurs, the "climatic change" theories (and other dinosaur extinction theories) are weakened.

Criterion 2: Parsimony. Parsimony here means "the infrequent use of assumptions." If a few assumptions allow us to explain many things, then confidence in the explanation will be great. Conversely, if many starting conditions only help explain a few observations, or if we must often add new assumptions as new observations are made, then we will have little confidence in our explanation.

For example, another attempt to explain dinosaur extinction claims that a large asteroid or comet struck the earth. The asteroid, containing the rare element iridium, kicked up a worldwide dust cloud that blocked out sunlight for several years, reduced photosynthesis on the earth, and choked off the dinosaurs' food chain. Support for this theory comes from a thin but widely spread layer of clay in Europe, New Zealand, and elsewhere that contains iridium. This iridium-rich layer is found near many dinosaur fossils. An asteroid or comet striking the earth might explain the worldwide extinction of dinosaurs and a widely spread iridium layer near many dinosaur fossils. In other words, one starting condition (an impact of a large asteroid or comet) explains two important observations: dinosaur extinctions and the iridium layer. This is good.

But there are some hidden assumptions. While iridium is frequently found in some meteorites, it has obviously not been found in asteroids or comets, since they have never been captured. Therefore, we must assume that asteroids or comets have large amounts of iridium. Other iridium-rich layers have recently been found above and below the original layer. Did other asteroids strike the earth before the one that destroyed the dinosaurs? Why did the dinosaurs survive those earlier impacts? Why were no other extinctions associated with these other iridium layers? Each question can be answered by making new assumptions. However, by Criterion 2, this reduces our confidence in the theory.

Criterion 3: Prediction. A legitimate theory allows us to predict unusual things that we should soon see if we look in the right places and make the right measurements. Our confidence will be greatly increased or decreased by a prediction's confirmation or lack of confirmation. ***Predictions are the most important test of any scientific theory.*** Few evolutionists make predictions.

What predictions can be made based on the "climatic variation" and "impact" theories? Few, if any, have been made publicly. This does not inspire confidence in these explanations. Rarely do predictions accompany explanations of ancient, unobserved events.

However, some predictions can be associated with the impact theory. For example, a very large impact crater should be found whose age corresponds to the time of the extinction of dinosaurs. Extinctions should concentrate near the crater or, at least, in the hemisphere containing the crater. However, it is recognized that other extinctions that accompanied the dinosaurs' demise are uniformly distributed worldwide[18]—a point worth remembering.

For several years, no suitable crater could be found.[19] Finally in 1990, an impact site was proposed on the northern coast of Mexico's Yucatán Peninsula, centered near the village Chicxulub (CHICKS uh loob). No crater shape was visible, and evolutionists initially dated the site 40-50 million years earlier than is needed to explain the

dinosaur's extinction. However, circular magnetic and gravitational anomalies were found along with some debris from an impact. Therefore, impact advocates are, in effect, predicting that drilling in and around the Chicxulub site will reveal a buried impact crater.

Other dinosaur extinction theories have even more problems. Our purpose here is not to address this question but instead to show how scientific reasoning should be applied to unobserved and nonreproducible events. Incidentally, another theory on dinosaur extinction will soon become obvious—a theory relating to a global flood and the harsh conditions afterward. (For more on dinosaurs, see ***What about the Dinosaurs?*** on pages 164-166.)

Scientific explanations are never certain or final, and the overused word "prove" is never justified except possibly in mathematics or a court of law. Science is even less certain when dealing with ancient and unrepeatable events, since another starting condition might work as well or better. Perhaps we have overlooked a physical consequence or have improperly applied the laws of physics. Certainly we will never have all the data.

Unfortunately, this is the only way we can hope to understand unobservable and unrepeatable events using science. Ancient records cannot give ***scientific*** support for the truth or falsity of an ancient event. Such records may provide important ***historical*** support for those who have confidence in a particular ancient record. This, however, is not science. Our methodology here will be that of science.

The Hydroplate Theory: Assumptions

The previous section explained why assumptions are required to explain ancient, unrepeatable events. Three assumptions underlie the hydroplate theory.

Interconnected Continents. The first assumption has already been mentioned: Europe, Asia, Africa, and the Americas were joined across what is now the Atlantic Ocean. They were generally in the position shown in Figure 35 on page 80.

Subterranean Water. Before the 21 features (listed earlier) were formed, the earth had a large amount of salty, subterranean water—about half of what is now in the oceans. (See Figure 37.) This subterranean water was contained in ***interconnected chambers*** that collectively formed a thin, spherical shell. It averaged about $\frac{5}{8}$ of a mile in thickness and was located 10 miles below the earth's surface.

Figure 37: Cross-Section of Preflood Earth. Several aspects of the early earth are shown here at approximately the proper scale. The assumed shell of subterranean water would have been thinner under preflood mountains, since the crust bent downward under loads applied by mountains. Conversely, the subterranean water would have been thicker under preflood seas. If the average thickness of the water was as shown above, then half the earth's water was in the relatively thin subterranean chamber. The earth's curvature would not be apparent at this scale.

There is no need to assume the temperature of this water. Subsequent events, as you will see, suddenly increased the temperature of most subterranean water and the rock above. Many minerals and some gases were dissolved in this water, especially salt (NaCl) and carbon dioxide (CO_2).

Beneath the subterranean water was a layer of basaltic rock, and beneath the basalt was the top of the earth's mantle. An important distinction between the basalt and upper mantle was discovered in 1909 by seismologist Andrija Mohorovicic. He noticed that earthquake waves passing into the mantle suddenly increased in speed. This boundary, now called the Mohorovicic discontinuity, has for obvious reasons been shortened to *"The Moho."*

Increasing Pressure. The final assumption of the hydroplate theory is that the pressure in the layer of subterranean water was increasing. Many things could have caused this. For example, a very slight increase in the mantle's temperature, due to radioactive decay, would expand the mantle. This, in turn, would increase the pressure in the subterranean water. Another possibility is that an asteroid struck the earth and suddenly pressurized the subterranean water. All of this, however, is speculation. Simply labelling the increase in pressure as a starting assumption is probably best. All theories of past events have some assumptions or initial conditions. Usually they are hidden.

No attempt will be made to determine what caused these initial conditions. That would only present the next question, "What caused those causes?," ad infinitum.

Each reader must judge the ultimate cause, or, as Sir Isaac Newton wrote, "The First Cause." Instead, it will simply be assumed that (1) the continents were interconnected, (2) there was a large shell of salty, subterranean water, and (3) the pressure was increasing within that water.

It appears that all 21 features described earlier, such as major mountain ranges or the Grand Canyon, are consequences of these three basic assumptions. The chain of events that flow naturally from these starting conditions will now be described as an observer might relate them. For clarity, the events are divided into four phases.

The Hydroplate Theory: Events

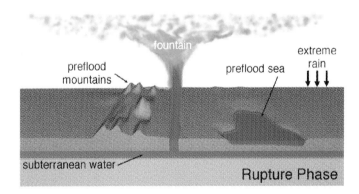

Figure 38: The Rupture Phase of the Flood. This rupture, which encircled the earth near what is now the Mid-Oceanic Ridge, was 46,000 miles long.

Rupture Phase. The increasing pressure in the subterranean water stretched the overlying crust, just as a balloon stretches when the pressure inside increases. Eventually, this shell of rock reached its failure point.[20] Failure began with a microscopic crack. Stress concentrations at both ends of the crack resulted in its rapid propagation at about 2 miles per second, nearly the velocity of sound in rock.[21] The crack followed the path of least resistance, generally along a great-circle path. The ends of the crack traveled in opposite directions, circling the earth in several hours.[22] The initial stresses were largely relieved when one end of the crack ran into the path left by the other end. In other words, the path traveled by this crack intersected itself (or formed a "T" or "Y") somewhere on the opposite side of the earth from where the rupture began.

Figure 39: Fountains of the Great Deep. For a global perspective of what this may have looked like, see page 68.

As the crack raced around the earth, the ten-mile-thick "roof" of overlying rock opened like a rip in a tightly stretched cloth. The pressure in the subterranean chamber immediately beneath the rupture suddenly dropped to almost atmospheric pressure. Water exploded with great violence out of the ten-mile-deep "slit," which wrapped around the earth like the seam of a baseball.

All along this globe-circling rupture, a fountain of water jetted supersonically into and above the atmosphere. The water fragmented into an "ocean" of droplets that fell to the earth great distances away. This produced torrential rains such as the earth has never experienced—before or after. Some jetting water rose above the atmosphere where the droplets froze. (See note 127 on page 131.) Huge masses of extremely cold, muddy "hail" fell at certain locations where it buried, suffocated, and froze many animals, including some mammoths.

Flood Phase. The extreme force of the 46,000-mile-long sheet of upward jetting water rapidly eroded both sides of

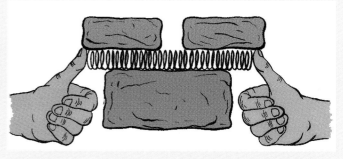

a) A spring, compressed by your hands, is enclosed by rock.

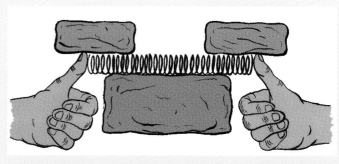

b) The spring remains aligned and compressed as the gap between the rocks increases.

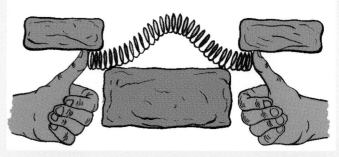

c) When the gap reaches a certain critical width, the spring suddenly buckles upward. Now consider thousands of similar springs lined up behind the first spring—all repeating in unison steps a-b. Newly exposed coils are soldered to the coils of the adjacent springs. The upbuckling of any one coil will cause adjacent springs to become unstable and buckle up themselves. They, in turn will lift the next coil, and so on, in ripple fashion.

Figure 40: Spring Analogy Relating to the Development of the Mid-Atlantic Ridge.

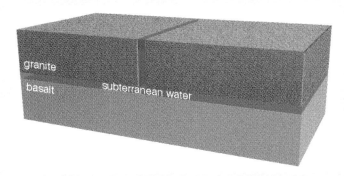

d) Rupture completed. Jetting water not shown.

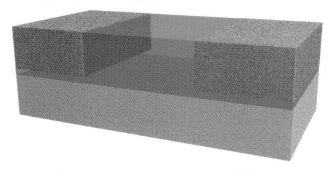

e) The rupture's path widens by erosion. Most of the earth's sediments are quickly produced by the outflow of the high velocity waters—the "Fountains of the Great Deep."

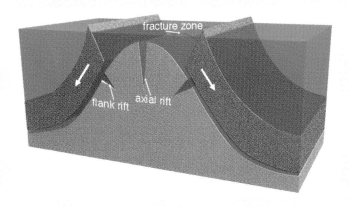

f) Continental drift phase begins. The Mid-Atlantic Ridge "springs" upward, releasing extreme amounts of stored, compressed energy. Fracture zones and rifts form along the ridge axis. (See Endnote 25 on page 95.) The massive hydroplates begin to accelerate downhill, riding on lubricating water.

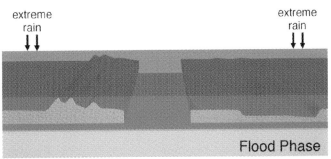

Flood Phase

Figure 41: The Flood Phase. Throughout the flood phase, the sediment in the escaping water increased until its volume nearly equaled the volume of water gushing out. These suspended particles quickly settled and buried plants and animals in a chaotic mixture. During this phase, a strange phenomenon, called ***liquefaction*** sorted sediments, animals, and plants into horizontal layers that are much wider and more uniform than those laid down today. The traces of these dead organisms are called fossils. Global liquefaction, a previously unknown phenomenon, will be explained on pages 134 - 145.

the crack. Eroded particles (or sediments) were swept up in the waters that gushed out from the rupture, giving the water a thick, muddy consistency. These sediments settled out over the earth's surface in days, trapping and burying many plants and animals, beginning the process of forming most of the world's fossils.

The rising flood waters eventually blanketed the water jetting from the rupture, although water still surged out of the rupture. Global flooding occurred over the earth's relatively smooth topography, since today's major mountains had not yet formed.

The temperature of the escaping subterranean waters increased by about 100°F as they were forced from the high pressure chamber. (See **Energy in Subterranean Water**, page 187.) The hot water, being less dense, rose to the surface of the flood waters. There, high evapora-

Figure 42: Salt Dome. Just as a cork placed at the bottom of a swimming pool will float up through water (which is denser), so also salt will float up through sediments (which are denser). As it does, much of the original layer of salt will flow horizontally and then up into the rising and expanding salt dome. If the salt and sediments are mushy and water saturated, friction will not impede this action very much. Often, the upturned (or bowl-shaped) layers next to the salt dome become traps in which oil collects. Thus, the location and understanding of salt domes has great economic value.

tion occurred, increasing the salt content of the remaining water. When it became supersaturated, salts precipitated into thick, pasty layers. Later, the pasty (low density) salt was blanketed by denser sediments. This created an unstable arrangement, much like having a layer of light oil beneath a denser layer of water. A slight jiggle will cause a plume of the lighter layer below to flow up through the denser layer above. In the case of salt, that plume is called a salt dome.

The pressure of the water decreased as it rose out of the subterranean chamber. Since high pressure liquids hold more dissolved gases than low pressure liquids, gases bubbled out of the escaping waters. This process occurs when a pressurized can of carbonated beverage is opened, quickly releasing bubbles of dissolved carbon dioxide. From the subterranean waters, the most significant gas that came out of solution was carbon dioxide. About 35% of the sediments were eroded from the basalt below the escaping water.[23] Up to 6% of basalt is calcium by weight. Calcium ions in the escaping water, along with dissolved carbon dioxide gas (carbonic acid), caused vast sheets of limestone ($CaCO_3$) to precipitate as the pressure dropped. (See technical note on page 188.)

The flooding uprooted most of the earth's abundant vegetation. Much of it was transported by the flood's currents to regions where it accumulated in great masses. Some vegetation even drifted to the South Pole. (A process described in a later chapter, pages 134-145, will explain how this vegetation was collected and sorted into thin layers within the sediments.) Later, during the continental drift phase, buried layers of vegetation were rapidly compressed and heated, precisely the conditions required to form coal and oil. The flood phase ended with the continents near the positions shown in Figure 35 and Figure 43.

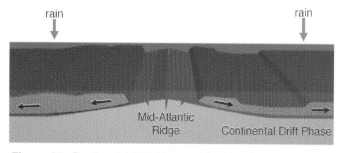

Figure 43: Continental Drift Phase of the Flood.

Continental Drift Phase. Material within the earth is compressed by the weight of overlying rock. Rock's slight elasticity gives it springlike characteristics.[24] The deeper the rock, the more tightly compressed the "spring"—all the way down to the center of the earth.

Figure 44: Birth of Mid-Atlantic Ridge.

During the flood phase, the rupture path widened as erosion continued. (See Figure 40e.) Eventually the width was so great that the compressed rock beneath the subterranean chamber was on the verge of springing upward. Centrifugal force, due to the earth's spin, is greatest at the equator and produces slightly greater "outward tugs" on this compressed rock where the rupture crossed the equator. The 46,000-mile-rupture path only crossed the equator at two places: one, in what is now the Pacific, and the other, in the Atlantic. However, the Atlantic location lies along the equator for 2000 miles. Its length and location, then, caused the initial instability to occur there. As the ridge rose, it lifted adjacent material just enough to cause it to become unstable and also spring upward. This process continued all along the path of the rupture, forming the Mid-Oceanic Ridge. Also formed were fracture zones and the strange offsets the ridge makes along fracture zones.[25] Soon afterward, the magnetic anomalies (Figure 32 on page 75) developed.[26]

The ridge rose several miles and elevated the granite plates along the flanks of the ridge. (See Figure 40f.) As the plates rose, they began to slide downhill. The plates were perfectly lubricated by subterranean water still escaping from beneath them. They slid east and west, because the Mid-Atlantic Ridge extends north and south. This process resembled the following:

A long train sits at one end of a very long track. If we could somehow just barely lift the end of the track under the train and the wheels were frictionless, the train would start rolling downhill. Then we could lift the track even higher, causing the train to accelerate even more. If this continued, the high-speed train would eventually crash into something. The long train of boxcars would suddenly decelerate, compress, and "jackknife."

Figure 45: Computer Animation of the **Rapid** Continental Drift Phase. The first frame (top) shows what parts of the earth looked like immediately following the flood phase. Since the rupture encircled the earth, a corresponding gap existed between the continental plates on the opposite side of the globe. The slowly rising Mid-Oceanic Ridge rose first in the Atlantic. This caused the plates to slide downhill on a layer of lubricating water, away from the widening Atlantic and into the gap on the opposite side of the earth. The continental drift phase ends (bottom frame) with the dramatic **compression event** that, among other things, squeezed up the earth's major mountains. These six frames simply rotate the present continents about the polar axis. Therefore, greater movement occurs at lower latitudes. Movement begins approximately from where the continents best fit against the base of the Mid-Atlantic Ridge (see Figure 35 on page 80) and ends in their present position.

Not shown are the consequences of the compression event. For example, the compression squeezed and almost doubled (actually increased 1.8 times) the average thickness of the continents. A corresponding shortening of the east-west distance of the major continents also occurred. Of course, mountainous regions thickened the most, but nonmountainous regions thickened as well. Regions that did not thicken and rise out of the water are now part of the ocean floor—usually the shallow ocean floor. (See Figure 28 on page 72.)

While it may seem strange to think of squeezing, thickening, and shortening granite, one must understand the gigantic forces required to decelerate the sliding continental plates. If the forces are great enough, granite deforms (much like putty) on a global scale. On a human scale, however, one would not see smooth, puttylike deformation; instead one would see and hear blocks of granite fracturing and sliding over each other. Some blocks would be the size of a small state or province, many would be the size of a house, and even more would be the size of grains of sand. Friction at the sliding surfaces would generate heat. At great depths the heat would be enough to melt rock. The liquid rock (magma) would squirt up and fill spaces between the blocks. This is seen in most places where the basement rocks are exposed, such as at the Black Canyon of the Gunnison (shown in Figure 49 on page 90) and in the inner gorge of the Grand Canyon.

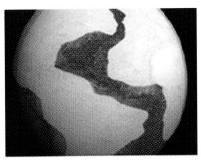
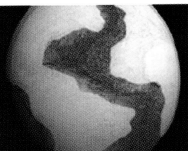
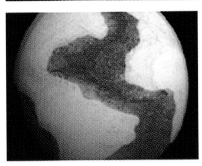
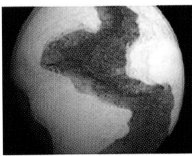
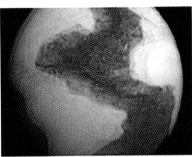
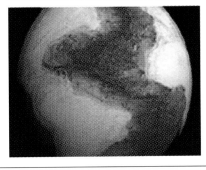

Continental plates accelerated away from the segment of the Mid-Oceanic Ridge now called the Mid-Atlantic Ridge. As they did, the Atlantic Ocean basin opened up. Eventually the drifting (actually accelerating) continental plates (or **hydroplates**) ran into resistances of two types. The first happened as the water lubricant beneath each sliding plate was depleted. The second occurred when a plate collided with something. For example, India literally collided with Asia, and the western coast of North America collided with a rising portion of the Mid-Oceanic Ridge. As each massive hydroplate decelerated, it experienced a gigantic **compression event**—buckling, crushing, and thickening each plate.

To illustrate how extreme the compression was, imagine yourself in a car traveling at 45 miles per hour. You gently step on the brake as you approach a stop light and brace yourself by straightening and stiffening your arms against the steering wheel. You might feel about 15 pounds of compressive force in each arm, just as you feel lifting 15 pounds above your head. If we could repeat your gentle deceleration at the stop light, but each time double your weight, the compressive force in your arms would also double each time. After six doublings, especially if you were sitting on a lubricated surface, your arm bones would break. If your bones were made of steel, they would break after nine doublings. If your arm bones were one foot in diameter and made of granite (a much stronger material), 17 doublings would crush them. This compression would be comparable to that at the top of each decelerating hydroplate. The compression at the base of the hydroplate exceeded the crushing strength of granite, even before the deceleration, simply due to the weight of the overlying rock. Consequently, the compression event at the end of the continental drift phase easily and continually crushed and thickened the hydroplates for many minutes. Mountains were quickly squeezed up.

Buckling occurred in the thinner portions of the hydroplates. Crushing and upward buckling formed major mountain ranges, while downward buckling formed oceanic trenches. As explained earlier, the forces

Figure 46: The upbuckling of a deep, rock floor has been observed. The floor of a limestone quarry buckled upward in Yorkshire, England in 1887.[27] The explanation is quite simple. Shale, which lay beneath the floor, consists of platelike particles that can slide over each other like playing cards in a deck. The weight of the quarry's walls squeezed shale toward the center of the quarry. Once the slightest upbuckling began, the limestone floor weakened, allowing the shale to push up even more.

For the cataclysm we are addressing, the "quarry" was 10 miles deep, hundreds of miles wide, and 46,000 miles long. It was eroded by the escaping, high-pressure water—the fountains of the great deep. Material in the mantle and core flowed under high, unbalanced pressure. Thus, the pressure at the base of the continents was transmitted to the subterranean chamber's floor, just as the pressure of the quarry's walls was transmitted through the shale to the floor of the limestone quarry. The upbuckled region is the globe-encircling Mid-Oceanic Ridge.

Mechanical and civil engineers call this phenomenon "the buckling of a beam on an elastic foundation."[28] It can be demonstrated by placing long bricks on top of a foam rubber mattress that is compressed in a rigid box. Slowly remove the bricks from the foam mattress, beginning at the center and moving outward. When enough bricks are removed, the mattress will suddenly spring upward, raising the remaining bricks. If these bricks were on a frictionless surface, they would slide downhill, just as the continents did during the continental drift phase.

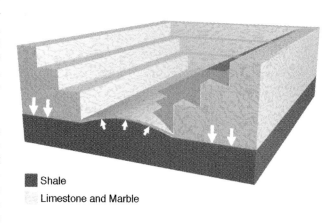

■ Shale
▨ Limestone and Marble

for this dramatic event could not be applied to stationary (static) continents resting on other rock. The force was dynamic, produced by rapidly moving hydroplates riding on lubricating water that had not yet escaped from below.

Naturally, the long axis of each buckled mountain and each trench was perpendicular to its hydroplate's motion—or parallel to the portion of the Mid-Oceanic Ridge from which it slid. Thus, the Rocky Mountains, Appalachians, and Andes have a north-south orientation. The Himalayas have a northwest-to-southeast orientation, because their hydroplate slid from the Mid-Indian Oceanic Ridge. Since most plates moved toward the Pacific basin, the Pacific is surrounded by trenches and mountain ranges that parallel each other.

Friction at the base of skidding hydroplates generated immense heat, enough to melt rock and produce massive volumes of magma. Crushing produced similar effects, as broken and compressed blocks and particles slid past each other. The deeper the sliding, the greater the pressure pushing the sliding surfaces together, and the greater the frictional heat generated. In some regions, the high temperatures and pressures formed metamorphic rock. Where this heat was intense, rock melted. This high pressure magma squirted up through cracks between broken blocks, producing other metamorphic

rocks. Sometimes it escaped to the earth's surface, producing volcanic activity and "floods" of lava outpourings, such as we see on the Columbia and Deccan Plateaus. This was the beginning of the earth's volcanic activity.

Other magma collected in pockets, which are now called magma chambers. Magma sometimes escapes from these chambers and produces volcanoes. Thus volcanic activity surrounds the Pacific Ocean in a region called "the ring of fire." This corresponds to the leading edges of the hydroplates where compression and crushing would have, in general, been the greatest. The heat remaining today is called geothermal heat.

Some subterranean water also flowed up into the cracks in the crushed granite. This is what was encountered in the deep holes drilled in Russia and Germany. (We noted earlier that surface water cannot penetrate down to those depths. This alone implies that subsurface water was its source.) We can now understand why the salt concentration in these cracks was about twice that of sea water. The preflood seas, which had little dissolved salt, diluted by about half the equal volume of salty, subterranean water that gushed out during the flood. Salty water that did not escape, therefore, has twice our present ocean's salt concentration.

Recovery Phase. *Where did the water go?* As the compression event began on a particular hydroplate, the continents began to thicken. Continents rose out of the water and mountains grew from the weakest, or most severely crushed and buckled, portions of the continents.[29] As they did, the flood waters over the continents receded.

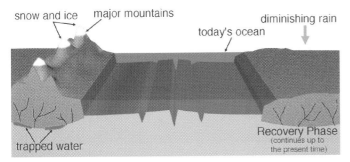

Figure 47: Recovery Phase of the Flood.

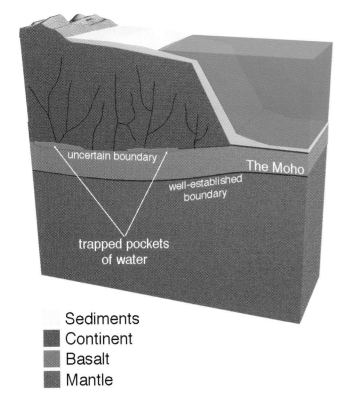

Sediments
Continent
Basalt
Mantle

Figure 48: This is a typical cross section of the continents and oceans as they appear today. Notice the relative depths of the Moho (the Mohorovicic discontinuity). It is deepest under the major mountains and shallowest under the ocean floor. Although geophysicists are uncertain of the exact location of some boundaries, most of these general characteristics are well established. Notice also that large pockets of water may be under major mountains.[30]

Simultaneously, the violent force of the upward surging subterranean water was "choked off" as the plates settled onto the floor of the subterranean chamber. Without

sinking hydroplates to produce the high pressure flow, water was no longer forced up. Instead, the deep basins between the continents became reservoirs into which the flood waters returned. As you will recall, these deep reservoirs were initially part of the basalt floor of the subterranean chamber, $10\frac{5}{8}$ miles below the earth's surface. Consequently, the surface of the ocean immediately after the flood was several miles lower than it is today. This provided wide land bridges between all continents, facilitating the migration of animals and people for perhaps several centuries. Drainage of the flood waters down the steep continental slopes eroded deep channels which today are called submarine canyons.

Hydroplates rested on some portions of this basalt floor, and water lay above other portions. Since the thickened hydroplates applied greater pressure to the floor than the water, the hydroplates depressed the basalt floor downward over the centuries. The material the sinking plates displaced caused the deep ocean floor to rise. (Imagine a water bed suddenly covered completely by two large adjacent plates. The denser plate will sink, lifting the other plate.)

As sea level rose, animals were forced to higher ground and were sometimes even isolated on islands far from our present continental boundaries. Classic examples of this are the finches and other animals Charles Darwin found on the Galapagos Islands, 650 miles off the coast of Ecuador. Darwin believed the finches were blown there during a giant storm. (While some may believe that story, it also requires that both a male and female finch ended up on the same island, or at least one pregnant female.)

The more sediments continents carried and the thicker continents grew during the crushing of the compression event, the deeper they sank. Of course, the Moho was depressed in the process. Newly formed mountains sank even more—slowly depressing the Moho beneath them to depths of 20-30 miles. (See Figure 48.) The Moho and mantle under the ocean floor rose along with the ocean floor. This is why continental material is so different from oceanic material, and why the Moho is so deep beneath mountains and yet so shallow beneath the ocean floor.

Many other things were far from equilibrium after the continental drift phase. Over the centuries, the new mountain ranges and thickened continental plates settled slowly to their equilibrium depth—just as a person's body sinks into a water bed. Sinking mountains increased the pressure under the crust on both sides of mountain ranges. Consequently, weaker portions of the overlying crust fractured and rose, forming plateaus, even on the ocean floor. In other words, *as continents and mountains sank, plateaus rose*. This and the compression event explain the seemingly strange aspects of plateaus noted by Kennedy on page 79.

A Picture with a Story

Here at the Black Canyon of the Gunnison in Colorado, rock cliffs are exposed for up to 2700 feet above the Gunnison River. Their marble-cake appearance comes from melted rock, primarily quartz, that was forced up through cracks in the darker rock.[31] To appreciate the size of this cliff, note that the trees at the top of the cliff are 10-15 feet tall.

Now let's put aside all prior opinions and ask, what must happen to cause this marble-cake pattern? First, deep magma must be present or be produced.

Figure 49: Black Canyon of the Gunnison.

Second, the black rock must be fractured. This obviously takes gigantic forces acting over a large area, but the forces must be of a special kind. A tensile (stretching) force would produce one or at most a few cracks. At the instant of breakage, each broken piece would scatter. (Try breaking something by pulling on it. The two pieces will fly apart.) This leaves us with only one viable type of force—compression.[32]

If the compressive forces acted slowly in all directions, no breaks would occur. A force that might break particles apart would be counterbalanced by another force. For example, deep sea creatures, living under high compressive pressure (inside and out), are not crushed. Also not crushed are many delicate pieces of pottery and other objects found in sunken vessels on the ocean floor.

If the compressive forces acted slowly but were almost evenly balanced, slight but slow movements would occur at the atomic level, a phenomenon called "creep." The rock would slowly flow like putty, until the forces evened out.

Some channels (or cracks) are wider than others. Normally, the largest channels should have provided the least resistance to the flow, and all the magma from below should have spilled out through them. (Pump a liquid into a closed container until something pops. You will only see one or at most a few major cracks, not many little cracks.) If the magma had been contained in a chamber below, just waiting for a crack to appear, the first crack should release all the magma, unless it solidified on its way up through the colder rock. But if all cracks occurred at once,

They also explain why plateaus are adjacent to major mountain ranges. For example, the Tibetan Plateau, the largest in the world, is next to the most massive mountain range in the world—the Himalayas. The Tibetan Plateau covers 750,000 square miles and rose 3 miles relative to the continent. The Colorado Plateau, next to the Rocky Mountains, and the Columbia Plateau, next to the Cascade Mountains, are other dramatic examples.

Drainage of the waters that covered the earth left every continental basin filled to the brim with water. Some of these postflood lakes lost more water by evaporation and seepage than they gained by rainfall and drainage from higher elevations. Consequently, they shrank over the centuries. A well-known example was former Lake Bonneville which became the Great Salt Lake.

Through rainfall and drainage from higher terrain, other lakes gained more water than they lost and thus overflowed their rims at the lowest point. The resulting erosion at that point on the rim allowed more water to flow over it. This eroded the cut in the rim even deeper and caused even more water to cut it faster. Thus, the downcutting process accelerated catastrophically. Eventually, the entire lake dumped through a deep slit which we today call a canyon. These waters emptied into the next lower basin, causing it to breach its rim and create another canyon. It was like falling dominoes. The most famous canyon of all, the Grand Canyon, was caused primarily by the dumping of what we will call **Grand Lake**. It occupied the southeast quarter of Utah, parts of northeastern Arizona, as well as small parts of Colorado and New Mexico. Grand Lake, standing at an elevation of then magma would fill most cracks. All of this leaves us with one conclusion for how the fractures occurred—***rapid crushing***.

Next, magma must squirt up very rapidly through the cracks in the black rock. If it happened slowly, or even at the rate a river flows, the front edge of the upward flowing magma would solidify (freeze) and the flow would stop. If water is dissolved in any molten rock, its melting or freezing point is lowered considerably. Thus, liquid quartz could better survive its cold, upward journey if it contained dissolved water.

Figure 50: Inner Gorge of the Grand Canyon. The same marble-cake pattern exists in the inner gorge of the Grand Canyon. However, the contrast in colors is less than at the Black Canyon of the Gunnison.

An individual channel (or vein) has a fairly uniform thickness. This reveals that the liquid's pressure exceeded the rock's pressure by nearly the same amount all along the channel. Again, this would not happen if the flow was slow or its consistency was like cold tar.

This marble-cake appearance occurs for at least the 50 miles exposed along the Gunnison River. Therefore, the amount of compressive force must have been about the same over at least those 50 miles. If the magma came from one spot below, it had a very long path to travel to fill cracks at least 25 miles away. Instead, the magma would tend to escape through the shortest cracks leading to the surface. Consequently, the source of the magma and water was probably spread out over an area directly below this phenomenon.

Because similar things are commonly seen where other deep basement rocks are exposed, we have to believe that either these gigantic forces "cropped up" many times at different places or this happened once on a continental or global scale. The parsimony criterion (looking for the simplest explanation) leads us to favor one big event. We will call this ***the compression event***.

This brief study allows us to conclude that ***this rock, visible for at least 50 miles, was rapidly crushed. Magma and its dissolved water, spread out below, were then quickly injected up through the cracks.***

In studying this ***effect***, "marble-cake rock," we tried to deduce its ***cause***. One can easily err in reasoning from effect back to its cause. Another approach, one we began on page 82, was to reason from cause to effect. We started with three assumptions and then asked what would be their logical consequences. It is also easy to make an error or overlook something, when reasoning from cause to effect—what will be called "forward reasoning." But when "forward reasoning" is consistent with "backward reasoning" (from effect to cause), then we can have much more confidence in our conclusion.

5,700 feet above today's sea level, spilled over and quickly eroded its natural dam 22 miles southwest of what is now Page, Arizona. In doing so, the western boundary of former Hopi Lake (elevation 5,950 feet) was eroded, releasing the waters that occupied the present valley of the Little Colorado River. In just a few weeks, more water was released over northern Arizona than is in all the Great Lakes combined.[33]

With thousands of large, high lakes after the flood, and a lowered sea level, many other canyons were carved. Some are now covered by the raised ocean. It appears likely that (1) the Mediterranean "Lake" dumped into the lowered Atlantic Ocean and carved a canyon at the Strait of Gibraltar, (2) the Black Sea carved out the Bosporus and Dardanelles, and (3) "Lake California" filling the Great Central Valley of California carved a canyon (now largely filled with sediments) under what is now the Golden Gate bridge in San Francisco. ***PREDICTION 1: The crystalline rock under Gibraltar, the Bosporus and Dardanelles, and the Golden Gate bridge is eroded into a V-shaped notch.***

Shifts of mass upon the earth created stresses and ruptures in and just beneath the earth's crust. This was especially severe under the Pacific Ocean, since the major continental plates all moved toward the Pacific. The portions of the plates that buckled downward were pressed into the earth's mantle. This produced the ocean trenches and the region called the "ring of fire" in and around the Pacific Ocean. The sharp increase in pressure under the floor of the Pacific caused ruptures and an outpouring of lava which formed submarine volcanoes called seamounts.

The beginning of earthquake activity also coincided with the end of the flood. Rock was buckled down into regions of higher temperature and pressure. Some minerals that compose a large fraction of the mantle undergo several types of phase transformation; that is, their atoms rearrange themselves into a denser packing arrangement when the temperature and pressure rise above certain thresholds. For example, olivine (a prominent mineral in the mantle) snaps into an atomic arrangement called spinel having about 10% less volume. The collapse begins at a microscopic point and creates a shock wave. A larger pocket of rock, that is already sufficiently heated, then exceeds its pressure threshold. The resulting implosion is a deep earthquake. Over the many centuries since this worldwide cataclysm, the downbuckled rock has slowly heated up, and it periodically implodes.[34]

The reverse process, sudden expansion, occurs at the uplifted Mid-Oceanic Ridge. There, some minerals slowly swell and rearrange themselves into a less dense packing arrangement. The swelling at the ridge and the shrinking at the trenches slides the skin of the earth in jerks along its "near-zero-shear-strength surface" 125 miles below the earth's surface. Earthquakes also occur under hydroplates wherever there has been a large, vertical displacement.

Shallow earthquakes involve a different phenomenon.[35] The following may explain what happens. Trapped, subterranean water, unable to escape during the flood, slowly seeps up through cracks and faults formed initially during the compression event. The higher this water migrates through cracks, the greater its pressure is in comparison to the walls of the crack trying to contain it. This spreads the cracked rock and causes the crack to grow. (This may explain why the ground often bulges slightly before an earthquake and why water levels sometimes change in wells.) Stresses build up in the crust as the Mid-Oceanic Ridges swell and trenches contract. Once the compressive stress has risen enough, the cracks have grown enough, and the degree of frictional locking of cracked surfaces has diminished enough, sudden movement occurs. The water then acts as a lubricant. (This explains why frictional heat was not found along the San Andreas Fault.) Sliding friction almost instantaneously heats the water, converts it to steam at an even higher pressure, and initiates a runaway process called a shallow earthquake. This movement of the remaining subterranean water produces imbalances and partial voids which trigger even deeper sudden movements. ***PREDICTION 2: Moderately deep holes, drilled along major faults in populated regions, will provide an easy escape for some of the seeping, high pressure, subterranean water near the hole. The***

frequency of shallow earthquakes in the region will diminish. Of course, stresses will continue to build up, but some of that energy will be dissipated by the flow of deep, viscous rock. (Rock gets progressively weaker as one moves from a depth of 10 miles down to 125 miles below the earth's surface. There its shear strength is almost zero.) ***Bleeding off subsurface water will reduce the runaway effect caused by the frictional heating of the lubricating water. Sudden increases in the water's depth in many of these holes may serve as a precursor to shallow earthquakes.***

Frictional heating at the base of sliding hydroplates and in movements within the rising ocean floors produced warm oceans, high evaporation rates, and heavy cloud cover. The elevated continents, which would require decades or centuries to sink to their equilibrium level, were consequently colder than today. Volcanic debris and the cloud cover shielded the earth's surface from much of the sun's rays, producing the ultimate "nuclear winter." At higher latitudes and elevations, such as the newly elevated and extremely high mountains, this combination of high precipitation and low temperatures produced very heavy snow falls—perhaps 100 times that of today. Large temperature differences between the cold land and warm oceans generated high winds that rapidly transported moist air up onto the elevated, cool continents where heavy snowfall occurred, especially over glaciated areas. As snow depths increased, periodic and rapid movements of the glaciers occurred in "avalanche fashion." During the summer months, rain fell instead of snow, causing the glaciers to partially melt and retreat, thus marking the end of that year's "*ice age.*"

Many seamounts grew up to the surface of the lowered ocean, where their peaks were eroded and flattened by wave action. These flat-topped or truncated cones are now call tablemounts. Their eroded tops are several thousand feet below today's sea level. Sea level continued to rise as the glaciers melted and retreated to their present positions. Glacial retreat continues today.

A Final Comment

Many details about the earth have been discussed up to this point. The hydroplate theory began with the three assumptions on page 82. What followed were consequences of those assumptions and the laws of physics. The events described followed logically from these assumptions, prior events, and experimental science.

Even more details have not been explained. Some are presently unknown. For example, what besides carbon dioxide and salt (NaCl), was dissolved in the subterranean water? Certainly those substances will account for the ore found in sedimentary rock. What percentage of the earth's water was in the subterranean chamber, and what was that water's temperature? What was the chamber's internal structure and exact depth?

In this short study, the descriptions of problems in the earth sciences and the hydroplate theory were specific enough for us to see the big picture and make predictions as large pieces of the puzzle were fit together. However, descriptions were general enough to accommodate other less significant details. For example, a computer simulation of global weather patterns following the flood should allow one to simulate the ice age and fine tune the rate at which continents sank and oceans cooled. Since that will

require many years of work and a powerful mainframe computer, bypassing it for now seems prudent.

Some unexplained details are on pages 102-145, where two of the 21 features described so far, **strata** and **frozen mammoths**, are greatly expanded. (The remaining nineteen topics are potential chapters for future editions of this book.) All topics will begin with a detailed description of that feature. Then all known explanations for the feature will be described and contrasted. So far, the many details and recognized problems associated with each feature, most of which have not been described here, seem to be best explained by the hydroplate theory. Time will tell.

References and Notes

1. Plate tectonics, as initially proposed, had 6-8 plates. This number has grown as followers of the theory have applied it to specific regions of the earth. Although textbooks usually mention only about a dozen plates, the theory now requires more than 100, most of them small.

    This reminds one of epicycles, used from 150-1543 A.D. to explain planetary motion. Ptolemy explained that planets revolved about the earth on epicycles—wheels that carried planets and rode on the circumference of other wheels. As more was learned about planetary motion, more epicycles were required to fit Ptolemy's geocentric theory. Of course, any theory can fit facts if the theory has enough variables.

    Both the plate tectonic theory and the hydroplate theory involve plates moving over the globe. Plate tectonics has plates somehow moving slowly and continuously for hundreds of millions of years. Hydroplates, using an understood mechanism, moved rapidly toward the end of a global flood and today are moving extremely slowly (but in jerks).

    As historians of science know, old theories frequently accumulate many anomalies—discoveries that do not fit the theory. These problems do not overthrow the old theory until a new theory comes along that can explain all that the old theory did **plus** the anomalies. [See Thomas S. Kuhn, *The Structure of Scientific Revolutions* (Chicago: The University of Chicago Press, 1970).] Plate tectonics is becoming more complex as new information is learned, a sign that "epicycles" are with us again. This has caused a growing number of international scientists to announce that "*a lot of phenomena and processes are incompatible with this theory* [plate tectonics] . . . *we must develop competitive hypotheses.*" [A. Barto-Kyriakidis, editor, *Critical Aspects of the Plate Tectonics Theory*, Vol. I (Athens, Greece: Theophrastus Publications, 1990), p. v.]

2. W. Jason Morgan, "Rises, Trenches, Great Faults, and Crustal B," *Journal of Geophysical Research*, Vol. 73, No. 6, 15 March 1968, p. 1973.

3. Ken C. Macdonald and P. J. Fox, "Overlapping Spreading Centers," *Nature*, Vol. 302, 3 March 1983, pp. 55-58.

•   Richard Monastersky, "Mid-Atlantic Ridge Survey Hits Bull's-eye," *Science News*, Vol. 135, 13 May 1989, p. 295.

4. Richard Monastersky, "Reservoir Linked to Deadly Quake in India," *Science News*, Vol. 145, 9 April 1994, p. 229.

5. Mark D. Zoback, "State of Stress and Crustal Deformation Along Weak Transform Faults," *Philosophical Transactions of the Royal Society of London*, Vol. 337, 15 October 1991, pp. 141-150.

6. Arthur D. Raff, "The Magnetism of the Ocean Floor," *Scientific American*, October 1961, pp. 146-156.

7. Richard S. Lewis, *A Continent for Science: The Antarctic Adventure* (New York: Viking Press, 1965), p. 134.

•   Quinn A. Blackburn, "The Thorne Glacier Section of the Queen Maud Mountains," *The Geographical Review*, Vol. 27, 1937, p. 610.

•   Ernest Henry Shackleton, *The Heart of the Antarctic*, Vol. 2 (New York: Greenwood Press, 1909), p. 314.

•   Stefi Weisburd, "A Forest Grows in Antarctica," *Science News*, Vol. 129, 8 March 1986, p. 148.

8. Lewis, p. 130.

9. Carl K. Seyfert and Leslie A. Sirkin, *Earth History and Plate Tectonics*, 2nd edition (New York: Harper & Row, 1979), p. 312.

10. Richard A. Kerr, "Looking—Deeply—into the Earth's Crust in Europe," *Science*, Vol. 261, 16 July 1993, pp. 295-297.

•   Richard A. Kerr, "German Super-Deep Hole Hits Bottom," *Science*, Vol. 266, 28 October 1994, p. 545.

•   Richard Monastersky, "Inner Space," *Science News*, Vol. 136, 21 October 1989, pp. 266-268.

•   Richard A. Kerr, "Continental Drilling Heading Deeper," *Science*, Vol. 224, 29 June 1984, p. 1418.

11. Yevgeny A. Kozlovsky, "Kola Super-Deep: Interim Results and Prospects," *Episodes*, Vol. 1982, No. 4, pp. 9-11.

12. The geothermal gradient in continental regions far from volcanoes varies from 10-60°C per km.

13. Harvey Blatt, *Sedimentary Petrology* (New York: W. H. Freeman and Co., 1982), pp. 3, 6, 241.

14. John V. Walther and Philip M. Orville, "Volatile Production and Transport in Regional Metamorphism," *Contributions to Mineralogy and Petrology*, Vol. 79, 1982, pp. 252-257.

15. George C. Kennedy, "The Origin of Continents, Mountain Ranges, and Ocean Basins," *American Scientist*, Vol. 47, December 1959, pp. 493-495.

16. Kenneth J. Hsu, *The Mediterranean Was a Desert* (Princeton, New Jersey: Princeton University Press, 1983).

17. Moving continental-sized plates in an east-west direction requires much less energy than moving them in a north-south direction. This is because the earth is not a perfect sphere but is flattened at the poles and bulges at the equator. Consequently, a plate moving from a polar region to the equator must bend and stretch—requiring much more energy. Advocates of the plate tectonic theory claim that India broke away from Antarctica and drifted northward across the equator and "crashed" into Asia! Never explained are where this additional energy came from or why north-south cracks are not apparent in India. (Of course, the word "crashed," as used in plate tectonics, is a gross exaggeration. You will soon see why continents did crash, in the true sense of the word.)

18. *"Taken together, our analyses indicate that the end-Cretaceous mass extinction was a globally uniform event."* David M. Raup and David Jablonski, "Geography of End-Cretaceous Marine Bivalve Extinctions," *Science*, Vol. 260, 14 May 1993, p. 973.

19. The popular press has made several announcements of possible craters that might explain the extinction of dinosaurs. After the initial fanfare, other discoveries were usually made which falsified the candidate impact site.

20. At the time of this rupture, the strain energy in the crust would have been about 2×10^{29} ergs. The released compressive energy, as the Mid-Oceanic Ridge sprung upward, was about 10^{33} ergs. (This is explained beginning on page 84.) Only a small fraction of this was needed to form the mountains. One can obtain a feel for these amounts of energy by comparing them with two of the most violent volcanic eruptions of modern times. The energy release from Krakatoa in 1883 has been estimated at 10^{25} ergs, and that from Tambora in 1815 was about 8.4×10^{26} ergs. [Gordon A. Macdonald, *Volcanoes* (Englewood Cliffs, New Jersey: Prentice-Hall, 1972), p. 60.]

21. B. R. Lawn and T. R. Wilshaw, *Fracture of Brittle Solids* (New York: Cambridge University Press, 1975), pp. 91-100.

22. Tensile cracks propagate at about half the velocity of sound in rock. [See the prior reference.] The speed of sound in Precambrian granite is 5.23 km/sec. [Robert S. Carmichael, *Handbook of Physical Properties of Rocks*, Vol. 2 (Boca Raton, Florida: CRC Press, 1982), p. 310.] Using 6371 kilometers as the mean radius of the earth, one end of the crack would circumscribe the globe in just over four hours.

Therefore, two ends moving in opposite directions along a wiggly path that approximates a great circle would require about half as much time, or just over two hours.

$$\frac{2\pi \times 6371 \text{ km}}{5.23 \frac{\text{km}}{\text{sec}} \times 3600 \frac{\text{sec}}{\text{hr}}} = 2.13 \text{ hours}$$

Of course, the pressure that ruptured the crust would begin dropping in the subterranean chamber immediately after the rupture began. This pressure drop would propagate through the liquid shell at the velocity of sound in water. Since the velocity of sound in water is only about one-third of that in rock, the crack would race ahead of the pressure drop in the water below. (In this respect, the example of a rupturing balloon is not analogous with the rupture of the earth's crust.) If the rupture began somewhere near Alaska, the rupture path would race ahead of any pressure drop in the water for the entire path of what is now the Mid-Oceanic Ridge. One "T" or "Y" would be formed.

23. Much erosion occurred as the subterranean waters flowed out from under the crust. Consider a semi-infinite plate, settling at a velocity V and overlying a layer of water of thickness t. A drop of water exactly below the center of the plate will not move, since it is "undecided" whether to flow to the right or left. However, the further a particle is from the center, the faster it will flow. A simple conservation of mass calculation shows that the water particles that are a distance x from the center of the plate will move with an average velocity of

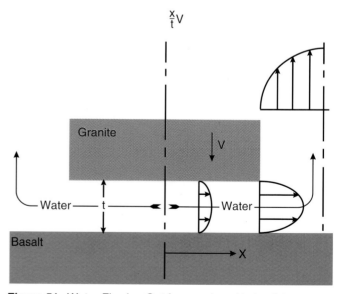

Figure 51: Water Flowing Out from under a Hydroplate.

Constrictions in the flow channel, such as below the preflood mountains, will produce higher flow velocities and, therefore, greater erosion at that constriction. Thus, constrictions would tend to be removed. Since the frictional drag on the horizontal flow increases as the plate approaches its basalt foundation, so will its sediment load per unit volume. (Erosion varies at least as the 4th power of velocity.) Consequently, the volume of water escaping will sharply decrease and the plate will fall more and more slowly.

Once a water particle flows out from under the plate and begins to flow upward, it accelerates. This is because of the imbalanced pressure acting from below. The greatest erosion from the upward expanding flow will be at the top of the plate, where the water's velocity is the greatest. The erosion patterns will be as shown in Figure 52.

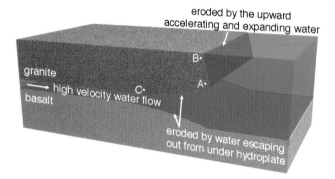

Figure 52: Regions of Greatest Erosion.

Once the plate finally settles onto its basalt foundation, it will have a continental shelf and a continental slope. (See Figure 53 below and compare with Figure 30 on page 74.)

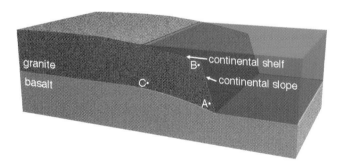

Figure 53: Continental Shelf and Continental Slope Formed.

Twenhofel and Mead reported that the chemical composition of the earth's sedimentary rock can best be matched by taking 65 parts of granite and 35 parts of basalt. [William H. Twenhofel, *Treatise on Sedimentation*, 2nd edition (New York: Dover Publications, 1961), pp. 2-3; W. J. Mead, "The Average Igneous Rock," *Journal of Geology*, Vol. 22, November-December, 1914, pp. 772-778.] This is a remarkable statement, since the quantities of what turns out to be ten chemical elements can be related to two parameters: an amount of granite and an amount of basalt. From the above, we can now see why this happens. For every 65 parts eroded above the subterranean chamber, 35 parts of

basalt were eroded under the subterranean chamber. This produced almost all the earth's sediments and sedimentary rock.

24. Compressed solids, liquids, and gases store energy. Springs are common examples. If a force, F, compresses some material by a small amount, D, the additional energy stored in the material is F x D. If the compressed material is rock, D will be very small, but F could be huge. The product of the two could be large. The compressed energy stored in the earth's mantle and core is immense. (See note 20 on page 94.)

25. As the Mid-Oceanic Ridge rose, its surface was stretched in two perpendicular directions. Since rock is weak in tension, two types of cracks grew, each perpendicular to a direction of stretching. Both types of cracks are shown in Figure 44 on page 86, Figure 40f on page 85, and on the map on page 72.

Just as the tops of the coils of the spring are further apart on page 84 in (c) than (a) or (b), so the surface of the ridge was stretched perpendicular to its axis. One can also feel this type of stretching by grabbing a phone book firmly in both hands and arching it. The outer, or convex, cover is placed in tension.

The other type of stretching was along the ridge axis. A circle's circumference increases as its radius grows. Likewise, the total length of the ridge's crest was stretched as the ridge moved further from the center of the earth.

Again, each type of crack began as a microscopic opening with stress concentrations at both ends. As the ridge rose, both types of cracks grew perpendicular to each other. The cracks along the ridge axis, called **axial rifts**, began at different locations along the ridge crest. Later, **flank rifts**, also parallel to the ridge axis, formed further down the flanks of the ridge. This sequence occurred because the greatest curvature, and therefore tension in the surface of the ridge, was at the crest. When rifts ran into the perpendicular cracks, called **fracture zones**, they stopped growing. Fracture zones always began at the crest, since there the ridge was furthest from the center of the earth. Therefore, fracture zones never ran into rifts, but rifts sometimes ran into fracture zones. These cracks are still growing, although at a much reduced rate. This is due to cooling and thermal contraction, and it accounts for much of the earthquake activity along the ridge.

As the ridge rose, hundreds of short axial rifts began growing at different places along the rupture path. The more the ridge rose, the longer and wider these cracks became. This created a line of bending weakness which caused the ridge to rise symmetrically with the axial rift. In general, each axial rift did not align with the next axial rift. For this reason and because rifts ran into fracture zones, the Mid-Oceanic Ridge has an offset pattern.

Growing axial rifts also explain overlapping spreading centers (OSCs), where two portions of the ridge axis overlap. Macdonald and Fox, who first reported on OSCs, demonstrated how the overlaps occur. (See reference 3, page 93.) They took a knife and made two parallel cuts in a sheet of frozen wax—one cut ahead of the other. The sheet was then pulled in the direction perpendicular to both cuts, causing the cuts to grow toward each other. As the cracks grew past each other, their ends began turning toward the other crack. Sometimes they intersected. (See Figure 31 on page 74.) This suggests that OSCs were formed by lengthening axial rifts as the ridge rose. OSCs are completely inconsistent with the plate tectonic theory.

Another test of the hydroplate theory vs. the plate tectonic theory concerns the cross-sectional profile of fracture zones. The hydroplate theory says that fracture zones are tensional features formed when the ridge suddenly rose and was stretched parallel to the ridge axis. Cracks grew from the surface downward. Consequently, their profile should be V-shaped or trough-shaped. See Figure 54 (a). If the crack is relatively shallow, it will be V-shaped. If it is deep, it will be trough-shaped since the pressure is so great at the base of the crack that the rock flowed as it was pulled apart. On the other hand, the plate tectonic theory says that a fracture zone is one kind of boundary between two adjacent plates. If so, the profile should look as shown in Figure 54 (b). Having made these two predictions jointly with one of the founders of the plate tectonic theory (the late Robert S. Dietz on April 30, 1986), we set out to determine the actual shape of fracture zones. The true profiles confirm the hydroplate prediction. [See Tjeerd H. van Andel et al., "The Intersection Between the Mid-Atlantic Ridge and the Vema Fracture Zone in the North Atlantic," *Journal of Marine Research*, Vol. 25, No. 3, 15 September 1967, pp. 343-351. See also A. A. Meyerhoff and Howard A. Meyerhoff, "Tests of Plate Tectonics," *Plate Tectonics: Assessments and Reassessments*, editor Charles F. Kahle, p. 108.] Dietz urged this author to publish these results.

This exercise also produced two other surprising confirmations of the hydroplate theory. First, the fracture zone profiles that were examined were trough-shaped near the ridge axis where, according to hydroplate theory, the fracture should be deepest. At the ends of the fracture zones, the profiles were V-shaped. The second surprise was the presence of undeformed, layered sediments inside fracture zones. If the opposite sides of a fracture zone are sliding past each other, as plate tectonics claims, one would expect that sediments caught between sliding plates would be highly deformed.

Textbooks frequently claim that earthquakes in fracture zones occur only between the two offset ridge axes, where the plates (according to plate tectonics) are moving in opposite directions. This is not true. To the contrary, earthquakes occur all along fracture zones, as the hydroplate theory predicts.

A final confirmation of the hydroplate explanation comes from the picture on page 73. The SEASAT map shows that fracture zones lack mass. Figure 54 (a), not Figure 54 (b), fits this observation.

26. Basalt contains magnetite and hematite which make basalt highly magnetic. A magnetic material will lose its magnetism if its temperature exceeds a certain amount,

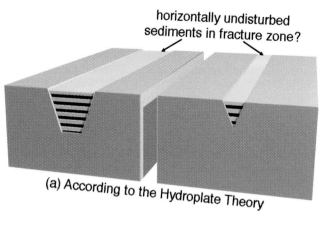

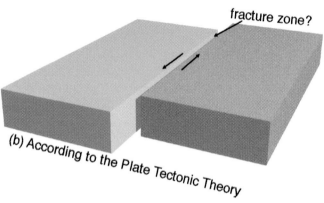

Figure 54: Two Possible Cross-Sections of Fracture Zones.

called the **Curie point.** The Curie point for basalt is near 578°C.

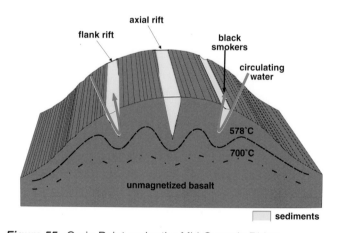

Figure 55: Curie Point under the Mid-Oceanic Ridge.

A typical cross section of the Mid-Oceanic Ridge is shown in Figure 55. In general, the ridge's temperature increases with depth. However, the walls of these cracks in the Mid-Oceanic Ridge are cooled by cold water that circulates down into and up out of them by natural convection. The cracks act as chimneys; the hotter rock below serves as the fire. After several thousand years of cooling, the constant temperature line corresponding to the Curie point should be as shown by the long dashed line. Notice that more magnetized material would be near each fracture.

Magnetic anomalies would also occur perpendicular to the ridge—along fracture zones. Naturally, if a device that measures magnetic intensity (a *magnetometer*) is towed across the ridge, it will show the magnetic anomalies of Figure 32 on page 75. These magnetic anomalies, however, are not magnetic reversals.

Incidentally, the hot water that rises from these sediment filled cracks probably accounts for the jets of up to 400°C water that shoot up from the ocean floor. Such black smokers are often aligned parallel to the ridge axis and are intermittent as one would expect from the above explanation. **PREDICTION 3: Fracture zones and axial and flank rifts will always be along lines of high magnetic intensity. PREDICTION 4: The magnetic intensity above black smokers slowly increases because the recently fractured rock below is cooling.**

27. T. McKenny Hughes, "Bursting Rock Surfaces," *Geological Magazine*, Vol. 3, 1887, pp. 511-512.

28. J. P. Den Hartog, *Advanced Strength of Materials* (New York: McGraw-Hill, 1952), pp. 141-171.

29. The compression event formed mountains by bending and crushing hydroplates at their weakest regions. When a long, thin object, such as a yardstick, is steadily compressed, no bending or displacement occurs until the compressive force reaches a certain critical amount. Once this threshold is exceeded, the yardstick (or any compressed beam or plate) "snaps" into a bowed position or more accurately, into the shape of one-half of a sine wave. As further compression occurs, the amplitude of the sine wave increases. Buckling at one portion of the hydroplate would cause adjacent portions to also bend.

The crushing of the hydroplate also pushed up linear mountain chains. Where the compression exceeded the crushing strength of granite, the plate thickened and shortened. The collapse of strength in the crushed region increased the load on adjacent regions perpendicular to the direction of compression, causing them to fail and the length of the mountain chain to grow. Therefore, bending and crushing rapidly lifted mountain chains.

30. Obviously, as mountains buckled up, the remaining water under the plate tended to fill in large voids. Much of that pooled water should also remain in cracked and contorted layers of rock. (See Figure 47 on page 89 and Figure 48 on page 89.) This would largely explain the reduced mass beneath mountains that gravity measurements have shown for over a century. **PREDICTION 5: Volumes of pooled water will be found beneath the major mountains. This water will contain large amounts of salts and carbon dioxide. PREDICTION 6: Salty water will be frequently found to fill cracks in granite 5-10 miles below the earth's surface, where surface water should not be able to penetrate.**

In past years, the United States Government has considered funding a 3-year, 45-million dollar project to drill a deep hole into the southern Appalachian Mountains. The hole was intended:

". . . to test among other things, the hypothesis that a sheet of crystalline rock about 10 kilometers thick was shoved 225 kilometers westward over underlying sedimentary rock by a continental collision. In 1979, despite the seeming improbability that such a thin sheet would hold together like that, deep seismic reflection profiling revealed a layer that is presumably the previously proposed boundary between the crystalline sheet and the underlying sedimentary rock. The hole would penetrate this reflector of seismic waves at a depth of about 8 or 9 kilometers and return samples to verify its nature." [Richard A. Kerr, "The Deepest Hole in the World," *Science*, Vol. 224, 29 June 1984, p. 1420.]

Of course, the hydroplate theory provides an explanation for why and how a thin sheet of rock was moved westward. It was not "shoved" for the reasons given in the technical note on page 186. It gained its velocity by gravitational sliding and, therefore, incurred no internal stresses. The thrusting of an 8-9 kilometer layer for 225 kilometers should no longer be an enigma. Consequently, this $45,000,000 project is unnecessary.

From another point of view, such a drilling project may be extremely dangerous. If the prediction of water under the buckled portions of mountains is correct, then this drilling project might have disastrous consequences. Upward escaping, high-pressure water would quickly erode and greatly enlarge the drilled hole. As the water escaped from beneath the mountain range, voids would be created. Earthquakes would occur such as the earth has not experienced in modern times.

31. Some geologists have wondered if quartz migrated out of the black rock. One look at the sharp contact between the light veins and the dark host rock should remove that possibility from further consideration. Incidentally, quartz is the first common mineral to melt as rock heats up and the last to solidify as it cools.

32. Other forces, such as viscous, electrical, magnetic, and gravitational forces, can be eliminated on other grounds. Since few would even entertain them as a means of breaking so much rock, we will not discuss them.

33. Marble Canyon was eroded by the waters of Grand Lake, while the Grand Canyon was eroded by the waters of both Grand and Hopi Lakes. In 1988, this author, using geological and topological features, discovered and announced the location of the former Grand Lake. This explanation was published for the first time in the fifth edition of *In the Beginning* (1989). Hopi Lake had been described previously. [See R. B. Scarborough, "Cenozoic Erosion and Sedimentation in Arizona," *Arizona Bureau of Geology and Mineral Technology*, 16 November 1984.]

The catastrophic dumping of Grand Lake took place through what is now the gap between Echo Cliffs and Vermilion Cliffs. Before this natural dam eroded, those two cliffs were a single face of a block-faulted mountain. The release of these vast waters first eroded hundreds of meters of relatively soft Mesozoic sediments off northern

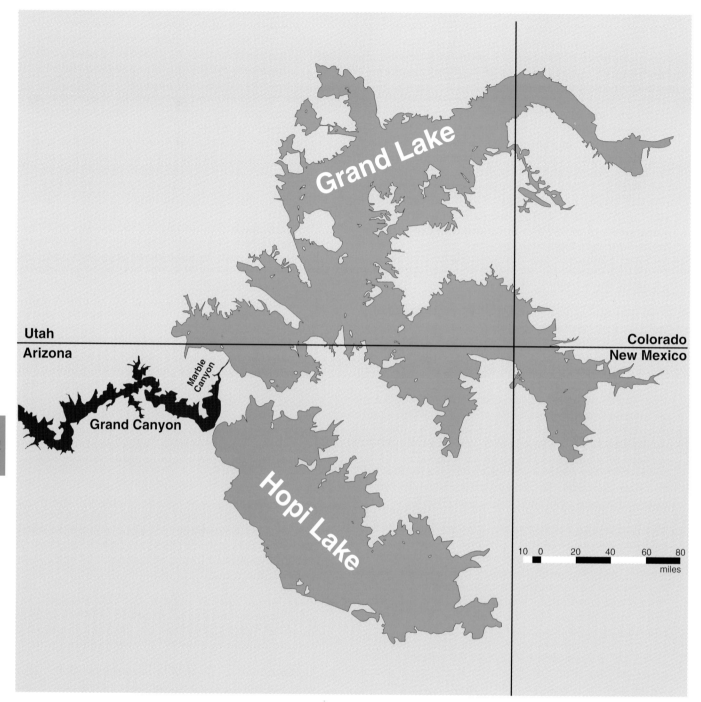

Figure 56: Grand and Hopi Lakes.

Arizona. Once completed, the downcutting through the hardened Kaibab limestone began. *As it eroded deeper beneath the water table, more water, under greater pressure, was released from the water-saturated sediments flanking the canyon.* Subsurface flow, mass wasting, and slumping were extreme. The weight of material removed from northern Arizona produced isostatic uplifts that account for the uplift of the Kaibab Plateau, much faulting and volcanism, and the "barbed" canyons. This is why the strata dip away from Marble Canyon and Grand Canyon. The timing of this event is uncertain. Perhaps it took place a century or two after the flood.

What are *barbed canyons*? Side streams usually enter their main streams at acute angles. However, the drainage through the "barbed" canyons enters the Colorado River at obtuse angles. These canyons are called "barbed" because on a map their backward orientation gives them the appearance of barbed wire. Except for a rare cloud burst directly overhead, little drainage occurs through these giant canyons. So what cut them, and why are they backwards? The answer lies in the northward dip of the land shortly after the vast weight of rock suddenly eroded to the south by the dumping of Grand and Hopi Lakes. Thus, the

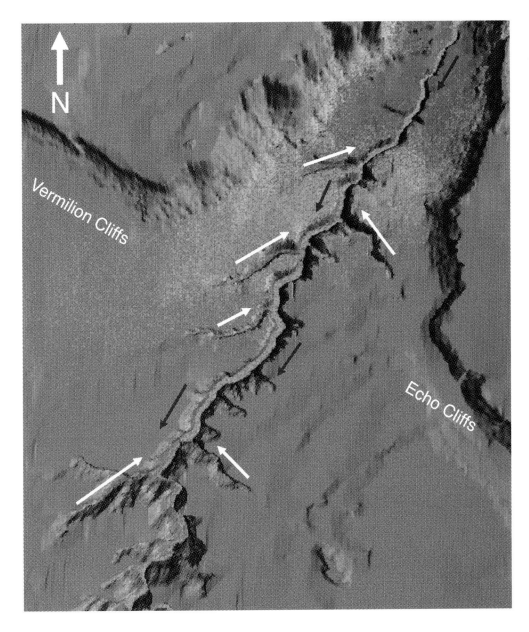

Figure 57: "Funnel" from Above. This computer generated picture resembles a photograph taken from 35,000 feet above the "barbed" side canyons feeding into the Colorado River. The water that carved the barbed canyons flowed (yellow arrows) in the opposite direction to that of the Colorado River today (red arrows). Note 33 on page 97 explains how this happened.

Notice the "funnel" in the top right corner. A giant, high-pressure hose, placed above the upper right corner of this picture and squirting in the direction of the red arrows, would carve the funnel nicely.

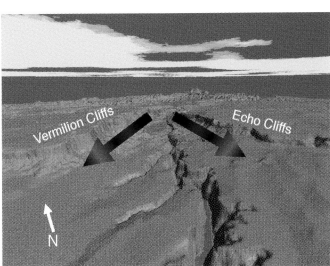

Figure 58: "Funnel" between Vermilion and Echo Cliffs. This computer generated picture is based on actual U.S. Geological Survey Digital Elevation Models (DEM) with an accuracy of 30 feet. The picture appears as it would at an elevation of 13,000 feet above the ground. Marble Canyon, in the center, separates Vermilion Cliffs from Echo Cliffs. The funnel-shaped region, bounded by blue arrows, marks where Grand Lake breached its boundary and dumped its contents over northern Arizona. Marble Canyon and the Grand Canyon (30 miles to the southwest) were carved in weeks. Grand Lake was located northeast of the blue arrows, behind the "funnel."

surface drainage pattern was reversed for the waters spilling out of Echo and Vermilion Cliffs and elsewhere. (See Figure 57 and Figure 58 on page 99.)

34. Deep earthquakes occur at depths of 400-650 kilometers, where the pressure is so great that cracks should not be able to open. Instead, any concentrated stress that might cause an earthquake should slowly and quietly deform the rock, thereby removing that stress. How then do deep earthquakes occur? This has perplexed geophysicists for decades.

To solve this problem, most advocates of plate tectonics now accept that sudden phase changes, such as from olivine to spinel, must produce deep earthquakes. This requires transporting cold olivine down into hotter regions of higher pressure. They believe their slowly subducting plates move cold rock down to depths where it heats up, suddenly changes phase and "shrinks" to spinel, then implodes as a deep earthquake. (Remember, they do not know how a plate could subduct, whether it is pushed, pulled, or dragged. Nor, do they understand the problems shown on page 185.)

There is another problem. The points of origin of a deep earthquake can now be precisely located. A single, deep earthquake sometimes originates over a broad, horizontal zone that could not fit within a plate. Yet, plate tectonics claims that deep earthquakes occur within subducted plates. [*"The deepest quakes should be confined to a thin layer at the center of a descending slab—and the Bolivian quake was just too big to fit."* Richard A. Kerr, "Biggest Deep Quakes May Need Help," *Science*, Vol. 267, 20 January 1995, pp. 329-330.]

Notice that this fits with the hydroplate theory. As stated earlier, during the compression event at the end of the continental drift phase, the earth's crust was buckled down near what are now oceanic trenches. Olivine in the preflood mantle was pushed deeper by perhaps 10-30 kilometers. This movement generated frictional heat and transported olivine to a higher pressure region. After enough heating, olivine becomes unstable, contracts to form spinel, and produces deep earthquakes. A chain of implosions sometimes occurs in a region that could not fit inside a hypothetical subducted plate.

35. The existence of two mechanisms for earthquakes is best shown by their distribution with depth. Earthquakes occur most frequently at 35 km and 600 km and are sharply reduced above and below these depths. Aftershocks also cluster near these depths. [See Cliff Frohlich, "Deep Earthquakes," *Scientific American*, Vol. 260, January 1989, p. 52.]

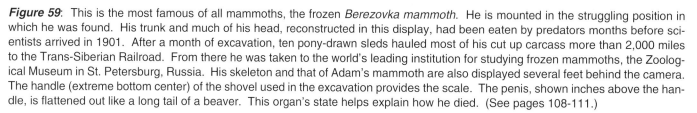

Figure 59: This is the most famous of all mammoths, the frozen *Berezovka mammoth*. He is mounted in the struggling position in which he was found. His trunk and much of his head, reconstructed in this display, had been eaten by predators months before scientists arrived in 1901. After a month of excavation, ten pony-drawn sleds hauled most of his cut up carcass more than 2,000 miles to the Trans-Siberian Railroad. From there he was taken to the world's leading institution for studying frozen mammoths, the Zoological Museum in St. Petersburg, Russia. His skeleton and that of Adam's mammoth are also displayed several feet behind the camera. The handle (extreme bottom center) of the shovel used in the excavation provides the scale. The penis, shown inches above the handle, is flattened out like a long tail of a beaver. This organ's state helps explain how he died. (See pages 108-111.)

Frozen Mammoths

For centuries, stories have been told of frozen carcasses of huge, elephantlike animals called **mammoths**,[1] buried in the tundra of northeastern Siberia.[2] These mammoths, with curved tusks sometimes more than 13 feet long, were apparently so fresh-looking that many believed they were simply large moles living underground. Some called them "ice-rats."[3] People thought that when mammoths surfaced and saw daylight, they died. Dr. Leopold von Schrenck, Chief of the Imperial Academy of Sciences at Petrograd (today's St. Petersburg, Russia), published the following account in 1869: "The mammoth . . . is a gigantic beast which lives in the depths of the earth, where it digs for itself dark pathways, and feeds on earth . . . . They account for its corpse being found so fresh and well preserved on the ground that the animal is still a living one."[4] Some even thought rapid tunneling by mammoths produced earthquakes.[5]

This was an early explanation for the frozen mammoths. As people learned other strange details, the theories multiplied. Unfortunately, theories that explained some details could not explain others. In fact, some proposed explanations, such as the one above, appear ludicrous in light of new knowledge.

To learn what produced the frozen mammoths, we must first understand much of what is known about them. This is summarized immediately below. From this we will distill the key details requiring an explanation. Then we will examine nine proposed theories. While many will seem initially plausible, their flaws will become apparent when we systematically compare how effectively they explain each detail. Finally, we will see that one theory—the hydroplate theory—introduced in the preceding section, best explains all the details.

General Description

What is Found. Since 1800, at least ten scientific expeditions have excavated fleshy remains of the extinct mammoth.[6] Most fleshy remains were buried in the permafrost of northern Siberia, inside the Arctic Circle. Six were found in Alaska. Only a few complete carcasses have been discovered. Usually wild animals had eaten the exposed parts before scientists arrived. In 1977, the first of two complete baby mammoths was found—a 6-12 month old male named "Dima." His flattened,[7] emaciated,[8] but well-preserved body was enclosed in a lens of ice, six feet below the surface of a gentle mountainous slope.[9] "Portions of the ice were clear and others quite brownish yellow with mineral and organic particles."[10] Silt, clay, and small particles of gravel were found throughout his digestive and respiratory tracts (trachea, bronchi, and lungs).[11]

If we expand our horizon even further by looking for the frozen soft tissue of other animals, we learn that several rhinoceroses have been found in the same regions. Some were remarkably preserved. (Table 2 on page 105 summarizes fifty-seven reported mammoth and rhinoceros discoveries.) Other fleshy remains come from a horse,[12] a young musk ox,[13] a wolverine,[14] voles,[15] squirrels, a bison,[16] a rabbit, and a lynx.[17]

If we now look for the bones and ivory of the mammoth, not just preserved flesh, the number of discoveries becomes enormous, especially in Siberia and Alaska. Nikolai Vereshchagin, the Chairman of the Russian Academy of Science's Committee for the Study of Mammoths, estimated that more than half a million tons of mammoth tusks were buried along a 600-mile stretch of the Arctic coast.[18] Since the typical tusk weighs 100

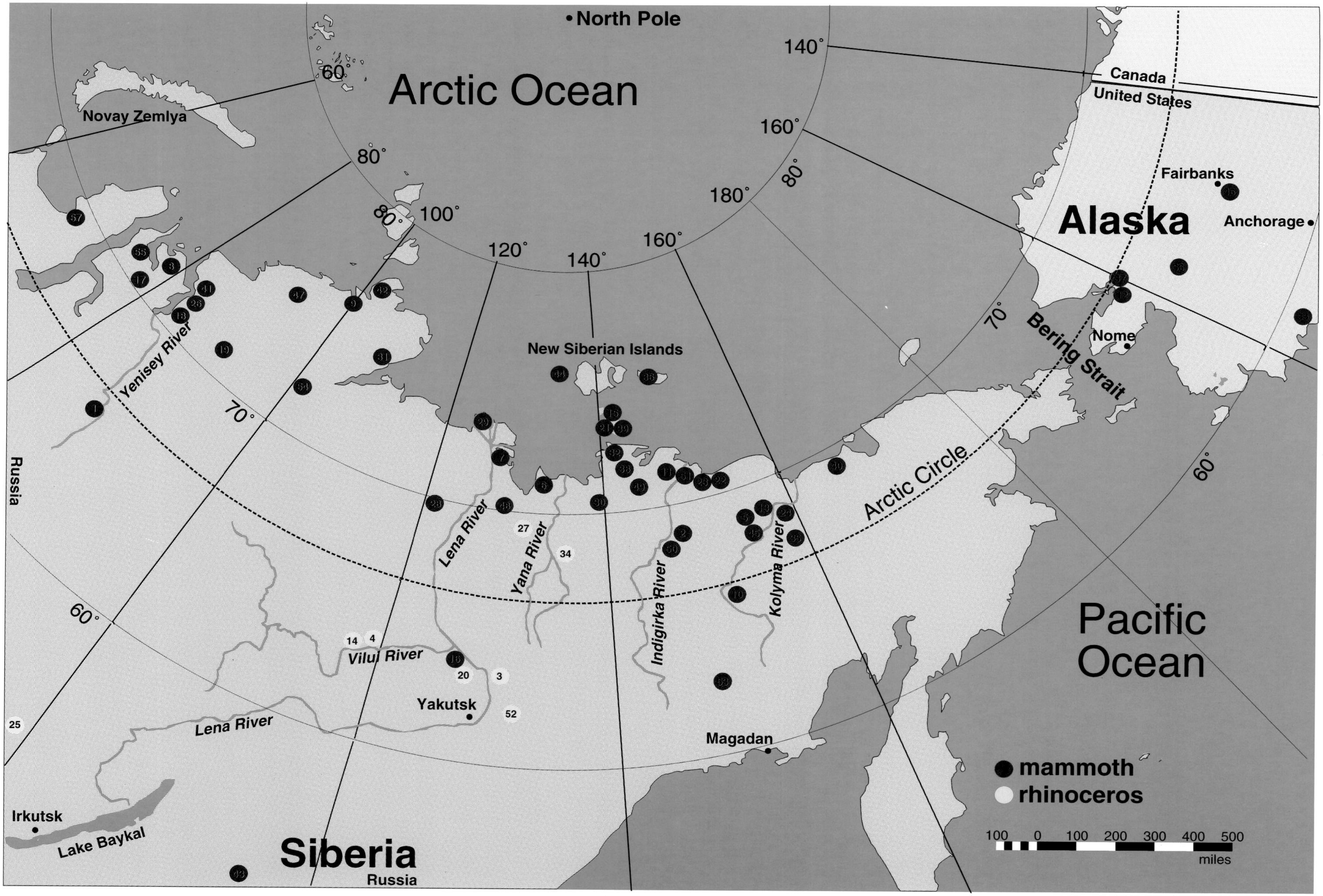

Figure 60: Map of Frozen Mammoth and Rhinoceros Finds.

Table 2: Reports of Frozen Mammoths and Rhinoceroses

	Date[a]	Name[b]	Description (Pertains to mammoths unless stated otherwise.)	Reference[c]
1	1693[d]	Ides	frozen head and leg[e]	Ides, 25-27
2	1723	Messerschmidt	frozen head and big pieces of skin with long hair	Breyne, 138
3	1739	Laptev	several rhinoceros heads	T, 22
4	1771	Pallas	complete rhinoceros; apparently suffocated; hairy head and two feet recovered	Eden[19]; H, 44, 82, 184
5	1787	Sarychev	complete when first seen; upright[e]	H, 82-83; T, 23
6	1800	Potapov	"on the shores of the Polar Sea"; skin and hair recovered	T, 25
7	1805	Adams	complete when first seen; 70-year-old male; 35,800 RCY; upright[e]	T, 23-25; H, 83-85
8	1839	Trofimov	complete; in a river bank; recovered; hair, bones, pieces of flesh and brain	H, 85; T, 26
9	1843	Middendorff	a half-grown mammoth; most of the flesh had decayed, eyeball recovered	H, 85-86; Eden, 104
10	1845[d]	Khitrof	well-preserved when found; food between teeth	H, 86
11	1846	Benkendorf	complete; upright; See page 108.	HD, 32-38; D, 97-103
12	1847[d]	Goodridge	AK; "a skull with a quantity of hair"	Maddren[20]
13	1854	Khitrovo	a foot, covered with hair; from a mammoth in good condition	T, 27
14	1858	Vilui	rhinoceros; a complete skeleton with some ligaments	T, 27
15	1860	Boyarski	upright in the face of an island's coastal cliff	T, 32
16	1861[d]	Golubef	"a huge beast covered with skin" in a river bank	H, 86
17	1864	Schmidt-1	PC; only skin and hair recovered a year later	T, 28; D, 108-110
18	1865	Koschkarof	PC; largely decomposed a year later	H, 86-87
19	1866	Schmidt-2	recovered on a lake shore; bones and hair of different lengths	T, 28; P, 8
20	1866	Kolesov	a large mammoth or rhinoceros, covered with skin	T, 27
21	1866	Bunge-1	"pieces of skin and plenty of hair"	T, 32
22	1869	Von Maydell-1	PC; upright; three years later, only a large hairy hide recovered	D, 80-95; H, 87-89
23	1869	Von Maydell-2	PC; only two legs found a year later	D, 80-95; H, 87-89
24	1870	Von Maydell-3	PC; only a leg was recovered three years later	D, 80-95; H, 87-89
25	1875	Tscherski	rhinoceros found in the frozen ground in a cave; hair and a piece of hide recovered	T, 29
26	1876	Nordenskiold	inch thick hide near skull of a musk sheep	Nordenskiold, 310; H, 89
27	1877	Von Schrenck	complete rhinoceros; the head was thoroughly studied; apparent suffocation	H, 89; T, 30-31
28	1879	Bunge-2	tusks chopped off; only reported to authorities four years later	T, 31
29	1884	Bunge-3	PC; first seen by natives 27 years earlier; two inch thick skin claimed	T, 16, 31
30	1886	Toll-1	23 years after natives' discovery, a few soft parts and hair were recovered	T, 32
31	1889	Burimovitch	reportedly complete; Toll's bad health prevented him from reaching the site	T, 33
32	1893	Toll-2	damaged bones, hairy skin, and other hair	T, 33
33	1894	Dall	AK; disintegrated muscle tissue, bones, and 300 pounds of fat	Dall[21]
34	1901	Pfizenmayer	rhinoceros; "a few fragments of ligaments and other soft parts"	P, 53-54; T, 35
35	1901	Berezovka	almost complete; upright; late summer death; 44,000 RCY; See page 108.	HE, 611-625; D, 111-136
36	1902	Brusnev	hair recovered, mixed with mud	T, 36
37	1908	Quackenbush	AK; pieces of flesh; tendons, skin, tail, and hair recovered	A, 299; Q, 107-113
38	1908	Vollosovitch-1	small female; pieces scattered; died at end of summer; 29,500 and 44,000 RCY	P, 146-164; D, 211-212
39	1910	Vollosovitch-2	late summer death; well-preserved eye, four legs, trunk, food in stomach	P, 241-246; T, 37-38
40	1910	Soloviev	PC; young mammoth; reported to but not pursued by scientists	T, 39
41	1913	Goltchika	PC; "dogs and foxes got at it and ate pretty well all the lot"	T, 38; D, 212
42	1915	Transehe	PC; found in 30-50 foot cliff on the Arctic Ocean; never excavated	T, 39; Transehe[22]
43	1922	Kara	carcass reported to scientists, but only hard parts remained four years later	T, 39-40
44	1923	Andrews	ivory traders sold skull still containing ligaments to British museum	T, 39
45	1924	Middle Kolyma	scrap of trunk remained; no record of original discovery	VT, 19; G, 26
46	1948	Fairbanks Creek	AK; 200 pound six-month old; head, trunk, and one leg; 15,380 RCY and 21,300 RCY	A, 299-300; G, 38-41
47	1949	Taimir	50-year-old male; tendons (11,500 RCY), hair, and an almost complete skeleton	VT, 20; Lister and Bahl[23]
48	1960	Chekurov	carcass of a young female, very small tusks, hair dated at 26,000 RCY	Vinogradov[24]
49	1970	Berelekh	a cemetery of at least 156 mammoths; minor hair and flesh remains	U, 134-148; S, 66-68
50	1971	Terektyakh	pieces of muscle, ligament, and skin; some around head	S, 67
51	1972	Shandrin	old; 550 pounds of internal organs and food preserved; 32,000 RCY and 43,000 RCY	U, 67-80; G, 27-29
52	1972	Churapachi	old rhinoceros, probably a female, "lower legs were in fair condition"	G, 34-37
53	1977	Dima	complete; 6-8 month-old male; 26,000 RCY and 40,000 RCY; See page 103.	G, 7-24; U, 40-67
54	1978	Khatanga	male; 55-60 years old, left ear, two feet; trunk in pieces; 45,000 RCY and 53,000 RCY	U, 30-40; G, 24-27
55	1979	Yuribei	12-year-old female; green-yellow grass in stomach; hind quarters preserved	U, 12-13, 108-134; VT, 22
56	1983	Colorado Creek	AK; two males; bones, hair, and gut contents recovered; 16,150 RCY and 22,850 RCY	Thorson and Guthrie[25]
57	1988	Mascha	3-4 month old female; complete except for trunk, tail, and left ear	LB, 46-47; VT, 25

Abbreviations: A=Anthony, AK=found in Alaska, D=Digby, G=Guthrie, H=Howorth, HD=Hornaday, HE=Hertz, LB=Lister and Bahl, P=Pfizenmayer, PC=possibly complete when first seen, Q=Quackenbush, RCY=radiocarbon years (most radiocarbon ages are from VT: 17-25), S=Stewart, 1977, T=Tolmachoff, U=Ukraintseva, VT=Vereshchagin and Tikhonov

Footnotes: a. *Usually the year of excavation. First sighting often occurred earlier.* **b.** *The name given is usually that of the discoverer, a prominent person involved in reporting the discovery, or a geographical name such as that of a river.* **c.** *No more than the two best references are given. The more complete reference is listed first.* **d.** *An approximate date.* **e.** *Referred to other carcasses but details are lacking.*

pounds, this implies that more than five million mammoths lived in this small region. Even if this estimate is high and represents thousands of years of accumulated remains, we can see that large herds of mammoths must have thrived along the Arctic coast. Many more existed elsewhere. Mammoth bones and ivory are also found throughout Europe, North and Central Asia, in North America, and as far south as Mexico City.

Dense concentrations of mammoth bones, tusks, and teeth are also found on remote Arctic islands. Obviously, today's water barriers were not always there. Many have described these mammoth remains as the main substance of the islands.[26] Even if these reports are exaggerated, what could account for any concentration and preservation of bones and ivory on barren islands well inside the Arctic Circle? More than 200 mammoth molars were dredged up with oysters from the Dogger Bank in the North Sea.[27]

Finally, throughout northern Europe, Asia, and parts of North America, we see the bones of many other animals along with those of mammoths. A partial listing includes: tiger,[28] antelope,[29] camel, horse, reindeer, giant beaver, giant ox, musk sheep, musk ox, donkey, badger, ibex, woolly rhinoceros, fox, giant bison, lynx, leopard, wolverine, Arctic hare, lion, elk, giant wolf, ground squirrel, cave hyena, bear, and several kinds of birds. Friend and foe, as well as young and old, are found nearby; carnivores, sometimes buried with herbivores. Were their deaths related? Rarely are animal bones preserved. Since bones of so many different animals were, there may be a connection.

Former Environment of Frozen Mammoths. There is a common misconception that the mammoth lived in areas of extreme cold. This widespread belief comes primarily from popular drawings showing mammoths living comfortably in snowy, Arctic regions. The artists, in turn, were influenced by earlier opinions based on the mammoth's hairy coat, thick skin, and a 3.5 inch layer of fat under the skin. However, animals with these characteristics do not necessarily live in cold climates. Let's examine these characteristics more closely:

Hair. The mammoth's hairy coat no more implies an Arctic adaptation than a woolly coat does for a sheep. The mammoth lacked erector muscles that fluff-up an animal's fur and creates insulating air pockets. Neuville, who conducted the most detailed study of the skin and hair of the mammoth, wrote: "It appears to me impossible to find, in the anatomical examination of the skin and [hair], any argument in favor of adaptation to the cold."[30] The long hair on a mammoth's legs hung to its toes.[31] Had it walked in snow, snow and ice would have caked on its hairy "ankles." Each step into and out of snow would have

pulled or worn away the "ankle" hair. All hoofed animals living in the Arctic, including the musk ox, have fur, not hair, on their legs.[32] Fur, especially oily fur, holds a thick layer of stagnant air (an excellent insulator) between the snow and skin. With the mammoth's greaseless hair, much more snow would touch the skin, melt, and increase the heat transfer 10 - 100 fold. Later refreezing would seriously harm the animal.

Skin. The skin of the mammoth and elephant are very similar in thickness and structure.[33] Both lack oil glands, making them vulnerable to cold, damp climates. Today, it appears that all Arctic mammals have both oil glands and erector muscles—equipment **absent** in the mammoths.[34]

Fat. The amount of fat under the skin says little about an animal's habitat. Some animals living in temperate zones, such as the rhinoceros, have thick layers of fat, while many Arctic animals, such as reindeer and caribou, have little fat. Thick layers of fat under the skin simply show that **food was plentiful**. Abundant food also suggests a temperate climate.

Elephants. The elephant—a close approximation to the mammoth[35]—is a tropical, not an Arctic animal. It requires "a climate that ranges from warm to very hot," and "it gets a stomachache if the temperature drops close to freezing."[36] Newborn elephants are susceptible to pneumonia and must be kept warm and dry at all times.[37] Hannibal, who crossed the Alps with 37 elephants, lost all but one due to cold weather.[38]

Temperature. The **average** January temperature in northeastern Siberia is about -28°F (60°F **below** the freezing point)! During the ice age, it was colder. The long, slender trunk of the mammoth was particularly vulnerable to cold weather. A six-foot-long nose could not survive even one cold night, let alone an eight-month-long Siberian winter. For the more slender trunk of a young mammoth, the heat loss would be even more harmful. An elephant usually dies if its trunk is seriously injured.[39]

Water. If the mammoth lived in an Arctic climate, its drinking water in the winter must have come from eating snow or ice. A wild elephant requires 30-60 gallons of water each day.[40] The heat needed to melt snow or ice and warm it to body temperature would consume about half a typical elephant's calories. Unlike other Arctic animals, the trunk would bear much of this thermal stress. Nursing elephants require about 25% more water.

Salt. How would a mammoth that lives in an Arctic climate satisfy its considerable salt appetite? Elephants dig for salt using their sharp tusks.[41] In the rock-hard permafrost this would be almost impossible, summer or winter, especially with the curved tusks of the mammoth.

Nearby Plants and Animals. The easiest and most accurate way to determine an extinct animal or plant's environment is to identify familiar animals and plants buried nearby. For the mammoth this includes rhinoceroses, tigers, bison, horses, antelope, a 90-foot-tall fruit tree,[42] and temperate species of grasses. All live in warm climates. Some frozen remains are of burrowing animals, such as voles, who would not burrow in rock-hard permafrost. Even larvae of the warble fly have been found in a frozen mammoth's intestine—larvae identical to those found in tropical elephants today.[43] No one argues that the animals and plants buried near the mammoths were adapted to the Arctic. Why then do so for mammoths?

Sudden Freezing and Rapid Burial. Before examining other facts, we can see three curious problems. First, northern Siberia today is cold, dry, and desolate. How could thousands, if not millions, of mammoths and many other animals feed themselves? Apparently their surroundings were more temperate and moist. If so, why did the climate change?

Second, the well-preserved mammoths and rhinoceroses must have been completely frozen soon after death or their soft, internal parts would have quickly decomposed. Guthrie has observed that "an unopened animal continues to decompose after a fresh kill, even at very cold temperatures, because the thermal inertia of its body is sufficient to sustain microbial and enzyme activity as long as the carcass is completely covered with an insulating pelt and the torso remains intact."[44] Since mammoths had such large reservoirs of heat, the freezing temperatures must have been extremely low.

Finally, their bodies were buried and protected from predators, including birds and insects. But burial could not have occurred if the ground were frozen as it is today. Again, this implies a major climate change, but now we can see that it must have changed suddenly. How were these huge animals quickly frozen and buried—almost exclusively in muck, a dark soil containing decomposed animal and vegetable matter?

Muck. Muck is a major geological mystery. It covers one-seventh of the earth's land surface—all surrounding the Arctic Ocean. Muck occupies treeless, generally flat terrain, with no surrounding mountains from which the muck could have eroded. Russian geologists have in

some places drilled through 4,000 feet of muck without hitting solid rock. Where did so much eroded material come from?

Oil prospectors, drilling through Alaskan muck, have "brought up an 18-inch long chunk of tree trunk from almost 1,000 feet below the surface. It wasn't petrified—just frozen."[45] The nearest forests are hundreds of miles away. Williams describes similar discoveries in Alaska:

Though the ground is frozen for 1,900 feet down from the surface at Prudhoe Bay, everywhere the oil companies drilled around this area they discovered an ancient tropical forest. It was in frozen state, not in petrified state. It is between 1,100 and 1,700 feet down. There are palm trees, pine trees, and tropical foliage in great profusion. In fact, they found them lapped all over each other, just as though they had fallen in that position.[46]

How were trees buried under a thousand feet of hard, frozen ground? We are faced with the same series of questions that we first saw with the frozen mammoths. Again, we are driven to the conclusion that there was a sudden and dramatic change in climate accompanied by rapid burial in muck, now frozen solid.

Figure 61: Vast, floating remains of forests have washed up on the coasts of the New Siberian Islands, well inside the Arctic Circle and thousands of miles from comparable forests today. This driftwood was washed ashore on Bolshoi Lyakhov Island, one of the New Siberian Islands. The wood was probably buried under the muck that covers northern Siberia. North flowing Siberian rivers, during the early summer flooding, eroded the muck, releasing the buried forests. "Fossil wood," as it is called, is a main source of fuel and building material for many Siberians.

Figure 62: Here driftwood is at the mouth of the Kolyma River, on the northern coast of Siberia. Today no trees of this size grow along the Kolyma. Leaves, and even fruit (plums), have been found on such floating trees.[47] One would not expect to see leaves and fruit if these trees had been carried far by rivers.

Some Specifics

We cannot minimize the frozen mammoth mystery by saying, "Only a few complete mammoths have been reported." One good case would be enough. Undoubtedly, hundreds of past discoveries went unreported, because many Siberians believed that looking at a mammoth's face brought death or misfortune. Fear of being forced by scientists to dig a mammoth out of the frozen ground also suppressed other discoveries. Besides, Siberia and Alaska are sparsely populated and relatively unexplored. Flowing rivers are the primary excavators, so man has only seen a small sample of what was buried there. Siberian geologists report that "work at the gold mines uncovers frozen mammoths every year, but since the arrival of scientists can delay and complicate the mining, most are lost to science."[48]

Widespread freezing and rapid burial are also inferred when commercial grade ivory is found. Ivory tusks, unless frozen and protected from the weather, dry out, lose their animal matter and elasticity, crumble, crack, and become useless for carving.[49] The trade in mammoth ivory has prospered since at least 1611 over a wide geographical region, from which an estimated 96,000 mammoth tusks have been exported.[50] Therefore, the extent of the freezing and burial is wider than most people have imagined.

The Benkendorf Mammoth.[51] In May 1846, a surveyor named Benkendorf and his party were camped in Siberia on the Indigirka River. The spring thaw and the unusually heavy rains caused the swollen river to erode a new

channel. Benkendorf noticed a large object bobbing slowly in the water. As the "black, horrible, giantlike mass was thrust out of the water [they] beheld a colossal elephant's head, armed with mighty tusks, with its long trunk moving in an unearthly manner, as though seeking something lost therein." They tried to pull the mammoth to shore with ropes and chains but soon realized that its hind legs were anchored, actually frozen, in the river bottom *in a standing position*.

Figure 63: Depiction of the Rescue of the Benkendorf Mammoth.

Twenty-four hours later, the river thawed and eroded the river bottom, freeing the mammoth. The team of fifty men and their horses pulled the mammoth onto dry land, twelve feet from the shore. The 13-foot tall, 15-foot long beast was fat and perfectly preserved. Its "widely opened eyes gave the animal an appearance of life, as though it might move in a moment and destroy [them] with a roar." They removed the tusks and opened its *full* stomach containing "young shoots of the fir and pine; and a quantity of young fir cones, also in a chewed state . . ." Hours later and without warning, the river bank collapsed, because the river had slowly undercut the bank. The mammoth was carried off toward the Arctic Ocean, never to be seen again.

The Berezovka Mammoth. The most famous, accessible, and perhaps studied mammoth is a fifty-year-old[52] male, found in a freshly eroded bank, 100 feet above Siberia's Berezovka River in 1900. A year later an expedition, led by Dr. Otto F. Herz, painstakingly excavated the frozen body and transported it to the Zoological Museum in St. Petersburg, Russia.[53] (See Figure 59 on page 102.)

Berezovka was upright, although his back was excessively humped and his straightened hind legs were rotated forward at the hips into an almost horizontal position. This strange, contorted position was further exaggerated by his raised and spread front legs. Several ribs, a shoulder blade, and pelvis were broken.[54] Amazingly, the long bone in his right foreleg was crushed into about a dozen pieces, without noticeably damaging the surrounding tissue.[55] His shaggy, wirelike hair, some of which was twenty inches long, was largely intact.[56] His erect penis was horizontally flattened.[57] (This organ in an elephant is round, S-shaped, and never horizontal.[58])

What can we conclude from these unusual details? To crush a long, slender rod (which the long leg bones resemble) requires axial compression while the rod (or bone) is encased in some material that will prevent bending and snapping. To demonstrate this, place a straight stick vertically on a table and see how difficult it is to compress and break it into a dozen or so pieces. Instead, it will snap at the weakest point. If the stick has a slight bend, as do the long leg bones, crushing becomes almost impossible. Something must prevent the stick or bone from bending as the compressive load is applied. Apparently, Berezovka's leg bone was severely compressed along its length while encased in some fairly rigid medium.[59]

Penile erection, under the above conditions, suggests death by slow suffocation. Tolmachoff concluded that, "The death [of Berezovka] by suffocation is proved by the erected male genital, a condition inexplicable in any other way."[60] But why was the penis horizontally flattened? It had to be pressed between two horizontal surfaces, one of which was probably his abdomen. Again, there apparently was considerable vertical compression throughout some medium that encased the entire body.

Suffocation is also implied with four other frozen giants in this region. Vollosovitch (Table 2) concluded that his second mammoth, buried with a penile erection on Bolshoi Lyakhov Island, also suffocated.[61] A third example is provided by Dima, whose "pulmonary alveoli suggested death by asphyxia" after "great exertion just before death."[62] The Pallas rhinoceros also showed symptoms of asphyxiation.

The blood-vessels and even the fine capillaries were seen to be filled with brown coagulated blood, which, in many places still preserved its red colour. This is exactly the kind of evidence we look for when we want to know whether an animal has been drowned or suffocated. Asphyxia is always accompanied by the gorging of the capillaries with blood.[63]

Von Schrenck's rhinoceros was found with expanded nostrils and an open mouth. The investigators concluded "that the animal died from suffocation, which it tried to avoid by keeping the nostrils wide asunder."[64] In all, three mammoths and two rhinoceroses apparently suffocated. No other cause of death has been shown for the remaining frozen giants.[65]

Sanderson describes another strange aspect of Berezovka.

Much of the head, which was sticking out of the bank, had been eaten down to the bone by local wolves and other animals, but most of the rest was perfect. Most important, however, was that the lips, the lining of the mouth and the tongue were preserved. Upon the last, as well as between the teeth, were portions of the animal's last meal, which for some almost incomprehensible reason it had not had time to swallow. The meal proved to have been composed of delicate sedges and grasses . . .[66]

Another account states that the mammoth's "mouth was filled with grass, which had been cropped, but not chewed and swallowed."[67] The grass froze so rapidly that it still had "the imprint of the animal's molars."[68] Hapgood's translation of a Russian report mentions eight well-preserved bean pods and five beans found in its mouth.[69]

Twenty-four pounds of undigested vegetation were removed from the Berezovka mammoth and analyzed by the Russian scientist, V. N. Sukachev. He identified more than forty different species of plants: herbs, grasses, mosses, shrubs, and tree leaves. Many no longer grow that far north; others grow both in Siberia and Mexico. Dillow draws several conclusions from these remains:

- *The presence of so many varieties* [of plants] *that generally grow much to the south indicates that the climate of the region was milder than that of today.*

- *The discovery of the ripe fruits of sedges, grasses, and other plants suggests that the mammoth died during the second half of July or the beginning of August.*

- *The mammoth must have been overwhelmed suddenly with a rapid deep freeze and instant death. The sudden death is proved by the unchewed bean pods still containing the beans that were found between its teeth, and the deep freeze is suggested by the well-preserved state of the stomach contents and the presence of edible meat* [for wolves and dogs].[70]

Table 3: Mammoth Myths vs. Mammoth Facts

Mammoth Myths	Facts
1. Fresh buttercups were in the mouth and stomach of the Berezovka mammoth.	Its stomach contained three **seeds** from plants that produce delicate, yellow buttercups. Fragments of other flowers were in its stomach. No large flowers were in its mouth.
2. People have been served mammoth steaks.[71]	These reports persist but are never specific enough to verify. For example, Lydekker reported that "sleigh dogs, as well as Yakuts themselves, have often made a hearty meal on mammoth flesh thousands of years old."[72] Lydekker never visited Russia, let alone Siberia. The following report by Herz appears valid. Herz wrote in his diary that the Berezovka mammoth "looks as fresh as well-frozen beef or horse meat. It looked so appetizing that we wondered for some time whether we should not taste it, but no one would venture to take it into his mouth, and horse flesh was given in the preference. The dogs cleaned up whatever mammoth meat was thrown them."[73] In 1982, construction workers in Siberia uncovered a frozen mammoth (not listed on page 105) and fed it to their dogs.[74]
3. Mammoths are encased in ice. Their preservation is complete.	Charles Lyell, often called the father of geology, popularized this myth by writing that mammoth remains are found in icebergs and frozen gravel.[75] There are very few reports of complete ice encasement.[76] Other mammoths were near or partially in ice. Herz and Pfizenmayer only **believed** their Berezovka mammoth was once fully encased in ice. Most frozen mammoths are found partially preserved in frozen muck.
4. The mammoth's small ears, short tail and legs, and anal flap reduced its heat loss in cold Arctic air. This shows that the mammoth was an Arctic animal.	Animals with large ears and long tails, such as hares and foxes, survive quite well in the Arctic. The legs and tails of Arctic foxes are similar to those of foxes living in warmer climates. While there is a slight correlation between small ears and cold habitats, other factors play a stronger role, such as metabolic efficiency, food availability, and adjustable insulation. The African elephant also has a prominent anal flap.[77] There is no fossil evidence that these features ever changed to support the Arctic adaptation claim.
5. Mammoths used their long curved tusks to remove snow from plants they ate on the ground. Most tusks show these wear marks.	Wild elephants live far from snow, yet they also have wear marks on their shorter, less vulnerable tusks. Mammoth tusks do not show extreme abrasion from being scraped over rocky soil in search of food under snow. (Besides, shoveling snow with a long, curved stick is a good way to break the stick.) A wild elephant spends about 16 hours a day eating and searching for food.[78] If food were buried under snow, there would not be enough hours in the day to forage for the necessary food. Any food found would presumably be consumed as well by other mammoths in the herd.
6. The curve in the mammoth tusks almost forms a circle.	"Not one tusk in ten forms a third of a circle, not one in twenty even a semicircle."[79] Artists and museums have popularized this misconception.
7. The wool on woolly mammoths protected them from the Arctic cold.	The term "woolly" is misleading since true wool has tiny, overlapping scales that interlock and trap air, making it an excellent insulator. Unlike sheep's wool, mammoth "wool" is only short, coarse under-hair. Mammoth hair, some of it long and bristly, has relatively few fibers per square inch.
8. The mammoth's thick skin and hairy body protected it from the Siberian cold.	See the earlier section entitled **Former Environment of Frozen Mammoths** on page 106.
9. Mammoths were larger than today's elephants.	Mammoths were larger than Indian elephants, but smaller than the African elephants. Usually, mammoths' tusks and heads were larger than those of all elephants.[80]
10. Larger animals generate more heat per unit of their body's surface area. Therefore, the mammoth would stay warm, even in the Arctic winter.	The first sentence is true. However, an Arctic mammal must avoid having its warm skin melt snow, as explained earlier. The mammoth's skin would tend to melt snow, especially if it lay down. Its high ground pressure would have compressed and reduced the insulation provided by its hair. (Elephants doze standing up, but when they feel safe, they will lie down for a few hours of sleep.) Sick or injured mammoths, unable to stand, would probably not have survived. Young mammoths were even more vulnerable. They generated less heat per unit of surface area and probably spent more time lying down. Newborn mammoths, wet and initially unable to walk, could not have survived for long lying on permafrost, especially if they were born during the long winter. (Elephants are born at all times of the year.)

At normal body temperatures, the stomach acids and enzymes break down vegetable material within an hour. What inhibited this process? The only plausible explanation is for the stomach to cool to about 40°F in ten hours or less.[81] But since the stomach is protected inside a warm (96.6°F for elephants) body, how cold must the outside air become to drop the stomach's temperature to 40°F? Experiments have shown that the outer layers of skin would have had to drop **suddenly** to at least -175°F![82]

Independently, Sanderson concluded, "The flesh of many of the animals found in the muck must have been very rapidly and deeply frozen, for its cells [had] not burst[83]. . . Frozen-food experts have pointed out that to do this, starting with a healthy, live specimen, you must suddenly drop the temperature of the air surrounding it down to a point well below minus 150 degrees Fahrenheit."[84]

The ice layer directly under the Berezovka mammoth contained some hair still attached to his body. Below his right forefoot was "the end of a very hairy tail . . . of a bovine animal, probably [a] bison."[85] Also under the body were "the right forefoot and left hind foot of a reindeer . . . . The whole landslide on the Berezovka [River] was the richest imaginable storehouse of prehistoric remains."[86] In the surrounding, loamy soil was an antelope skull,[87] "the perfectly preserved upper skull of a prehistoric horse to which fragments of muscular fibre still adhered,"[88] tree trunks, tree fragments, and roots.[89] This vegetation differed from the amazingly well-preserved plants in the mouth and stomach.

Geographical Extent. We should also notice the broad geographical extent over which these strange events occurred. (See map on page 104.) They were probably not separate, unrelated events. As Sir Henry Howorth stated:

The instances of the soft parts of the great pachyderms being preserved are not mere local and sporadic ones, but they form a long chain of examples along the whole length of Siberia, from the Urals to the land of the Chukchis [the Bering Strait], so that we have to do here with a condition of things which prevails, and with meteorological conditions that extend over a continent.

When we find such a series ranging so widely preserved in the same perfect way, and all evidencing a sudden change of climate from a comparatively temperate one to one of great rigour, we cannot help concluding that they all bear witness to a common event. We cannot postulate a separate climate cataclysm for each individual case and each individual locality, but we are forced to the conclusion that the now permanently frozen zone in Asia became frozen at the same time from the same cause.[90]

Actually, northern portions of Asia, Europe, and North America contain "the remains of extinct species of the elephant [mammoth] and rhinoceros, together with those of horses, oxen, deer, and other large quadrupeds."[91] So the event may have been even more widespread than Howorth believed.

Rock Ice. In Alaska and Siberia, scientists[92] have found a strange type of massive ice in and under the muck containing mammoth remains. Tolmachoff called it "rock ice."[93] Rock ice often has a yellow-tinge and contains round or elongated bubbles. Some bubbles are connected, while others, more than two centimeters long, are vertically streaked.[94] Rock ice, when exposed to the sun, showed "a polyhedral, granular structure at the surface, and these granules could usually be easily rubbed off with the finger."[95] It looked "like compacted hail."[96] Mammoth remains have been found above, below, beside, partially in,[97] and, in one case, within[98] rock ice.

Horizontal layers of rock ice are most easily seen in bluffs along the Arctic coast and nearby rivers.[99] Some subsurface ice layers are more than two miles long and 150 feet thick.[100] A several-foot-thick layer of structureless clay or silt is sometimes above the rock ice. How was this clay or silt deposited? If it settled out of a lake or stream, as normally happens, it should have many thin layers, but it does not. Furthermore, the slow settling of clay and silt through water should have provided enough time for the water to melt all the ice below. Sometimes rock ice contains plant particles[101] and thin layers of sand or clay. Had the water frozen in a normal way, the dirt would have settled out and the vegetable matter would have floated upward. Apparently, this rock ice froze rapidly and was never part of a lake or stream.

Several feet beneath the Berezovka mammoth and muck was a layer of rock ice, sloping for more than 180 feet down to the river. Herz and Pfizenmayer,[102] in digging into it, reported perhaps the strangest characteristic of the rock ice.

Deeper down in the cliff the ice becomes more solid and transparent, in some places entirely white and brittle. After remaining exposed to the air even for a short time this ice again assumes a yellowish-brown color and then looks like the old ice.[103]

Obviously, something in the air (probably oxygen) was reacting chemically with something in the ice. Besides wondering what the reactants were, there is a more basic question. Why was air (primarily oxygen and nitrogen) not already dissolved in the ice? Just as liquid water dissolves table salt, sugar, or many other solids, water also dissolves gases in contact with it. For example, virtually all water and ice on earth are nearly saturated with air. Had air been dissolved in Herz's rock ice before it changed to a yellowish-brown color, the chemical reaction would have already occurred.

Table 4: *Characteristics of Rock Ice vs. Three Types of Ice*

Some Characteristics of Ice [a]	Type 1: A body of stationary or slowly moving liquid water freezes. Examples: frozen rivers and lakes, ice cubes, sub-surface water [b]	Type 2: Water vapor condenses and freezes on microscopic particles in air, forming a type of ice called snow. (Its volume can decrease enormously by compaction, partial melting, and refreezing.) Examples: glaciers, icebergs, ice on winter roads	Type 3: Many small particles of liquid water freeze while moving rapidly through cold air or outer space. Examples: hail, sleet, windblown spray just above a choppy lake	Characteristics of Rock Ice [c]
Bubble Numbers and Sizes	a few the size of a pin head	many tiny air pockets	large pockets trapped between ice particles	many large bubbles [d]
Bubble Percentage	less than 6%	for glacier ice: about 6%	much more than 6%	16%
Dissolved Air	saturated	saturated	depends on water source	undersaturated
Degree of Granularity	no grains	very tiny grains	very granular	very granular, "like compacted hail"
Color	usually clear	usually white	depends on the impurities dissolved in the liquid [e]	usually has a yellow tinge
Dirt Content	slight	very little when it first forms	depends on the liquid water's dirt content [e]	dirt and plant particles easily seen

a. *Ice has other characteristics. For example, the atoms in ice can take on nine known crystalline patterns, depending upon the temperature and pressure at which the ice formed. They are called: Ice I, Ice II, Ice IX, etc. Unfortunately, the crystallographic structure of rock ice is not yet known. Only the characteristics listed in the table are known for rock ice.*

b. *Many subsurface ice features are not rock ice: ice wedges, segregated ice (Taber ice), vein ice, pingos, and glaciers covered with dirt. Their characteristics, especially their shapes and sizes, clearly differentiate them from rock ice and show how they formed.*

c. *For details see: Cantwell, "Ice Cliffs," pp. 345-346; Cantwell, "Exploration," pp. 551-554; Dall, pp. 107-109; Digby, pp. 93-95, 116, 120-124, 151; Dubrovo, p. 630; Herz, pp. 613, 616, 618, 622; Howorth, p. 53; Maddren, pp. 15, 32, 38-40, 51-54, 58-64, 67-117; Pfizenmayer, 88-90; Quackenbush, pp. 97-103; and Tolmachoff, pp. 51-55.*

d. *Sometimes these bubbles are connected or form vertical streaks. Their shapes apparently formed over centuries as gravity deformed the ice plastically.*

e. *Hail, sleet, and ice formed from a lake or ocean spray usually have very little visible dirt or impurities. Ice formed from sprays from other sources might have impurities, color, and dissolved minerals.*

Table 4 compares the characteristics of rock ice with those of the three generic types of ice. A careful study of this table shows that rock ice is a type 3 ice. Since such thick layers of rock ice still exist, an enormous amount of water must have frozen while moving through cold air or outer space.

Yedomas and Loess. The Siberian frozen mammoths are frequently found in strange hills, 30-200 feet high, which Russian geologists call yedomas. For example, the mammoth cemetery, containing the remains of 156 mammoths, was in a yedoma.[104] (See line 49 in Table 2 on page 105.) It is known that these hills were formed under cold, windy conditions, since they are composed of a powdery, homogeneous soil, honeycombed with thick veins of ice. Sometimes the ice, which several Russian geologists have concluded was formed simultaneously with the soil, accounts for 90 percent of the yedoma's volume.[105] Some yedomas contain many broken trees "in the wildest disorder."[106] The natives call them "wood hills" and the buried trees "Noah's wood."[107] Yedoma soil has a high salt and carbonate content,[108] contains tiny plant remains, and is comparable to muck.[109] The Berezovka mammoth was found in a similar soil.[110]

Recently, this soil has been identified as loess[111] (a German term, pronounced "LERSE"). Little is known about its origin. Most believe it is a windblown deposit spread under cold, glacial conditions over wide (almost global) geographical areas. However, Siberia was scarcely glaciated, and normal winds would deposit it too slowly to protect so many frozen animals from predators. Loess often blankets formerly glaciated regions, such as Wisconsin, Illinois, Iowa, Kansas, and Alaska. It lacks internal layering (stratification) and is found at all elevations—from just above sea level to hillsides at 8,000 feet elevation. Since loess is at many elevations and its tiny particles are not rounded by thousands of years of exposure to water and wind, some have proposed that loess came recently from outer space.[112] Loess, a fertile soil rich in carbonates, has a yellow tinge caused by the oxidation of iron-bearing minerals since it was deposited.[113] The Yellow River and the Yellow Sea of China are so named because of the loess suspended in them.

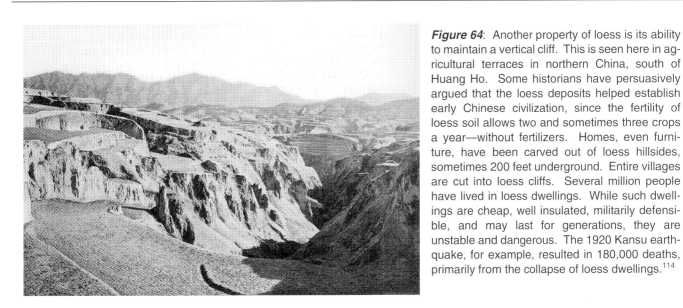

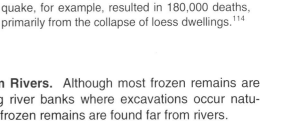

Figure 64: Another property of loess is its ability to maintain a vertical cliff. This is seen here in agricultural terraces in northern China, south of Huang Ho. Some historians have persuasively argued that the loess deposits helped establish early Chinese civilization, since the fertility of loess soil allows two and sometimes three crops a year—without fertilizers. Homes, even furniture, have been carved out of loess hillsides, sometimes 200 feet underground. Entire villages are cut into loess cliffs. Several million people have lived in loess dwellings. While such dwellings are cheap, well insulated, militarily defensible, and may last for generations, they are unstable and dangerous. The 1920 Kansu earthquake, for example, resulted in 180,000 deaths, primarily from the collapse of loess dwellings.[114]

Why is there an apparent relationship between frozen mammoths, yedomas, and loess?

Conclusion. This brief survey raises several intriguing but perplexing problems. What killed the mammoths, and how were they buried in such a peculiar manner? Some must have frozen within hours after their death, since significant decay or mutilation by scavengers did not occur. However, during that late summer or early fall, the conditions in Siberia were not cold. What happened?

Details Requiring an Explanation

Listed below is a summary of the hard-to-explain details relating to the frozen mammoths. Any satisfactory theory for the frozen mammoths should be able to explain them.

Abundant Food. A typical wild elephant requires about 330 pounds of food per day and spends about 16 hours a day eating. Therefore, vast quantities of food would have been required to support the estimated 5,000,000 mammoths that lived in just a small portion of northern Siberia. The Adams mammoth (a male), discovered in 1799, "was so fat ... that its belly hung below its knees."[115]

Warm Climate. Abundant food requires a temperate climate—much warmer than northern Siberia today. Only a small percentage of the food found in Berezovka's mouth and stomach grows near the Arctic Circle today. Furthermore, the flower fragments in its stomach show that it died during warm weather. Despite the popular misconception, the mammoth was a temperate, not an Arctic, animal.

Away From Rivers. Although most frozen remains are found along river banks where excavations occur naturally, some frozen remains are found far from rivers.

Yedomas and Loess. Frozen mammoths are frequently found in yedomas and loess. What accounts for this and the strange properties of yedomas and loess?

Multi-Continental. Soft parts of large animals have been preserved over a 3,000 mile wide zone spanning two continents. It is unlikely that many unrelated local events would produce such similar results over such a broad geographical area.

Elevated Burials. Mammoth and rhinoceros bodies are often found on the highest levels of generally flat, low plateaus.[116] Dense concentrations of mammoth and rhinoceros remains in yedomas and the interior of Arctic islands are examples of this. Dima was discovered in a mountainous region.

Frozen Muck. Mammoth carcasses are almost exclusively encased in frozen muck.[117] Also buried in the muck are huge deposits of trees and other animal and vegetable matter. The origin of muck is a mystery.

Rock Ice. Strange, granular ice containing clay, sand, and a large volume of air pockets is sometimes found near frozen mammoths. It apparently is a type 3 form of ice. (See Table 4 on page 112.)

Sudden Freezing. Some frozen mammoths and rhinoceroses still had food preserved in their mouths, stomachs, or intestines.[118]

Suffocation. At least three mammoths and two rhinoceroses appear to have suffocated. No other cause of death has been established for the remaining frozen giants.

What Happened?

Two strange, but admittedly secondary, reports may relate to the frozen mammoth problem. Each is so surprising that one might dismiss it as a mistake or hoax, just as with any single hearsay report of a frozen and buried mammoth. Nevertheless, since both reports are so similar yet originated from such different sources, it is probably best to reserve judgement. Each report was accepted as credible and published by an eminent scientific authority. Each involved the sudden freezing of a river *in apparent defiance of the way bodies of water freeze*. Each contained frozen animals in transparent ice, yet natural ice is rarely transparent. Each discovery was in a cold, remote part of the world. One was in the heart of Siberia's frozen mammoth country.

The brief reports will be given exactly as they were written and translated. The first was published by the former Soviet Academy of Sciences. Alexander Solzhenitsyn, winner of the Nobel Prize for Literature in 1970, recalled this report (as best he could remember it) in the first paragraph of his preface to *The Gulag Archipelago*. Unfortunately, Solzhenitsyn did not give the report's date, so this author began a difficult search. The report was finally located in Moscow's Lenin State Library.

Y. N. Popov, the author of this report, was discussing the scientific importance of finding mammals frozen in Siberia. He then described some frozen fish:

Figure 65: Frozen Fish.

There are some cases of finds of not only dead mammals, but also fishes, unfortunately lost for science. In 1942, during road construction in the Liglikhtakha River valley (the Kolyma Basin) an explosion opened a subterranean lens of transparent ice encasing frozen specimens of some big fishes. Apparently the explosion opened an ancient river channel with representatives of the ancient ichthyological fauna [fish]. The superintendent of construction reported the fishes to be of amazing freshness, and the chunks of meat thrown

Dirty Lungs. Dima's digestive and respiratory tract contained silt, clay, and small particles of gravel. Apparently, the air Dima breathed and the food he ate contained such matter for minutes or hours before his death.

-150°F. The temperature surrounding some mammoths must have plunged to at least -150°F.

Large Animals. The frozen remains are usually from the larger, stronger animals such as mammoths and rhinoceroses.

Summer-Fall Death. Vegetation in the stomachs and intestines of preserved mammoths imply that they died in the late summer or early fall,[119] perhaps in August,[120] or even late July.[121]

Animal Mixes. The bones of many types of animals, friends and foes, are frequently found near the mammoths.

Upright. Several frozen mammoths, and even mammoth skeletons,[122] were found upright. Despite this posture, the Berezovka mammoth had a broken pelvis, shoulder blade, and *a crushed* leg. Surprisingly, he was not lying on his side in a position of agony.

Vertical Compression. The crushed leg bone and the horizontally flattened penis of the Berezovka mammoth show that he experienced severe vertical compression after his death. Dima was also compressed and flattened.

Seventeen pieces of the problem are now before us. Fitting this centuries-old jigsaw puzzle together will be the final task. As we will see, many clever and surprising proposals have been made. However, most theories address only a few pieces of the frozen mammoth puzzle.

Theories Attempting to Explain the Frozen Mammoths

Nine theories have been proposed to explain the frozen mammoth puzzle; some are quite imaginative. Each theory will be described as it would be by the referenced advocate, usually the theory's author. We will then construct a special table (Table 5 on page 117) showing *out by the explosion were eaten by those present.*[123]

The second report comes from M. Huc, a missionary traveler in Tibet in 1846. Sir Charles Lyell, the "father of geology," also quoted this same story in the eleventh edition of his *Principles of Geology*. After many of Huc's party had been frozen to death, the survivors pitched their tents on the banks of the Mouroui-Oussou (which lower down becomes the famous Blue River). Huc reported:

> *At the moment of crossing the Mouroui-Oussou, a singular spectacle presented itself. While yet in our encampment, we had observed at a distance some black shapeless objects ranged in file across the great river. No change either in form or distinctness was apparent as we advanced, nor was it till they were quite close that we recognized in them a troop of the wild oxen. There were more than fifty of them encrusted in the ice. No doubt they had tried to swim across at the moment of congelation [freezing], and had been unable to disengage themselves. Their beautiful heads, surmounted by huge horns, were still above the surface; but their bodies were held fast in the ice, which was so transparent that the position of the imprudent beasts was easily distinguishable; they looked as if still swimming, but the eagles and ravens had pecked out their eyes.*[124]

Any explanation for these strange discoveries must recognize that streams freeze from the top down.[125] The

Figure 66: Frozen Oxen Found in Tibet in 1846.

ice formed insulates the warmer liquid water below. The thicker the ice grows, the harder it is for the liquid's heat to pass through the ice layer and into the cold air. Freezing a stream fast enough to trap more than fifty upright oxen **in the act of swimming across**, seems impossible, especially since a stream's velocity (and thus its tendency to freeze) varies considerably across its width. Freezing a river so fast that many large fish are frozen, edible, and underground, defies belief. However, the similarities with the frozen mammoths are so great that these reports may be related. A simple explanation of how it may have happened will follow shortly.

how well each theory fits the pieces of the puzzle together. You can make the critical judgments yourself and even modify the table. For comparison, this author's opinions will be explained.

Fruitful theories answer not only the obvious, initial questions but also more perplexing and seemingly unrelated problems. This will be the case with the frozen mammoth mystery. In trying to learn why an extinct animal is sometimes frozen and buried, we will answer broader questions and may even uncover a sequence of dramatic, global events.

Fruitful theories also generate surprising predictions for testing the theory. Keep this in mind as we examine all nine explanations. With each, ask yourself, "What predictions can this theory make?" If few predictions are forthcoming, the theory is probably weak.[126] (If theories could not be published unless they included clearly enumerated predictions, we would be mercifully spared many distractions and false ideas.)

Hydroplate Theory. (For a more complete description of the hydroplate theory, first read pages 70-100.) The

rupture of the earth's crust passed between Alaska and Siberia in minutes. During the next few hours, some of the upward jetting, subterranean water from "the fountains of the great deep" went above the atmosphere where the effective temperature is several hundred degrees below zero Fahrenheit.[127] Much of the resulting ice fell in a gigantic "hail storm." Some animals were suddenly buried, suffocated, frozen, and compressed by tons of cold, muddy ice crystals. The mud in this ice prevented it from floating as the flood waters submerged these regions after days and weeks. The thick blanket of ice preserved many animals during the flood phase. After the flood waters drained off the continents, the icy graves in warmer climates melted, and their contents decayed. However, many animals, buried in what are now permafrost regions, were preserved.

Lake Drowning Theory.[128] No catastrophe occurred. The well-preserved mammoths, with food in their stomachs and between their teeth, died suddenly, probably from asphyxiation resulting from drowning in a partially frozen lake, river, or bog. Such burials preserve animal tissue, and even humans, for many thousands of years.

Figure 67: A Yedoma. These Siberian hills, called yedomas, are honeycombed with ice. The layering that is seen within yedomas (for example, to the left of the man) suggests that high winds accompanied the deposition of the material. Remains of mammoths and other animals are frequently found in yedomas.

The ice and mud was not deposited as hills. Instead, it was deposited as one thick layer. Later the ice began to melt in spots. The more it melted, the thinner the layer became, causing lakes to collect in the depressions. The presence of lakes accelerated the melting below them. What is now left, after thousands of years of summer melting, are these hills. Since some yedoma are 200 feet tall, the initial deposition in the windy environment was probably at least 200 feet thick.

Crevasse Theory. Some mammoths fell into ice crevasses or deep snowdrifts. This protected them from predators, while ice preserved them for thousands of years.[129]

Mud Burial Theory. In Siberian summers, the top foot or so of tundra thaws, so larger animals, even man, can easily become stuck—standing upright. Herds of mammoths, rhinoceroses, and buffalo made summer migrations to northern Siberia and Alaska. Some became stuck in this mud; others were overwhelmed and suffocated in mudslides. Still others died for various reasons and were then buried in slow mudflows during several summer thaws. Sudden cold spells—sometimes followed by long, cold winters—froze and preserved many of them.[130]

River Transport Theory. The mammoths and other animals lived further south in the temperate zone of Asia where food was abundant. Their remains floated from Central Siberia on the north-flowing rivers during local floods.[131]

Extinction-by-Man Theory. Man exterminated the mammoths—just as man almost exterminated the buffalo. Man, in hunting the mammoths, pursued and pushed them north into Siberia and Alaska. There they died from harsh weather, lack of food, or the direct killing by man.[132]

The Bering Barrier Theory. At the peak of the last ice age, the Bering Strait was closed as ice accumulated on continents, lowering sea level by 300 feet. This newly created land bridge allowed people and animals, including mammoths, to migrate between Siberia and Alaska and onto Arctic islands. Since the warmer Pacific waters could no longer mix through the Bering Strait with the cold Arctic Ocean, the Pacific waters became even warmer and the Arctic waters even colder. The resulting heavy evaporation from the Pacific caused extreme snow falls on the higher, colder land masses north of the Bering

Table 5: Theories Proposed to Explain the Frozen Mammoths.

Each number in this table refers to an amplifying explanation in the following pages.

Detail to be Explained	Hydroplate	Lake Drowning	Crevasse	Mud Burial	River Transport	Extinction by Man	Bering Barrier	Shifting Crust	Meteorite
Abundant Food						53	65		80
Warm Climate		10	17				65		
Away from Rivers				29	42				
Yedomas and Loess	1	11	18	30	42	54	66	74	81
Elevated Burial	2		19	31	43	55			
Multi-Continental		11	18	30	42		67		
Rock Ice	3	12	20	32	44	56	68	75	82
Frozen Muck	2	11	21	30	42	57	69	76	81
Sudden Freezing		13	22	33					
Suffocation	4		18			58	70		81
Dirty Lungs	5	14	23	34	45	59	71		
-150° F	6	13	24	30	42	54	67	74	83
Large Animals	6		25		42	54	72	74	
Summer-Fall Deaths					46			77	
Animal Mixes	2	15	26	35		60			84
Upright	7	11	27	36	47	54			
Vertical Compression	7	16	18	37	42	54	67	74	81
Other	8-9		28	38-41	48-52	61-64	73	78-79	85

Key

Theory explains this detail.	Theory has moderate problem with this detail.	Theory has serious problems with this detail.

barrier. Mammoths and others were buried in severe snow storms early one fall. As the ice age ended, heavy rains washed soil down on top of compacted snow deposits, forming rock ice. Some frozen mammoths and rock ice are still preserved. Since this last ice age, glacial melting raised sea levels and reestablished the Bering Strait.[133]

Shifting Crust Theory. Before the last ice age, the Hudson Bay was at the North Pole. Siberia and Alaska were further south and supported large herds of mammoths with abundant vegetation. The earth's crust shifted, moving Siberia northward. Since the earth is slightly flattened at the poles and bulges at the equator, the shifting earth's crust produced many ruptures. Volcanic gas was thrown above the atmosphere where it cooled and descended as a super-cold "blob." Airborne volcanic dust lowered temperatures on the earth and caused phenomenal snow storms. Mammoths and other animals living in Siberia and Alaska were suddenly frozen and buried in the extremely cold snow. Some are still preserved.[134]

Meteorite Theory. At the end of the last ice age, a large iron meteorite hit the earth's atmosphere. The resulting heat temporarily melted the top layers of the frozen tundra, causing mammoths to sink into muck. The poor visibility caused others "to blunder to their deaths in the icy bogs."[135]

Table 5

Table 5 on page 117 summarizes how well each theory explains the many strange things associated with the frozen mammoths. Each column corresponds to a theory and each row represents a strange detail requiring an explanation. A green box means that, in this author's opinion, the column's theory provides a reasonable explanation for the detail represented by that row. Yellow and red boxes indicate moderate and serious problems. The number in a cell refers to an amplifying explanation below.

Readers may make their own judgments and independently assess each theory's plausibility. For example, if you feel a detail or theory has been omitted or misstated, add to or correct it. This tabular approach focuses future discussions on the areas of critical disagreement. It also motivates one to keep all details and competing theories in mind—encouraging balance and thoroughness. Often a disagreement becomes moot when one realizes other facts opposing some theory. When a theory is proposed, usually only the details supporting it and opposing a competing theory are mentioned. Table 5 on page 117 is an attempt to analyze all published theories and all known diagnostic details.

In seeking the cause of many strange and related details, one is tempted to use a separate explanation for each detail. Throughout the history of science, experience has shown that the simplest theory explaining the most details is most likely to be correct. For example, a sudden rash of fires in a city may all be unrelated. However, most investigators would instinctively look for a common explanation. Another example occurred centuries ago. To explain a newly discovered detail of planetary motion required, in effect, a new theory. Later, one theory (Newton's Law of Gravitation) provided a simple explanation for all these motions.

Relating to the Hydroplate Theory

1. Yedomas and Loess. (These terms are explained on page 112.) Immediately after the rupture, the salty, subterranean water began flowing horizontally toward the rupture. The tremendous pressure in the subterranean chamber accelerated the escaping water to high speeds, rapidly eroding the rock bounding the chamber and rupture. Thus the water expelled up through the rupture and into the atmosphere was filled with dirt fragments of various sizes. As you will see, the higher a droplet rose, the more likely it was to lose the larger particles carried inside. Therefore, the droplets that rose above the atmosphere and froze contained the powdery dirt particles that comprise yedoma hills and the world's loess.

First, imagine that you are a water droplet jetting up through the rupture and atmosphere. What would you see and feel? The atmospheric pressure drops as you go higher, causing water to evaporate from your surface and reducing your size slightly. The evaporation cools you just as drying perspiration cools a person or evaporation units cool homes in dry climates. Flowing past you are gases—some air, but primarily water vapor (steam) from the evaporation of other water droplets. This "gusting wind" strikes you from differing directions, each time dragging your skin around toward the opposite, or downstream, side. This creates a strong and complicated circulation within your body and chaotic waves on your surface. Your ride is bumpy. Sometimes you fragment into two or more pieces, but the smaller a piece is, the stronger the molecular forces (the surface tension) holding it together.

Now pretend you are one of the smallest of hundreds of dirt particles in a small, buffeted, water droplet. The swirling currents within your droplet cause the other particles in the droplet to dart around you chaotically. Being one of the smallest of these particles, you are not jostled as much as the larger particles.[136] Each gust tends to shake the larger particles out of the droplet. When you finally arrive high above the atmosphere and your droplet freezes, only the smallest dirt particles remain. Since you are encased in ice, you are protected from water erosion that would round and smooth your sharper corners.

Eventually most of this ice fell to the earth in a giant hail storm as the flood began. The high winds tore up trees and pulverized vegetation that mixed with the muddy hail. Many animals froze and suffocated. When the ice melted, it left behind tiny, angular, dirt particles (now called loess) and some dissolved salts. Years later, the thick layers of muddy hail began melting in many isolated locations. Further melting around these spots accelerated as melt water collected in these depressions during subsequent melting seasons. Today's hilly yedomas remain. Therefore, in Arctic regions where little summer melting occurs, the loess, salt, vegetation, and mammoth remains were largely preserved in cold yedomas.

At the periphery of formerly glaciated areas, where ice sheets most recently melted, loess is commonly found. It is especially abundant along the downwind side of ice age drainage channels, such as the Mississippi River. In warmer climates, wind often retransported the loess, rain leached the salts from the soil, and the organic material decayed. *PREDICTION 7: High concentrations of loess particles will be found in the bottom several hundred feet of ice cores drilled in Antarctica and Greenland.* The bottom layers of Greenland, Canadian, and Antarctic ice sheets contain up to 50 times more microparticles than the glacial ice above.[137] The ice crystals containing them are much smaller than normal glacial ice crystals. This suggests that the hail that buried and froze the mammoths was smaller than normal hail. Another study[138] found that the lower portion of the Greenland ice sheet contains abnormally high amounts of dust, sea salt, and other chemicals consistent with that in the subterranean water chamber.

2. Elevated Burials, Frozen Muck, and Animal Mixes. When a space ship reenters the earth's atmosphere, aerodynamic friction melts a thin layer of the vehicle's leading surface. The liquid film then flows off the spaceship into the atmosphere. This localized absorption and removal of heat, called ablation, protects the rest of the vehicle from the friction and heat.

Likewise, frictional heating melted the first ice particles falling into the atmosphere. Muddy rain, accompanied by high winds, fell first, forcing many different animals to higher ground. Some of these high burial grounds are now the Arctic islands containing dense concentrations of mammoth bones and ivory. Prey and predator sought protection from the greater common enemy—rising waters. Larger animals, such as mammoths and rhinoceroses, in rushing to higher ground, may have crushed and buried the smaller animals in warmer sediments. This may explain the antelope skull under the Berezovka mammoth.

Fine sediments in the muddy rain and ice mixed with the torn up surface vegetation and formed *muck*. This soupy mixture, along with ripped up forests, flowed into valleys and other low areas, smoothing the topography into flat, low plateaus. Later this muck froze, preserving to this day its distinguishing organic component and its loesslike inorganic component. *PREDICTION 8: Muck on the Siberian plateaus should have a wide range of thicknesses. The greatest thickness will be in former valleys. Preflood hilltops will have the thinnest layers of muck. Drilling or seismic reflection techniques should confirm this.*

3. Rock Ice. Table 4 on page 112 shows why rock ice is a type 3 ice. As was stated on page 83, the subterranean waters contained large quantities of dissolved salt and carbon dioxide. The carbon dioxide contributed to the carbonates found in loess. *PREDICTION 9: Rock ice is salty.*[139]

Before the flood, the subterranean water was sealed off from the atmosphere and, therefore, probably contained no dissolved air. As "the fountains of the great deep" exploded up through the atmosphere, the rapid and steady evaporation from the rising liquid forced gases away from, rather than toward, each rising liquid particle. Thus, the water that froze above the atmosphere had no dissolved air but still had dissolved carbon dioxide. Both froze to become a mixture of water ice and frozen carbon dioxide, or "dry ice."

Ice absorbs air very slowly, especially the inner portion of a large volume of falling ice particles. Therefore, little air was absorbed as the hail fell to the earth. Once the ice was on the warm ground, some "dry ice" and water ice slowly evaporated as white clouds. As the ice depth increased to perhaps several hundred feet, these clouds billowed up through gaps between the ice particles, forcing out any air that might have been between the ice particles. Eventually, the weight of the topmost layers of ice essentially sealed the lower ice from the air above. This explains why Herz saw the ice under Berezovka turn yellow-brown as it came in contact with (and reacted chemically with) air for the first time. *PREDICTION 10: The bubbles in rock ice will be found to contain less air and much more carbon dioxide than normal.*

The ice ages followed the flood. Since then, the surface of the ground in Alaska and Siberia melts slightly each summer. In some parts of Alaska and Siberia, this included several feet of rock ice. When a layer of this dirty ice melted, the water drained away, leaving particles of dirt and vegetation behind. The remaining clay and silt provided an insulating blanket, causing less ice to melt each year. Most of the unsorted and unstructured clay and silt above rock ice came from melted rock ice. *PREDICTION 11: The dirt and organic particles in rock ice will closely resemble those in the overlying muck.*

4. Suffocation. Suffocation occurred in several ways: (a) physical burial by falling ice particles, (b) breathing too much carbon dioxide gas from evaporating "dry ice," and (c) freezing lung tissue, thereby preventing the diffusion of oxygen into and carbon dioxide out of the lungs.

5. Dirty Lungs. The extreme winds beginning at the time of the rupture created a gritty atmosphere for a few hours before the rain and ice reached Dima. This is why his entire digestive and respiratory tracts contained silt, clay, and small particles of gravel.

6. -150°F and Large Animals. As the mass of "hail" fell into the atmosphere, it pushed forward and displaced large volumes of air, creating violent down drafts and additional surface winds. Larger, stronger animals, such as mammoths and rhinoceroses, best withstood the driving rain, wind, and cold as they sought safety. They were still standing as the colder hail began piling up at various places—hail whose temperature was about -150°F, corresponding to the temperature above the atmosphere. This "supercold" ice pressing against their bodies rapidly froze even their warm stomachs and internal organs.

Some muddy hail fell to the bottoms of streams, rivers, and lakes. It did not float, because it contained dirt. Its extreme coldness absorbed so much heat that lakes and streams, and the animals therein, quickly froze. (See **What Happened?** on pages 114 and 115.)

7. Upright and Vertical Compression. The massive and violent hail storm buried mammoths and rhinoceroses alive—many standing up and compressed from all sides. Babies were flattened. Exposed parts of adult bodies, unsupported by bone, were vertically flattened. Sometimes even strong bones were crushed by axial compression. Encasement in muddy ice maintained the alignment of Berezovka's leg bone as it was crushed lengthwise.

Ice slowly flows downhill as, for example, in glaciers. Such a flow, pushing Berezovka's body—tail first, would explain his forward swept hind legs, humped back, displaced vertebrae, and spread front legs bent at the "wrists."

8. Other. The hydroplate theory states that the frozen animals were buried in muddy hail at the onset of the flood. During the following months, sedimentary layers and their fossils were deposited on top of this ice and sorted by liquefaction. (See pages 134-145.) ***PREDICTION 12: One should never find marine fossils, layered strata, coal seams, or limestone directly beneath undisturbed rock ice or frozen carcasses.*** This is a severe test for this theory since a few crude geologic maps of Siberia imply that marine fossils lie within several miles of the frozen remains. How accurate are these geologic maps, and what deposits are *directly beneath* frozen carcasses?

Sedimentary layers generally extend over large areas and sometimes contain distinctive fossils. One can construct a plausible geologic map of an area (a) if many deep layers are exposed, as for example in the face of a cliff or

the bank of a river, (b) if similar vertical sequences of fossils and rock types are found in nearby exposures, and (c) if no intervening crustal movement has occurred. If all three conditions are satisfied, then it is reasonable to assume that the layers with similar distinctive fossils are connected. Finally, if such layers pass beneath any frozen carcass, this explanation for the frozen mammoths will have a serious problem. This author is not aware that these four conditions were ever satisfied in northern Siberia, one of the most unexplored regions on the earth.

Nor is there any known report of marine fossils, layered strata, limestone deposits, or coal seams directly beneath any frozen mammoth or rhinoceros remains. Tolmachoff, in his chapter on the geology of the Berezovka site, wrote that "Marine shells or marine mammals have never been discovered in [deposits having frozen mammoths]."[140] Also, Hern von Maydell, reporting on his third frozen mammoth, wrote, "despite my thorough search, not a single shell or fossil was found."[141] The sediments beneath the Fairbanks Creek mammoth down to bedrock contained no marine fossils, layered strata, coal seams, or limestone.[142]

9. Other. According to the hydroplate theory, all the frozen mammoths and rhinoceroses died at the same time. However, the radiocarbon ages vary. See Table 2 on page 105. For an explanation of radiocarbon dating and its assumptions, see page 151. Those pages explain why 40,000 radiocarbon years (RCY) is a typical radiocarbon age for most frozen remains, and why 40,000 radiocarbon years probably correspond to about 5,000 actual years. A slight amount of contamination of the remains, for example by ground water, would lower their radiocarbon age considerably, especially something living before or soon after the flood. This probably explains why different parts of the first Vollosovitch mammoth had widely varying radiocarbon ages—29,500 and 44,000 RCY. One part of Dima was 40,000 RCY, another was 26,000 RCY, and the "wood found immediately around the carcass" was 9,000 - 10,000 RCY. The lower leg of the Fairbanks Creek mammoth had a radiocarbon age of 15,380 RCY, while its skin and flesh were 21,300 RCY.[143] The two Colorado Creek mammoths had radiocarbon ages of 22,850 ± 670 and 16,150 ± 230 years respectively. Since a bone fragment at one burial site fit precisely with a bone at the other site 30 feet away, and the soil had undergone considerable compression and movement, it seems likely they died simultaneously. ***PREDICTION 13: Blind radiocarbon dating of different parts of the same mammoth will continue to give radiocarbon ages that differ by more than statistical variations would reasonably permit.*** (See page 59 for an explanation of blind testing.) ***Contamination by ground water will be most easily seen if the samples came from widely separated parts of the***

mammoth's body with different water absorbing characteristics.

Relating to the Lake Drowning Theory

(The reader may wish to read only the discussions concerning the theories of personal interest.)

10. Warm Climate. Frozen lakes or rivers do not exist in a warm climate during the late summer or early fall. Many additional weeks of freezing temperatures are needed to form ice thick enough for a large, hoofed animal to venture far enough from shore to drown. Yet, the vegetation in the digestive tracts of various large animals shows that the weather was warm when they died.

11. Yedomas and Loess, Multi-Continental, Frozen Muck, and Upright. The lake drowning theory does not explain the relationship of mammoths with yedomas and loess, why these peculiar events occurred over such wide areas on two continents, where so much muck originated, why it contains buried forests, or why so many mammoth bodies and skeletons are found upright.

12. Rock Ice. The ice near several carcasses was not lake or river ice. It was type 3 ice, not type 1 ice.

13. Sudden Freezing and -150°F. Yes, burial in peat bogs can retard bacterial decay and preserve bodies for thousands of years. However, only a rapid and extreme temperature drop can stop the destructive activity of enzymes and stomach acids.

14. Dirty Lungs. Drowning in a lake would not cause gravel to enter Dima's lungs. Nor could silt, clay, and gravel work its way throughout Dima's intestines after a sudden drowning.

15. Animal Mixes. If mammoths occasionally fell through the ice on a lake, why are the bones of so many types of animals from temperate latitudes found together? Why do prey lie near their predators? Large, hoofed animals seldom venture out on frozen lakes.

16. Vertical Compression. Falling into a lake would not produce the vertical compression found in Dima and Berezovka.

Relating to the Crevasse Theory

17. Warm Climate. The contents of Berezovka's stomach showed that he lived in a warm climate, not one containing ice crevasses. Furthermore, tree fragments and roots were found beneath him. Trees do not grow near icy crevasses. Glacial climates prevent tree growth. Many animals and plants buried in northern Siberia and Alaska only live in temperate climates today. Besides, mammoths are not Arctic animals.

18. Yedomas and Loess, Multi-Continental, Suffocation, and Vertical Compression. The crevasse theory does not explain the relationship of mammoths with yedomas and loess, why these peculiar events occurred over such wide areas on two continents, why some of these huge animals suffocated, or what caused the vertical compression found in Dima and Berezovka.

19. Elevated Burial. Falling into a crevasse or being transported downhill in a glacier would not herd mammoths up onto islands or up near the higher elevations of flat, low plateaus. Furthermore, crevasses form only on steep slopes.

20. Rock Ice. Mammoths are sometimes buried near type 3 ice. Crevasses only have type 2 ice. In contrast to rock ice, glaciers and crevasses almost always occur on steep slopes.

21. Frozen Muck. Mammoths were found primarily in frozen muck, not ice. Where did all the muck come from, and why are so many large trees buried in it?

22. Sudden Freezing. Let us assume that after Berezovka had eaten beans at the base of a glacier, he climbed up to a crevasse, fell in, and died. His stomach acids and enzymes would have destroyed his food in about an hour. Since crevasses are not at the base of glaciers, Berezovka's long trip up the glacier and subsequent freezing must have been unbelievably rapid. Furthermore, what could motivate a grazing beast to climb up a long, steep, icy slope?

23. Dirty Lungs. Falling into a crevasse would not put gravel in Dima's lungs or silt, clay, and gravel throughout Dima's intestines.

24. -150°F. Snow is a surprisingly good insulator. Transferring heat through glacial snow is a relatively slow process, as those who have lived in igloos know. Transferring heat from a solid object, such as the body of a mammoth, to stagnant air is also a slow process. Both conditions would exist if a mammoth fell into a crevasse. The steep walls of a crevasse would shield the body from cold winds, and the glacial ice would insulate the mammoth from sharp drops in the outside temperature. Eventually the carcass would freeze, but the vast residual heat in its huge body would delay freezing and cause putrefaction. Hoyle's comment, therefore, comes as no surprise:

I have been informed that, today, when reindeer fall down crevasses in the Greenland ice, they are subsequently found to be in an unpleasantly putrefied condition. It seems that, no matter how cold the air is, the body heat of the dead animal is sufficient to promote bacterial decomposition.[144]

The warmer, internal parts of the body, such as the stomach, would experience even more decay than the outer layers. Furthermore, this theory cannot begin to explain a sudden temperature drop to -150°F.

25. Large Animals. The crevasse theory does not explain why primarily larger animals fell into the icy crevasses and froze. Actually, the larger the animal, the greater its reservoir of stored heat and the slower it would cool. Therefore, the larger animals should experience greater and more rapid decay.

26. Animal Mixes. If an occasional mammoth fell into an ice crevasse, why are the bones of so many types of animals found together? While some might argue that an adult mammoth climbed up a glacier, why would a baby such as Dima? Why would a rhinoceros? A heavy, low-slung rhinoceros should not be able to walk in deep snow. Beavers, squirrels, and birds do not fall into crevasses, but all have been found near mammoths.

27. Upright. Herz, who excavated and analyzed the Berezovka mammoth, felt that it had fallen into a crevasse since it had several broken bones and was frozen. This might explain why the mammoth was found in an upright, although contorted, position. Normally, with a broken pelvis, a broken shoulder, a few broken ribs, and a crushed leg bone, it should have been lying on his side. However, it is strange that a fall would break bones in different parts of the body. To break so many bones requires many large forces. The blow received from a fall might explain a few fractures, but probably not all, especially the aligned crushed-fracture of the leg.

28. Other. Only a few mountains in northeastern Siberia show evidence of former glaciers.

Relating to the Mud Burial Theory

29. Away From Rivers. A very large mudslide, such as might occur near a river bank, is required to suffocate and bury large animals. Yet frozen remains of mammoths are sometimes found far from rivers, on high ground where river mud could not reach, or in the interior of hilly islands. Besides, northern Siberian rivers transport relatively little mud.[145]

30. Yedomas and Loess, Multi-Continental, Frozen Muck, and -150°F. The mud burial theory does not explain the relationship of mammoths with yedomas and loess, why these peculiar events occurred over such wide areas on two continents, where so much muck originated, why it contains buried forests, or what caused the rapid drop in temperature to -150°F.

31. Elevated Burials. Mud burials, especially those caused by mudslides, would not explain why mammoth and rhinoceros carcasses are sometimes found on the highest levels of generally flat, low plateaus. Mud moves very slowly, if at all, on flat, low plateaus. Rhinoceroses do not live far above the level of rivers or oceans.

32. Rock Ice. Burial in mud that later froze would produce type 1 ice, not type 3 ice.

33. Sudden Freezing. The coldest a mud flow could be is 32°F. Presumably, the air would be even warmer than 32°F. If mud, a good insulator, suddenly buried the Berezovka mammoth, the contents of its stomach would stay warm for too long. It would take about 20 times too long for its stomach to cool enough to stop the destructive action of the acids and enzymes on the vegetable matter. In other words, burial in even cold, flowing mud could not freeze a mammoth rapidly enough. Even if the atmospheric temperature dropped to -200°F after the mammoth was buried, the freezing would not be rapid enough to overcome the insulating effect of the mud.

34. Dirty Lungs. One researcher used the mud burial theory to explain why Dima had silt, clay, and small particles of gravel throughout his respiratory and digestive tract.[146] While these particles might enter the upper digestive tract, they would not enter the lungs and the lower digestive tract. Such particles would need to be in the air for several hours, as would occur during sustained high winds.

35. Animal Mixes. Many animals, such as beavers, marmots, voles, and squirrels, whose bones lie alongside those of the mammoth, do not create enough ground pressure to sink into mud.

36. Upright. The upright Berezovka mammoth apparently suffocated. Burial in a mudslide might explain the suffocation, but it would not explain the upright posture. Becoming stuck in shallow mud might explain the upright posture, but it would not explain the suffocation. The Benkendorf mammoth and others were also upright. (See Table 2 on page 105.)

37. Vertical Compression. Burial in a typical mud flow would not flatten Dima or produce the severe vertical compression found in Berezovka.

38. Other. Elephants rarely become stuck in mud. This is because their feet expand as weight is placed on them, and narrow as they are lifted. In northern Siberia only a thin layer of soil thaws in the summer.

39. Other. A large animal trapped in mud would probably live for hours, if not days. Therefore, food should not be preserved in its mouth and digestive tract, as occurred for a rhinoceros and several mammoths.

40. Other. Large animals buried in mud flows should frequently show marks of scavengers on the top parts of their body where mud had not yet reached. No known report has described such a pattern.

41. Other. Rhinoceroses do not migrate as this theory presupposes.

Relating to the River Transport Theory

42. Away From Rivers, Yedomas and Loess, Multi-Continental, Frozen Muck, -150°F, Large Animals, and Vertical Compression. The river transport theory does not explain why frozen mammoths are not exclusively found along rivers, why there is a relationship between mammoths, yedomas, and loess, why these peculiar events occurred over such wide areas on two continents, where so much muck originated, why it contains buried forests, why the temperature suddenly dropped to -150°F, why primarily the larger animals were frozen and preserved, or what caused the vertical compression found in Dima and Berezovka.

43. Elevated Burials. Rivers would not deposit large carcasses on the higher levels of plateaus. A few mammoths are found 1,000 feet above the nearest rivers.[147]

44. Rock Ice. With the river transport theory, one would expect to find type 1 ice, not type 3 ice.

45. Dirty Lungs. Drowning in a local flood might cause silt and clay to enter Dima's lungs, but it would not explain the gravel in his lungs. Nor would drowning distribute these particles throughout his intestine.

46. Summer-Fall Deaths. How could so many animals, washed far north by rivers, get buried in hard, frozen muck? Bloating promotes floating. Even if flooding rivers buried mammoths under sediments that froze the following winter, their bodies would have experienced considerable decay after a summer or fall death. Besides, river flooding usually occurs in the spring, not late summer or fall, and rivers do not deposit muck. The organic component in muck would separate and float to the surface of a river.

47. Upright. Mammoths, transported by rivers, would not be deposited upright, as some were.

48. Other. No fossils of water animals have been reported in deposits containing frozen mammoths.[148]

49. Other. The teeth and tusks of the mammoths found south of Siberia differ considerably from those in Siberia. Therefore, the many northward flowing rivers did not transport southern mammoths during floods.

50. Other. Cold Siberian and Alaskan rivers would minimize the buildup of gas in a decaying carcass. This is why "bodies ordinarily do not float in very cold water."[149] Even if these remains floated for hundreds of miles, why were some found along very short rivers flowing directly into the Arctic Ocean?[150] Why was their long hair not worn off? Why are the mammoths found on the New Siberian Islands in the Arctic Ocean, more than 150 miles from the mainland? Their bones do not show the wear associated with transport or water erosion. If an unusually strong river carried the floating carcasses to these islands, the carcasses should have been found only along beaches. Instead, remains are found in the interior of islands, the largest of which is 150 miles long and 75 miles wide.[151]

51. Other. Parts of six frozen mammoths have also been found in Alaska where rivers do not originate in warm climates.

52. Other. Elephants are, and presumably mammoths were, excellent swimmers.

Relating to the Extinction-by-Man Theory

53. Abundant Food. There is little precedent for believing that man will push any animal population into a harsh environment having little food. Only Dima, a baby, appeared underfed. Most frozen mammoths, complete enough to evaluate, were well fed.

54. Yedomas and Loess, -150°F, Large Animals, Upright, and Vertical Compression. The extinction-by-man theory does not explain the relationship of mammoths with yedomas and loess, the sudden drop in temperature to -150°F, why primarily the larger animals were frozen and preserved, why so many mammoth bodies and skeletons were upright, or what caused the vertical compression found in Dima and Berezovka.

55. Elevated Burials. Even if man pushed these animals north into Siberia and Alaska, why would a disproportionate number be buried on the higher elevations of generally flat plateaus?

56. Rock Ice. With this theory, one would expect type 1 or 2 ice, not type 3 ice.

57. Frozen Muck. If man killed the mammoths, how were they and even forests buried in such widespread layers of frozen muck? Where did the muck come from?

58. Suffocation. If humans killed mammoths and rhinoceroses, why did at least five suffocate?

59. Dirty Lungs. Being hunted by man would not explain silt, clay, and small gravel particles in Dima's respiratory and digestive tracts.

60. Animal Mixes. Mammoth remains are often found near bones of animals that man would probably not have simultaneously pursued. Examples include horses, tigers, badgers, bears, wolves, hyenas, lynxes, etc. Nor is it likely that man would have pursued the slow, lumbering rhinoceros. Why would animals that man normally does not hunt die while man was killing mammoths? Why would a hunted horse be frozen?[152] Today, wild horses live in only mild climates.

61. Other. It is doubtful that primitive man could have exterminated the formidable mammoth in a remote, frigid, and vast region. Yes, man almost exterminated the less imposing buffalo—with guns in a temperate climate. Apparently, no human remains (even bones or teeth), no weapons (arrows or knives), and no other artifacts (pottery, utensils, or art) have been found alongside frozen mammoth and rhinoceros remains. Nor are the distinctive marks of man's ax or knife clearly seen on mammoth bones and ivory. If man exterminated the mammoths, some signs of human activity should occasionally be found among the millions of mammoth remains. When humans try to capture or kill large animals, they often dig deep pits. This would be extremely difficult in permafrost.

62. Other. Humans in today's heavily populated areas might try to exterminate mammoths and rhinoceroses. However, it is difficult to imagine man doing this thousands of years ago in the barren and sparsely populated regions of northern Siberia.

63. Other. Humans do not travel to desolate regions for food, especially food difficult to preserve and transport. Even if man occupied these regions, his motive for killing mammoths and rhinoceroses would not have been for food, since less dangerous and more desirable game was available. In Africa today, man has no great desire for

elephant or rhinoceros meat. In fact, before the day of the rifle and the ivory market, man generally avoided these huge animals. If man killed the mammoth for its ivory tusks, why did he kill the rhinoceros? Why were so many valuable tusks left behind?

64. Other. The mammoth remains found south of Siberia differ considerably from those in Siberia, especially the teeth and tusks. This implies that the mammoths did not migrate northward for their summer feeding and were not driven there by man.

Relating to the Bering Barrier Theory

65. Abundant Food and Warm Climate. This theory describes events during the peak of the last ice age when northern Siberia and Alaska would not have had abundant vegetation and a warm climate. Many animal and plant species found there live only in temperate climates today; mammoths are not Arctic animals. The more complete mammoths appeared well fed.

66. Yedomas and Loess. Soils washed down on top of ice would show stratification and some sorting of a wide range of particle sizes. Loess, in contrast, consists of very fine and uniform dirt particles. Besides, the ice in yedomas is mixed in with the loesslike soil.

67. Multi-Continental, -150°F, and Vertical Compression. The Bering barrier theory does not explain why these peculiar events occurred over such wide areas on two continents, the rapid drop in temperature to -150°F, or the vertical compression found in Dima and Berezovka.

68. Rock Ice. This theory might explain buried layers of glacial ice (type 2 ice), but it does not explain rock ice (type 3 ice).

69. Frozen Muck. This theory says that mammoths were buried in a gigantic snow storm. Actually they are buried primarily in frozen muck. Where does so much muck come from, and why does it contain buried forests?

70. Suffocation. Animals caught in a sudden snow storm would die of starvation and exposure, not suffocation.

71. Dirty Lungs. Sudden snow falls would remove dust from the air and bury other dirt particles under a blanket of snow. How then did silt, clay, and gravel enter Dima's digestive and respiratory tracts?

72. Large Animals. Sudden snow storms would preferentially entomb and freeze the smaller animals.

73. Other. The prevailing winds at the Bering Strait blow to the east. Therefore, one would expect that storms from the Pacific would dump snow primarily on Alaska, not Siberia. However, 90 percent of the frozen mammoths and all the frozen rhinoceroses are in Siberia.

Relating to the Shifting Crust Theory

74. Yedomas and Loess, -150°F, Large Animals, and Vertical Compression. The shifting crust theory does not explain the relationship of mammoths with yedomas and loess, why the temperature dropped suddenly to -150°F, why primarily the larger, harder to freeze, animals were frozen and preserved, or why vertical compression was found in Dima and Berezovka.

75. Rock Ice. This theory might explain type 2 ice near mammoths, but not type 3 ice.

76. Frozen Muck. If a gigantic snow storm buried many mammoths, why are almost all carcasses encased in frozen muck? Where does so much muck come from, and why does it contain buried forests?

77. Summer-Fall Death. Shifting the earth's crust would produce ruptures in both northern and southern hemispheres. The volcanic activity and storms should have been equally intense in both hemispheres. However, since this catastrophic event probably occurred in July or August, summer storms should have occurred in the northern hemisphere and winter storms in the southern hemisphere. Therefore, we should find parts of frozen carcasses in the southern hemisphere, not the northern hemisphere.

78. Other. Frozen remains of mammoths and other animals were found in northern Alaska. If the crust shifted (as Hapgood describes) with the Hudson Bay moving from the North Pole to its present position, Alaska would not move northward. Why then would northern Alaska suddenly shift from a temperate to an Arctic climate?

79. Other. The places where the earth's crust ruptured should be visible today. They are not. There is no independent evidence that Siberia shifted north and Canada shifted south. Furthermore, what would cause such a shift?

Relating to the Meteorite Theory

80. Abundant Food. This theory places the mammoth extinction at the sudden end of the ice age. However, to support such large herds and many other animals, vegetation must have been plentiful in Alaska and Siberia. Temperate vegetation would not have been abundant in those Arctic regions during the last ice age.

81. Yedomas and Loess, Frozen Muck, Suffocation, and Vertical Compression. The meteorite theory does not explain the relationship of mammoths with yedomas and loess, where so much muck originated, why it contains buried forests, why some of these huge animals appear to have suffocated, or what caused the vertical compression found in Dima and Berezovka.

82. Rock Ice. The meteorite theory might explain why type 1 ice melted and allowed mammoths to sink into icy bogs; it would not produce type 3 ice.

83. -150°F. This theory tries to explain a sudden warming trend. It does not explain why the temperature went *suddenly* in the other direction to -150°F.

84. Animal Mixes. A sudden warming at the end of the ice age might have caused some animals "to blunder to their deaths in the icy bogs."[153] It would not explain why this happened to so many different types of animals—animals that are quick, surefooted, or highly mobile (such as birds).

85. Other. The jump in atmospheric temperature required to rapidly melt the permafrost to a depth necessary to bury a 13-foot-tall mammoth would have also incinerated their bodies.

Final Thoughts

Students of the earth sciences are frequently discouraged from considering alternative explanations such as we have with the "frozen mammoths." Too often, students are told what to think, rather than taught how to think. Why is this? Permit one person's opinion.

Before the birth of the field of geology in the early 1800s, a common explanation for major geological features was a global flood. Such explanations were repugnant to many early geologists for three reasons. First, many geologists were opposed to the Bible which spoke of a global flood. Second, flood explanations seemed (and sometimes were) scientifically simplistic. Finally, a global flood is an unrepeatable catastrophe which cannot be scientifically studied directly.

Rather than appear closeminded by disallowing flood explanations, a more subtle approach was simply to disallow global catastrophes. This solved all three objections above and was more justifiable since experimental repeatability is the foundation of modern science. By definition, catastrophes are rarely repeated. Besides, large scale events are difficult to reproduce in the laboratory. The flaw in this exclusionary logic is that catastrophes involve many phenomena and leave widespread wreckage and strange details that require an explanation. (You have seen many relating to the frozen mammoths.) Most of these phenomena are testable and repeatable on a smaller scale. Some are so well tested and understood that mathematical calculations and computer simulations can be easily made at any scale.

How were catastrophes disallowed? The small but growing number of academic chairs in geology were primarily given to those who supported the anti-catastrophe principle. These professors did not advance students who espoused catastrophes. The rare advocate of a global flood was branded a "Biblical literalist" or "fuzzy thinker." Geology professors also influenced, through the peer review process, papers that could be published. Textbooks soon reflected their orthodoxy, so few students became "fuzzy thinkers." This practice continues to this day, since a major criterion for selecting professors is the number of their publications.

This anti-catastrophe principle is called **uniformitarianism**. For more than 150 years, it was summarized by the phrase, "The present is the key to the past." In other words, only processes observable today and acting at present rates can be used to explain past events. Because some catastrophes, such as large impacts from outer space, are now fashionable, many now recognize uniformitarianism as a poor and arbitrary assumption.[154]

However, this presents a dilemma. Since uniformitarianism is foundational to geology, should the entire field be reexamined? Uniformitarianism was intended to banish the global flood. Will the death of uniformitarianism allow scholarly consideration of evidence that implies a global flood? Most geologists are repulsed by such a possibility. They either deny that a problem exists or hope it will go away. Some want to redefine uniformitarianism to mean that only the laws of physics observed today can be used to explain past geological events—an obvious principle of science long before uniformitarianism was sanctified. The problem will not go away, but will fester even more until enough geologists recognize that catastrophes were not the problem. Early geologists simply, and arbitrarily, wanted to exclude a global flood, not catastrophes in general.

Ruling out catastrophes in general (and the flood more specifically), even before all facts are in, has stifled much study and understanding. The "frozen mammoth issue" is only one of many examples. Disallowing catastrophes has also developed a mind-set where strange observations are ignored, or considered unbelievable, rather than viewed as important **diagnostic details** worthy of testing and consideration. Those who express disbelief at some diagnostic details associated with the frozen mammoths may have adopted this mind-set.

Table 5 on page 117 is a broad target for anyone who wishes to grapple with ideas. Notice that it invites, not suppresses, critiques. All theories should be subject to critique and refinement. We can focus on the more likely theories, on any misunderstandings or disagreements, on the diagnostic details that need further verification, and on the expensive process of testing predictions. With the predictions of various theories clearly enumerated, field work becomes more exciting and productive. Most importantly, those who follow us will have something to build upon. They will not be told what to think.

References and Notes

1. Some people split mammoths into various species, such as *Mammuthus primigenius* (the woolly mammoth) and *Mammuthus columbi* (the Columbian mammoth). Members of a species can produce fertile offspring with others in the species, but not with another species. Obviously, no one can say that the woolly mammoth could not produce fertile offspring with the Columbian mammoth or even that the Columbian mammoth did not have a hairy coat similar to the woolly mammoth. Their differences, if any, were slight. Artificially "creating" new species without solid medical or experimental justification seems unwise.

African and Asian elephants are officially different species, and yet on at least one occasion they interbred successfully. If they had occupied the same territory in the wild, no doubt other hybrids would have been born. (Unfortunately, the one known offspring died ten days after birth. This has no bearing on the fact that African and Asian elephants should not be designated as two species.)

● According to *Webster's Third New International Dictionary* (Unabridged; 1964 edition, p. 1369), the word "mammoth" comes from "mamma," which means "earth" to the Yakut people of northeastern Siberia. "Mammoth" also relates to the word "behemoth" used in Job 40:15 to describe a huge animal. Supporting this view are:

♦ Henry H. Howorth, *The Mammoth and the Flood* (London: Samson Low, Marston, Searle, and Rivington, 1887), pp. 2-4, 74-75.

♦ A. E. Nordenskiold, *The Voyage of the Vega Round Asia and Europe*, translated from Swedish by Alexander Leslie (New York: Macmillan and Co., 1882), p. 302.

♦ Willy Ley, *Exotic Zoology* (New York: The Viking Press, 1959), p. 152.

2. E. Ysbrants Ides, *Three Years* [of] *Land Travels from Moscow Over-Land to China* (London: W. Freeman, 1706) English Edition, p. 26. In 1692, Czar Peter the Great directed Ides to explore the vast eastern region of Russia. When Ides returned, he reported that mammoths were found, *sometimes whole*, "among the hills," along four named rivers and the Arctic coast. He described one person's specific discovery of a head "somewhat red, as tho' they were tinctured with blood" and a forefoot, cut from a leg, as big around as a man's waist.

● One of the earliest descriptions, written in 1724, was authenticated by Dr. Daniel Gottlieb Messerschmidt, a naturalist sent to Siberia by Czar Peter the Great to inquire, among other things, into the frozen mammoth stories. Although Messerschmidt did not personally see the frozen partial remains, he had an eye witness, Michael Wolochowicz, describe the find in a short report. The report's credibility is enhanced by its similarity with many thoroughly verified accounts by scientific teams in subsequent years. [See John Breyne, "Observations on the Mammoth's Bones and Teeth Found in Siberia," *Philosophical Transactions of the Royal Society of London*, Vol. 40, January-June 1737, pp. 125-138.]

3. E. W. Pfizenmayer, *Siberian Man and Mammoth*, translated from the German by Muriel D. Simpson (London: Black & Son Limited, 1939), p. 4.

4. Howorth, p. 76.

5. Basset Digby, *The Mammoth* (New York: D. Appleton and Company, 1926), pp. 17-18, 79.

6. Most recently, five expeditions occurred in the 1970s, two in the 1980s, and one in 1990.

7. Ian Redmond, *Elephant* (New York: Alfred A. Knopf, 1993), p. 10.

8. Dima may have suffered from one of the many problems common to baby elephants; mortality among baby elephants is very high. During their first year of life, the mortality rate varies between 5 and 36 percent. [See S. Keith Eltringham, *Elephants*, editor Jeheskel Shoshani (Emmaus, Pennsylvania: Rodale Press, 1992), p. 102.]

9. Valentina V. Ukraintseva, *Vegetation Cover and Environment of the "Mammoth Epoch" in Siberia* (Hot Springs, South Dakota: the Mammoth Site of Hot Springs, 1993), pp. 12-13.

● N. A. Dubrovo et al., "Upper Quaternary Deposits and Paleogeography of the Region Inhabited by the Young Kirgilyakh Mammoth," *International Geology Review*, Vol. 24, No. 6, June 1982, p. 630.

10. R. Dale Guthrie, *Frozen Fauna of the Mammoth Steppe* (Chicago: the University of Chicago Press, 1990), pp. 9, 13.

11. Guthrie, pp. 9, 13.

12. Ukraintseva, pp. 80-98.

● Guthrie, pp. 10, 30-32.

13. *Science News Letter*, Vol. 55, 25 June 1949, p. 403.

14. John Massey Stewart, "Frozen Mammoths from Siberia Bring the Ice Ages to Vivid Life," *Smithsonian*, 1977, p. 67.

15. N. K. Vereshchagin and G. F. Baryshnikov, "Paleoecology of the Mammoth Fauna in the Eurasian Arctic," *Paleoecology of Beringia*, editors David M. Hopkins et al. (New York: Academic Press, 1982), p. 276.

16. Harold E. Anthony, "Nature's Deep Freeze," *Natural History*, September 1949, p. 300.

17. Michael R. Zimmerman and Richard H. Tedford, "Histologic Structures Preserved for 21,300 Years," *Science*, Vol. 194, 8 October 1976, pp. 183-184.

18. Stewart, p. 68.

19. Charles H. Eden, *Frozen Asia* (New York: Pott, Young & Co., 1879), pp. 97-100.

20. A. G. Maddren, "Smithsonian Exploration in Alaska in 1904 in Search of Mammoth and Other Fossil Remains," *Smithsonian Miscellaneous Collections*, Vol. 49, 1905, p. 101.

21. W. H. Dall, "Presentation to the Biological Society of Washington, 247 Meeting," *Science*, 8 November 1895, pp. 635-636.

22. N. A. Transehe, "The Siberian Sea Road: The Work of the Russian Hydrographical Expedition to the Arctic 1910-1915," *The Geographical Review*, Vol. 15, 1925, p. 392.

23. Adrian Lister and Paul Bahn, *Mammoths* (New York: Macmillan, 1994), p. 46.

24. A. P. Vinogradov et al., "Radiocarbon Dating in the Vernadsky Institute I-IV," *Radiocarbon*, Vol. 8, 1966, pp. 320-321.

25. Robert M. Thorson and R. Dale Guthrie, "Stratigraphy of the Colorado Creek Mammoth Locality, Alaska," *Quaternary Research*, Vol. 37, No. 2, March 1992, pp. 214-228.

26. Howorth, pp. 50-54.

27. Ley, p. 169.

28. I. P. Tolmachoff, *The Carcasses of the Mammoth and Rhinoceros Found in the Frozen Ground of Siberia* (Philadelphia: The American Philosophical Society, 1929), p. 71.

29. Maddren, p. 60.

30. H. Neuville, "On the Extinction of the Mammoth," *Annual Report Smithsonian Institution*, 1919, p. 332.

31. Nikolai K. Vereshchagin and Alexei N. Tikhonov, *The Exterior of Mammoths* (Yakutsk, Siberia: Merelotovedenia Institute, 1990), p. 18. (Russian)

- Pfizenmayer, p. 162.

- Hair on the rhinoceros leg also hung to the feet. (See Eden, pp. 99-100.)

32. Hans Krause, *The Mammoth—In Ice and Snow?: Cold-Adaptation of Woolly Mammoth: Fact or Fiction?* (Stuttgart: self-published, 1978), p. 53.

33. Neuville, pp. 327-338.

34. Krause, pp. 51-52.

35. The mammoth is closely related to the African and Indian elephants. A comparative study of 350 mitochondrial DNA nucleotides from each of the three shows that the "woolly" mammoth, Dima, differed from both African and Indian elephants by only four or five nucleotides. [See Jeremy Cherfas, "If Not a Dinosaur, a Mammoth?", *Science*, Vol. 253, 20 September 1991, p. 1356.] A recent Japanese study extracted longer strands of nuclear DNA which showed the mammoth to be more closely related to the Indian elephant than the African elephant.

36. Ralph S. Palmer, "Elephant," *The World Book Encyclopedia*, Vol. 6 (U.S.A.: Field Enterprises Educational Corporation, 1973), pp. 178, 178d.

37. Daphne Sheldrick, *Elephants*, editor Jeheskel Shoshani, (Emmaus, Pennsylvania: Rodale Press, 1992), p. 115.

38. Harold Lamb, *Hannibal: One Man Against Rome* (New York: Doubleday & Company, Inc., 1958), pp. 83-108.

39. Redmond, p. 19.

40. Redmond, p. 27.

41. Redmond, p. 42.

42. Digby, p. 151.

43. Stewart, p. 68.

44. Guthrie, p. 84.

45. Anonymous, "Much About Muck," *Pursuit*, Vol. 2, October 1969, pp. 68-69.

46. Lindsey Williams, *The Energy Non-Crisis*, 2nd edition (Kasilof, Alaska: Worth Publishing Co., 1980), p. 54.

47. Anonymous, "Much About Muck," p. 69.

48. Lister and Bahn, p. 47.

49. R. Lydekker, "Mammoth Ivory," *Annual Report of the Board of Regents of the Smithsonian Institution for the Year Ending June 30, 1899* (Washington, D.C.: Government Printing Office, 1901), pp. 361-366.

50. Vera Rich, "Gone to the Dogs," *Nature*, Vol. 301, 24 February 1983, p. 647.

51. Two very similar accounts describe this discovery. [See Digby, pp. 97-103, or William T. Hornaday, *Tales from Nature's Wonderlands* (New York: Charles Scribner's Sons, 1926), pp. 32-38.] The latter was translated from a Russian report held in the American Museum of Natural History.

52. Ages of mammoths, elephants, and mastodons can be approximated by counting the rings in their tusks. This method was first used on Berezovka. [See Vereshchagin and Tikhonov, p. 17.] Some scientists question whether one ring always equates to one year.

53. Peter the Great, Russia's most famous and influential czar, founded this museum and initiated formal mammoth studies. His strong interest in science, and mammoths in particular, led in 1714 to the systematic study and exhibition in St. Petersburg of unusual and exotic animals.

54. Herz, pp. 617, 620, 622.

- Digby, pp. 123, 126, 131.

55. Personal communication from Alexei N. Tikhonov, zoologist and mammoth specialist at the Zoological Institute, Russian Academy of Sciences, St. Petersburg, 12 November 1993.

56. Vereshchagin and Tikhonov, p. 17.

57. Herz, p. 623.

- Digby, p. 182.

58. Jeheskel Shoshani, "Anatomy and Physiology," *Elephants*, pp. 79, 80, 97.

59. Some readers may want to consider other explanations for the crushed leg bone such as impacts or pinching forces perpendicular to the crushed bone. The flesh surrounding the bone was not visibly mangled, and the leg was still in its shoulder socket. Axial compression might crush a short, weak beam. However, to crush a long beam requires considerable lateral support.

60. Tolmachoff, p. 35.

61. Tolmachoff, p. 57.

62. Guthrie, p. 13.

63. *Proceedings of the Berlin Academy*, 1846, p. 223, cited by Howorth, p. 184.

64. Leopold Von Schrenck, *Memoirs of St. Petersburg Academy*, Vol. 17, pp. 48-49, cited by Howorth, p. 185.

65. William R. Farrand, "Frozen Mammoths and Modern Geology," *Science*, 17 March 1961, p. 734.

66. Ivan T. Sanderson, "Riddle of the Frozen Giants," *Saturday Evening Post*, 16 January 1960, p. 82.

67. A. S. W., *Nature*, Vol. 68, 30 July 1903, p. 297.

68. Lister & Bahn, p. 74.

69. Charles H. Hapgood, *The Path of the Pole* (Philadelphia: Chilton Book Company, 1970), p. 267.

70. Joseph C. Dillow, *The Waters Above: Earth's Pre-Flood Vapor Canopy* (Chicago: Moody Press, 1981, pp. 371-377.

71. One questionable report is contained in a brochure distributed at an exhibit of some mammoth remains that toured the United States in 1992. The brochure stated, "Portions of a mammoth thousands of years old that was discovered in permafrost were defrosted, cooked and served at a banquet honoring scientists." Hapgood (*The Path of the Pole*, p. 261) made a similar statement but mentioned the name of the man who claimed to have eaten mammoth steak in Moscow.

72. Lydekker, p. 363.

73. O. F. Herz, "Frozen Mammoth in Siberia," *Annual Report of the Board of Regents of the Smithsonian Institution* (Washington, D.C.: Government Printing Office, 1904), p. 621.

74. Rich, p. 647.

75. Charles Lyell, *Principles of Geology* (New York: Verlag Von J. Cramer, reprint edition, 1970), p. 97.

76. Guthrie, pp. 9, 11, 12, 20.

 • Georges Cuvier, *Essay on the Theory of the Earth*, Reprint Edition (New York: Arno Press, 1978), pp. 274-276.

77. Krause, p. 88.

78. S. Keith Eltringham, "Ecology and Behavior," *Elephants*, editor Jeheskel Shoshani, p. 126.

79. Digby, 171.

80. Henryk Kubiak, "Morphological Characters of the Mammoth," *Paleoecology of Beringia*, editors David M. Hopkins et al. (New York: Academic Press, 1982), p. 282.

81. Dillow, pp. 380-381.

82. Dillow, pp. 383-396.

83. When an animal dies and decay begins, the decomposition of each cell's amino acids produces water that ruins the meat's taste. The water expands as it freezes. If a cell freezes after enough water has accumulated, the expansion will tear the cell, showing that a certain amount of time elapsed between death and freezing. This characteristic was absent in the Berezovka mammoth, and the meat was edible—at least for dogs. Apparently, these mammoths froze before decay set in.

84. Sanderson, 1960, pp. 82, 83.

85. Pfizenmayer, pp. 105-106.

86. Ibid., pp. 105-105.

87. Maddren, p. 60.

88. Pfizenmayer, p. 176.

89. Herz, pp. 613, 615.

90. Howorth, p. 96.

91. Maddren, p. 87.

92. L. S. Quackenbush, "Notes on Alaskan Mammoth Expeditions of 1907 and 1908," *Bulletin American Museum of Natural History*, Vol. 26, pp. 87-127.

 • Tolmachoff, pp. 51-55.

 • Herz, pp. 615, 616, 618.

93. Some have called it "fossil ice." Pfizenmayer, who participated in the Berezovka excavation, called it "diluvial ice." The term "diluvial," refers to the biblical flood (deluge). A common belief among Russian Siberians was that the frozen mammoths were killed and buried during the biblical flood, after which the Siberian weather became much colder. For these reasons, the term "diluvial" is often associated with buried animals and ice in Siberia. Even today, geologists use the word "diluvium" to refer to glacial deposits believed in the 1800s to be laid down during Noah's flood.

 Baron Eduard Toll, in the late 1800s, may have been the first to write about this strange ice. He called it "stone ice." Toll and his three companions disappeared in 1903 while on a mammoth expedition to Bennett Island, one of the Arctic islands off the north coast of Siberia. A rescue attempt was unsuccessful. Toll's diary, found on Bennett Island three years later, reported that another frozen mammoth had been discovered (not listed in Table 2). Few details were given. The diary also mentioned that the explorers had just killed their remaining dogs for food. (See, for example, Digby, p. 147.)

94. Herz, p. 618.

95. Quackenbush, p. 101.

96. W. H. Dall, "Extract from a Report to C. P. Patterson, Supt. Coast and Geodetic Survey," *American Journal of Science*, Vol. 21, 1881, p. 107.

97. A. S. W., p. 297.

98. Dubrovo et al., pp. 630, 632.

99. One of the earliest reports of these thick layers of buried ice came from the expedition led by Lieutenant J. C. Cantwell. He concluded that, *"The formation of the remarkable ice-cliffs in the lower country* [of northern Alaska] *is, however, a geological nut which the writer admits his inability to crack."* "Ice-Cliffs on the Kowak River," *National Geographic Magazine*, 1896, pp. 345-346. See also J. C. Cantwell, "Exploration of the Kowak River," *Science*, Vol. 4, 19 December 1884, pp. 551-554.

 Some, but not all, of these reported ice layers may be the vertical faces of ice wedges. When found along coast lines, the two are easily confused. As the Arctic winter approaches and temperatures drop, the ground contracts. Sometimes the ground splits open with a loud crack. Water later fills the vertical crack, freezes, and forms an ice wedge. Years later this fracture, which is a vertical plane of weakness, might be exposed along a coast line by the undercutting of waves. Viewed from a boat far from the coast, the side of the ice wedge might seem to be the edge of a horizontal layer of ice. By tracing the ice inland for thousands of feet, the "ice wedge explanation" can be rejected. This was done by Dall (p. 107) and Maddren (pp. 15-117).

100. Dall, p. 107.

- Maddren, p. 104.

- Cantwell, "Ice-Cliffs," p. 345.

101. Cantwell, "Ice-Cliffs," p. 346.

102. Pfizenmayer, pp. 89-90.

103. Herz, p. 618.

104. Stewart, p. 68.

105. *"The yedoma deposits could only have been formed by cryogenous-eolian* [cold and windy] *processes."* V. K. Ryabchun, "More about the Genesis of the Yedoma Deposit," *The Second International Conference on Permafrost: USSR Contribution, 13-28 July 1973* (Washington, D.C.: National Academy of Sciences, 1978), pp. 816-817.

106. Adolph Erman, *Travels in Siberia*, Vol. 1 (London: Longman, Brown, Green, and Longmans, 1848), pp. 379-380.

107. Nordenskiold, pp. 26, 311.

108. Ryabchun, p. 817.

- S. V. Tomirdiaro, "Evolution of Lowland Landscapes in Northeastern Asia During Late Quaternary Time," *Paleoecology of Beringia,* editors David M. Hopkins et al. (New York: Academic Press, 1982), pp. 29-37.

109. Paul A. Colinvaux, "Land Bridge of Duvanny Yar," *Nature*, Vol. 314, 18 April 1985, p. 581.

110. A. I. Popov, "Origin of the Deposits of the Yedoma Suite on the Primor'Ye Floodplain of Northern Yakutia," *The Second International Conference on Permafrost: USSR Contribution*, 13-28 July 1973 (Washington, D.C.: National Academy of Sciences, 1978), p. 825.

111. S. V. Tomirdiaro, "Cryogenous-Eolian Genesis of Yedoma Deposits," *The Second International Conference on Permafrost: USSR Contribution*, 13-28 July 1973 (Washington, D.C.: National Academy of Sciences, 1978), pp. 817-818.

- Colinvaux, p. 582.

- Tomirdiaro, "Evolution of Lowlands," p. 22-37.

- Troy L. Péwé, *Origin and Character of Loesslike Silt in Unglaciated South-Central Yakutia, Siberia, U.S.S.R.*, Geological Survey Professional Paper 1262 (Washington, D.C.: United States Government Printing Office, 1983).

112. John B. Penniston, "Note on the Origin of Loess," *Popular Astronomy*, Vol. 39, 1931, pp. 429-430, and "Additional Note on the Origin of Loess," *Popular Astronomy*, Vol. 51, 1943, pp. 170-172.

113. Richard Foster Flint and Brian J. Skinner, *Physical Geology* (New York: John Wiley & Sons, Inc., 1974), p. 190.

114. Don DeNevi, *Earthquakes* (Millbrae, California: Celestial Arts, 1977), pp. 56, 67.

115. Digby, p. 107.

116. Tolmachoff, p. 51.

- *"Experience has also shown that more* [and better mammoth bones] *are found in elevations situated near higher hills than along the low coast or on the flat tundra."* Ferdinand von Wrangell, *Narrative of an Expedition to the Polar Sea, in the Years 1820, 1821, 1822, & 1823*, 2nd edition (London: James Madden and Co., 1884), p. 275.

117. Sanderson, 1960, p. 82.

- Tolmachoff, pp. 51, 59.

118. Tolmachoff, p. 48.

- Tolmachoff, pp. 49, 62.

119. Stewart, "Frozen Mammoths from Siberia," p. 68.

120. John Massey Stewart, "A Baby That Died 40,000 Years Ago Reveals a Story," *Smithsonian*, 1978, p. 126.

121. Hapgood, p. 268.

122. Tolmachoff, pp. 26, 56-57.

- Howorth, pp. 61, 82-83, 158, 185.

123. Y. N. Popov, "New Finds of Pleistocene Animals in Northern USSR," *Nature*, No. 3, 1948, p. 76. This is the former Soviet (not the British) journal *Nature*.

124. M. Huc, *Recollections of a Journey through Tartary, Thibet, and China, During the Years 1844, 1845, and 1846*. Vol. 2 (New York: D. Appleton & Company, 1852), pp. 130-131.

- Charles Lyell, *Principles of Geology*, 11th edition, Vol. 1 (New York: D. Appleton and Company, 1872), p. 188. Some earlier editions did not contain this report.

125. Streams, rivers, lakes, and oceans freeze from the top down, because water reaches its maximum density at 39°F—seven degrees *above* its normal freezing point. As cold air further lowers the water's temperature, water defies the behavior of most liquids and expands. This less dense water "floats" on top of the denser water. Eventually it freezes into ice, which is even less dense.

We are fortunate that water behaves in this unusual way. If water continued to contract as it became colder and froze (as most substances do), ice would sink. Bodies of water would freeze from the bottom up. The overlying liquid water would insulate the ice and delay its melting during the summer. Each winter more ice would collect at the bottom of a lake, stream, or ocean. This would first occur at polar latitudes, but over the years would spread toward the equator as surface ice reflected more of the sun's rays back into space, cooling the earth. Sea life would eventually cease. Evaporation and rain would diminish, turning the land into a cold, lifeless desert.

126. For example, one might ask, "What predictions can the theory of organic evolution make? Few, if any, although Darwin predicted that the gaps in the fossil record would soon be filled. Obviously, he was wrong. Evolutionists today are quick to explain why they make no predictions. Evolution happens over geologic time—*so slowly that we cannot see it* on a human time scale, even after breeding thousands of generations. When asked why gaps exist throughout the fossil record, their typical answer is that evolution happens *so rapidly that we cannot capture it* as a fossil. When asked why we cannot see a beneficial mutation that produces increased complexity and viability, the answer is again an appeal to geologic time. **Unwillingness to make predictions shows a lack of scientific rigor and confidence. Successful predictions are a clear test of the fruitfulness and strength of a scientific theory.**

127. Confusion exists when temperatures are given for outer space. For example, an atmospheric physicist might say the temperature two hundred miles above the earth's surface is 2,000°F. However, a mercury thermometer, shielded from the direct rays of the sun, might register a drastically colder -150°F. The confusion results from different definitions of temperature and different ways of transferring heat.

The physicist defines temperature as the average kinetic energy of gas molecules. Since molecules in the extreme upper atmosphere are heated by the sun's direct rays, they travel very fast and register a very high temperature. Typically they travel several miles before colliding with another molecule, so little slows them down. However, the air transfers little of its heat, because the air is so thin (only 1/100,000,000,000 as dense as that at sea level).

A thermometer two hundred miles above the earth's surface might read a frigid -150°F, because it *radiates* so much heat into far outer space, where the effective temperature is close to absolute zero (-460°F). A thermometer temporarily warmer than -150°F would radiate more heat into far outer space than it receives from the rare impact of fast air molecules. Consequently, its temperature would drop. Only when the thermometer's temperature drops to -150°F will the heat added by the fast gas molecules balance the heat lost by radiation. An astronaut without a heated space suit would "feel" the same temperature as the thermometer.

The temperature is even colder inside a packet of mineral ladened water that was suddenly expelled two hundred miles above the earth. A small fraction of the liquid will rapidly evaporate into the vacuum of outer space, cooling the liquid, just as perspiring cools your skin. Water's temperature drops 1°F for every thousandth of its volume

that evaporates. This is a strong effect, because the faster (or hotter) liquid molecules jump out of the liquid, expending much of the liquid's energy in overcoming the intermolecular attraction. The water would not freeze until it was below its normal freezing point because (a) the water circulates, and (b) the minerals in solution lower the freezing point just as antifreeze prevents your car's radiator fluid from freezing. Once frozen, evaporation would continue, although at a slower rate. Evaporation from a solid object (a process called sublimation) lowers the water's temperature even more. Consequently, this additional heat rejection mechanism (evaporation) would lower the water's temperature below that of the thermometer.

128. Tolmachoff, p. 64.

129. Charles Lyell, the most influential founder of modern geology, advocated this theory to explain some frozen mammoths. [See Charles Lyell, *Principles of Geology* (New York: Verlag Von J. Cramer, reprint edition, 1970), pp. 96-99.] Herz also used it to explain the Berezovka mammoth. [See Herz, p. 614.]

130. Tolmachoff, pp. 56, 57.

131. This theory was first proposed by Ides. Middendorff, Lyell, and Bunge also favored it in some instances. [See Tolmachoff, pp. viii-ix, 56.]

132. Tolmachoff, p. 66.

133. George M. Dawson, "Notes on the Occurrence of Mammoth-Remains in the Yukon District of Canada and in Alaska," *The Quarterly Journal of the Geological Society of London*, Vol. 50, 1894, pp. 1-9.

134. Hapgood, 1970, pp. 249-270.

- Charles H. Hapgood, "The Mystery of the Frozen Mammoths," *Coronet*, September 1960, pp. 71-78.

- Sanderson, 1960, p. 83.

135. Fred Hoyle, *Ice* (New York: The Continuum Publishing Company, 1981), pp. 159, 160.

136. Smaller particles have a much greater ratio of viscous-to-inertial forces acting on them. Thus, the liquid appears much more sticky and syruplike to smaller particles. Sudden movements of the droplet carry the smaller dirt particles with the liquid, while the larger particles, which have higher inertial forces, could be thrown out of the liquid.

137. Niels Reeh, "Was the Greenland Ice Sheet Thinner in the Late Wisconsinan Than Now?", *Nature*, Vol. 317, 31 October 1985, p. 797.

- R. M. Koerner and D. A. Fisher, "Discontinuous Flow, Ice Texture, and Dirt Content in the Basal Layers of the Devon Island Ice Cap," *Journal of Glaciology*, Vol. 23, No. 89, 1979, pp. 209-219.

138. P. A. Mayewski et al., "Changes in Atmospheric Circulation and Ocean Cover over the North Atlantic During the Last

41,000 Years," *Science*, Vol. 263, 25 March 1994, pp. 1747-1751.

139. Besides being salty, rock ice will contain carbon dioxide and many dissolved minerals, will have a crystallographic structure showing that it formed at very low pressures and temperatures, and will have large hydrogen and oxygen isotope anomalies. Large oxygen anomalies (a lower ratio of O^{18}/O^{16} than is found in ocean water) have already been reported at the bottom of ice cores on Devon Island in Arctic Canada. The same ice layer has a high silt content. [See Koerner and Fisher.] The bottom ice in some ice wedges in Siberia has already been found to be abnormally salty. [See Yu. K. Vasilchuk and V. T. Trofimov, "Cryohydro-chemical Peculiarities of Ice Wedge Polygon Complexes in the North of Western Siberia," *Permafrost: Fourth International Conference Proceedings* (Washington, D.C.: National Academy Press, July 17-22, 1983), pp. 1303-1308.]

140. Tolmachoff (pp. 51-55) reported that, "The uppermost position of mammoth-bearing deposits . . . cover the sediments of the Arctic transgression." This has caused some confusion in North America where "transgression" means the advance of the sea over the land. Such an advance might lay down sediments and fossils unconformably. To Europeans (and presumably the European-trained Tolmachoff) the term "transgression" simply means an unconformity—basically, dirt that is not layered. [See "transgression," in Robert L. Bates and Julia A. Jackson, editors, *Glossary of Geology*, 2nd edition (Falls Church, Virginia: American Geological Institute, 1980), p. 660.] In other words, the rocks under the mammoths are not stratified. Tolmachoff attributed this to glacial activity, but described nothing that is diagnostic of glacial activity.

141. Digby, p. 93.

142. Troy L. Péwé, *Quaternary Geology*, Geological Survey Professional Paper 835 (Washington, D.C.: United States Government Printing Office, 1975), pp. 41-42.

143. Troy L. Péwé, *Quaternary Stratigraphic Nomenclature in Unglaciated Central Alaska*, Geological Survey Professional Paper 862 (Washington, D.C.: United States Government Printing Office, 1975), p. 30.

144. Hoyle, p. 160.

145. Howorth, p. 182.

146. Guthrie, p. 17.

147. Tolmachoff, p. 52.

148. Tolmachoff, p. 52.

149. Hapgood, p. 258.

150. Howorth, p. 61.

151. Hapgood, 1970, p. 257.

152. Guthrie, pp. 30-32.

153. Hoyle, p. 160.

154. *"As is now increasingly acknowledged, however, Lyell* [the father of geology] *also sold geology some snake oil. He convinced geologists that because physical laws are constant in time and space and current processes should be consulted before resorting to unseen processes, it necessarily follows that all past processes acted at essentially their current rates (that is, those observed in historical time). This extreme gradualism has led to numerous unfortunate consequences, including the rejection of sudden or catastrophic events in the face of positive evidence for them, for no reason other than that they were not gradual."* Warren D. Allmon, "Post-Gradualism," *Science*, Vol. 262, 1 October 1993, p. 122.

Figure 68: This empty concrete tank floated up from just below ground level, because the ground turned to a dense liquidlike substance during a 1964 earthquake in Niigata, Japan. This was the first time geologists recognized the phenomenon of *liquefaction*, which had undoubtedly occurred in most other large earthquakes. Liquefaction has even lifted empty tanks up through asphalt pavement[1] and raised pipelines and logs out of the ground.[2] In other words, buried objects that are less dense than the surrounding soil rise buoyantly when that soil liquefies. What would happen to buried animals and plants in temporarily liquefied sediments?

Figure 69: In the Niigata, Japan, earthquake, building number 3 sank in and tipped 22 degrees as the ground partially liquefied. Another building, seen at the red arrow, tipped almost 70 degrees, so much that its roof is nearly vertical.

Strata: Consequence of Liquefaction

Sedimentary rocks are distinguished by layers, called strata. Fossils almost always lie within these layers. Both characteristics, strata and sorted fossils, are largely a consequence of a little-known and poorly-understood phenomenon called ***liquefaction*** (lik-wuh-FAK-shun).

We will first consider several common situations that cause liquefaction on a small scale. After understanding why liquefaction occurs, we will see that a global flood would produce massive liquefaction on a worldwide scale. Finally, a review of other poorly-understood features in the earth's crust will confirm that global liquefaction did occur.

Examples of Liquefaction

Quicksand. Quicksand is a simple example of liquefaction. Quicksand is sand up through which spring-fed water flows. The upward flowing water lifts the sand grains very slightly, surrounding each grain with a thin film of water. This cushioning gives quicksand, and other liquefied sediments, a spongy, fluidlike texture.

Contrary to popular belief, and as shown in many films, a person or animal stepping into deep quicksand will not sink out of sight forever. They will quickly sink in—but only so far. Then they will be lifted, or buoyed up, by a force equal to the weight of the sand and water displaced. The more they sink in, the greater the lifting force.[3] This buoyancy force acts in the same way upon a person floating in a swimming pool. However, quicksand's buoyancy is almost twice that of water, because the weight of the displaced sand and water is almost twice that of water alone. As we will see, the buoyancy of fluidlike sediments will explain why fossils have experienced a degree of vertical sorting and why sedimentary rocks all over the world are so typically layered.

Earthquakes. Liquefaction is frequently seen during, and even minutes after, earthquakes. During the Alaskan Good Friday earthquake of 1964, liquefaction caused most of the destruction within Anchorage, Alaska. Much of the damage during the San Francisco earthquake of 1989 resulted from liquefaction. Although geologists can describe the consequences of liquefaction, they appear to have little understanding of why it happens. Levin describes it as follows:

> *Often during earthquakes, fine-grained water-saturated sediments may lose their former strength and form into a thick mobile mudlike material. The process is called liquefaction. The liquefied sediment not only moves about beneath the surface but may also rise through fissures and "erupt" as mud boils and mud "volcanoes."*[4]

Strahler says that in a severe earthquake:

> *. . . the ground shaking reduces the strength of earth material on which heavy structures rest. Parts of many major cities, particularly port cities, have been built on naturally occurring bodies of soft, unconsolidated clay-rich sediment (such as the delta deposits of a river) or on filled areas in which large amounts of loose earth materials have been dumped to build up the land level. These water-saturated deposits often experience a change in property known as liquefaction when shaken by an earthquake. The material loses strength to the degree that it becomes a highly fluid mud, incapable of supporting buildings, which show severe tilting or collapse.*[5]

These are accurate descriptions of liquefaction, but they do not explain why it happens. Once we understand the mechanics of liquefaction, we can identify two other situations where liquefaction would have occurred massively and continuously for weeks or months—all over the earth.

Visualize a box filled with small, angular rocks. If the box was so full that you could not put its lid on, you could shake the box and cause the rocks to settle into a denser packing arrangement. Now repeat this thought experiment, only this time all the spaces between the rocks are filled with water. As you shake the box and the rocks settle into a denser arrangement, water will be forced up to the top by the weight of the falling rocks. If the box is tall so that many rocks fall, the force of the rising water will increase, and the topmost rocks will be lifted by water pressure for as long as the water flow continues.

This is similar to an earthquake in a region having loose, water-saturated sediments. Once upward flowing water lifts the topmost sediments, the next level of sedimentary particles no longer has the weight of the topmost particles pressing down on them. This second layer can then be more easily lifted by the force of upward flowing water. This, in turn, unburdens the third layer of sediments, etc. The particles are no longer in solid-to-solid contact, but are now suspended in and lubricated by water, so they can slip by each other with ease.

Wave-Loading—A Small Example. You are walking barefooted along the beach. As each ocean wave comes in, water rises from the bottom of your feet to your knees. When the wave returns to the ocean, the sand beneath your feet becomes very loose and mushy, causing your feet to sink in. Walking becomes difficult. This temporarily mushy sand is a small example of liquefaction that most people have experienced.

Why does this happen? At the height of each wave, water is forced down into the sand. As the wave returns to the ocean, the water forced into the sand gushes back out. In doing so, it lifts the topmost sand particles, forming the mushy mixture.

If you submerged yourself under breaking waves but just above the seafloor, you would see sand particles rise slightly above the floor as each wave trough approached. Water just above the sand floor also moves back and forth horizontally with each wave cycle. Fortunately, the current moves toward the beach as liquefaction lifts the sand particles above the floor. Thus, sand particles are continually nudged upslope, toward the beach. If this did not happen, beaches would not be sandy.[6]

Wave-Loading—A Medium-Sized Example. During storms, high waves have caused liquefaction on parts of the sea floor. This has resulted in the failure of pipelines buried offshore.[7]

As a large wave passes over a buried, offshore pipe, the water pressure increases above it. This, in turn, forces more water into the porous sediments. As the wave peak passes and the wave trough approaches, the stored, high-pressure water in the sediments begins to flow upward. This lifts the sediments and causes liquefaction. The buried pipe, in floating upward, breaks.

Wave-Loading—A Large Example. On November 18, 1929, an earthquake struck the continental slope off the coast of Newfoundland. Minutes later, transatlantic phone cables began breaking sequentially. The exact time and location of each break were recorded. It was reported to have been a 65 mile-per-hour current of muddy water that snapped 12 cables in 28 places as it swept 400 miles down the continental slope from the earthquake's epicenter.

Geologists became very interested in this event. If thick muddy flows could travel that fast and far, they could erode long submarine canyons and do other geological work. Such hypothetical flows, called "turbidity currents," now constitute a large field of study within geology.

One problem with the 65 mile-per-hour, turbidity current explanation is that even the best nuclear powered submarines cannot travel at that speed, and the average slope of the ocean floor in that area off the coast of Newfoundland is less than 2 degrees.[8] Also, some broken cables were at a higher elevation than the ocean floor nearest to the earthquake. It seems much more likely that a large wave (called a tsunami[9]) radiated out from the epicenter at the time of the earthquake. Liquefaction, occurring below the expanding wave, left segments of the transatlantic cables without support, and caused them to snap.

Two other examples of liquefaction will soon follow. One gigantic example was caused by wave loading for weeks or months. For now, we can see that *liquefaction occurs whenever water is forced up through loose sediments with enough pressure to lift the topmost sedimentary particles.*

Liquefaction During the Flood

The flooded earth would have had enormous, unimpeded waves, especially tidal waves caused by the gravitational attraction of the sun and moon. Today, most of the energy in tidal waves is dissipated as they reach coast lines. A flooded earth would have no coast lines, so that much of the tidal energy would be carried around the earth to reinforce the next tidal wave. Under these conditions, tidal wave heights of almost a hundred feet have been simulated by computer.[10] (Today, the average tidal amplitude is only 30 inches. Record tides of more than 50 feet occur at the Bay of Fundy in eastern Canada because of the unusual shape of that bay.)

During the flood, at high tide or during other large waves, water would have been forced into the ocean floor by two mechanisms. First, water is slightly compressible. Therefore, water in the saturated sediments below the wave is compressed like a spring. Second, under wave peaks, water is forced, not just down into the sediments below, but laterally through the sediments, in the direction of decreasing pressure. As the wave height diminishes, and the local pressure is reduced, that compressed water reemerges as upward flowing water. Since the sediments were laid down through water, the maximum buoyancy would have acted on each particle. Thus, the bed of sediments would have been loosely packed and would have held much water.

Throughout the flood phase, a liquefaction cycle due to tides alone must have taken place every 12 hours and 25 minutes, the length of today's tidal cycle. Half the time, water would have been pushed down into the sediments, being stored for the other half-cycle, the discharge half, in which water would flow upward. Only during part of this discharge half would the water's upward velocity have been sufficient to cause liquefaction. When it did, many interesting things would happen.

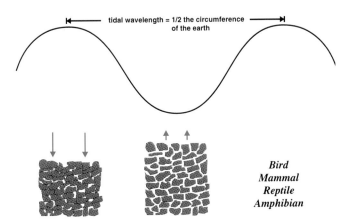

Figure 70: Global Liquefaction. The liquefaction cycle begins at the left with water being forced down into the sea floor at high tide. During the next 6 hours, as low tide approaches, that stored water is released. As it flows up through the sea floor, the sediments are lifted, beginning at the top of the sedimentary column. Once liquefaction begins, lighter particles are free to move up and denser particles to move down. This sorting occurred for many hours each day and for many days. Not only were sedimentary particles sorted into vast, thin layers, but also sorted were dead organisms buried in the sediments. In one experiment by Dr. Leonard R. Brand, a bird, a mammal, a reptile, and an amphibian were buried in thick, muddy water. Their natural settling order was as shown above.[11] This happens to be "the evolutionary order," but, of course, evolution did not cause it.

A Closer Look at Liquefaction

A thick layer of sediments provides a high resistance to water trying to flow up through it, because the water must flow through extremely narrow, twisting passages. Therefore, high pressure is needed to force water up through a thick layer of sediments. Usually, the required high pressure is provided by the weight of the falling sediments.

Water flowing up through a bed of sediments with enough velocity will lift and support each sedimentary particle with water pressure. Rather than thinking of the water as flowing up through the sediments, we can think of the sediments as falling through a very long column of water. The slightest difference in a particle's density, size, or shape will cause it to fall at a slightly different speed than an adjacent particle. Therefore, these particles are continually changing their relative positions until the water's velocity or pressure drops below a certain value or until nearly identical particles are adjacent to each other and fall at the same speed. *This sorting accounts for the layering that is so typical in sedimentary rocks.*

Such sorting also explains why several investigators have observed horizontal strata in large mud deposits from recent local floods.[12] Liquefaction occurred as the mud settled through the water (or as the water was forced up through the mud).

To understand liquefaction better, the author built the apparatus shown in Figure 71 on page 138. The 10-foot-long metal arm pivoted like a teeter-totter from the top of the four-legged stand. Suspended from each arm was a 5-gallon container, one containing water and one containing a mixture of different sediments. A 10-foot pipe connected the mouths of the two containers.

By gently inclining the metal arm to raise the water tank, water flowed from that tank down through the pipe and up through the bed of sediments in the other tank. If the flow velocity exceeded a very low threshold,[13] the sediments would swell slightly as liquefaction began. If an object, having the density of a dead animal or plant, was buried in the sediment tank, it would float to the top of the tank. Once water started to overflow the sediment tank, the metal beam had to be tipped so the water flowed back into the water tank. After repeating this process for 10 or 15 minutes, the mixture of sediments became visibly layered. The longer liquefaction continued, the sharper the boundaries became between different sedimentary layers.

Another phenomenon, which will be called *lensing*, was anticipated and observed in the sediment tank. Some

Figure 71: Liquefaction Demonstration. When the wooden blocks at the top of the horizontal beam are removed, the beam can rock like a teeter-totter. When the far end of the beam is tipped up, water flows from the far tank down through the pipe and up into a container at the left, holding a mixture of sediments. Once liquefaction begins, plants and dead animals buried in the sediment container will float up through the sediments. Sedimentary particles fall or rise relative to each other and begin to sort themselves out into layers of like particles. The same would happen to plants and animals buried in the flood sediments. Their sorting and later fossilization might give the mistaken impression that fossils in higher layers were organisms that evolved millions of years after lower organisms.

sedimentary layers were more porous and permeable than other layers. If water could flow more easily through a lower layer than it could through the layer immediately above it, a lens of water accumulated at their interface. Water lenses were usually at small angles to the horizontal. In such lenses, the water always flowed uphill.[14]

During the flood, liquefaction probably lasted for many hours twice a day. In a liquefaction column, many thick water lenses would have formed. Organisms would have floated up to the lens immediately above. Those of similar size, shape, and density (usually of the same species) would have been swept at similar rates along a nearly horizontal channel and spread out for many miles.[15] Water's buoyant force is much less than that of liquefied sediments, so water alone would have been less able to lift dead organisms into the denser sedimentary layer immediately above the lens.

Once the liquefaction phase of that cycle ended, the water flow would dissipate and the lens would collapse. The layers would settle tightly together, leaving fossils of one species spread over a wide surface which geologists would call a **horizon**. Thousands of years later, this would give most investigators the false impression that the species died long after the layers below were deposited and long before the layers above were deposited. When a layer with many fossils covered a vast area, it would be mistaken as an extinction event or, perhaps, as a boundary between geologic periods.

Frequently, animals or plants, similar in size or shape, were found in two closely spaced horizons. It seemed obvious to early investigators that their subtle differences developed over the assumed long time interval between the horizons. Different species names were given to these organisms, although nothing was known about their inability to interbreed successfully. Complicated systems for naming the organisms began to develop. Later, in 1859, Charles Darwin proposed a mechanism, called natural selection, which he claimed would account for those subtle differences. If sorting by liquefaction produced those differences, then Darwin's explanation is irrelevant.

Questionable Principles. Early geologists learned that fossils found above or below another type of fossil in one location were almost always in that same relative position, even many miles away. This led to the belief that all the lower organisms lived, died, and were buried before the upper organisms. It was thought that a long time elapsed between the two burials, since sediments are deposited very slowly today. Each horizon became associated with a specific time, perhaps thousands of years earlier (or later) than the horizon above (or below) it. Great confidence in this interpretation was gained by finding so many examples of "the proper sequence" that the idea was called the **principle of superposition**. This "principle" is one of the two foundational principles of evolutionary geology.

The other foundational principle in evolutionary geology is the **principle of uniformity**. It states that all geological features can be explained by processes operating today.[16] For example, today rivers deposit sediments at river deltas. Over thousands or millions of years, sediments of a certain thickness would accumulate, which might explain thick layers of sedimentary rocks we now see.

In light of liquefaction, however, both "principles" appear to be seriously flawed. The sediments throughout a tall liquefaction column could have been re-sorted and deposited almost simultaneously by a large scale process that is **not** going on today.

Testing the Theories

How can the two conflicting explanations—liquefaction versus eons of time and the principles of superposition and uniformity—be tested?

- Many sedimentary layers can be traced over hundreds of thousands of square miles. On the other hand, river deltas, which are the most significant example of sedimentation we see today, are only a tiny fraction of that area. Liquefaction during a global flood accounts for the vast lateral expanses of layers. Current processes and eons of time do not.

- Some thick and extensive sedimentary layers have remarkable purity. The St. Peter sandstone, spanning about 500,000 square miles in the central United States, is composed of almost pure quartz, similar to the sand on a white beach. It is hard to imagine how any process, other than global liquefaction, could achieve this degree of purity over such a wide area.[17] Almost all other processes involve mixing, which destroys purity.

- Streams and rivers act on a small fraction of the available sediments and deposit them along a narrow line, but strata are not linear features. Liquefac-

tion during the flood acted on all sediments and sorted them over large areas in a matter of weeks or months.

- Sedimentary layers usually have boundaries that are sharply defined, parallel, and nearly horizontal. Thin, sharply defined layers are sometimes stacked vertically, thousands of feet deep. If each layer had been laid down thousands of years apart, erosion would have destroyed this parallelism. Again, liquefaction explains this common observation.

Sometimes these adjacent, parallel layers contain such different fossils that evolutionists must conclude that they were deposited millions of years apart. But again, the lack of erosion clearly shows that the layers were deposited rapidly. Liquefaction explains all of this.

- Varves are extremely thin layers which evolutionists claim, without much justification, are laid down annually in lakes. By counting tens of thousands of varves, they believe elapsed time can be determined. However, since varves are so uniform, show no evidence of the slightest erosion, and are deposited over wider areas than tiny "stream deltas," they are better explained by liquefaction. **PREDICTION 14: If representative corings are taken in the bottom of any large lake, they will not show laminations as thin, parallel, and extensive as the varves of the Green River formation.**

- Dead animals and plants quickly decay, are eaten, or are destroyed by the elements. Their preservation as fossils requires rapid burial in sediments thick enough to preserve their bodily form. This rarely happens today. When it does, such as in an avalanche or a volcanic eruption, the blanketing layers are not strata spanning hundreds of thousands of square miles. Liquefaction provides a mechanism for the rapid burial of trillions of fossils in appropriate layers. A similar statement can be made concerning fossilized footprints and tracks of many animals. (See also **Rapid Burial** on page 7.)

- Limestone layers, hundreds of feet thick, are sometimes found. The standard geological explanation is that those regions were covered by incredibly limy (alkaline) water for millions of years—a toxic condition not found anywhere on the earth today. Liquefaction, on the other hand, would have quickly sorted limestone particles into vast sheets. (See technical note on page 188.)

- Conventional geology likewise claims that coal layers, sometimes more than a hundred feet thick, first accumulated as thousand-foot thick layers of unde-

Figure 72: Transported Block. This large block, made of a very hard, dense material called quartzite, was transported horizontally and deposited in layers which, at the time, were soft sand. Other layers of sand then blanketed the block. Notice how the layers were deformed below the lower right corner and above the upper left corner. The easiest way to transport such a heavy block is in a liquefied (and thus very buoyant) sand/water mixture. The location of the block relative to its source is shown in Figure 76. It is proposed that the quartzite block was transported in the sliding sedimentary mass above the Precambrian-Cambrian interface during the compression event.

cayed vegetation. Nowhere do we see that happening today. Conversely, liquefaction would have quickly sorted vegetation buried during the early stages of the flood into thick layers, which would later become coal. Furthermore, coal layers often lie above and below a repeating pattern of other layers, called a cyclothem. These patterns are understandable in the context of liquefaction.

- Fossils are sorted vertically to some degree. Evolutionists believe this is a result of macroevolution. No known mechanism will cause macroevolution, and many evidences refute macroevolution. (See pages 2-15.) Liquefaction, an understood mechanism, would sort animals and plants. If liquefaction occurred, one would expect some exceptions to this sorting order, but if macroevolution happened, there should be no exceptions. Many exceptions exist. (See **Out-of-Place Fossils** on page 9.)

- Almost all animals are directly or indirectly dependent on plants for food. However, geological formations frequently contain many fossilized animals *without* fossilized plants.[18] How could they have survived? Apparently the fossilization process involved a sorting that treated plants and animals differently.

- The absence of meteorites in deep sediments is consistent only with a rapid deposition of all the sediments. (See **Shallow Meteorites** on page 25.)

Liquefaction During the Compression Event

While liquefaction operated cyclically throughout the flood phase, it acted massively once during the compression event, at the end of the continental drift phase. (See pages 70-100.)

Visualize a deck of cards sliding across the table. Friction from the table acts to slow the bottommost card. That card, in turn, applies a decelerating force on the second card from the bottom. If none of the cards slip, a frictional, deceleration force will finally be applied to the top card. But if a lubricant somehow built up between any two cards, the cards above the lubricated layer would not decelerate, but would slide over the decelerating cards below.

Similarly, the decelerating, granite hydroplates acted on the bottommost sedimentary layer riding on the hydroplate. Each sedimentary layer, from the bottom to the top, acted in turn to decelerate the topmost layer. As each layer decelerated, it was severely compressed. This is analogous to suddenly squeezing a water-saturated sponge. The sediments were forced into a denser packing arrangement, freeing water in the process. Angular sedimentary particles also broke as they were crushed together. As the broken fragments settled into the water-filled spaces between particles, more water was released. The freed water was then forced up through the sediments, causing massive liquefaction.

As the deceleration (and thus compression) of the sedimentary column increased, the layers became more and more fluid. Eventually, a point could be reached where the sediments were so fluid that slippage occurred above

Figure 73: Liquefaction Plume #1. Almost a hundred of these plumes are found in Kodachrome Basin State Reserve in south-central Utah, 10 miles east of Bryce Canyon National Park. I am standing at the bottom left of the plume.

Figure 74: Liquefaction Plume #2. The plume can be traced down through the large rock it is mounted on and then several hundred feet below the ground to horizontal sandstone layers.[19] After the plume pushed upward, cementing took place, with the sandstone plume being harder than the material it penetrated. Obviously, many of the layers the plume penetrated were softer and eroded away, leaving the plume exposed. (See Figure 79 on page 143.) One of my adult sons is standing at the bottom right of this plume.

a given level, as in our deck of cards. Below that level, compression and liquefaction would have been extreme. Fossils below that level would have floated up and collected at this level where sliding took place.

The lowest of these levels appears to be the Precam-brian-Cambrian interface. The Precambrian, where it exists, is famous for being a thick sedimentary layer containing almost no fossils. Fossils suddenly begin to be found just above the Precambrian-Cambrian interface at the beginning of the Cambrian. (See **Missing Trunk** on page 8.) Evolutionists interpret the Precambrian as about 90% of all geologic time—a vast period, they believe, without life, because fossils are almost never found in Precambrian sediments. Again, the thickness of sedimentary layers is mistakenly associated with passing time.

In the Grand Canyon, the Precambrian-Cambrian interface is an almost flat, horizontal surface that is exposed for 26 miles above the Colorado River. The layers above the Precambrian-Cambrian interface are generally horizontal, but the layers below are tipped at large angles, and their tipped edges are beveled off hori-zontally. It appears that, as slippage began during the compression event, the layers below the slippage plane continued to compress to the point where they buckled. The sliding sedimentary block above the slippage plane beveled off the layers that were being increasingly tipped.

Evolutionists have a different interpretation. The tipped, Precambrian layers represent a former mountain range,

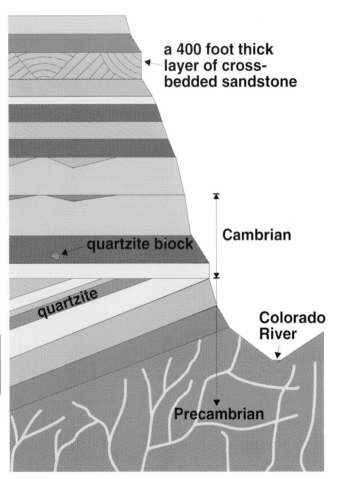

Figure 75: Cross-Bedded Sandstone. Dry sand can build up slopes of not much more than 32 degrees. Cross-bedded sandstone, such as shown here, often has much greater slopes. Therefore, the sand was probably wet when it took on this configuration.

Figure 77: Ayers Rock from the Air. Ayers Rock, located in central Australia, 225 miles southwest of Alice Springs, is one of the most popular tourist attractions in Australia. This mystery to geologists rises 1,140 feet from the desert floor and has a perimeter of 5.6 miles. The best explanation some geologists can muster is that the sand in Ayers Rock came from the Musgrave mountain range 60 miles to the north and was dumped by water in this spot. Later, they say, erosion carved out its present shape. However, most geologists admit they do not know the origin of Ayers Rock.

a 400 foot thick layer of cross-bedded sandstone

quartzite biock

quartzite

Cambrian

Colorado River

Precambrian

Figure 78: Ayers Rock from the Ground. Ayers Rock is explained within these pages as a huge liquefaction mound. Many large water vents, from which the water in the liquefied sediments exited the mound, are found in the sides of Ayers Rock. Today, these vents resemble shallow caves.

Figure 76: Grand Canyon Cross-Section. The tipped and beveled layers are part of the Precambrian. The beveled plane is sometimes called The Great Unconformity. A similar, but much smaller, example of tipped and beveled layers is shown in the cross-bedded sandstone in Figure 75. Beveling implies relative motion. Near the top of the Grand Canyon is a 400-foot-thick layer of cross-bedded sandstone.

layers are beveled almost perfectly horizontal, the top of the mountain must have eroded away. That, of course, would take a long time. Then millions of years would have had to have passed, so seas could have flooded the area, because fossils of sea-bottom life are found just above the Precambrian-Cambrian interface. Within various groups of layers above that, other fossils are found, which required different environments (such as deserts and lagoons), so obviously, greater time is needed.

because mountains today often have steeply tipped layers. (See Figure 33 on page 77.) Since the tipped

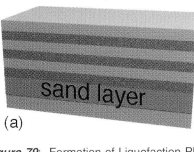
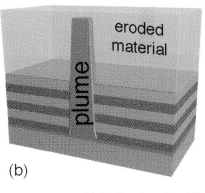
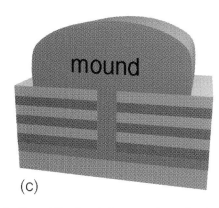

(a) (b) (c)

Figure 79: Formation of Liquefaction Plumes and Mounds. (a) During the global liquefaction of the flood phase, water saturated sediments were sorted into nearly horizontal layers. (b) As a result of the massive liquefaction during the compression event, a less dense sand/water layer would have tended to float up, as a plume, through denser overlying layers. (For a similar phenomenon, see Figure 42 on page 85.) Later, if the surface layers were not cemented as well as the sandstone plume, the surface layers could erode away leaving the plume exposed. (c) If the plume spilled out on the ground, a mound would form.

Figure 80: Small Water Vents. Some water vents, such as these, are the width of a pencil or smaller; others are so large and deep that a person can walk into them. Water vents are quite different from the shallow, bowl-like depressions frequently found on the top of formations. Those depressions are caused by normal wind and rain erosion.

Cross-bedded sandstone. Sand layers would have had the greatest water content, because sand grains are fairly rounded, leaving relatively large gaps for water between the particles. Therefore, the sand layers were the most fluid during the massive liquefaction that accompanied the compression event. Deceleration would have forced the sand forward, displacing the water backward. This compression of horizontal sand layers would have tipped, buckled, and beveled individual layers and groups of layers, forming what is known as cross-bedded sandstone. (See Figure 75.)

Figure 81: Medium-Sized Water Vents. If these holes were simply places where the rock was weakly cemented, one should find such holes on the tops of mounds. Instead, the tops are smooth. It is remarkable how uniform and hard the cementing is in mounds and cross-bedded sandstone. It is almost as if the cement was uniformly spread through water that saturated the sand. Some water vents on other mounds are as large as caves.

Liquefaction Plumes and Mounds. The large water content of liquefied sand layers would have made them quite buoyant. Whenever a low density, fluid layer (such as the compressed, water-sand mixture) underlies a denser, liquefied layer, the potential exists for the lighter fluid to float up in plumes through the denser fluid. These plumes of sand that penetrated overlying layers are seen in many places on the earth. (See Figures 73 and 74.)

When a deep, thick, sand layer is laterally extensive, the plume would spill out on the surface of the earth. This spilling-out would resemble volcanic action, only water-saturated sand would erupt, not lava. Small *liquefaction mounds*, as they will be called, appear when liquefaction occurs during earthquakes.[20] (See Levin's description on page 135.) Ayers Rock in central Australia appears to be a very large example of this. (See Figures 77 and 78.) As with liquefaction plumes, Ayers Rock also connects to a thick sandstone layer below ground. Many smaller, but similar, mounds are found throughout the southwestern United States.

All liquefaction mounds seem to have holes in their sides for releasing their stored water soon after they "erupted." The channels from which the water exited have collapsed except for the opening, which was under much less collapsing stress. Those holes now look like pock marks. Some have claimed they are erosion features from wind and rain. Obviously, wind and rain would smooth out the pock marks, not make them. Besides, the "pock marks," which will be called *water vents*, are found only in the sides of mounds, not the tops, where they should be if outside erosion formed them.

Summary

Liquefaction is associated with quicksand, earthquakes, and wave action. Liquefaction also played a major role in rapidly sorting sediments, plants, and animals during the flood. Indeed, *the global presence of sorted layers and fossils shows that a global flood occurred.* Massive liquefaction has also left other telltale signs such as cross-bedded sandstone, plumes, and mounds.

References and Notes

1. Ivars Peterson, "Liquid Sand," *Science News*, Vol. 128, 12 October 1985, p. 235.

2. Committee on Earthquake Engineering, George W. Housner, Chairman, Commission on Engineering and Technical Systems, National Research Council, *Liquefaction of Soils During Earthquakes* (Washington, D.C.: National Academy Press, 1985), pp. 25, 27.

3. Why is it called quick*sand*? Couldn't the same phenomenon occur with other sedimentary particles, such as clay? The reason "quick*clay*" is seldom seen is that springs rarely produce enough pressure to force water up through densely packed clay. Clay particles are flat and platelike. Since they stack on top of each other like playing cards, very little water can flow between the particles.

   Resistance to the flow of a fluid between solid particles increases enormously as the space between the particles becomes very small, as in clay. Sand particles, on the other hand, are more rounded, creating much larger gaps between particles. A pile of dry sand is so porous that air occupies 30-50% of its volume. Each sand particle deposited in water will be almost completely surrounded by water, so water can flow up through sand with relative ease.

   Some people and most animals caught in quicksand panic. Although they only sink to about half the depth they would in pure water (which is less buoyant) the thick, sand-water mixture creates a suction that opposes movement. Animals frequently die of exertion or starvation. If ever caught in quicksand, relax, let the sand-water mixture support your weight, be patient, and slowly swim out of it.

4. Harold L. Levin, *Contemporary Physical Geology*, 2nd edition (New York: Saunders College Publishing, 1986), p. 251.

5. Arthur N. Strahler, *Physical Geology* (New York: Harper & Row, Publishers, 1981), p. 202.

6. "Breakthroughs in Science, Technology, and Medicine," *Discover*, November 1992, p.14.

7. Experiments have demonstrated this phenomenon as well. See John T. Christian et al., "Large Diameter Underwater Pipeline for Nuclear Power Plant Designed Against Soil Liquefaction," *Offshore Technology Conference Preprints*, Vol. 2, Houston, Texas, 6-8 May 1974, pp. 597-606.

8. Bruce C. Heezen and Maurice Ewing, "Turbidity Currents and Submarine Slumps, and the 1929 Grand Banks Earthquake," Vol. 250, *American Journal of Science*, December 1952, pp. 849-873.

9. A tsunami is often confused with a tidal wave. Tsunamis are caused by undersea earthquakes or volcanic eruptions that initiate a wave. A tidal wave is a regularly occurring, long period wave caused by the gravitational action of the sun and moon on the earth.

10. M. E. Clark and H. D. Voss, "Resonance and Sedimentary Layering in the Context of a Global Flood," *Proceedings of the Second International Conference on Creationism*, Vol. 2 (Pittsburgh, Pennsylvania: Creation Science Fellowship, 1990), pp. 53-63.

    ● M. E. Clark, personal communication, 17 June 1995.

11. Leonard R. Brand, personal communication, 26 March 1996.

12 E. D. McKee et al., "Flood Deposits, Bijou Creek, Colorado, June 1965," *Journal of Sedimentary Petrology*, Vol. 37, September 1967, pp. 829-851.

13. Water would flow into the sediment tank at about a centimeter per second. With a longer column of sediments, the velocity is much slower. This author's computer simulations of liquefaction on the flooded earth showed typical velocities of about 0.1 centimeter per second. Liquefaction would begin at the top of a thick column of sediment and would grow downward as low tide approached. Several hundred feet of sediments would experience liquefaction at one time. If the sediment column grew by adding more sediments from the flood waters before the next liquefaction cycle began, the lowest sediments liquefied in the previous cycle might not experience liquefaction again. Thus, the least dense sediments will not all end up at the top of the sedimentary column.

14. The old adage that water only flows downhill is not always true. Water flowed uphill in the water lens because the pressure in the lowest part of the lens (where the weight of the overlying sediments was greatest) was greater than in the upper part of the lens.

15. Once a water lens began to form, it would spread rapidly. This is because the presence of a lens increases the flow into the lens from below, retards the flow of water escaping upward, and captures water in proportion to the lense's lateral extent.

    During liquefaction, each sedimentary particle, surrounded by a thin film of water, can rotate and vibrate. The water's flow around each irregular particle would vary, causing sudden pressure changes that would impart rapidly changing forces all around the particle. (These are the same fluid forces that lift the wing of an airplane and cause a baseball or golf ball to curve.) When one particle collided with an adjacent particle, the effect would ripple "down the line" to some extent.

    With all this "microagitation" and lubrication, particles would arrange themselves into a very dense packing arrangement that would free more water. More importantly, the close packing would later aid in cementing each horizontal stratum between water lenses into a very strong unit. (See the technical note on page 188.) This is why horizontal cracks (called joints) generally lie between strata.

    Why would there have been an increased flow of water up through the floor of the lens? The sedimentary layer just below a lens is "microagitated" only from below. Thus, the sediments just below the lens, being lifted by the flow from below and having nothing to bump into from above, are very loose and resist the flow from below less.

    Why would less water flow up through the roof of the lens? The particles just above the water lens are pushed up into the mass of sediments comprising the roof, compacting and increasing its resistance to the upward flow. There is also a migration of finer dust or organic material that will come up against the roof and block the flow through the roof. This bottommost layer of the roof is also less agitated, because no particles are "bumping" into it from below. The lack of agitation retards the flow, since more water is held closer to particle surfaces (deeper in a boundary layer) where the resistance to the flow is greatest.

    Evolutionists believe the interfaces between two adjacent strata represent a long time interval in which the environment changed so that some other sediments would be deposited. The sources of these new sediments are never thoroughly explained. New sediments, as opposed to reworked sediments, had to come from eroded crystalline rock. But as long as that crystalline rock was blanketed by sediments, it could not contribute new sediments. In other words, the more sediments are produced and deposited, the less sources are available to produce new sediments. How then did such large thicknesses of sediments and sedimentary rock build up—thickness **which average** a mile in thickness on the continents?

16. The most authoritative source for geological definitions is the *Glossary of Geology*. It defines uniformitarianism as:

    The fundamental principle or doctrine that geologic processes and natural laws now operating to modify the Earth's crust have acted in the same regular manner and with essentially the same intensity throughout geologic time, and that past geologic events can be explained by phenomena and forces observable today; the classical concept that "the present is the key to the past." Robert L. Bates and Julia A. Jackson, editors, *Glossary of Geology*, 2nd edition (Falls Church, Virginia: American Geological Institute, 1980), p. 677.

17. *"The widespread deposition of such clean sand* [in the St. Peter sandstone] *may seem strange to a modern observer, since there is no region on earth where a comparable pattern of deposition can now be found."* Steven M. Stanley, *Earth and Life through Time* (New York: W. H. Freeman and Company, 1986), pp. 355-356.

18. Ariel A. Roth, "Incomplete Ecosystems," *Origins*, Vol. 21, No. 1, 1994, pp. 51-56.

19. Dwight Hornbacher, *Geology and Structure of Kodachrome Basin State Reserve and Vicinity, Kane and Garfield Counties, Utah* (master's thesis, Loma Linda University, California, 1985).

20. George Sheppard, "Small Sand Craters of Seismic Origin," *Nature*, Vol. 132, 30 December 1933, p. 1006.

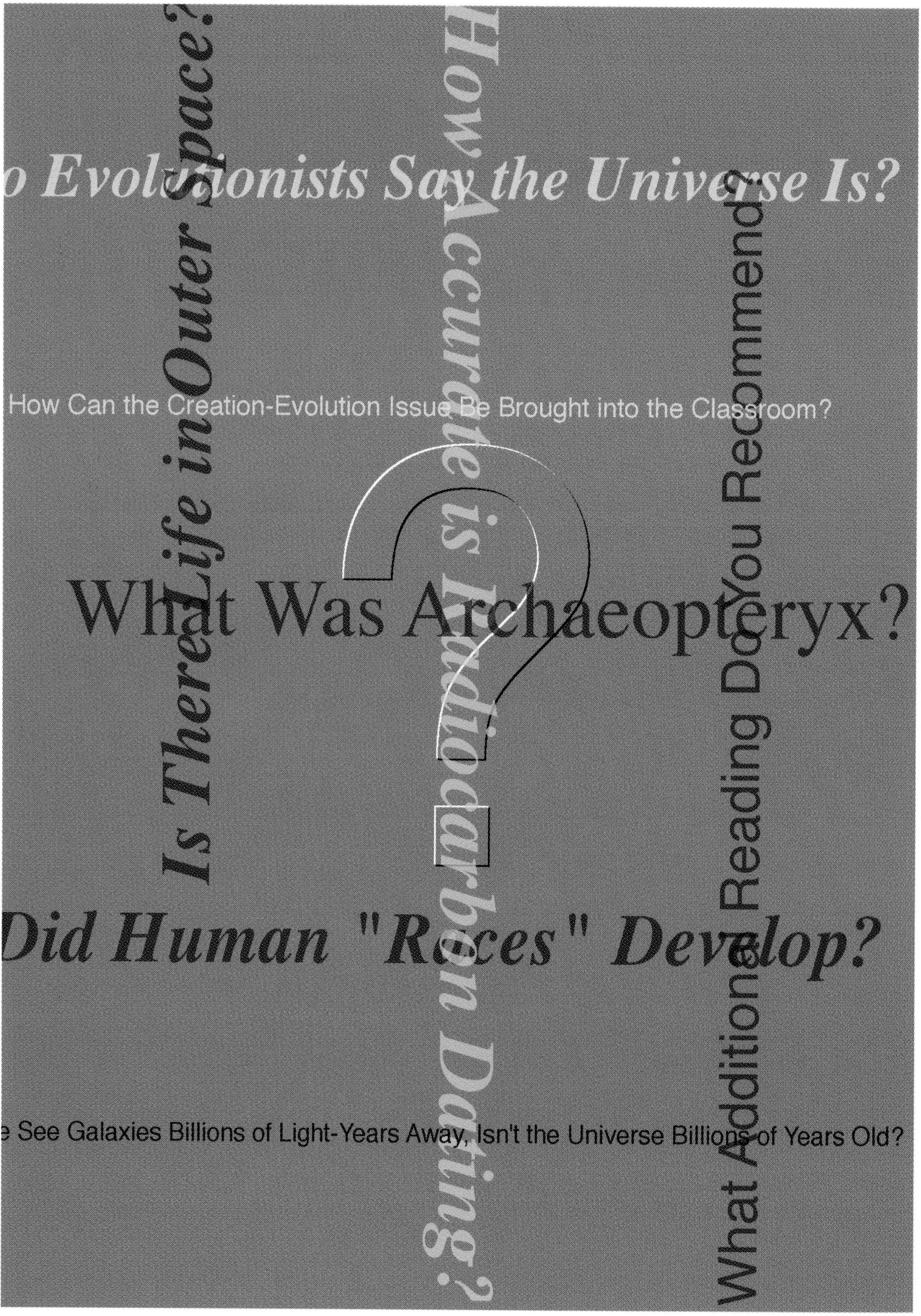

How Old Evolutionists Say the Universe Is?

Is There Life in Outer Space?

How Accurate is Radiocarbon Dating?

What Additional Reading Do You Recommend?

How Can the Creation-Evolution Issue Be Brought into the Classroom?

What Was Archaeopteryx?

Is There Life in Outer Space?

Did Human "Races" Develop?

e See Galaxies Billions of Light-Years Away, Isn't the Universe Billions of Years Old?

Figure 82

Part III:

Frequently Asked Questions

Most questions people have concerning origins are answered in Parts I and II. Of the questions that remain, the following are some of the most frequently asked of this author in seminars and public presentations.

What Was Archaeopteryx?

If reptiles evolved into birds, as evolution claims, there should have been thousands of types of animals more birdlike than reptiles and yet more reptilelike than birds. Evolutionists claim that *Archaeopteryx* (ark ee OP ta riks) is a transition between reptiles and birds, basically a feathered reptile. If so, it is the only transitional form between reptiles and birds. Furthermore, of the relatively few claimed intermediate fossils, this is the one most frequently cited by evolutionists and shown in almost all biology textbooks. Some say it is the most famous fossil in the world.

Archaeopteryx means ancient (*archae*) wing (*pteryx*). But the story behind this alleged half-reptile, half-bird is much more interesting than its fancy, scientific-sounding name or the details of its bones. If *Archaeopteryx* were shown to be a fraud, the result would be devastating for the evolution theory.

Since the early 1980s, several prominent scientists have charged that the two *Archaeopteryx* fossils with clearly visible feathers are forgeries.[1] Allegedly, thin layers of cement were spread on two fossils of a chicken-size dinosaur, called *Compsognathus* (komp SOG nuh thus). Bird feathers were then imprinted into the wet cement.

Were it not for these perfectly formed, modern feathers, that are visible only on two of the six known specimens,[2]

Figure 83: *Compsognathus*. While most dinosaurs were large, this one, *Compsognathus longipes,* was small—about the size of a domestic cat. The German scientist who discovered *Compsognathus*, Andreas Wagner, "recognized from the description [of *Archaeopteryx*] what seemed to be his *Compsognathus* but with feathers! He was extremely suspicious . . . ."[3] There is a long list of similarities between *Compsognathus* and *Archaeopteryx*.

Archaeopteryx would be considered *Compsognathus*.[4] The skeletal features of *Archaeopteryx* are certainly not suitable for flight, since no specimen shows a sternum (breast bone) which all birds, and even bats, must have to attach their large flight muscles. Finally, *Archaeopteryx* should not be classified as a bird.[5]

Figure 84: "Chewing Gum Blob." These raised spots have the appearance of pieces of chewing gum. They have no corresponding indentation on the mating face of the fossil. Probably some small drops of wet cement fell on the surface and were never detected or cleaned off by the forger.

The two fossils with feathers were "found" and sold for high prices by Karl Häberlein (in 1861 for 600 pounds) and his son, Ernst, (in 1877 for 36,000 gold marks) just as Darwin's theory and book, *The Origin of Species* (1859), were gaining popularity. While some German experts apparently thought the new (1861) fossil was a forgery, the British Museum (Natural History) bought it sight unseen.

Figure 85: Furcula of *Archaeopteryx*? The V-shaped bone is claimed to be the wishbone, or furcula, of *Archaeopteryx*. It is shaped more like a boomerang than the familiar wishbone in a chicken. A furcula acts as a spring—storing and releasing energy with each flap of a wing. Note the crack in the right arm of the furcula and the broken right tip—strange for a bird's flexible bone buried in soft sediments. Perhaps it broke when a forger chipped it out of another fossil. One must ask why the other *Archaeopteryx* specimens do not show a clear furcula. The counterslab, immediately above, does not appear to have a correspondingly smooth depression into which the raised furcula will fit.

Evidence of a forgery includes instances where the supposedly mating faces of the fossil (the main slab and counterslab) do not mate. The feather impressions are primarily on the main slab, while the counterslab in several places has raised areas that have no corresponding indentation on the main slab. These raised areas, nicknamed "chewing gum blobs," are made of the same fine grained material that is found only under the

feather impressions. The rest of the fossil is composed of a courser grained limestone. (See Figure 84 on page 148.)

Some might claim that *Archaeopteryx* has a wishbone, or furcula—a unique feature of birds. It would be more accurate to say that only the British Museum specimen has a visible furcula. It is a strange furcula, "relatively the largest known in any bird."[6] Furthermore, it is upside down, a point acknowledged by two giants of the evolutionist movement—T. H. Huxley (Darwin's so-called bulldog) and Gavin deBeer. As Fred Hoyle and N. Chandra Wickramasinghe stated, "It was somewhat unwise for the forgers to endow *Compsognathus* with a furcula, because a cavity had to be cut in the counterslab, with at least some semblance to providing a fit to the added bone. This would have to be done crudely with a chisel, which could not produce a degree of smoothness in cutting the rock similar to a true sedimentation cavity." [7] (See Figure 85.)

Many feather imprints show what has been called "double strike" impressions. Apparently, feather impressions were made twice in a slightly displaced position as the slab and counterslab were pressed together. (See Figure 86.)

Figure 86: Double Strike. A forger would have a delicate task positioning the counterslab on top of the slab with a cement paste in between the two slabs. The two halves of the fossil must mate perfectly. A last minute adjustment or slip would create a double strike, such as you see in the bottom right of this picture.

Honest disagreement as to whether *Archaeopteryx* was or was not a forgery was possible until 1986, when a definitive test was performed. An X-ray resonance spectrograph of the British Museum fossil showed that the material containing the feather impressions differed significantly from the rest of the fossil slab. The chemistry of this "amorphous paste" also differed from the crystalline rock in the famous fossil quarry in Germany where *Archaeopteryx* supposedly was found.[8] Few responses have been made to this latest, and probably conclusive, evidence.[9]

Fossilized feathers are almost unheard of, and several complete, flat feathers that just happened to be at the slab/counterslab interface is even more remarkable. Furthermore, there has been no convincing explanation for how to fossilize (actually encase) a bird in the 80% pure, Solnhofen limestone. One difficulty, which will be appreciated after reading about liquefaction on pages 134-145, is the low density of birds. Another is that limestone is precipitated from sea water, as explained on pages 188-189. Therefore, to be buried in limestone, the animal must lie on the sea floor—a rarity for a dead bird.

Significantly, two modern birds have recently been found in rock strata dated by evolutionists as much older than *Archaeopteryx*.[10] Therefore, according to evolutionary dating methods, *Archaeopteryx* could not be ancestral to modern birds.

Archaeopteryx's fame seems assured, not as a transitional fossil between reptiles and birds, but as a forgery. Unlike the Piltdown hoax, which fooled leading scientists for more than 40 years, the *Archaeopteryx* hoax lasted for 125 years. (See **"Ape-Men?"** on page 9.) Since the apparent motive for the *Archaeopteryx* deception was money, *Archaeopteryx* should be labeled as ***a fraud***. The British Museum (Natural History) gave life to both deceptions and must assume much of the blame. Those scientists who were too willing to fit *Archaeopteryx* into their evolutionary framework also helped spread the deception. Piltdown man may soon be replaced as the most famous hoax in all of science.

References and Notes

1. Dr. Lee Spetner first made this allegation in a meeting of orthodox Jewish scientists held in Jerusalem in July 1980. Spetner had studied the British Museum specimen in June 1978 and had pointed out the discrepancies to Dr. Alan Charig, Chief Curator of Fossil Amphibians, Reptiles, and Birds. [See "Is the *Archaeopteryx* a Fake?", *Creation Research Society Quarterly*, Vol. 20, September 1983, pp. 121-122.] Charig has consistently denied the forgery.

   For the most complete description and photographs of this evidence, see Fred Hoyle and N. Chandra Wickramasinghe, *Archaeopteryx, the Primordial Bird: A Case of Fossil Forgery* (Swansea, England: Christopher Davies, Ltd., 1986). This book also responds to counterclaims that *Archaeopteryx* was not a forgery.

2. Some defenders of *Archaeopteryx* will claim that three of the other four specimens also have feathers—the Teyler Museum specimen, the Eichstätt specimen, and the poorly preserved Maxberg specimen. Hoyle, Wickramasinghe, and Watkins put it bluntly. *"Only people in an exceptional condition of mind can see them."* [F. Hoyle, N. C. Wickramasinghe, and R. S. Watkins, "Archaeopteryx," *The British Journal of Photography*, 21 June 1985, p. 694.]

3. Ian Taylor, "The Ultimate Hoax: Archaeopteryx Lithographica," *Proceedings of the Second International Conference on Creationism*, Vol. 2 (Pittsburgh, Pennsylvania: Creation Science Fellowship, 1990), p. 280.

4. *". . . these specimens* [of *Archaeopteryx*] *are not particularly like modern birds at all. If feather impressions had not been preserved in the London and Berlin specimens, they* [the other specimens] *never would have been identified as birds. Instead, they would unquestionably have been labeled as coelurosaurian dinosaurs* [such as *Compsognathus*]. *Notice that the last three specimens to be recognized* [as *Archaeopteryx*] *were all misidentified at first, and the Eichstätt specimen for 20 years was thought to be a small specimen of the dinosaur Compsognathus."* John H. Ostrom, "The Origin of Birds," *Annual Review of Earth and Planetary Sciences*, Vol. 3, 1975, p. 61.

   • *"Apart from the proportions of its wings, the skeleton of Archaeopteryx is strikingly similar to that of a small, lightly built, running dinosaur, such as the coelurosaur Compsognathus."* Dougal Dixon et al., *The Macmillan Illustrated Encyclopedia of Dinosaurs and Prehistoric Animals* (New York: Macmillan Publishing Company, 1988), p. 172.

5. *"Phylogenetic analysis of stem-group birds reveals that Archaeopteryx is no more closely related to modern birds than are several types of theropod dinosaurs, including tyrannosaurids and ornithomimids. Archaeopteryx is not an ancestral bird, nor is it an 'ideal intermediate' between reptiles and birds. There are no derived characters uniquely shared by Archaeopteryx and modern birds alone; consequently there is little justification for continuing to classify Archaeopteryx as a bird."* R. A. Thulborn, "The Avian Relationships of *Archaeopteryx* and the Origin of Birds," *Zoological Journal of the Linnean Society*, Vol. 82, 1984, p. 119.

6. Larry D. Martin, "The Relationship of *Archaeopteryx* to other Birds," *The Beginnings of Birds: Proceedings of the International Archaeopteryx Conference of 1984* (Eichstätt, Germany: Jura Museum, 1985), p. 182.

7. Hoyle and Wickramasinghe, *Archaeopteryx, the Primordial Bird: A Case of Fossil Forgery*, p. 93.

?

8. N. Wickramasinghe and F. Hoyle, *"Archaeopteryx, the Primordial Bird?"*, *Nature*, Vol. 324, 18/25 December 1986, p. 622.

9. Two milligram-size samples of the fossil material were tested; one from a "feather" region and a control sample from a nonfeathered region. The British Museum *"contends that the amorphous nature of the feathered material is an artifact explainable by preservatives that they have put on the fossil."* [Lee M. Spetner, "Discussion," *Proceedings of the Second International Conference on Creationism* (Pittsburgh, Pennsylvania: Creation Science Fellowship, 1990), p. 289.] If this excuse were correct, then why were no "preservatives" found on the control specimen? Control specimens are tested for precisely this purpose—to dispel unique, last minute excuses. The British Museum has refused further testing, a shocking position for a scientific organization, and one which raises suspicions to the breaking point.

10. Tim Beardsley, "Fossil Bird Shakes Evolutionary Hypotheses," *Nature*, Vol. 322, 21 August 1986, p. 677.

● Alun Anderson, "Early Bird Threatens *Archaeopteryx*'s Perch," *Science*, Vol. 253, 5 July 1991, p. 35.

● Sankar Chatterjee, "Cranial Anatomy and Relationship of a New Triassic Bird from Texas," *Philosophical Transactions of the Royal Society of London, B*, Vol. 332, 1991, pp. 277-342.

How Accurate Is Radiocarbon Dating?

Radiocarbon dating can be quite accurate, and the techniques improve yearly. However, before accepting a radiocarbon date, one should understand how the technique works, its limitations, and its assumptions. One limitation is that the radiocarbon technique only dates material that was once part of an animal or plant. To understand the other capabilities and limitations of radiocarbon dating, we must first understand how it works and consider the flood.

Most carbon atoms weigh 12 atomic mass units. However, about one in a trillion carbon atoms weighs 14 atomic units. This carbon is called carbon-14. It is also called **radio**carbon since it is **radio**active. Half of it will decay in about 5730 years to form nitrogen. Half of the remainder will decay in another 5730 years, and so on.

Cosmic radiation striking the upper atmosphere converts about 21 pounds of nitrogen each year into radiocarbon (carbon-14). Most carbon-14 quickly combines with oxygen to form radioactive carbon dioxide, which then spreads throughout the atmosphere. Plants take in carbon dioxide, and thus incorporate both carbon-14 and normal carbon-12 into their tissues **in the same proportion as occurs in the atmosphere**. Carbon-14 then moves up the various food chains to enter animal tissue—again, in about the same ratio carbon-14 has with carbon-12 in the atmosphere.

When a living thing dies, it no longer takes in radiocarbon. Therefore, its radiocarbon clock begins "ticking" since the radiocarbon in its dead body steadily decreases with a half-life today of 5730 years. If one knew what fraction of the organism's carbon atoms were carbon-14 when it died, then one could attempt to date the time of death.

The key questions, then, are "Has the atmospheric ratio of carbon-14 to carbon-12 changed in the past, and if so, why and how much?"

The assumption usually made (but rarely acknowledged) is that the ratio of carbon-14 to carbon-12 in the atmosphere has always been about what it is today—about one in a trillion. But that may not have been true in the ancient past. For example, a worldwide flood would uproot and bury preflood forests. Afterwards, less carbon would be available to cycle between living things and the atmosphere. With less carbon-12 to dilute the carbon-14 that is continually forming in the upper atmosphere, the ratio of carbon-14 to carbon-12 in the atmosphere would slowly begin to increase. If the ratio of carbon-14 to carbon-12 doubled and we did not know it, radiocarbon ages of things living then would appear to us to be one half-life (or 5730 years) older than their true ages. If that ratio quadrupled, organic remains would appear 11,460 (2 x 5730) years older, etc. Consequently, a "radiocarbon year" would not correspond to an **actual** year.[1]

Another consequence of the flood would have greatly diluted the carbon-14 to carbon-12 ratio. The precipitation of limestone during the flood involved the release of vast quantities of dissolved carbon dioxide from the subterranean water chamber. (See pages 70 - 100 and the technical note on page 188.) Since that carbon was isolated from the atmosphere before the flood, it would have been free of carbon-14. Much of that released carbon dioxide undoubtedly mixed with some of the carbon dioxide in the preflood seas before all the limestone precipitated. This would have diluted the biosphere's ratio of carbon-14 to carbon-12, resulting in artificially old carbon-14 dates.

If all of this is true, the ratio of carbon-14 to carbon-12 should have been building up in the atmosphere since the flood. In fact, it should still be increasing. This is precisely what recent measurements show.[2]

Radiocarbon dating of organic-rich, sedimentary layers worldwide has consistently shown a surprising result. Radiocarbon ages do not increase steadily as we go down into layers of old (but postflood) organic matter, as one might expect. Instead, they increase at an accelerating rate.[3] In other words, the concentration of carbon-14 decreases rapidly with depth. The concentration of carbon-14 starts unexpectedly low just after the flood, as represented in the lower organic layers, and increases more rapidly than expected as the centuries passed. For the reasons mentioned above, the rapidity and direction of this change is what we would expect in the centuries after a worldwide flood.

One way to infer how the atmospheric concentration of carbon-14 changed in the past is by tree-ring dating. Some types of trees, that grow at high elevations and have a steady supply of moisture, reliably add only one ring each year. In other environments, multiple rings can be added in a year.[4] The thickness of a tree ring depends on the tree's growing conditions, which will naturally vary from year to year. Some rings may even show frost or fire damage. By comparing sequences of ring thicknesses in two different trees, a correspondence can sometimes be shown. Ring patterns will correlate strongly for two trees of the same species that grew near each other at the same time. Weaker correlations (or less confident matches) exist between trees of different species growing simultaneously in different environments. Claims are frequently made that wood growing today can be matched up with some scattered pieces of dead wood so that tree-ring counts can be extended back more than 8,600 years. This may not be true.

These claimed "long chronologies" begin with either living trees or dead wood that can be accurately dated by historical methods. This carries the chronology back perhaps 3,500 years. Then the more questionable links

are established based on the judgment of a tree-ring specialist. Standard statistical techniques could establish just how good the dozen or more supposedly overlapping tree-ring sequences are. However, tree-ring specialists refuse to subject their judgments to these statistical tests, and they have not released their data so others can carry out these statistical tests.[5]

Several laboratories in the world are now equipped to perform a much improved radiocarbon dating procedure. Using atomic accelerators, the carbon-14 atoms in a specimen can now be actually counted. This gives more precise radiocarbon dates with even smaller specimens. The standard, but less accurate, radiocarbon dating technique only attempts to count the rare disintegrations of carbon-14 atoms, which are sometimes confused with other types of disintegrations. This new atomic accelerator technique has consistently detected at least small amounts of carbon-14 in every organic specimen—even materials that evolutionists claim are millions of years old, such as coal. The minimum amount of carbon-14 found is so consistent among various specimens that contamination can probably be ruled out. If the specimens were millions of years old, virtually no carbon-14 would remain in them.

Eleven human skeletons, the earliest known human remains in the western hemisphere, have been dated by this new "accelerator mass spectrometer" technique. All eleven were dated at about 5000 radiocarbon years or less![6] If more of the claimed evolutionary ancestors of man are tested and are also found to contain carbon-14, a major scientific revolution will occur, and thousands of textbooks will become obsolete. ***PREDICTION 15: Hominid and dinosaur bones that have retained enough carbon to be dated by this precise technique will be shown to be relatively young in blind tests.***

Radiocarbon dating is becoming increasingly important in interpreting the past. However, one must understand how it works and especially how a flood as proposed in this book would have affected radiocarbon dating.

References and Notes

1. A radiocarbon year would also not equal a calendar year if, for example, the half-life of carbon-14 has changed, if carbon-12 or carbon-14 was added to, or leached from, the specimen being dated, or if the rates of formation or decay of carbon-14 differed.

2. In 1952, when Willard Libby first published his work on radiocarbon dating, he called attention to the critical assumption that the ratio of carbon-14 to carbon-12 has been constant. He tested that assumption by making various measurements and calculating how rapidly carbon-

14 was forming and decaying. Surprisingly, carbon-14 seemed to be forming faster than it was decaying. That would mean that there was less carbon-14 in the atmosphere in the past. If we did not know that, we would falsely conclude that the lack of carbon-14 in dead animals and plants was because much time had passed.

Libby believed his measurements were in error, since he thought the earth was so old that a balance between formation and decay must exist. He tried to justify this as follows: *"If the cosmic radiation has remained at its present intensity for 20,000 or 30,000 years, and if the carbon reservoir has not changed appreciably in this time, then there exists at the present time a complete balance between the rate of disintegration of radiocarbon atoms and the rate of assimilation of new radiocarbon atoms for all material in the life-cycle."* [See Willard F. Libby, *Radiocarbon Dating* (Chicago: University of Chicago Press, 1952), pp. 4-9.]

Recently, others have duplicated Libby's measurements with much greater accuracy. They concluded that the out-of-balance condition is real and even worse than Libby believed. **Radiocarbon is forming 28-37% faster than it is decaying.** [See Melvin A. Cook, "Nonequilibrium Radio-Carbon Dating Substantiated," *Proceedings of the First International Conference on Creationism,* Vol. 2 (Pittsburgh, Pennsylvania: Creation Science Fellowship, 1986), pp. 59-68.] Notice that this is what we would expect from the flood.

3. Robert H. Brown, "Implications of C-14 Age vs. Depth Profile Characteristics," *Origins*, Vol. 15, No. 1, 1988, pp. 19-29.

4. W. S. Glock and S. Agerter, "Anomalous Patterns in Tree Rings," *Endeavor*, Vol. 22, January 1963, pp. 9-13.

5. The oldest living thing known is a bristlecone pine in the White Mountains of California. The American Forestry Association estimates that it is 4600 years old. Amazingly, it is not part of any "long chronology."

6. R. E. Taylor et al., "Major Revisions in the Pleistocene Age Assignments for North American Human Skeletons by C-14 Accelerator Mass Spectrometry," *American Antiquity*, Vol. 50, No. 1, 1985, pp. 136-140.

Since We See Galaxies Billions of Light-Years Away, Isn't the Universe Billions of Years Old?

The logic behind this common question has several hidden assumptions. Probably the most questionable assumption is that starlight has always traveled at the same speed. Has it? Has the speed of light always been 186,000 miles per second or, more precisely, 299,792.458 kilometers per second? One simple test is to compare the historic measurements of the speed of light.

Historical Measurements. During the last 300 years, at least 164 separate measurements of the speed of light have been published. Sixteen different measurement techniques were used. Astronomer Barry Setterfield of Australia has studied these measurements, especially their precision and experimental errors.[1] His results show that **the speed of light has apparently decreased so rapidly that experimental error cannot explain it!** In the seven instances where the same scientists measured the speed of light with the same equipment years later, a decrease was always reported. The decreases were often several times greater than the reported experimental errors. This author has conducted other analyses that weight (or give significance to) each measurement according to its accuracy. Even after considering the wide range of accuracies, it is hard to see how anyone can claim, with any statistical rigor, that the speed of light has remained constant.[2]

M. E. J. Gheury de Bray, writing in the official French astronomical journal in 1927, was probably the first to propose a decreasing speed of light.[3] He based his conclusion on measurements spanning 75 years. Later, he became more convinced and twice published his results in *Nature,*[4] possibly the most prestigious scientific journal in the world. He emphasized, "If the velocity of light is constant, how is it that, **invariably**, new determinations give values which are lower than the last one obtained . . . . There are twenty-two coincidences in favour of a decrease of the velocity of light, while there is not a single one against it."[5] [emphasis in original]

Although the speed of light has only decreased a percent or so during the past three centuries, the decrease is statistically significant since measurement techniques can detect changes that are thousands of times smaller. Of course the older measurements have greater errors. However, the trend of the data is startling. The speed of light apparently increases the further back one looks in time. The rate of change is high. Several mathematical curves seem to fit these three centuries of data. Projecting these curves back in time, the speed of light becomes so fast that conceivably the light from distant galaxies could reach Earth in several thousand years.

There is no physical reason why the speed of light must be constant.[6] Most of us simply assumed that it is, and of course, changing old ways of thinking is sometimes difficult. Russian cosmologist, V. S. Troitskii, at the Radiophysical Research Institute in Gorky, is also questioning some old beliefs. He concluded, independently of Setterfield, that **the speed of light was ten billion times faster at time zero!**[7] Furthermore, he attributed the cosmic background radiation and most redshifts to this rapidly decreasing speed of light. Setterfield reached the same conclusion concerning redshifts by a completely different approach. If either Setterfield or Troitskii is correct, the big bang theory will fall (with a big bang).

Figure 87: This atomic clock at the United States National Institute of Standards is named NIST-7. If its time were compared with a similar clock three million years from now, they would differ by about one second! Because of this remarkable precision, NIST-7 is the reference time piece for all U.S. space missions. NIST-8, which is being planned now, will reduce this error even more by cooling the vibrating atoms nearly to absolute zero. Despite the extreme precision of atomic clocks, we have no assurance that they are not all drifting relative to "true" time. In other words, we can marvel at the precision of atomic clocks, but we cannot be certain of their accuracy.

Atomic vs. Orbital Time. Why would the speed of light decrease? T. C. Van Flandern, working at the U.S. Naval Observatory, showed that atomic clocks are apparently slowing relative to orbital clocks.[8] Orbital clocks are based on orbiting astronomical bodies, especially Earth's one-year period about the sun. Before 1967, one second of time was defined by international agreement as 1/31,556,925.9747 of the time it takes Earth to orbit the sun. Atomic clocks are based on the vibrational period of the cesium-133 atom. In 1967, a second was redefined as 9,192,631,770 oscillations of the cesium-133 atom. Van Flandern showed that if atomic clocks are "correct," then the orbital speeds of Mercury, Venus, and Mars are increasing; consequently, the gravitational "constant" should be changing. However, he noted that if orbital clocks are "correct," then the gravitational constant is truly constant, but atomic vibrations **and** the speed of light are decreasing. The drift between the two types of clocks is only several parts per billion per year. But again, the precision of the measurements is so good that the discrepancy is probably real.

There are four reasons why orbital clocks seem to be correct and why atomic frequencies are probably slowing very slightly.

- If a planet's orbital speed increased (and all other orbital parameters remained the same), then its energy would increase. This would violate the law of conservation of mass-energy.

- If atomic time is slowing, then clocks based on the radioactive decay of atoms should also be slowing. Radiometric dating techniques would give ages that are too old. This would bring radiometric clocks more in line with most other dating clocks. (See pages 24-29.) This would also explain why no primordial isotopes have half-lives less than 50 million years. Such isotopes simply decayed away when radioactive decay rates were much greater.[9]

- If atomic clocks and Van Flandern's study are correct, the gravitational "constant" should change. Statistical studies have not detected these variations.

- If atomic frequencies are decreasing, then five "properties" of the atom, such as Planck's constant, should also be changing. Statistical studies of the past measurements of four of the five of these "properties" support both the magnitude and direction of this change.[10]

For these reasons, orbital clocks seem to be more **accurate** than the extremely **precise** atomic clocks.[11]

Many of us were skeptical of Setterfield's initial claim, since the decrease in the speed of light apparently ceased in 1960. Large, one-time changes seldom occur in nature. The measurement techniques were precise enough to detect any decrease in the speed of light after 1960, if the trend of the prior three centuries had continued. Later, Setterfield realized that beginning in the 1960s, atomic clocks were used to measure the speed of light. If atomic frequencies are decreasing, then both the measured quantity (the speed of light) and the measuring tool (atomic clocks) are changing at the same rate. Naturally, no relative change would be detected, and the speed of light would be constant in atomic time—but not orbital time.

Misconceptions. Does the decrease in the speed of light conflict with the statement frequently attributed to Albert Einstein that the speed of light is constant? Not really. Einstein's theory of special relativity assumes that the speed of light is independent of the velocity of the light source. This is called Einstein's Second Postulate. Many have misinterpreted this to mean that "Einstein said that the speed of light is constant." Imagine two spaceships traveling away from each other. An astronaut in one

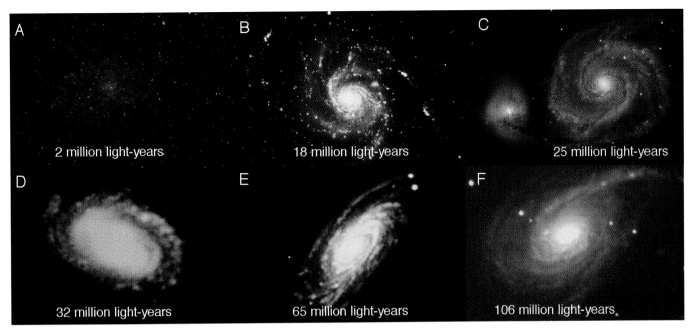

Figure 88: The arms in these six representative spiral galaxies have about the same amounts of twist. Their distances from Earth are shown in light years. One light-year, the distance light travels in one year, equals 5,879,000,000,000 miles. For the light from all galaxies to arrive at Earth tonight, the further galaxies had to release their light long before the closer galaxies. Therefore, the further galaxies did not have as much time to rotate and twist their arms. Conversely, the closer galaxies should have the most twist. Of course, if the speed of light was a million times faster in the past, the furthest galaxies did not have to send their light much before the nearest galaxies. The twists in spiral galaxies should be similar. This turned out to be the case. The galaxies are: A) M33, or NGC 598; B) M101, or NGC 5457; C) M51, or NGC 5194; D) NGC 4559; E) M88, or NGC 4501; and F) NGC 772. All distances are taken from R. Brent Tully, *Nearby Galaxies Catalog* (New York: Cambridge University Press, 1988).

spaceship suddenly shines a flashlight at the other spaceship. Einstein claimed that the beam will strike that spaceship at the same speed as it would if the two spaceships were traveling toward each other. This paradox has some experimental support.[12] Setterfield, on the other hand, says that while the speed of light has decreased *over time*, at any instant all light beams travel at the same speed, regardless of the velocity and location of their sources.[13]

Some people give another explanation for why we see distant stars in a young universe. They believe that light was created between Earth and each star. Of course, a creation would immediately produce completed things. Seconds later, they would look older than they really were. This is called "creation with the appearance of age." The concept is sound. However, for starlight, it is probably not an acceptable explanation for two reasons:

- Very bright, exploding stars are called "supernovas." If starlight, apparently from a supernova, were created en route to Earth and did not originate at the surface of the star, then what exploded? If the image of an explosion was only created on that beam of light, then the star never existed, and the explosion never happened. Only a relatively short beam would have been created near Earth. One finds this hard to accept.

- Every hot gas radiates a unique set of precise colors, called its ***emission spectrum***. The gaseous envelope around each star also emits specific colors that identify the chemical composition of the gas. Since all starlight has emission spectra, this strongly suggests that a star's light originated at the star—not in cold, empty space. Each beam of starlight also carries other information, such as the star's spin rate, magnetic field, surface temperature, and the chemical composition of the cold gases between the star and Earth. For these reasons, starlight seems to have originated at stellar surfaces, not in empty space.

Surprising Observations. Starlight from distant stars and galaxies is redshifted—meaning that the light is redder than it should be. (Most astronomers have interpreted the redshifted light to be a wave effect, similar to the pitch of a train's whistle that is lower when the train is going away from an observer. The greater the redshift, the faster stars and galaxies are supposedly moving away from us.) Since 1976, William Tifft, a University of Arizona astronomer, has found that the redshifts of distant stars and galaxies typically differ from each other by fixed amounts.[14] This is very strange if stars are moving away from us. It would be as if galaxies could travel only at specific speeds, jumping abruptly from one speed to another, without passing through intermediate speeds. If stars are not moving away from us at high speeds, the big bang theory will fall, along with most other beliefs in the field of cosmology. Many other astronomers, not believing Tifft's results, have done similar work, only to reach the same conclusions as Tifft.

Atoms behave in a similar way. That is, they give off tiny bundles of energy (called quanta) of fixed amounts—and nothing in between. So Setterfield believes that the "quantization of redshifts," as many refer to the phenomenon, is an atomic effect, not a strange recessional velocity effect. If a property of space is slowly removing energy from all emitted light, it would do so in fixed increments. This would also redshift starlight, with the furthest star's light being redshifted the most. Furthermore, it would also slow the velocity of light and the vibrational frequency of the atom, all of which is observed. Setterfield is currently working on a theory to tie all of this together. **PREDICTION 16: The redshifts of some specific, distant galaxies will undergo abrupt decreases.**

Another surprising observation is that most distant galaxies look remarkably similar to nearer galaxies. For example, galaxies are fully developed and show no signs of evolving. This puzzles astronomers.[15] If the speed of light has decreased drastically, these distant, yet mature, galaxies no longer need explaining.

A Critical Test. How can we test whether the speed of light has decreased a millionfold? If it has, **we should observe events in outer space in extreme slow motion.** Here is why.

Consider a time in the distant past when the speed of light was, say, a million times faster than it is today. On a hypothetical planet, billions of light-years from Earth, a light started flashing toward Earth every second. Each flash then began a very long trip to Earth. Since the speed of light was a million times greater than it is today, those initial flashes were spaced a million times further apart in distance than they would have been at today's slower speed of light.

Thousands of years have now passed. Throughout the universe, the speed of light has slowed to today's speed, and the first of those flashes—strung out like beads sliding down a long string—are approaching Earth. The distances separating adjacent flashes have remained constant during these thousands of years, because the moving flashes slowed in unison. Since the first flashes to strike Earth are spaced so far apart, they will strike Earth every million seconds. In other words, we are seeing past events on that planet (the flashing of a light) in slow motion. If the speed of light has been decreasing since the creation, then the further out in space we look, the more extreme this slow motion becomes.

As one example, galaxies would be seen in slow motion. Galaxies that appear to spin at a rate of once every 200 million years would be spinning much faster. This might explain the partial twist seen in all spiral galaxies. If the speed of light has not decreased, and there is no slow-motion effect, then why do billion-year-old spiral galaxies, at all distances, show about the same twist? (See Figure 88 on page 155.)

Most stars in our galaxy are binary; that is, they and a companion star are in a tight orbit around each other. If there is a "slow-motion effect," the orbital periods of binary stars should tend to increase with increasing distance from Earth. **PREDICTION 17: The Hubble Space Telescope will find that binary stars at great distances have very long orbital periods, showing that they are in slow motion.**

References and Notes

1. Trevor Norman and Barry Setterfield, *The Atomic Constants, Light, and Time* (Box 318, Blackwood, South Australia, 5051: self-published, 1987).

2. Two creationist physicists have claimed that the speed of light has not changed. See, for example:

   Gerald E. Aardsma, "Has the Speed of Light Decayed?", *Impact*, No. 179 (El Cajon, California: The Institute for Creation Research), May 1988.

   Gerald E. Aardsma, "Has the Speed of Light Decayed Recently?", *Creation Research Society Quarterly*, Vol. 25, June 1988, pp. 36-40.

   Robert H. Brown, "Statistical Analysis of the Atomic Constants, Light and Time," *Creation Research Society Quarterly*, Vol. 25, September 1988, pp. 91-95.

   These calculations contain mathematical errors which, if corrected, would support the hypothesis that the speed of light has decreased. I have discussed these matters with each author. The following professional statisticians have verified my conclusions or have reached similar conclusions independently:

   Michael Hasofer, University of New South Wales, Sidney 2033, Australia.

   David J. Merkel, 11 Sunnybank Road, Aston, Pennsylvania 19014, U.S.A.

Alan Montgomery, 218 McCurdy Drive, Kanata, Ontario K2L 2L6, Canada.

3. "The Velocity of Light," *Science*, Vol. 66, Supplement x, 30 September 1927.

4. M. E. J. Gheury de Bray, "The Velocity of Light," *Nature*, 24 March 1934, p. 464.

● M. E. J. Gheury de Bray, "The Velocity of Light," *Nature*, 4 April 1931, p. 522.

5. Ibid., p. 522.

6. No physical law prevents anything from exceeding the speed of light. In two published experiments, the speed of light was apparently exceeded by as much as a factor of 100! The first experiment involved radio signals which, of course, are a type of light. Counterexplanations are being proposed for these surprising results, but so far, no one has repeated the experiment or shown it to be false. [Alexis Guy Obolensky, personal communication.] The second report referred to a theoretical derivation and a simple experiment that permitted electrical signals to greatly exceed the speed of light. This derivation follows directly from Maxwell's equations. The special conditions involved extremely thin electrical conductors with very low capacitance and inductance. For further details see:

♦ P. T. Pappas and Alexis Guy Obolensky, "Thirty Six Nanoseconds Faster Than Light," *Electronics and Wireless World*, December 1988, pp. 1162-1165.

♦ Harold W. Milnes, "Faster Than Light?", *Radio-Electronics*, Vol. 54, January 1983, pp. 55-58.

A strange quantum effect also causes light, in certain situations, to slightly exceed the normal speed of light. [See Julian Brown, "Faster Than the Speed of Light," *New Scientist*, 1 April 1995, pp. 26-29. This has also been reported in the popular press. See Sharon Begley, "Faster Than What?," *Newsweek*, 19 June 1995, pp. 67-69.]

7. V. S. Troitskii, "Physical Constants and the Evolution of the Universe," *Astrophysics and Space Science*, Vol. 139, No. 2, December 1987, pp. 389-411.

8. T. C. Van Flandern, "Is the Gravitational Constant Changing?", *The Astrophysical Journal*, Vol. 248, 1 September 1981, pp. 813-816.

● T. C. Van Flandern, "Is the Gravitational Constant Changing?", *Precision Measurement and Fundamental Constants II*, editors B. N. Taylor and W. D. Phillips, National Bureau of Standards (U.S.A.), Special Publication 617, 1984, pp. 625-627.

9. Some who believe in an old universe have a different explanation. Those isotopes are extinct because so much time has passed. However, this explanation raises a counterbalancing question: How did those isotopes, and 97 percent of all elements, form? The standard answer is that these elements appeared during supernova explosions. This is actually speculation, since essentially no supporting evidence has been found. Besides, all supernova remnants we see in our galaxy appear to be less than 10,000 years old. This is based on the well-established decay pattern of a supernova's light intensity in the radio-wave frequency range. [Keith Davies, "Distribution of Supernova Remnants in the Galaxy," *Proceedings of the Third International Conference on Creationism* (Pittsburgh, Pennsylvania: Creation Science Fellowship, 1994), pp. 175-184.]

10. Alan Montgomery and Lambert Dolphin, "Is the Velocity of Light Constant in Time?", *Galilean Electrodynamics*, Vol. 4, No. 5, September-October 1993, pp. 93-97.

11. "Precision" should not be confused with "accuracy." Atomic clocks are very precise, but not necessarily accurate. They keep very consistent time with each other, and each atomic clock can subdivide a second into nine billion parts. This is remarkable **precision**. But what if this entire global network of atomic clocks is drifting—speeding up or slowing down? Precision, while impressive, does not imply accuracy.

12. Kenneth Brecher, "Is the Speed of Light Independent of the Velocity of the Source?", *Physical Review Letters*, Vol. 39, No. 17, 24 October 1977, pp. 1051-1054.

13. The light beams are considered to be traveling in a vacuum. Light travels at slightly slower speeds when it travels through any substance, such as air, water, or glass.

● Another question concerns Einstein's well-known formula, $E=mc^2$, which supposedly gives the energy (E) released when a nuclear reaction annihilates a mass (m). If the speed of light (c) decreases, then one might think that either E must decrease or m must increase. Not necessarily.

In the universe, time could flow according to either atomic time or orbital time. Under which standard would $E=mc^2$ be a true statement? Mass-energy would be conserved under both; in other words, the energy or mass of an isolated system would not depend on how fast time passed. Obviously, $E=mc^2$ would be absolutely true in atomic time where c is constant, but not in orbital time where c decreases. Let's now see why $E=mc^2$ will be approximately correct even in orbital time.

Nuclear reactions convert mass to energy. Unfortunately, the extremely small mass lost and large energy produced cannot be measured precisely enough to test whether $E=mc^2$ is absolutely true. Even if mass and energy could be precisely measured, this formula has embedded in it ***an experimentally-derived, unit-conversion factor*** that requires a time measurement by some clock. Which type of clock should be used: an orbital clock or an atomic clock? Again, we can see that $E=mc^2$ is "clock dependent."

If c has decreased (the orbital time standard), neither length, electrical charge, nor temperature standards would change. Therefore, chemical and nuclear reactions would not change. However, the **speed** of nuclear reactions, and to a slight extent chemical reactions, would change, since the vibrational frequencies of atoms would change. Also, radioactive decay rates, which depend on the vibrational frequency of the atom, would decrease if c decreased.

14. W. G. Tifft, "Properties of the Redshift. III. Temporal Variation," *The Astrophysical Journal*, Vol. 382, 1 December 1991, pp. 396-415.

15. "Most Distant Galaxies: Surprisingly Mature," *Science News*, Vol. 119, 7 March 1981, p. 148.

How Old Do Evolutionists Say the Universe Is?

In the late 1920s, evolutionists believed that the universe was 2 billion years (b.y.) old. Later, radiometric dating techniques gave much older ages for certain rocks on Earth.[1] Obviously, a part of the universe cannot be older than the universe itself. This contradiction was soon removed by devising a rationale for increasing the age of the universe.

A similar problem is now widely acknowledged. (See **Big Bang?** on page 19.) If a big bang occurred, it happened 8-12 b.y. ago. If stars evolved, some stars are 16 b.y. old.[2] Obviously, stars cannot be older than the universe.

Figure 89: Globular clusters are spherical concentrations of stars with stellar densities thousands of times greater than in our portion of the Milky Way Galaxy. This globular cluster, called M 13, is about 22,000 light-years away.

A lesser known problem of this type also exists. Let's suppose the universe is 10 b.y. old. This is not enough time for certain extremely distant stars and galaxies to form and transmit their light to Earth. The light from these distant objects shows that they contain many chemical elements heavier than hydrogen and helium, such as carbon, iron, and uranium. A big bang would have produced essentially only hydrogen and helium. Consequently, the first generation of stars would not contain any heavy chemical elements. Evolutionists, therefore, believe that the heavier 97% of the chemical elements in the universe were produced inside stars, especially when some exploded as supernovas at the end of their lifetimes. Much later, a second generation of stars supposedly formed from that exploded debris. These were the first stars, then, to have visible heavy elements. If a big bang happened, there must be enough time afterwards to:

a. form the first generation of stars;
b. have many of those stars pass through their complete life cycles then finally explode as supernovas to produce the heavier chemical elements;
c. recollect, somehow, enough of that exploded debris to form the second generation of stars; and finally
d. transmit their light immense distances to Earth.

Some new and sophisticated light-gathering instruments have enabled scientists to discover many extremely distant galaxies and quasars. The current distance record is held by a quasar that has a mixture of heavy elements at its surface.[3] Its light has taken 93% of the age of the universe to reach us, assuming constancy in the speed of light as the evolutionists always do. This means that only the first 7% of the age of the universe is available to accomplish the events that evolutionists believe happened—events a-c above. Only 0.7 b.y. would be available in a 10 b.y. old universe. Few evolutionist astronomers believe that such slow processes as a-c above, if they happened at all, could happen that quickly.[4]

Evolutionists can undoubtedly resolve these time contradictions—but at the cost of rejecting some cherished theory. Perhaps they will accept the possibility that light traveled much faster in the past. (Evidence already exists to support this revolutionary idea. See page 153.) Perhaps they will conclude that the big bang never occurred, or that heavy elements were somehow in the first and only generation of stars, or that redshifts do not always imply a recessional velocity, or that stellar evolution does not occur. Each of these ideas is consistent with a recent creation.

Most evolutionists are unaware of these contradictions. However, as more powerful telescopes begin peering many times further into space, more attention will be focused on these problems. If scientists find, as one might expect, even more distant stars and galaxies with heavy elements, problems with the claimed age of the universe will no longer be the secret of a few evolutionists.[5]

References and Notes

1. Arthur N. Strahler, *Science and Earth History* (Buffalo, New York: Prometheus Books, 1987), pp. 102, 129.

2. Ivan R. King, "Globular Clusters," *Scientific American*, Vol. 252, June 1985, pp. 79-88.

3. Ron Cowen, "Quasars: The Brightest and the Farthest," *Science News*, Vol. 139, 4 May 1991, p. 276.

4. Jeff Kanipe, "Galaxies at the Confusion Limit," *Astronomy*, December 1988, pp. 56-58.

● R. F. Carswell, "Distant Galaxy Observed," *Nature*, Vol. 335, 8 September 1988, p. 119.

5. Dietrick E. Thomsen, "Farthest Galaxy Is Cosmic Question," *Science News*, Vol. 133, 23 April 1988, pp. 262-263.

● M. Mitchell Waldrop, "The Farthest Galaxies: A New Champion," *Science*, Vol. 241, 19 August 1988, p. 905.

● Dietrick E. Thomsen, "Galaxies in a Primitive State," *Science News*, Vol. 133, 23 January 1988, p. 52.

● M. Mitchell Waldrop, "Pushing Back the Redshift Limit," *Science*, Vol. 239, 12 February 1988, pp. 727-728

Is There Life in Outer Space?

Those who believe there is life in outer space usually base that belief on the following reasoning:

> Life evolved on Earth. Since the universe is so immense and contains so many heavenly bodies, life probably evolved on some other planet as well.

There are several flaws in this reasoning. First, it assumes that life evolved on Earth. Actually, a great deal of evidence shows that life is so complex that it could not have evolved—anywhere! (See pages 2-15.) Over the last 130 years, our culture has been so saturated with evolution that many have uncritically believed it. Subsequently, they concluded that life must have also evolved on at least a few of the many extraterrestrial bodies.

Yes, there are many stars, and a very small fraction *may* have planets.[1] However, the probability of just one living cell forming by natural processes is so infinitesimal, *even considering the vast number of stars*, that the likelihood of life spontaneously occurring anywhere in the visible universe is virtually zero!

Despite popular and influential science fiction books and films, such as: *Star Wars, E.T., Star Trek, 2001,* and *Close Encounters of the Third Kind*, there really is no scientific evidence for any extraterrestrial life. Hundreds of millions of tax dollars have been spent trying to find life in outer space. Conditions outside Earth are more destructive than probably anyone suspected before space exploration began: deadly radiation, poisonous gases, extreme gravitational forces, gigantic explosions, and the absence of the proper atmospheres and specific chemical elements. Just the temperature extremes in outer space would make almost any kind of life either so hot that it would vaporize or so cold that it would be completely rigid, brittle, and dead. Unfortunately, these physical realities do not stir the imagination as well as science fiction and evolutionary stories.

"Bioastronomy" and "exobiology" are the studies of life in outer space. (They are the only fields of science without evidence or subject matter.) People in these fields are searching for signals from outer space that would imply an intelligent source. Radio telescopes linked with computers simultaneously search millions of radio frequencies for a non-random, nonnatural, extraterrestrial signal—any short sequence of information. Yet these researchers do not understand that the long sequence of information in the DNA of every living thing also implies an intelligence—a vast intelligence. But if these researchers ever accepted the evidence for this intelligent designer, the evolutionary premise for their search would disappear.

If life evolved in outer space as easily as some people believe, many extraterrestrial "civilizations" should exist. Some should even be technologically superior to ours. Any superior civilization within our galaxy would probably have already explored and colonized our solar system, at least with mechanical robots. Since this apparently has not happened, there is further reason to believe that extraterrestrial life does not exist, certainly not within our Milky Way Galaxy.

There have been many stories of unidentified flying objects (UFO's). However, almost all have been traced to natural or manmade causes. Even if technically advanced flying objects exist, they may be of terrestrial, not extraterrestrial, origin. The United States, for example, developed and flew the "superfast" and "super-secret" SR-71 aircraft for about a decade before almost any senior military officers in the United States knew such technology was possible. The evidence that UFO's are from extraterrestrial civilizations, although not disproved, has not been verified and usually relies on the truthfulness and rationality of a few alleged witnesses.

Is there life in outer space? Probably not. Many people enjoy speculating on this subject, and some want to believe there is life in outer space—usually life that is superior to ours. They may be right. However, there is little rational basis for this belief.

References and Notes

1. As of January 1996, some have claimed to have found a few planets outside our solar system. While further studies may verify these impressive finds, decades of similar previous announcements have turned out, on further study, to have been false alarms of many kinds.

   For example, a famous false alarm concerned Barnard's star that appeared to wobble due to the gravitational attraction of orbiting planets. Later it was shown that the telescope probably wobbled, not the star. In 1984, major radio and television networks reported that a team of astronomers at Kitt Peak National Observatory had discovered the first planet outside the solar system. Other astronomers, after months of searching, could not verify the claim. Two years later, the original astronomers acknowledged that atmospheric turbulence probably fooled them, since even they could not find their "planet." In July of 1991, British astronomers reported a star that wobbled with a six-month period. They claimed, and the excited media announced, discovery of the first planet outside our solar system. Later, these astronomers retracted their claim. It was Earth that wobbled slightly, not the star. There have been other false alarms. Unfortunately, the media typically sensationalizes each report and hardly ever retracts them when they are disproven.

   One aspect of the January 1996 announcement has gone largely unnoticed. Very sensitive instruments detected a few stars that wobble, apparently because of the gravitational attraction of **unseen** bodies orbiting them—perhaps planets. The measurements, based on the slight cyclic changes in color of these stars, only indicates the star's wobble towards and away from Earth. The key question that is overlooked is, "How is the plane of the orbiting body oriented?" If the body orbits in a plane that is parallel to our line of sight to the star, then the orbiting body is small enough to be a planet and still cause the wobble. However, if the orbital plane is nearly perpendicular to our line of sight, a much more massive body is needed to cause the wobble. Such a body would be so massive that it would be a small dim star called a brown dwarf—it would not be a planet. Stars often orbit other stars. We must await additional confirmation before we can confidently assert that planets exist outside the solar system.

How Did Human "Races" Develop?

Today, common usage of the word "race" refers to groups of people with distinguishing physical characteristics such as skin color, shape of eyes, and type of hair. Unfortunately, the term "race" was applied to different groupings of humans, even though there is only one race—the human race. This term came into popular usage with the growing acceptance of evolutionism in the late 1800s.

To appreciate how minor these human variations are, consider the large variations in the dog family. (See Figure 2 on page 2.) Most varieties of domestic dogs have been produced during the past 300 years. Dogs may be white, black, red, yellow, spotted, tiny, huge, hairy, almost hairless, cute, or not-so-cute. Their temperaments and abilities also vary widely. Since the domestic dog can interbreed with the wolf, the coyote, the dingo, and the jackal, all are part of the dog kind. By comparison, human variations are few and minor. The vast number of genes in every kind of life permits these variations, allowing successive generations to adapt to environmental changes. Without this design feature, extinctions would be much more common. Besides, wouldn't life be much less interesting without variations within each kind?

The following three mechanisms probably account for most of the so-called "racial" characteristics.

1. Natural Selection. This well-established phenomenon is not a mechanism for macroevolution, as a century of experimentation has shown, although it is an important mechanism for microevolution. Natural selection filters out certain parental genes in successive generations, producing offspring with slightly different characteristics and less genetic variability. For example, a fair-skinned person living near the equator is susceptible to several health risks, such as skin cancer. Consequently, the fair-skinned person at low latitudes has slightly less chance of living to reproductive age and passing on his or her genes for light skin color to a child. A similar situation exists for dark-skinned people living in the polar latitudes. Their dark skin screens out sunlight and tends to deprive them of vitamin D_3 which forms in skin exposed to sunlight. Absence of vitamin D_3 produces rickets. Therefore, over many generations, dark-skinned people tend to live near the equator and light-skinned people tend to live at the higher latitudes.

There are exceptions, however. Eskimos (Inuits) have dark skin and yet live in Arctic latitudes. Their diet, which includes fish-liver oils containing large amounts of vitamin D_3, prevents rickets.

2. Cultural Preference. This takes the form of likes (as in mate selection) or dislikes (as in prejudices).

- **Likes.** The old saying that "beauty is in the eye of the beholder" probably plays a major role in explaining "racial" characteristics. In other words, a person's cultural upbringing appears to influence mate selection along "racial" lines. This has been demonstrated in geese. Blue snow geese live in one region of the Arctic, and white snow geese live in another. Eggs from each colony were hatched in an incubator. The goslings were then raised by "foster parents" of the opposite color. The young geese later showed a mating preference for geese having the color of their foster parents. In another experiment, the foster parents were painted pink. Again there was a mating preference for the color the young geese saw as they were growing up, even though that color was artificial. The old song "I Want a Girl Just Like the Girl That Married Dear Old Dad" illustrates the point.

- **Dislikes.** Humans also have prejudices—some people more than others. Prejudices based on physical appearances have caused wars, genocide, forced segregation, and voluntary isolation. Adolf Hitler had a fanatical hostility toward Jews and a strong preference for the supposedly Aryan characteristics of tall, blond, blue-eyed people. This led to his extreme and repugnant steps to exterminate the former and increase the latter. An example of voluntary isolation occurs in Africa. The pygmies, who are typically $4\frac{1}{2}$ feet tall, live separately from the Watusi, whose people are sometimes seven feet tall. Yet, they may live within several hundred miles of each other. These and hundreds of other prejudicial actions, operating over several thousand years, resulted in the geographical isolation of people with certain physical appearances.

3. Small, Isolated Populations. A population of people (or any other form of life) has a large set of genetic characteristics. If a few members of this population move to an isolated region, such as an island, they will have a different and smaller set of genetic characteristics (or a smaller range of genetic potential) than the entire population. As a result, subsequent generations on that island will have different traits from the original population.

This can be illustrated by a barrel filled with marbles—half white and half black. Let's say that each marble represents a person, and the color of the marble represents a gene for that person's skin color. If pairs of marbles are

?

drawn at random and placed on separate islands, about half the islands will have marbles of just one color—white or black. If each pair of marbles represented a husband and wife, this would be somewhat analogous to the dispersion and isolation that would occur after a global disaster with few survivors. Each person carries genes for skin color. If a husband and wife ended up having the same genes for dark or light skin color, then all their descendants would tend to have dark skin or light skin. The color of the marbles could just as well represent any other genetic characteristic.

Actually, the genetics of this process are more complicated than this simple illustration. For example, at least four genes determine skin color, not just one. Nevertheless, there are thousands of traits, each of which might cluster in an isolated geographic region if small groups broke off from the larger population. Thus, specific characteristics can easily arise from a few isolated people.

For the past 130 years, evolutionism told us that man supposedly ascended from some apelike ancestor. According to evolutionism, some early humans branched off sooner than others, and therefore, they looked different, acted differently, and had different physical and mental abilities. This is *racism*, a highly prejudicial school of thought that tends to dehumanize fellow human beings. One cannot say that evolutionists today are racists. Racism is unpopular today, and public acknowledgment of it is even more so. However, many evolutionists in the several generations following Darwin, and Charles Darwin himself, were racists. The theory of evolution provides a very convincing rationale to justify racism.[1]

Creation provides quite a different historical perspective. If we are all descended from an original male and female, we are all cousins. Think what the world would be like if everyone realized that!

References and Notes

Figure 90: Faces. A few members of the human race from the following locations: top row, left to right: Japan, Tibet, Borneo, Holland; second row: Ireland, China, Rwanda, Korea; third row: New Zealand, Bali, Okinawa, Israel; fourth row: United States of America, Australia, India, Egypt; bottom row: Molucca Islands, Canada, Greece, Guatemala. Visualize all without the minor variations in dress, hair style, age, and skin color. How different are we? The differences are small; the ways we are alike are great. People continents apart laugh alike and cry alike.

1. *"Biological arguments for racism may have been common before 1859, but they increased by orders of magnitude following the acceptance of evolutionary theory."* Stephen Jay Gould, *Ontogeny and Phylogeny* (Cambridge, Massachusetts: The Belknap Press of Harvard University Press, 1977), p. 127.

● Roger Lewin, *Bones of Contention* (New York: Simon & Schuster, Inc., 1987), pp. 266-267.

?

What about the Dinosaurs?

This frequent question, asked in just this way, implies many questions related to dinosaurs—a word meaning "terrible lizards." When did they live? What killed the dinosaurs? What were they like? There were about 300 different types of dinosaurs. Most were large; some even gigantic. One adult dinosaur was as tall as a five-story building. However, some were small, about the size of a chicken. (See page 148.)

If we focus on one question, "When did they live?", most of these other questions will fall into place. There are two common, but quite different, answers. Evolutionists say that dinosaurs lived and died at least 60 million years before man evolved. Others believe that the earth is young and that man coexisted with the dinosaurs. If we look at the evidence, sorting out these two very different answers should be easy.

Did the dinosaurs live and die at least 60 million years before man evolved? Almost all textbooks that address the subject say so. Movies and television vividly portray this. One even hears it at Disney World and other amusement parks. Some will say that every educated person believes this. We frequently hear stories that begin with phrases such as, "Two hundred million years ago, as dinosaurs ruled the earth, . . ." But none of this is evidence; some of it is an appeal to authority. (Evidence must be visible, measurable, and verifiable.)

Did man and dinosaurs live at the same time? Scientists in the former Soviet Union have reported a layer of rock containing more than 2000 dinosaur footprints alongside tracks "resembling human footprints."[1] Obviously, both types of footprints were made in mud or sand that has since hardened into rock. If they are human footprints, then man and dinosaurs lived at the same time. Similar discoveries have been made in Arizona.[2] If it were not for the theory of evolution, few would doubt that these footprints were made by humans.

On April 25, 1977, a Japanese fishing ship, off the east coast of New Zealand, caught a huge monster that had been dead for about a month. From a depth of 900 feet, the foul-smelling animal was hauled on board and disengaged from the net. One crew member was alert enough to take five photographs, one of which is shown in Figure 91. He also sketched the animal. (See Figure 92.) The rotting corpse weighed 4,000 pounds and was 32 feet long. A piece of its flipper was cut off before the ship's captain had the putrid carcass thrown overboard to avoid contaminating the ship's cargo of fresh fish.

When the photographs were developed and shown to local scientists, no one could identify the animal. A panel of eminent marine scientists was asked to study it. The piece of flipper was analyzed chemically as similar to that of a fish or reptile but not a mammal, such as a whale. The animal's neck was too long to be a fish. Furthermore, it had vertebrae, as Figure 92 shows—something not present in many fish, including sharks. The opinion that the monster was a plesiosaur grew as all other contenders failed to fit the criteria, especially its size and the presence of four flippers. Finally, the Japanese government commemorated the discovery of an apparent plesiosaur with a postage stamp shown in Figure 93.

Other governments directed their fishing ships in the area to the spot where the find of a century had been thrown overboard. An estimated twenty Japanese, eight South Korean, and thirty Russian ships participated. Reportedly, the Russian crew members were told that if they found the monster but could not stand its smell, they (not the monster) must go overboard. Neither the monster nor any of its kind were found.[3]

If the Loch Ness monster exists, it too could be a plesiosaur. There are other reports, not yet confirmed by physical evidence and teams of scientists, of dinosaurs living today. For the past three centuries, reports have come from Zaire in western Africa that dinosaurs exist in remote swamps. These stories are often from educated people, eyewitnesses, and others who can quickly describe dinosaurs. Although they did not personally see dinosaurs, two expeditions, led by biochemist Dr. Roy Mackal of the University of Chicago, verified many of these accounts, some from scientists.[4] If the accounts are correct, then man and dinosaurs are contemporaries.

Consider the interesting question of dragon legends. Most ancient cultures have stories or artwork of dragons that strongly resemble dinosaurs.[5] *The World Book Encyclopedia* states that:

> *The dragons of legend are strangely like actual creatures that have lived in the past. They are much like the great reptiles* [dinosaurs] *which inhabited the earth long before man is supposed to have appeared on earth. Dragons were generally evil and destructive. Every country had them in its mythology.* [6]

The simplest and most obvious explanation for so many common descriptions of dragons from around the world is that man once knew the dinosaurs.

Figure 91: Apparent Plesiosaur. This animal was caught by a Japanese fishing ship manned by eighteen crewmen off the coast of New Zealand in 1977. The subject made front-page news for weeks in Japan. In North America and Europe, this photograph was barely seen because the common perception, based ultimately on the theory of evolution, is that it could not have been a plesiosaur. According to the theory of evolution, plesiosaurs have been extinct for 66 million years.

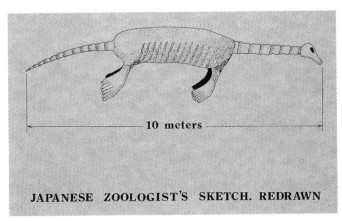

JAPANESE ZOOLOGIST'S SKETCH. REDRAWN

Figure 92: Sketch of the Monster. Notice the large bones, or vertebrae, in its neck and the four flippers of almost equal size. Before learning of these details, some thought the monster was a giant shark, such as the basking shark. Overlooked was the fact that the backbone of a shark, and many other fish, is one long piece of cartilage. Furthermore, the basking shark lives mainly in the Arctic Ocean, 7,500 miles and half a globe away. Some thought the monster was a giant seal, but the largest seal on record (a male southern elephant seal) is only 21 feet long. Besides, a seal has only two flippers and is a mammal.

Figure 93: Japanese Postage Stamp. This stamp celebrated 100 years of scientific discoveries. The greatest of 1977 was the discovery of an apparent plesiosaur.

Figure 94: Drawing of Plesiosaur from the Fraas Stuttgart Museum.

What caused the extinction of dinosaurs? The flood did. Since dinosaur bones are found among other fossils, dinosaurs must have been living when the flood began. There are dozens of other dinosaur extinction theories, but they all have recognized problems. (See pages 81-82.) Most of the food chain was buried in the flood. Therefore, many large dinosaurs that survived the flood probably had difficulty feeding themselves and became extinct.

Most, if not all, dinosaurs hatched from eggs. The largest dinosaur eggs ever found were a foot long. Hatchlings, even after a year of growth while on the Ark, would be quite easy to handle.

Possibly dinosaurs became very large, because they lived to great ages. Reptiles, unlike other animals, continue to grow throughout their lives. Perhaps large dinosaurs, which are similar to reptiles in many ways, were just old.

References and Notes

1. Alexander Romashko, "Tracking Dinosaurs," *Moscow News*, No. 24, 1983, p. 10.

2. Paul O. Rosnau et al., "Are Human and Mammal Tracks Found Together with the Tracks of Dinosaurs in the Kayenta of Arizona?", Parts I and II, *Creation Research Society Quarterly*; Vol. 26, September 1989, pp. 41-48 and December 1989, pp. 77-98.

- Before 1986 many thought dinosaur tracks and human tracks were together along the banks of the Paluxy River in Texas. Some, but not necessarily all, of the humanlike tracks were apparently made by a portion of a dinosaur's foot. The film (*Footprints in Stone*) and book (*Tracking Those Incredible Dinosaurs* by John Morris) which popularized the man-track idea have been withdrawn. A few creationists still maintain that some manlike tracks were made by humans. However, this author believes that the Paluxy tracks should be studied more and many questions satisfactorily answered before claiming that human tracks are along the Paluxy River.

- In Uzbekistan, 86 consecutive horse hoofprints were also found beside supposedly 90-100 million-year-old dinosaur tracks. Evolutionists have almost as much difficulty believing that horses and dinosaurs lived together as they do man and dinosaurs. Horses allegedly did not evolve

until many millions of years after the dinosaurs became extinct. See Y. Kruzhilin and V. Ovcharov, "A Horse from the Dinosaur Epoch?", *Moskovskaya Pravda* [*Moscow Truth*], 5 February 1984. For a report of quadruped hoofprints alongside 1000 dinosaur prints supposedly 210 million years old, see Richard Monastersky, "A Walk along the Lakeshore, Dinosaur-Style," *Science News*, Vol. 136, 8 July 1989, p. 21.

3. John Koster, "What Was the New Zealand Monster?", *Oceans*, Vol. 10, November-December 1977, pp. 56-59.

4. Roy P. Mackal, *A Living Dinosaur?* (New York: E. J. Brill, 1987).

- "Living Dinosaurs?" *Science 80*, November 1980, pp. 6-7.

- Jamie James, "Bigfoot or Bust," *Discover*, March 1988, pp. 44-53.

5. Lorella Rouster, "The Footprints of Dragons," *Creation Social Science and Humanities Quarterly*, Fall 1978, pp. 23-28.

6. Knox Wilson, "Dragon," *The World Book Encyclopedia*, Vol. 5, 1973, p. 265.

?

How Can I Become Involved In This Issue?

People who learn about the case for creation and the adverse and far-reaching consequences of evolutionism frequently ask, "What can I do?" Some people incorrectly feel this is merely a scientific issue that must be left to others. Actually, each of you, with your unique circumstances, interests, and abilities, can do something to help expose these evolutionary myths. Here are several possibilities.

Understand the Problem.

Evolutionary theories and interpretations are usually taught as if they were facts. Teachers, textbooks, and the media frequently convey the attitude that evolution is the only scientific and intellectually respectable view of origins. Students are implicitly presented with a choice, a false dichotomy—"Are you going to hold a narrow-minded religious belief, or are you going to accept a scientific explanation?" Evolution is thus protected from competent criticism, and students are kept ignorant of its many shortcomings. Valid scientific explanations are ignored (see pages 2-66). Students who were taught this way are now teachers, professors, publishers, and textbook writers. Their position, prestige, and income are threatened by the creation movement, so they choose to ignore the scientific evidence opposing evolution and supporting creation.

Learn More, and Teach Others.

Tell your friends what you have learned. Encourage them to learn more about the creation-evolution issue. Many excellent books are available—some at your local libraries and book stores. (See the recommended reading list on pages 174-175.) Learn more yourself. This will help you be more effective in talking with your friends.

Talk to Educators.

Talk or write to the teachers, school officials, and school-board members in your community. Ask them such questions as: Are you aware of the many fallacies concerning the theory of evolution that we have all been taught? Are you teaching the scientific evidence that points to creation? *Why not teach all the science?* Are you aware that the great majority of the American public want both evolution and creation taught? Are you aware that more than 85% of the public do not want only evolution taught?[1] Our message to educators should be:

- Teach all the science at the appropriate grade level.

- Teach students to think critically: to examine evi-

dence, to test alternative hypotheses, to question, to identify hidden assumptions, to think accurately, and to reach their own conclusions.

- Teachers should become technically up to date and learn the evidence concerning origins.

- Teachers have a serious responsibility for the accuracy of what they say in their classrooms, especially about the subject of origins.

Many educators mistakenly believe that most scientific creationists want to legislate their views into the classroom. *Assure teachers and professors that most scientists who are creationists do not advocate legislation that would force certain views to be taught.* Even if every legislature in the country required teachers to present both creation and evolution, the hostility and ridicule that would accompany such forced teaching of creation would be very damaging. The scientific evidence for creation is so strong that education and persuasion are by far the more effective and lasting approach.

Explain to friends and educators that most creationists advocate the following:

- *No religious doctrines or writings should be taught or ridiculed in the public schools.*

- *All the major scientific evidence dealing with origins should be brought out at the appropriate grade levels.*

- *When a theory of origins is presented, any reasonable opposing evidence should also be presented.*

Propose the Origins Research Project.

Encourage science teachers and professors, as well as members of boards of education and boards of trustees, to add an Origins Research Project to their curriculum (see page 169). Such a project, in which each student decides which theory of origins he or she feels is best supported by the scientific evidence, could be one of the most interesting, maturing, and valuable projects that the students ever experience. The project is appropriate at the high school, college, and graduate school level, can be tailored in many ways to fit a variety of school or classroom situations, requires no special teacher training, involves very little cost, favors no theory of origins, is not restricted to just two models (creation and evolution), focuses only on scientific evidence, completely removes

?

any concern about bringing religion into public schools, involves only a moderate amount of classroom time, and includes a variety of materials from which the instructor can choose.

Challenge Evolutionists.

Encourage knowledgeable evolutionists to enter either written or oral debates on this question of origins. If they decline, make a point of asking, "Why won't evolutionists debate the scientific evidence?" Do not argue with such evolutionists until you are familiar with the evidence. If you are not, refer these evolutionists to those who are.

Inform the Media.

Write letters to television stations and newspaper and magazine editors. Compliment them whenever they provide accurate and balanced coverage of the creation-evolution issue. Provide polite and reasoned criticisms when they assume evolution to be a fact or when they avoid the scientific evidence. In the case of television, send a copy of your letter to the program's advertisers. Inform the advertisers and media officials of the public's positions on the issue of origins.[2]

References and Notes

1. Many organizations have surveyed public attitudes on the teaching of origins. The results are remarkably consistent, regardless of whether creationist, evolutionist, or some other organization conducted the survey. Typically, responses are as follows:

   5% I would like only evolution taught.

   15% I would like only creation taught.

   70% I would like both creation and evolution taught.

   10% No opinion, or teach neither.

2. Gallup has conducted three polls of the beliefs in the United States concerning origins. People were given four choices:

   - The Creation Position: God created man pretty much in his present form at one time within the last 10,000 years.

   - The Theistic Evolution Position: Man has developed over millions of years from less advanced forms of life, but God guided this process, including man's creation.

   - The Atheistic Evolution Position: Man has developed over millions of years from less advanced forms of life. No God participated in this process.

   - No Opinion

Table 6: Gallup Poll Results

	1982	1991	1993
Creation	44%	47%	47%
Theistic Evolution	38%	40%	35%
Atheistic Evolution	9%	9%	11%
No Opinion	9%	4%	7%

Notice how few people are atheistic evolutionists, and yet this position dominates the media and many schools. It is noteworthy that despite the monopolistic teaching of evolution, so many are creationists.

Some will incorrectly claim that almost all scientists believe in evolution. The only survey of scientists of which this author is aware, involved chemists. Less than half (48.3%) said that "it was possible that humans evolved in a continuous chain of development from simple elements in a primordial soup." A slight majority (51.7%) said that "supernatural intervention played a role." [Murray Saffran, "Why Scientists Shouldn't Cast Stones," *The Scientist*, 5 September 1988, p. 11.]

How Can the Creation-Evolution Issue Be Brought into the Classroom?

Bringing the scientific evidences for creation into the public classroom has always been legal.[1] Nevertheless, many teachers wonder how to do this. Schools should be places of inquiry, where students are taught to analyze all sides of an issue. Few academic subjects have greater

inherent interest for high school, college, or graduate school students than the origins question. The fact that it is controversial is, therefore, not a liability but an asset.[2] The origins question, then, is an ideal vehicle for developing analytical skills.[3] An excellent way to develop these skills is "The Origins Research Project."

The Origins Research Project

Introduction. The Origins Research Project may be one of the most interesting and exciting projects your students ever experience. It will certainly be one they will remember the rest of their lives. It will demonstrate how scientific inquiry works while building upon one of the most basic and natural questions a person ever asks: "How did everything begin?" Each student is (a) to decide which theory of origins best fits the scientific evidence, and (b) to write a paper presenting his or her reasoning. Religious beliefs, while possibly important to the student's overall conclusion, are not to be a part of this paper. Neither is there any right or wrong answer. Instead, breadth of research, critical thinking, sound logic, and detailed comparisons of the data with the various theories should be the basis for evaluating the student's work.

The following description of the Origins Research Project has been written in a generalized form, so it can be used at the high school, college, or graduate school levels in either secular or religious schools. You can tailor this project to the time available, your student's needs, and your objectives.

Purpose. The purposes of this project are (a) to help each student develop analytical skills in science, (b) to integrate many seemingly diverse topics and fields of science into a meaningful, maturing, and exciting investigation which the student largely controls, and (c) to permit academic study in an important area of science without infringing on diverse religious views that are the prerogatives of the individual and the home. Since strongly held views will be presented on both sides of this question of origins, the student will develop, probably for the first time, strong, reasoned, and confident disagreement with some scientific authorities and textbook authors. This experience, which even most scientists or engineers do not have until they are well into their first major research effort, is one of the most maturing that an education can provide. Unfortunately, the typical classroom experience, especially in the sciences, is that of learning or absorbing a fixed body of knowledge—not that of evaluating the evidence and deciding which of several scientific explanations is most plausible.

The Project. Each student is to write a paper stating which theory of origins he or she feels is best supported by the scientific evidence and why. The first sentence of the paper will be, "I believe that the scientific evidence best supports _____." The blank space, for example, might contain one of the following:

- the theory of evolution

- the theory of creation

- a modified theory of evolution

- a modified theory of creation

(Possible definitions of "evolution" and "creation" are on page 172.) Any student who feels that the evidence supports a theory other than evolution or creation should define that theory. Students should understand that their conclusions, based upon an examination of only some scientific evidence, may differ from their religious views (theism, atheism, or the many variants of each). The scope of this project is not to resolve such differences but rather to learn to examine scientific evidence. Limitations and uncertainties in science, especially when dealing with ancient events that had no observers and cannot be repeated, will become apparent before the project is completed.

The Role of the Teacher. The teacher's primary role is (a) to develop each student's analytical skills in science, (b) to prevent religious aspects from entering into any classroom discussions, and (c) to challenge and stimulate the student's thinking. Teachers should frequently ask thought-provoking questions such as:

- What assumptions are being made?

- Can those assumptions be tested?

- Do other scientists agree?

- What are some other explanations?

- What evidence is there for other conclusions?

The teacher's role is not to teach the material. The scope of the subject matter is so broad that it would be unreasonable to expect teachers to master it quickly enough to teach it. Furthermore, most teachers probably have presuppositions that could easily bias the student's decision-making process. Students will frequently ask (sometimes subtly) what the teacher believes. A suggested response is:

Don't be concerned with what I believe. What matters in this class is how thoroughly you examine the scientific evidence on both sides of this issue. I am not interested in your specific conclusion; I am only interested in the thoroughness and logic you use to reach your conclusion. You are on your own.

The teacher's goal is to **teach students how to think, not what to think**.

Teacher Options:

1. Select the resources to be made available to the students.

2. Decide the length of the written paper. This decision should be based upon the student's academic level, the scientific fields the student should explore, and the objectives of the teacher. For a high school physics, biology, or modern science course, 1000 words might be a minimum. For a graduate student majoring in science education or geology, 40 type-written pages might not be sufficient.

3. Determine the beginning and ending dates for the Origins Research Project. The project should be long enough to allow the student to reflect on the subject, to do the depth of reading and library research the teacher desires, and to write the paper. It is suggested that the Origins Research Project span 1- 4 months and be completed in time to allow one week for grading. This project can be completed using a minimum of three classroom periods.

4. Specify the writing and grading standards. The required quality of the written paper and its adherence to the school's style manual should be established. Schools that have a well-integrated curriculum may want English teachers to grade the papers from a writing standpoint and science teachers to grade the papers from a scientific stand-point. If, among the teachers available for grading, at least one is an evolutionist and one is a creationist, then students could have their papers graded by a teacher who holds their basic view of origins (creation or evolution).

5. Establish the weight that will be assigned to this graded project. It should be commensurate with the research effort that the teacher desires and the student motivation that will be needed, possibly one-third to one-sixth of the course grade. Some students have been allowed to complete the Origins Research Project in lieu of taking the final exam.

Resource Materials. Many resources are available to help students form their conclusions. Teachers and school officials are encouraged to examine the following list of resources and select those they feel are appropriate for their learning situations. Regardless of which specific resources or activities the teacher selects, every effort should be made to provide a balance between at least the two basic scientific models of origins—evolution and creation.

1. Video Tape
"The Great Debate: Evolution vs. Creation" (50 minutes). This excellent video features a debate between Professor Evolution and Dr. Creation, each played by Terry Mondy, a public high-school biology teacher. Entertaining, informative, interesting, and accurate. Appropriate for high school through college audiences. Available for purchase from Terry Mondy, 6305 Ojibwa Lane, McHenry, IL 60050 for $24.95, plus $3.00 for mailing and handling.

2. Books for student reference:
 a. From the evolution perspective:[4]

 • Charles Darwin, *The Illustrated Origins of Species* by Charles Darwin, abridged and introduced by Richard E. Leakey, Hill & Wang, 1979.

 • Nicholas Hotton, *The Evidence of Evolution*, The Smithsonian Series, American Heritage Publishing Co., 1968.

 • F. C. Howell, *Early Man*, Time-Life Books, 1973.

 • Robert Jastrow, *Until the Sun Dies*, Warner Books, 1977.

 • Ruth Moore, *Evolution*, Time-Life Books, 1970.

 b. From the creation perspective:

 • Walt Brown, *In the Beginning: Compelling Evidence for Creation and the Flood*, Special Edition, Center for Scientific Creation, 1996.

 • Duane T. Gish, *Challenge of the Fossil Record*, Master Books, 1985.

 • Henry M. Morris and Gary E. Parker, *What is Creation Science?*, Master Books, 1982.

 c. Which contrast the creation and evolution perspectives:

 • Richard Bliss, *Origins: Two Models, Evolution/Creation,* Master Books, 1978.

 • Richard Bliss and Gary E. Parker, *Origin of Life, Evolution/Creation*, Master Books, 1979.

 • Richard Bliss, Gary E. Parker, and Duane T. Gish, *Fossils: Key to the Present, Evolution/Creation*, Master Books, 1980.

?

● Francis Hitching, *The Neck of the Giraffe,* Ticknor & Fields: New Haven and New York, 1982. (Also see the article excerpted from this book: "Was Darwin Wrong?", *Life*, April 1982, pp. 48-52.)

● R. L. Wysong, *The Creation-Evolution Controversy*, Inquiry Press, 1978.

d. Other helpful books:

● Michael Denton, *Evolution: A Theory in Crisis,* Burnett Books Limited (London), 1985.

● William R. Fix, *The Bone Peddlers: Selling Evolution*, Macmillan Publishing Co., 1984.

● Fred Hoyle and Chandra Wickramasinghe, *Evolution from Space*, Simon and Schuster, 1981.

● Norman Macbeth, *Darwin Retried: An Appeal to Reason*, Harvard Common Press, 1971.

● Gordon Rattray Taylor, *The Great Evolution Mystery*, Harper and Row, 1983.

3. Outside Speakers
The local school may invite, for separate appearances, outside experts to the school to answer students' questions. These experts would usually be an evolutionist and a creationist scientist. It is not recommended that teachers assume this role and defend one point of view. Teachers are encouraged to create an atmosphere of inquiry by stimulating and motivating their students to arrive at their own conclusions independently.

Having expert witnesses just before the students begin writing their papers will help the students concentrate on unresolved questions. It might be instructive, especially at the high school level, to formulate questions beforehand during classroom time. The students who favor evolution should question the creationist witness, and the students who favor creation should question the evolutionist witness. This will increase the level of interest and the desire to adequately prepare. Both questioning sessions could be done simultaneously in different rooms if time is a consideration.

4. Student Debates
Miniature student debates are an excellent way to increase student interest and involvement in this project. Each student could be given five minutes to state his or her case regarding some category of evidence, followed by two-minute rebuttals. A sign-up sheet could be posted for students to seek an opponent to debate selected topics. One such debate

each week, lasting possibly 15-20 minutes, could provide an important stimulus for all students. Care must be taken at the high school level to prevent debates from becoming disorderly. At all levels, videotaping during nonclassroom time can be effectively used. This would allow the teacher to select only the best debates for classroom viewing.

5. Bulletin Board Displays
Students should be encouraged to bring to class any magazine, newspaper, or journal articles on the subject of origins. After they have been posted on a bulletin board for several days, discussions concerning the quality of the articles, the evidence cited, and the identification of hidden assumptions can be very informative. Letters to the editor by students could provide additional interest. (The teacher may want to offer an incentive for any student's letter that is published. Perhaps excuse the student from some other writing exercise.)

Questions and Answers

Q: Are there approaches I could take other than having my students write a major paper?

A: Yes. Students could be exposed to the same scientific evidence by being asked to do one or more of the following:

● Summarize or outline what they feel are the most convincing evidences for the various theories of origins.

● Make an oral presentation of a specified length.

● List a specified number of evidences for creation and evolution.

● Prepare a poster or display dealing with one or more of the evidences for creation or evolution.

● Write a short critique of (a) any viewpoint expressed by a prominent creationist or evolutionist, (b) a museum display that relates to the origins issue, (c) a recent newspaper or magazine article, or (d) a chapter in a textbook.

Q: How can creation be dealt with scientifically?

A: Scientists employ a common but special type of reasoning when they try to explain past, unrepeatable events that had no observers. They first develop a model—or what some scientists call a "working hypothesis." This is simply a description of what they think happened. Once the model is defined, especially when alternative models are available, observations and measurements can be made that will help raise or lower the model's plausibility.

There are many possible models of origins. However, the two basic models, creation and evolution, can be defined as follows:

The Creation Model of Origins:

- Everything in the universe, including the stars, the solar system, the earth, life, and man, came into existence suddenly and recently, in essentially the complexity we see today.

- Genetic variations are limited.

- The earth has experienced a worldwide flood.

The Evolution Model of Origins:

- Over billions of years, the universe, the solar system, the earth, and finally, life developed from disordered matter through natural processes.

- Random mutations and natural selection brought about the present diversity of living things from single-celled life.

- Man descended from a common ancestor with apes.

Neither creation nor evolution can explain scientifically what happened at the ultimate beginning (represented by the region in red in Figure 95). The evolution model is completely silent concerning the origin of matter, space, energy, time, and the laws of chemistry and physics. The furthest back in time that most evolutionists claim to go is to a hypothetical "big bang." They admit that they are scientifically blind prior to such an event. Creationists likewise have no scientific understanding of what happened physically during the creation event. Nevertheless, to the right of the shaded region, both models can be tested against the evidence. For any assumed starting condition in the past, scientists frequently ask if the laws of physics and chemistry would produce many details of what we see today. These are certainly scientific questions that give us insight into our beginnings.

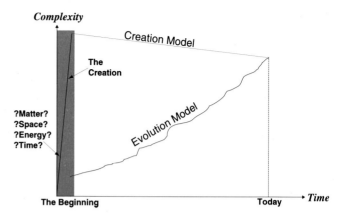

Figure 95: Comparison of Creation and Evolution on the Complexity Scale.

Q: How can those high school students who are underachievers or poorly motivated carry out this project?

A: Students who have difficulty carrying out a full-scale research project will understand and enjoy the video tape described on page 170. They may also be directed to any one of the three illustrated booklets written by Richard Bliss. These books, which have been tested in hundreds of classrooms, are written at the 8th or 9th grade level. Most students reading below this level can read portions of these books.

Teachers who see students having difficulty may want to limit them to a narrow topic, such as the fossil record, and might help them formulate questions, such as:

- How do evolutionists explain the fossil record?

- How do creationists explain the fossil record?

- How are fossils formed?

- Are there other explanations?

- Where are fossils formed today?

- What details are found in the fossil record?

- Do these observations better fit the creation or the evolution explanation?

The answers to these questions could form an outline for a student's paper. If the student requires more guidance, references and page numbers could be included with each question.

Many students, when arriving at their conclusions, are quite surprised to find that their verdicts differ from those of various scientists—either creationists or evolutionists.

The confidence these students have that their answers are correct and the answers of one group of scientists are incorrect produces self-confidence and increased interest and awareness. Students frequently want to explore other aspects of the origins controversy on their own. Generating this sense of excitement and discovery should be an objective of every science curriculum.

Q: What would the minimum project involve at the high school level?

A: The following is an inexpensive way to structure this project so that only three classroom periods are needed. These three classes should be spread out over at least a three-week period.

Day 1:

- Pass out the assignment sheets which (a) state the length, format, grading criteria, and due dates for the outline and final 1000-word paper, (b) define "creation" and "evolution," and (c) list the resources available in the school library.

- Describe selected resources.

- Show the video tape "The Great Debate: Evolution or Creation." (See page 170.)

- Explain science methodology when dealing with past events that were not observed and cannot be repeated. (See Figure 95.)

Day 2:

- Have the students conduct one or two debates.

- Lead an informal discussion of the issue. Emphasize the importance in science of basing conclusions on evidence.

- Remind the students that their outlines are due in ___ days.

Day 3:

- Comment on the quality of students' outlines.

- Discuss articles posted on the bulletin board.

- Remind the students that their final papers are due in ___ days.

References and Notes

1. As recently as 1987, the Supreme Court of the United States held: *"Moreover, requiring the teaching of creation science with evolution does not give schoolteachers a flexibility that they did not already possess to supplant the present science curriculum with the presentation of theories, besides evolution, about the origin of life."* "Edwards, Governor of Louisiana, et al. v. Aguillard et al.", *Supreme Court of the United States*, No. 85-1513, argued 10 December 1986, decided 19 June 1987, p. 1.

2. Richard Alexander, evolutionist and professor of zoology and curator of insects at the University of Michigan, proposed a similar idea.

   No teacher should be dismayed at efforts to present creation as an alternative to evolution in biology courses; indeed, at this moment creation is the only alternative to evolution. Not only is this worth mentioning, but a comparison of the two alternatives can be an excellent exercise in logic and reason. Our primary goal as educators should be to teach students to think and such a comparison, particu-larly because it concerns an issue in which many have special interests or are even emotionally involved, may accomplish that purpose better than most others. Richard D. Alexander, "Evolution, Creation, and Biology Teaching," *American Biology Teacher*, Vol. 40, February 1978.

3. Analytical skills in science include observing; classifying; measuring; explaining; predicting; applying mathematics; designing investigations and experiments; collecting and analyzing data; drawing conclusions; identifying assumptions; contrasting alternative explanations; formulating definitions, questions, hypotheses, and models; and the willingness to retract prior conclusions when the evidence warrants it.

4. School libraries usually have many books dealing with evolution, which can be used to supplement those suggested here.

What Additional Reading Do You Recommend?

Books:

Origin by Design, **Harold G. Coffin with Robert H. Brown (Review and Herald Publishing, 1983).**
> Coffin and Brown have written an easy-to-read layman's book on geology. This "history of the earth," for high-school level and above, contains more than thirty chapters on a variety of topics, including fossils, coal, ancient man, polystrate fossils, and animal adaptation and survival.

Evolution: A Theory in Crisis, **Michael Denton (Harper and Row, 1986).**
> Denton, who has a Ph.D. in molecular biology, is an active medical researcher. Since he is not a creationist, Denton's hard-hitting and authoritative arguments take on even greater force. He deals at length with the absence of transitional fossils, homology, molecular biology, genetics, design in nature, taxonomy, and the historical development of evolutionary thought. Denton believes that, "Ultimately the Darwinian theory of evolution is no more nor less than the great cosmogenic myth of the twentieth century." Although written in layman's language, it takes a thoughtful reader with some familiarity with biology to get the most out of this book.

The Bone Peddlers: Selling Evolution, **William R. Fix (Macmillan Publishing Co., NY, 1984).**
> William Fix is neither a creationist nor a scientist. Nevertheless, he has written an entertaining, accurate, readable, and critical attack on the evolutionist claim that humans descended from apelike creatures. Since Fix opposes both creation and evolution, he proposes "psychogenesis," a new idea without scientific merit. Fortunately, the two chapters that deal with this bizarre idea do not detract from the other twenty chapters.

Evolution: The Challenge of the Fossil Record, **Duane T. Gish (Master Books, 1985).**
> This book replaces and expands on Gish's earlier book *Evolution: The Fossils Say No!*. Evolutionists usually point to the fossil record as their best evidence. The author takes each category of the alleged fossil evidence and exposes the fallacies. Gish, a Ph.D. biochemist, is probably best known for his many public debates with evolutionists. By the evolutionist's own admission, they usually lose such debates.

Darwin on Trial, **Phillip E. Johnson (Regnery Gateway, 1991).**
> Berkeley law professor Johnson looks at the evidence for evolution with a dispassionate eye for logic and proof. He finds that many scientists have prematurely accepted Darwin's theory as fact and then scrambled to find evidence for it, unsuccessfully. Johnson maintains that although many difficulties have mounted for evolution, these scientists have clung to the theory out of fear of encouraging "religious fundamentalism" and in the process have turned belief in Darwinism into their own religion.

Speak to the Earth: Creation Studies in Geoscience, **editor George F. Howe (Presbyterian and Reformed Publishing Company, 1975).**
> Contains twenty-six selected articles on geoscience from the *Creation Research Society Quarterly* from 1969-1974. Major topics include paleontology and origins, evidence for catastrophes, and thermodynamics.

Scientific Studies in Special Creation, **editor Walter E. Lammerts (Presbyterian and Reformed Publishing Company, 1971).**
> A collection of articles from the *Creation Research Society Quarterly* during its first five years, 1964-1969. It contains thirty-one technical articles on genetics, botany, stratigraphy, radiometric dating, biblical topics, and many other subjects.

Darwin Retried: An Appeal to Reason, **Norman Macbeth (Harvard Common Press, 535 Albany St., Boston, MA 02118, 1971).**
> Norman Macbeth, an attorney, examines evolution more from a logical basis than a scientific basis. He exposes the fallacies just as a trial lawyer would in court. Macbeth gained his insights by attending the private monthly meetings of the experts at New York's American Museum of Natural History. The public would be surprised at how openly these experts acknowledge the problems of evolution, at least in their private meetings. Macbeth is amazed that this information ·is not filtering down to the 2nd and 3rd echelons—textbook writers and professors.

Macbeth claims that "any fool can see that evolution died years ago," and yet, teachers do not know it.

Scientific Creationism (Public School Edition), editor Henry M. Morris (Master Books, 1974).

The editor and prime contributor is Henry M. Morris, founder of the Institute for Creation Research in San Diego. Some consider him to be the father of and the prime driving force behind the modern creationist movement. He has written or coauthored more than forty books and hundreds of articles. Assisting Morris was the scientific staff at the Institute for Creation Research and dozens of other technical consultants. Although parts are out-of-date, *Scientific Creationism* is ideal for an informed layman or teacher at any level who wants a general and clear explanation of much of the scientific evidence supporting creation.

What Is Creation Science?, Henry M. Morris and Gary E. Parker (Master Books, 1982).

This is really two books in one. Part I is essentially Gary Parker's earlier book, *Creation: The Facts of Life*. Parker, who has a doctorate in biology, has a casual and lucid style that provides appealing explanations for creation evidences in the life sciences. Part II, by Henry Morris, deals with the physical sciences. Much of the material in Part II repeats other books of Morris. This readable book is an ideal gift for anyone you feel should reexamine the subject of origins, especially if they wonder "what difference does it make" or feel that "science favors evolution."

The Creation-Evolution Controversy, R. L Wysong (Inquiry Press, 1880 North Eastman, Midland, MI 48640, 1976).

This is both a thorough and balanced treatment of the creation-evolution controversy from a scientific and logical point of view. Wysong, a veterinarian and professor of human anatomy, has accumulated, documented, and explained a massive amount of data in a readable form for high school and adult levels. The book is not typeset.

Many fine books are no longer in print, but may be available in libraries. Some books to look for are:

♦ *Ape-Men: Fact or Fallacy?*, M. Bowden

♦ *Handy Dandy Evolution Refuter*, **Robert E. Kofahl**

♦ *The Mystery of Life's Origin: Reassessing Current Theories*, **Charles B. Thaxton, Walter L. Bradley, and Roger L. Olsen**

Periodicals:

Creation Ex Nihilo Technical Journal, P.O. Box 6330, Florence, KY, 1-800-350-3232.

Also published by the Creation Science Foundation of Australia. This journal covers more technical aspects of science as they relate to creation and the flood.

Creation Research Society Quarterly, P.O. Box 969 Ashland, OH 44805-0969.

This scientific journal is highly recommended for anyone who wishes to stay abreast of some of the latest technical developments in the growing field of creation. It is published in March, June, September, and December. Annual subscription rates vary depending on your status (student, non-voting member, etc.).

Origins, The Geoscience Research Institute, Loma Linda University, Loma Linda, CA 92350.

Origins is a small, attractive publication that is produced twice a year. It contains reports of research by some capable scientists. Topics usually deal with the earth sciences. More creationists need to become aware of the Geoscience Research Institute's research and writings.

Origins Research, Access Research Network, P.O. Box 38069, Colorado Springs, CO 80937-8069.

This newspaper-style publication, issued twice a year, was formerly published by Students for Origins Research. Its articles do not require specialized knowledge, although it is written for a college level audience.

?

How Do Evolutionists Respond to What You Say?

They generally ignore it. A few will criticize the evidences in forums where I cannot respond. Once every year or so, a knowledgeable evolutionist will agree to an oral, strictly scientific debate. These debates are usually lively, but always cordial. Unfortunately, little can be covered in a $2\frac{1}{2}$-hour debate, and the substance of the debate cannot be widely distributed, studied, and recalled by others as it could if it were in writing.

The biggest single step that I believe could be taken to clarify the creation-evolution controversy is to have a thorough, written, publishable debate. Both sides would lay out their case, much as I have in **The Scientific Case for Creation** on pages 2 - 66. Then each side would respond, point-by-point, to the case for the other side. Both sides would have the right to publish the finished exchange. I have sought such a dialogue since 1980, but have not had a serious and qualified taker. Many leading evolutionists know of the offer. When I speak at universities and colleges, I offer students a $200 finder's fee, if they can find an evolutionist professor who will complete such a debate. I am repeating that offer here to the first student who can find such a science professor.

Several excuses are given.

1. "I don't have time."

   Response: Many do not have time, and of course, they need not participate. Nevertheless, others have the time to write books attacking and misrepresenting creationist positions. Many are teaching what I feel are outdated evolutionary ideas and refuse to place themselves in a forum where they must defend what they are teaching. **If you are going to teach something, you ought to be willing to defend it**, especially if taxpayers are paying your salary.

2. *"I don't know enough about evolution."* (Carl Sagan's answer) or *"I am only qualified in one aspect of evolution."*

   Response: A team of people could participate in the evolutionist side of the debate.

3. "I don't want to give a creationist a forum."

   Response: Of the thousands of scientific controversies, the creation-evolution controversy is the only one I know where some scientists refuse to exchange and discuss the evidence. That is an unscientific, closeminded position.

4. "Creation is a religious idea. It is not science."

   Response: Creation certainly has religious implications, but much scientific evidence bears on the subject. Only the scientific aspects would be permitted in this written debate. An umpire would remove any religious, or antireligious, comments from the exchange. If my only comments were religious, the umpire would strike them from the debate. I would have nothing to say, and the evolutionist would win by default. (Incidentally, evolution also has religious implications.)

5. "Any debate should be in refereed science journals."

   Response: The journals you refer to are controlled by evolutionists. They would not provide a platform for such a lengthy debate. Nor do they publish any research questioning evolution and supporting creation. The publishers of these journals would be severely criticized by many of their clientele and advertisers if they did. (The few evolutionists who participate in oral debates often admit how much they are criticized by other evolutionists for participating in a debate.) In a well-publicized case, one journal, *Scientific American*, withdrew a contract to hire a very qualified assistant editor when it was learned he was a creationist.

If anyone wishes to explore the written debate idea further, I would welcome a letter regarding the debate. But if you are going to ask a qualified evolutionist to participate, watch out for the excuses.

How do evolutionists respond to the scientific case for creation? Most try to ignore it. As you can see from the above excuses, even qualified evolutionists avoid a direct exchange dealing with the scientific evidence.

?

Technical Notes

How Long Would It Take the Moon to Recede from the Earth to Its Present Position?

Evolutionists believe the earth and moon are 4.6 billion years old—an immense amount of time. They claim that with enough time bacteria will change into people. We have all heard some evolutionists say, "Given enough time, anything can happen." This simplistic attitude overlooks two things. First, most conceivable events will not happen because they would violate well-established laws of science.[1] Second, if 4.6 billion years have elapsed, many things should have occurred that obviously have not. Rather than "time being the hero of the plot," as one prominent evolutionist stated,[2] immense amounts of time cause problems for evolution as you will now see.

Most dating techniques, including the majority that indicate young ages, make the three basic assumptions given on page 21. The following dating technique has few, if any, major assumptions. It relies basically on only the law of gravity and one undisputed and frequently repeated measurement. *We will look at the forces causing the moon to spiral farther and farther away from the earth. Then we will see that this spiraling action could not have been happening for the length of time evolutionists say the earth and moon have been around.*

It will be shown that if the moon began orbiting the earth as closely as possible, it would move to its present position in 1.2 billion years. Stated another way, if we could run the clock backwards, the moon would spiral into the earth in only 1.2 billion years. Those astronomers who know of this problem call it "the lunar crisis."[3] Notice that this conclusion does not say that the earth-moon system is 1.2 billion years old. It only says that the earth-moon system must be *less than* 1.2 billion years old. Had the moon begun orbiting the earth at something greater that its minimum possible distance, its age would be even less—perhaps much less. Obviously, something is wrong with either the law of gravity or evolutionists' belief that the earth-moon system is 4.6 billion years old. Most astute people would place their confidence in the law of gravity, which has been verified by tens of thousands of experiments.

What causes tides? If the moon's gravity attracted equally every particle in and on the earth, there would be no tides. Tides are caused by slight differences in the moon's gravitational forces throughout the earth.[4] In Figure 96, the moon pulls more on ocean particle A, directly under the moon, than it does the center of the earth, C, because A is closer. While both A

and C are pulled toward the moon, A, being closer, is pulled with slightly more force and thus moves proportionally further. Therefore, water particle A moves farther from the center of the earth, creating a tidal bulge. Likewise, water particle B, on the far side of the earth, is pulled with slightly less force than C. This difference pulls the earth away from B, creating the far tidal bulge.

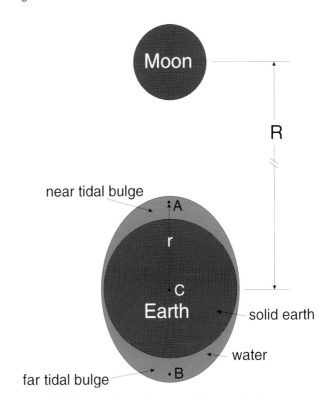

Figure 96: Why the Moon Produces Tides on Earth.

How does the height of ocean tides relate to the earth-moon separation distance (R)? According to Newton's law of gravitation, the moon's gravitational force pulls on the earth's center of mass with a force proportional to $1/R^2$. Water particle A directly under the moon is one earth radius (r) closer, so it is pulled by a force proportional to $1/(R-r)^2$. The difference between these forces is proportional to

$$\frac{1}{(R-r)^2} - \frac{1}{R^2} = \frac{R^2-(R-r)^2}{(R^2)(R-r)^2} = \frac{2rR-r^2}{(R^2)(R-r)^2} \qquad (1a)$$

Since r is much less than R, the numerator on the right is almost 2rR and its denominator is almost R^4. Therefore, the force difference producing the tides and the tide heights are approximately proportional to

$$\frac{2rR}{R^4} = \frac{2r}{R^3} \qquad (1b)$$

Because the earth's radius (r) is constant, we can conclude that the height of the tides is proportional to $1/R^3$. For example, if the earth-moon distance were suddenly doubled, the tides caused by the moon would only be 1/8th as high.[5]

How do tides affect the moon's orbit and the earth's spin rate? Surprisingly, the tidal bulges do not line up directly under the moon as shown in Figure 96. This is because the spinning earth drags the bulges out of alignment as shown in Figure 97. If the earth spun faster in the past, as we will see, the misalignment would have been even greater.

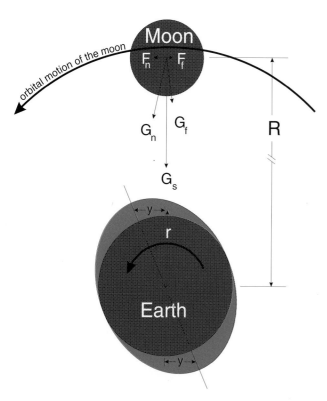

Figure 97: Rotated Tidal Bulges.

Another surprise is that tides do not occur just in the oceans. The solid earth also has two tidal bulges. They too are misaligned because changes in the moon's gravity do not instantaneously alter the stretching of the earth. (We cannot see "solid tides" because we and everything near us rise and fall by the same amount relative to the center of the earth.) Since only 0.02% of the earth's mass is water, "solid tides" alter the orbits of near satellites ten times more than water tides.[6] Which

of the two types of tides changes the moon's orbit more is still an open question.

Let's think of the earth as composed of two parts: a spherical portion (gray in Figure 97) and the tidal bulges—both water and solid tides.[7] G_s is the gravitational attraction of the earth's *spherical* portion on the moon. Since G_s is aligned with the centers of the earth and moon, it does not alter the moon's orbit. However, the near tidal bulge, because it is offset, pulls the moon in a direction shown by G_n, with a component, F_n, in the direction of the moon's orbital motion. F_n accelerates the moon in the direction it is moving, flinging it into an increasingly larger orbit. The far tidal bulge has an opposite but slightly weaker effect—weaker because it is farther from the moon. The *far* bulge produces a gravitational force, G_f, and a retarding force on the moon, F_f. The net strength of this accelerating force is $(F_n - F_f)$. It can also be thought of as a thrust pushing the moon tangential to its orbit, moving the moon farther from the earth. This accelerating force gives us a way to calculate an *upper limit* on the age of the moon. Today's recession rate has been precisely measured at 3.82 cm/yr, but as you will see, it was much faster in the past.[8]

Conversely, the moon's net gravitational pull applies an equal and opposite force on the earth's tidal bulges, slowing the earth's spin. In other words, the earth was spinning faster in the past.

How does $(F_n - F_f)$ relate to the earth-moon separation distance?

$$\frac{F_n}{G_n} \approx \frac{y}{R-r} \qquad\qquad \frac{F_f}{G_f} \approx \frac{y}{R+r}$$

$$G_n = \frac{Gmm_b}{(R-r)^2} \qquad\qquad G_f = \frac{Gmm_b}{(R+r)^2}$$

where y is the misalignment distance of each tidal bulge, m is the moon's mass, m_b is the mass of each tidal bulge, and G is the gravitational constant. Solving for $(F_n - F_f)$:

$$(F_n - F_f) \approx 6rGmy\left(\frac{m_b}{R^4}\right)$$

Equation 1b showed the mass of a tidal bulge, m_b, is proportional to $1/R^3$, that is

$$m_b = \frac{C_1}{R^3}$$

where C_1 is the constant of proportionality. Therefore,

$$(F_n - F_f) \approx 6rGmy\left(\frac{C_1}{R^7}\right) \qquad (2)$$

The velocity of the moon (or any orbiting body that can be considered in a circular orbit) is

$$V = \sqrt{\frac{G(M+m)}{R}}$$

where M is the earth's mass (or the mass of the central body).

Differentiating both sides with respect to time (t) and solving for $\frac{dR}{dt}$ gives

$$\frac{dR}{dt} = (-2)\left(\frac{dV}{dt}\right)\frac{R^{\frac{3}{2}}}{\sqrt{G(M+m)}}$$

Since the moon's tangential acceleration $\left(\frac{dV}{dt}\right)$ is equal to $(F_n - F_f)/m$, which is known from equation (2)

$$\frac{dR}{dt} \approx (-2)\left(6rGy\frac{C_1}{R^7}\right)\frac{R^{\frac{3}{2}}}{\sqrt{G(M+m)}} \qquad (3)$$

The displacement of the tidal bulge (y), as mentioned earlier, is proportional to the difference in the earth's spin rate (ω) and the angular velocity of the moon (ω_L). In other words,

$$y = C_2(\omega - \omega_L) \qquad (4)$$

Substituting (4) into (3) and replacing all the constants by C gives

$$\frac{dR}{dt} \approx \frac{C(\omega - \omega_L)}{R^{\frac{11}{2}}} \qquad (5)$$

C is found by using today's values (subscript t).

$$C = \left(\frac{dR}{dt}\right)_t \frac{R_t^{\frac{11}{2}}}{(\omega - \omega_L)_t} \qquad (6)$$

All we need now is to determine how $(\omega - \omega_L)$ varies with R. From Kepler's third law:

$$\omega_L = \sqrt{\frac{G(M+m)}{R^3}} \qquad (7)$$

Applying the law of conservation of angular momentum gives

$$P\omega + \frac{Mm}{M+m}R^2\omega_L = L \qquad (8)$$

where the constant L is the angular momentum of the earth-moon system, and P is the earth's polar moment of inertia. Combining (7) and (8) gives

$$\omega = \frac{L}{P} - \frac{Mm}{P}\sqrt{\frac{GR}{M+m}} \qquad (9)$$

Substituting (6), (7), and (9) into (5) gives us the final equation. Since it has no closed form solution, it will be solved numerically. The iteration steps begin by setting the clock to zero and R to its present value of 384,400 km. Then time is stepped backwards in small increments until the moon crashes into the earth.

$$R_{i+1} = R_i - \left[\frac{C}{R_i^{\frac{11}{2}}}(\omega - \omega_L)_i\right]dt \qquad \text{from (5)}$$

$$t_{i+1} = t_i + dt$$

$$\omega_{i+1} = \frac{L}{P} - \frac{Mm}{P}\sqrt{\frac{GR_i}{M+m}} = \frac{L}{P} - b\,R_i^{\frac{1}{2}} \qquad \text{from (9)}$$

$$(\omega_L)_{i+1} = \sqrt{G(M+m)}\,R_i^{-\frac{3}{2}} = a\,R_i^{-\frac{3}{2}} \qquad \text{from (7)}$$

The QuickBasic program that solves this is shown in the box on page 180. The answer is 1.2 billion years.

Two complicated effects were neglected, which would further reduce this upper limit for the moon's age.

1. Evolutionists believe the earth formed by gravitational accretion of smaller bodies. If so, the impacts would have left a molten earth. The earth, throughout its history, would have been less rigid that it is today. The tidal bulges would have been larger, causing the moon to spiral away from the earth even faster than we calculated here.
2. Tidal stretching of the solid earth produces internal frictional heating which reduces the earth's spin velocity. A greater value for ω in the past would have increased the tidal misalignment and the moon's recession over what we assumed above. This would have been especially severe if the earth had been less rigid in the past.

If we could incorporate these effects into the above analysis, the upper limit on the moon's age would be even less. Again, all of this does not say that the moon is about 1.2 billion years old. Instead, the maximum possible age for the moon is about 1.2 billion years. It could be much less such as 6,000 to 10,000 years.

One might argue that 1.2 billion years ago the moon was captured by the earth or blasted from the earth by an extraterrestrial collision.[9] (Other difficulties with these and other evolutionary theories on the moon's origin are discussed under **Origin of the Moon**, page 18.) These events would have placed the moon in a very elongated orbit. Today, the moon is in a nearly circular orbit.[10] The only known way to circularize an elongated lunar orbit is a highly improbable encounter with another gravitational body near the earth—a body that has since disappeared.[11] Further compounding such an improbability is the need for this to happen to the other 62 moons in the solar system. Worse yet, the tidal forces, discussed above, act to elongate even further the moon's orbit. Therefore, it is highly unlikely that the moon (a) was captured, (b) was blasted from the earth by an extraterrestrial collision, or (c) somehow began orbiting the earth 1.2 billion years ago. Its orbit is too circular.

What implication would a 1.2 billion year old moon have for organic evolution and the age of the earth? If the moon somehow began orbiting the earth 1.2 billion years ago, its close proximity to the earth would have created extreme tides many miles high.[12] They would have eroded mountains and smoothed the earth, especially at low latitudes. Little, if any, geological evidence supports this and much opposes it. Evolutionists claim that certain fossils are 2.8 - 3.5 billion years old. Had the moon begun orbiting the earth 1.2 billion years ago, such fossils would have been pulverized by the havoc of gigantic tides. Tides exceeding a mile in height would have swept the earth twice a day for millions of years. Evidently the moon did not originate near the earth. This further reduces the maximum age of the moon.

Every dating technique must assume how fast the dating clock has always ticked and the clock's initial setting. For example, radiometric techniques assume a constant rate of radioactive decay. This analysis on the moon's recession only assumes that the law of gravity has been constant. Neither assumption can be proven, but there is no doubt which assumptions scientists would favor. If Newton's law of gravitation did not hold in the past, our scientific foundations would crumble. If the moon is less than 1.2 billion years old, only some preconceptions must be altered. But that's progress.

PROGRAM

```
DEFDBL A-Z          'DOUBLE PRECISION
dt = 10             'TIME INCREMENT (yr)
G = 6.64E-08        'THE GRAVITATIONAL CONSTANT (km³ gm⁻¹ yr⁻²)
LOP = 13486.23      'ANGULAR MOMENTUM OF EARTH-MOON SYSTEM / P (1/yr)
ME = 5.97E+27       'MASS OF THE EARTH (gm)
mm = 7.35E+25       'MASS OF THE MOON (gm)
P = 8.068E+34       'THE EARTH'S POLAR MOMENT OF INERTIA (gm km²)
R = 384400          'TODAY'S EARTH-MOON SEPARATION DISTANCE (km)
Rdot = .0000382     'TODAY'S RATE OF CHANGE OF R (km/yr)
w = 2301.22         'TODAY'S ANGULAR VELOCITY OF THE EARTH'S SPIN (rad/yr)
wL = 83.993         'TODAY'S ANGULAR VELOCITY OF THE MOON'S ROTATION (rad/yr)
t = 0               'TIME, THE NUMBER OF YEARS AGO (yr)

a = SQR(G * (ME + mm))
b = ME * mm * SQR(G / (ME + mm)) / P
c = Rdot * R ^ 5.5 / (w - wL)        'FROM (6)

'marching solution begins

DO
  R = R - (c * (w - wL) / R^5.5) * dt 'FROM (5)
  IF R < 9827 THEN LPRINT "The upper limit on the moon's age is"; t; "years.": END
  w = LOP - b * SQR(R)               'FROM (9)
  wL= a * R ^ -1.5                   'FROM (7)
  t = t + dt
LOOP
```

OUTPUT

The upper limit on the moon's age is **1,198,032,540** years.

References and Notes

1. If you disagree, hold a rubber ball at arm's length and release it. Of the many possible paths the ball could conceivably take (actually an infinite number), it will follow only one. Compress the ball between two surfaces. Of the many possible ways the ball might deform, it will deform in the one way that minimizes its stored energy. These are consequences of physical laws. Even an infinite amount of time will not permit anything to happen, especially for protons to turn into planets, plants, and people.

2. George Wald, "The Origin of Life," *Scientific American*, Vol. 191, August 1954, p. 48.

3. Two international conferences have attempted to address this problem. See P. Brosche and J. Sündermann, editors, *Tidal Friction and the Earth's Rotation* (New York: Springer-Verlag, 1978) and P. Brosche and J. Sündermann, editors, *Tidal Friction and the Earth's Rotation II* (New York: Springer-Verlag, 1982). The studies presented were of mixed quality; none were aware of the effect described in equations 4-9, and all left this recognized problem somewhat "out of focus."

4. Since we are only concerned with the earth-moon interaction, the sun's lesser tidal effect will be omitted.

5. Once R is fixed, the tide's height at a specific location depends on many other factors, especially the shape of the coast line. Record tides are found at the Bay of Fundy in eastern Canada. There the tide sometimes rises and falls more than 50 feet. The average tidal amplitude on the open ocean is about 30 inches. Inland lakes have practically no tides. Lake Superior, for example, has two inch tides. Tidal bulges also occur in the atmosphere and in the

solid earth. Relative to the center of the earth, the foundation of your home (and everything around it) may rise and fall as much as nine inches, depending on your latitude.

6. A. Cazenave, "Tidal Friction Parameters from Satellite Observations," *Tidal Friction and the Earth's Rotation II*, editors P. Brosche and J. Sündermann (New York: Springer-Verlag, 1982), p. 8.

7. The earth's mountain ranges and equatorial bulge can be disregarded in this analysis, since they do not contribute to the moon's recession.

8. Laser beams have been bounced off arrays of corner reflectors left on the moon by three teams of Apollo astronauts and the Russian Lunakhod 2 vehicle. Knowing the speed of light today and the length of time for the beam to travel to the moon and back gives the moon's distance. This has been successfully done more than 8,300 times since August 1986. Adjusting for many other parameters that affect the moon's orbit gives its recession rate: 3.82±.07 cm/yr. (See J. O. Dickey et al., "Lunar Laser Ranging: A Continuing Legacy of the Apollo Program," *Science*, Vol. 265, 22 July 1994, p. 486.) This recession was first observed in 1754 by observing the moon's increasing orbital period. For details see Walter H. Munk and Gordon J. F. MacDonald, *The Rotation of the Earth* (Cambridge, England: Cambridge University Press, 1975), p. 198.

9. The other evolutionary theories on the moon's origin require it to have an age of 4.6 billion years. Since we have seen that the moon cannot be older than 1.2 billion years, and it may be much younger, these other theories can be disregarded.

10. Today, the moon's eccentricity is 0.0549. A perfect circle has zero eccentricity. An extremely elongated elliptical orbit has an eccentricity of 0.9999. An egg-shaped orbit has an eccentricity of about 0.25.

11. Most people, even scientists, do not appreciate the difficulty of placing a satellite in a nearly circular orbit. For an artificial satellite to achieve such an orbit, several "burns" are required at just the right time, in just the right direction, and with just the right thrust. Most planets and moons have nearly circular orbits. How could this have happened?

12. What would the tidal height be if the earth-moon distance (R) approached 9,827 km—the sum of the earth's and moon's radii? (The issue of whether the moon would be pulled apart if it were ever this close to Earth will be bypassed. It depends on many factors, including the moon's tensile strength, its rotation rate, and a subject called Roche's limit.)

From equation 1, the tidal height varies as $1/R^3$. The average height of tides on the open ocean today (with R = 384,400 km) is 30 inches or 0.76 meters. (See endnote 5, above.) Therefore, if R were ever 9,827 km, the tidal height would be

$$0.76 \times 10^{-3} \left(\frac{384,400}{9,827} \right)^3 = 45.5 \text{ km} = 28 \text{ miles}$$

Tides over a mile high would occur if R < 30,000 km = 18,774 miles.

How Much Dust and Meteoritic Debris Should the Moon Have If It Is 4,600,000,000 Years Old?

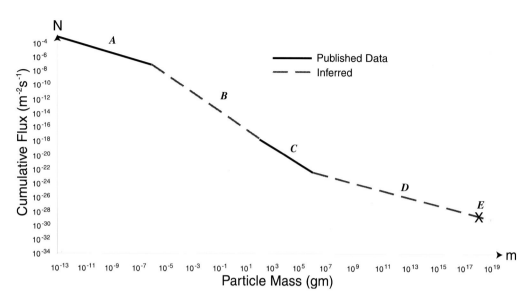

Figure 98: Cumulative Meteoritic Flux vs. Particle Mass.

In 1981, I had a conversation with Dr. Herbert A. Zook of the U.S. National Aeronautics and Space Administration (NASA). He had been intimately involved in estimating the thickness of the dust layer on the moon before the first Apollo moon landing. He also helped analyze the lunar material brought back from the moon. Of the many interesting things he told me and sent me by mail, one is critical in answering the above question.

NASA did not realize until the moon dust and rocks were analyzed that only one part in 67 (or 1.5%) of the debris on the moon came from outer space. The rest was pulverized moon rock. In hindsight, this makes perfect sense. Meteorites that strike the moon travel about seven times faster than a bullet—averaging 20 km/sec. When they strike the moon, they are not slowed down by an atmosphere (as on earth), because the moon has no atmosphere. Therefore, the projectile, regardless of size, instantaneously vaporizes upon impact and kicks up a cloud of pulverized moon rock.[1] The vaporized meteorite then condenses on the pulverized moon rocks. This was determined by slicing moon rocks and finding them coated by meteoritic material—material rich in nickel. Uncoated moon rocks have practically no nickel. In this way, NASA arrived at the factor of 67.[2]

The Data

How much meteoritic material is striking the moon? More specifically, how many particles (N) **greater than** a certain mass (m) pass through a square meter on the moon's surface each second? This is called the cumulative flux. The data is usually reported on a coordinate system as shown in Figure 98. Logarithmic scales are used because so many more smaller particles strike the moon than larger particles.

Particle sizes vary widely. Most particles smaller than 10^{-13} grams are blown out of the solar system by solar wind. At the other extreme are the large crater forming meteorites. Measurements exist for the influx of meteoritic material in three regions across this broad range. The first will be called region A; the second will be called region C; and the last will be called point E. Regions B and D are interpolated between these known regions and are shown as the blue dashed lines in Figure 98.

Region A is based on impacts registered by a satellite 0.98 - 1.02 astronomical units from the sun.[3] The curve for Region A is

$$\log N_A = -10.08 - 0.55 \log m \quad (10^{-13} < m < 10^{-6} \text{ gm})$$

Seismometers placed on the moon provided the data for Region C.[4] The results, again where N_C is the number of particles per square meter per second that are greater than mass m, were

$$\log N_C = -15.12 - 1.16 \log m \quad (10^2 < m < 10^6 \text{ gm})$$

The equation for Region B is obtained by finding the line that joins the far right point in Region A with the far left point in Region C. That equation is

$$\log N_B = -14.77 - 1.33 \log m \quad (10^{-6} < m < 10^2 \text{ gm})$$

Point E is based on the fact that "there are 125 structures [craters] on the moon with diameters greater than 100 km."[5] The diameter of a large meteorite is about 12% of its crater's diameter. If the density of meteorites is 3 gm/cm³, then the mass of a meteorite that could form a crater 100 km in diameter would be

$$\frac{4}{3}\pi\left(\frac{0.12 \times 100 \text{ km}}{2}\right)^3 \left(\frac{10^5 \text{cm}}{\text{km}}\right)^3 \times 3 \frac{\text{gm}}{\text{cm}^3} = 2.71 \times 10^{18} \text{ gm}$$

The surface area of the moon is 3.8×10^{13} m^2. If the largest 125 meteorites struck the moon during the last 4.6×10^9 years, then the average cumulative flux at point E is

$$N_E = \frac{125}{4.6 \times 10^9 \times 365.24 \times 24 \times 3600 \text{ sec}} \times \frac{1}{3.8 \times 10^{13} \text{m}^2}$$

$$= 2.266 \times 10^{-29} \times \frac{1}{\text{m}^2 \text{sec}}$$

Point E connects to region C by the curve

$$\log N_D = -18.91 - 0.53 \log m \qquad (10^6 < m < 2.7 \times 10^{18} \text{ gm})$$

The task now is to integrate the total mass of meteoritic material in regions A, B, C, and D. To do this, we must convert these cumulative flux curves to the thickness of meteoritic material.

Integration

The general form of the cumulative flux curves is

$$\log N = a + b \log m$$

which is equivalent to

$$N = 10^a m^b = \int_m^\infty n \; dm$$

where n(m) is the distribution function of the number of particles of size m.

Differentiating both sides of the right equation above with respect to m gives

$$10^a \; (b) \; m^{b-1} = -n$$

Multiplying the number of particles (n) in a narrow mass range (dm) by the mass m and then integrating between m_1 and m_2 gives

$$\int_{m_1}^{m_2} n \times m \; dm = 10^a \left(\frac{b}{b+1}\right)(m_1^{b+1} - m_2^{b+1})$$

Within this mass range, the thickness (t) of pulverized meteoritic material that will accumulate on the moon's surface in 4.6×10^9 years, *if the influx has always been at today's rate*, is

$$t_{1-2} = 10^a \left(\frac{b}{b+1}\right)(m_1^{b+1} - m_2^{b+1})k$$

where

$$k = \frac{4.6 \times 10^9 \times 365.24 \times 24 \times 3600 \text{ sec}}{2 \frac{\text{gm}}{\text{cm}^3}} \left(\frac{m}{100 \text{ cm}}\right)^3$$

and the density of the pulverized lunar crust is 2 gm/cm^3.

The total thickness of meteoritic material *and pulverized moon rock* during 4.6×10^9 years is

$$(t_A + t_B + t_C + t_D) \; 67$$

since the ratio of the pulverized moon rocks to meteoritic material was 67. Table 7 gives the calculated values for the various thicknesses.

Table 7: Computed Thickness of Lunar Dust

Region	a	b	mass range (gm)	67 x t_{A-D} (meters)
A	-10.08	-0.55	10^{-13} to 10^{-6}	0.98
B	-14.77	-1.33	10^{-6} to 10^2	3.17
C	-15.12	-1.16	10^2 to 10^6	0.01
D	-18.91	-0.53	10^6 to 2.71×10^{18}	310.86

Total Thickness = 315.02 m

Discussion

The lunar surface is composed of a powdery soil, an inch or so thick, below which is 4-10 meters of regolith. Regolith is a range of material from fine dust up to blocks that are several meters across. Meteoritic bombardment, in forming a crater, overturns and mixes this soil-regolith, each time coating the outer surfaces with very thin layers of condensed meteoritic material.

The expected thickness of the soil-regolith, as shown in Table 7 where we assumed 4.6×10^9 billion years of bombardment *at only today's rate*, exceeds by about 50 times its actual thickness. Furthermore, most of this calculated thickness comes from Region D—meteorites larger than 10^6 grams but smaller than meteorites that can form craters 100 km in diameter. Why are A, B, and C so much smaller?

We assumed that the influx of meteoritic material, for Regions A, B, and C, has always been what it is today. Obviously, as time has passed, the influx has decreased enormously because moons and planets sweep meteoritic material up or expel it beyond the earth-moon neighborhood. Only point E did not have that assumption. Point E is based on meteorites we know struck the moon sometime in the past.

Therefore, the cumulative flux for Region D, which is influenced by point E, is less affected by the constant influx rate assumption. This appears to be why Region D contributed most of the expected thickness of soil-regolith in 4.6×10^9 years.

If the moon has steadily collected meteoritic material for 4.6×10^9 years, it should have at least 50 times more lunar soil and regolith than it does. If the influx rate has decreased, as is almost certain, the factor of 50 would increase and give even more reason to believe that the moon is much younger than 4.6×10^9 years old.[6]

Several people have published attempts to answer the question of this technical note. Those efforts have usually (a) overlooked the factor of 67 (b) failed to consider the larger meteorites ($m > 10^6$ gm), and (c) ignored the assumption that the influx rate has always been what it is today.

Conclusion

The above calculations cast serious doubt on the prevailing opinion that the meteoritic material and craters on the moon accumulated over 4.6 billion years. Several other explanations can also be addressed.

Could there have been a steady rain of meteoritic material over only 10,000 years? If the above calculations are repeated, replacing the 4.6×10^9 years with 10,000 years in the calculation for N_E and k, the expected thickness of lunar regolith and soil becomes about 23 meters. This number is also too large, although not as much as the 315 meters calculated above. Therefore, the steady rain of meteoritic material idea is probably wrong, even over a shorter time interval.

Could the bombardment of the moon have been an event rather than a steady rain? If we calculate just the material contributed by the 125 largest impacts, ***assuming the impactors were meteorites***, we find that the thickness of the lunar regolith and soil should be

$$\frac{125 \ (2.71 \times 18^{18} \text{gm}) \times 67}{(3.18 \times 10^{13} \text{ m}^2) \times 2\frac{\text{gm}}{\text{cm}^3}} \times \left(\frac{\text{m}}{100 \text{ cm}}\right)^3 = 299 \text{ meters}$$

This is also too large.

This author's conclusion is that the impactors were comets, not meteorites. Comets are large dirty snowballs (or muddy icebergs). Their water content would have vaporized and escaped the moon long ago.

What was the source of so many comets? Probably it was the "fountains of the great deep," which would have expelled large volumes of muddy water into elliptical solar orbits. (See pages 71-100.) The water would have quickly frozen and become comets. Much more will be said about this surprising proposal at a later time.

References and Notes

1. A meteorite traveling 20 km/sec has tremendous kinetic energy. Suddenly decelerating it to a "dead stop" would compress every atom in it and raise each particle's temperature to many hundreds of thousands of degrees Kelvin.

2. This number has also been published.

   "The content of meteoritic material in mature lunar soils is about 1.5 percent." Stuart Ross Taylor, *Lunar Science: A Post-Apollo View* (New York: Pergamon Press Inc., 1975), p. 92.

3. David W. Hughes, "Cosmic Dust Influx to the Earth," *Space Research XV*, 1975, pp. 531-539.

 • More recent work has confirmed the cumulative mass flux in the 10^{-9} to 10^{-4} gram size range. [See S. G. Love and

   D. E. Brownlee, "A Direct Measurement of the Terrestrial Mass Accretion Rate of Cosmic Dust," *Science*, Vol. 262, 22 October 1993, pp. 550-553.]

4. Taylor, p. 84.

5. Ibid., p. 93.

6. Evolutionists admit that the flux rate has decreased, at least in region C, by about a factor of ten.

   "This flux is about one order of magnitude less than the average integrated flux over the past three aeons, calculated on the basis of crater counts on young lunar maria surfaces." Ibid., p. 92.

Does Subduction Really Occur?

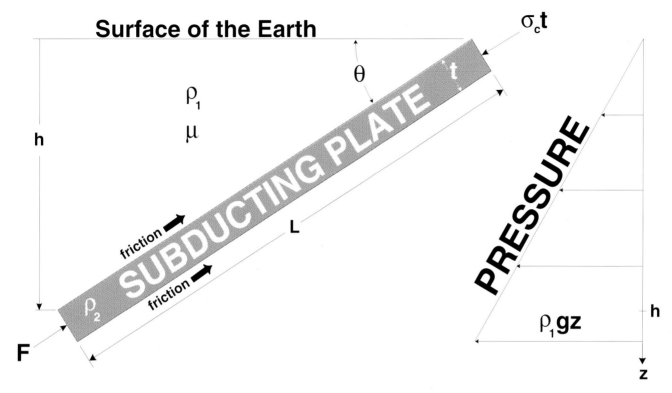

Figure 99: A Plate Trying to Subduct

A plate, which may or may not be subducting, has a length L, thickness t, a unit depth, and density ρ_2. It is inclined at an angle θ below the horizon and is pushed by a compressive stress σ_c through rock whose density is ρ_1. Solid-to-solid friction, with a coefficient of μ, is encountered to a depth h. The lithostatic pressure at a depth z is the mean density ρ_1 times z times the acceleration due to gravity g. A "drag" F opposes movement at the leading edge of the plate.

To make subduction as likely as possible, assume:

- The thrusting force, $\sigma_c t$, is perfectly aligned with the subduction angle θ.

- The thrusting force is the maximum possible, but does not exceed the crushing strength of the subducting slab.

For the plate to subduct, the sum of the forces down and to the left must exceed the sum of the forces up and to the right. That is:

{Net Thrust} + {Body Forces} >
{Friction on Top and Bottom Surfaces}

$$(\sigma_c t - F) + g(\rho_2 - \rho_1)L\, t\, \sin\theta \;>$$

$$\left(\rho_1 g \frac{h}{2} L \mu\right) + (\rho_1 g \frac{h}{2} + \rho_2 g\, t\, \cos\theta)L\, \mu$$

In dimensionless form, this simplifies to:

$$\frac{\left(\sigma_c - \dfrac{F}{t}\right)}{\rho_1\, g\, L\, \sin\theta} + \left(\frac{\rho_2}{\rho_1} - 1\right) > \left(\frac{L}{t} + \frac{\rho_2}{\rho_1}\mathrm{ctn}\,\theta\right)\mu$$

The coefficient of friction for rock against rock is about .6, and it is largely independent of the mineralogical composition and temperature up to about 350°C. [See Stephen H. Kirby and John W. McCormick, "Inelastic Properties of Rocks and Minerals: Strength and Rheology," *Handbook of Physical Properties of Rocks*, Vol. 2, editor Robert S. Carmichael (Boca Raton, Florida: CRC Press, 1982), pp. 151-152, 170.] Typical values for the above inequality are shown below.

$$\sigma_c = 1.3 \times 10^9 \; \frac{\text{dynes}}{\text{cm}^2} \qquad g = 980 \; \frac{\text{cm}}{\text{sec}^2}$$

$$\rho_2 = 3.5 \; \frac{\text{gm}}{\text{cm}^3} \qquad \rho_1 = 3.2 \; \frac{\text{gm}}{\text{cm}^3}$$

$$L = 350 \text{ km} \qquad t = 80 \text{ km}$$

$$\theta = 30° \qquad \mu = 0.6$$

To make subduction more likely, let's assume F = 0. Substituting these values in the above inequality gives the **false** statement that

$$0.024 + 0.094 > (4.375 + 1.894) \times 0.6$$

Since both the Net Thrust and the Body Force terms on the left-hand side are much less than 1, and the right-hand side is much greater than 1, **the inequality cannot be satisfied, so a pushing force will not cause subduction.**

Some believe that a pulling force causes subduction. They say, for example: "at a given depth, the subducting plate is colder and therefore denser than the mantle. The plate sinks through the mantle, like a dense rock falling through mud. As it falls, it pulls the rest of the plate."

This proposal overlooks the fact that the tensile strength of rock is much less than its compressive strength. If the pushing force, described above, cannot cause subduction, a pulling force certainly will not. **Therefore, subduction will not occur.**

Can Overthrusts Occur? Can Mountains Buckle?

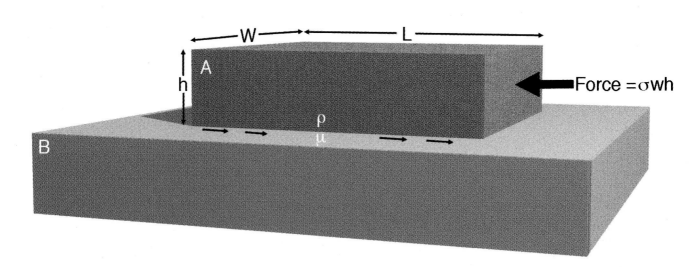

Figure 100: Frictional Locking of Two Slabs.

Slab A has a length, height, width, and density of L, h, w, and ρ respectively. It rests on horizontal surface B and is pushed from the right. The pressure or force trying to move slab A over surface B exerts a uniform stress that equals the maximum compressive strength σ_c of slab A.

Resisting the movement is the static friction at their interface having a coefficient of μ . For motion to occur, the pushing force must exceed the resisting force, that is:

$$\sigma_c\, w\, h > \rho g (L\, w\, h)\mu$$

The gravitational acceleration (g) is 980 cm/sec². The coefficient of static friction for most rocks is at least .6, if temperatures are less than about 350°C. [See Stephen H. Kirby and John W. McCormick, "Inelastic Properties of Rocks and Minerals: Strength and Rheology," *Handbook of Physical Properties of Rocks*, Vol. 2, editor Robert S. Carmichael (Boca Raton, Florida: CRC Press, 1982), pp. 151-152, 170.]

Using the properties of granite:

$$\rho = 2.7\,\frac{gm}{cm^3} \qquad \text{and} \qquad \sigma_c = 1.3 \times 10^9\,\frac{dynes}{cm^2}$$

$$L < \frac{\sigma_c}{\rho g \mu} = \frac{1.3 \times 10^9}{2.7 \times 980 \times 0.6} = 8.2 \times 10^5\,cm = 8.2\ km$$

In other words, if a slab of rock is longer than 8.2 km (5 miles), the pushed end will be crushed before movement begins. This result holds regardless of the other dimensions of the slab.

If rock must slide over unlubricated rock, overthrusts will not occur and mountains will not buckle. Since both appear to have happened (see for example Figure 33 on page 77), something must have lubricated the movement.

Energy in Subterranean Water

During the flood phase, the sinking hydroplates did work on the escaping subterranean water. This work W_h equaled the volume V of water expelled times the pressure p created by the weight of the hydroplate having a density ρ_h and height h or

$$W_h = p V = (\rho_h g h) V$$

where g is the acceleration due to gravity.

This work forced water out of the subterranean chamber with a high kinetic energy. Some of that energy elevated the water, having a density ρ_w by an amount h, reducing its energy by the potential energy E_p gained

$$E_p = \rho_w g h V$$

The remainder of the energy was converted to heat, raising the temperature of the currents of muddy subterranean water by an amount ΔT with

$$\Delta T = \frac{W_h - E_p}{m_w c_w + m_s c_s}$$

where m_w and m_s are the masses of escaping water and entrained sediments, and c_w and c_s are their specific heats. This gives

$$\Delta T = \left(\frac{\rho_h}{\rho_w} - 1\right)\frac{g h}{c_w\left(1 + \frac{m_s}{m_w} \times \frac{c_s}{c_w}\right)}$$

where the density of water, $\rho_w = \frac{m_w}{V}$. Using the following values:

$$\frac{\rho_h}{\rho_w} = 3.0 \qquad\qquad c_w = 1.00 \frac{cal}{gm\,^\circ C}$$

$$\frac{m_s}{m_w} = 1.5 \qquad\qquad h = 16 \times 10^5 cm$$

$$\frac{c_s}{c_w} = 0.23 \qquad\qquad g = 980 \frac{cm}{sec^2}$$

and the conversion factor, $2.39 \times 10^{-8} cal = 1 \times \frac{gm\ cm^2}{sec^2}$

The temperature change is

$$\Delta T = (3.0 - 1)\frac{980 \times 16 \times 10^5}{1(1 + 1.5 \times 0.23)} \times 2.39 \times 10^{-8} = 56^\circ C$$

Therefore, the subterranean water would have gained 56°C (or about 100°F) in exiting the subterranean chamber. Elevating water's temperature by this amount will increase its evaporation rate by about a factor of 20. The heavy evaporation of this salty water would have enriched the salt concentration in the hot surface waters, causing salt to precipitate into thick, pasty layers. This led to the formation of salt domes. (See page 79.)

Another source of energy would not have altered the water's temperature. Before the flood, the subterranean water contained stored compressive energy. This energy equaled the work that would have been done by a large piston compressing a volume of water $V + \Delta V$ to a pressure p in a cylinder. Compressibility β is defined as

$$\beta = \frac{p}{\left(\frac{\Delta V}{V}\right)}$$

For water $\beta = 2.75 \times 10^{10} \times \frac{dynes}{cm^2}$, and for the hydroplate $\rho_h = 3.0 \times \frac{gm}{cm^3}$. The subterranean water was compressed by 17%, or

$$\frac{\Delta V}{V} = \frac{\rho_h g h}{\beta} = \frac{3.0 \times 980 \times 16 \times 10^5}{2.75 \times 10^{10}} = 0.17$$

The work done, and thus the compressive energy stored in the subterranean water, was

$$W_c = \frac{1}{2} p \Delta V = \frac{p^2 V}{2\beta}$$

The cooling from the compressed water's expansion was about equal to the conversion of the compressed energy to heat. Therefore, no net temperature change would have resulted from the stored compressive energy.

How Is Limestone Produced?

Any satisfactory explanation for the world's sedimentary layers must also explain the enclosed limestone[1] layers. This requires answering two questions—rarely asked, and perhaps never answered.

- What was the source of the calcium and carbon in limestone? Remarkably, limestone holds more calcium and more carbon than today's atmosphere, oceans, coal and oil deposits, and living matter combined.

- What chemical reactions account for the deposition of vast, layered deposits of limestone within the sediments? The relative purity of these limestone layers suggests rapid precipitation. A simple, visual examination of limestone grains shows that few are ground-up sea shells or corals, as some believe.

Answering these questions in the context of the hydroplate theory will reveal answers to two other questions: How were sediments cemented together into rocks, and what was the source of the carbon dioxide (CO_2) needed to replenish the vegetation buried during the flood?

Calcium. The floor of the subterranean chamber consisted of basalt. A major mineral in basalt is calcium feldspar. Since the subterranean waters contained a large amount of dissolved salts, especially NaCl, there would have been an abundance of sodium ions in solution. Sodium ions appear to replace the abundant calcium ions in feldspar when given an opportunity. This would explain why basalts that erupted onto the ocean floor as magma have less calcium feldspars and more sodium feldspars than expected.

This suggests several sources for calcium ions in the flood waters.

1. Magma generated during the compression event released calcium ions by ion exchange when the magma contacted sea water.
2. Calcium diffused from the basalt floor into the subterranean water during the centuries before the flood.
3. Calcium ions were in the earth's subterranean and surface waters. Those ions may have been primordial, or they may have come from dissolved limestone itself.
4. Sediments eroded from the basalt floor, having a large surface-to-volume ratio, released calcium by ion exchange. The amount can be estimated as follows.

Basalt, which contains about 43% calcium feldspar, provided 35% of the earth's sediments. (See page 95.) The fractions of calcium in limestone ($CaCO_3$) and calcium feldspar ($CaAl_2Si_2O_8$) are $\frac{40}{100}$ and $\frac{40}{276}$, respectively. Approximately 12.5% of the earth's sediments are limestone. (See page 78.) Therefore, sediments, during their contact with sea water (number 4 above), could have released 44% of the calcium

needed for the earth's limestone. This percentage is derived from:

$$\frac{0.35 \times 0.43 \times \frac{40}{276}}{\frac{40}{100} \times 0.125} = 0.44$$

Some of it could have been released years after the flood. It seems reasonable that the other three sources listed above provided the remainder.

Carbon. We also assumed the subterranean waters held an abundance of dissolved CO_2. This has some independent support since the second most abundant gas escaping from volcanoes today is CO_2. Approximately 20% of volcanic gases, by volume, is CO_2, and 70% is steam. (See Gordon A. Macdonald, p. 50.) This water and CO_2 may be a remnant of the subterranean water. If not, what could possibly be the source of the carbon? Carbon is rarely found in basement or igneous rocks.

The subterranean water could have held the needed carbon. The solubility of CO_2 in water, as a function of pressure and temperature, is shown in Table 8. The present oceans contain 1.43×10^{24} grams of water. We also assumed the subterranean chamber held about half this water. At a depth of 16 kilometers, its pressure would have been more than 4000 atmospheres. Extrapolating in Table 8 to that pressure, the solubility of CO_2 would have been about 10 grams of CO_2 for every 100 grams of water. For every 44 grams of CO_2 there are 12 grams of carbon. Therefore, the subterranean chamber could have held

$$\frac{1}{2} \times 1.43 \times 10^{24} \times \frac{10}{100} \times \frac{12}{44} = 1.95 \times 10^{22}$$

grams of carbon.

Table 8: Solubility of Carbon Dioxide in Water [2]

Pressure (Atmospheres)	Parts (Weight) CO_2 Soluble in 100 Parts Water				
	18° C	35° C	50° C	75° C	100° C
25	3.7	2.6	1.9	1.4	1.1
50	6.3	4.4	4.0	2.5	2.0
75	6.7	5.5	4.5	3.4	2.8
100	6.8	5.8	5.1	4.1	3.5
200	---	6.3	5.8	5.3	5.1
300	7.4	---	6.2	5.8	5.7
400	7.8	7.1	6.6	6.3	6.4
700	---	---	7.6	7.4	7.6

Bolin[3] has estimated that there are more than 10^{22} grams of carbon in the earth's sediments, primarily as carbonates, not just limestone. Therefore, the subterranean waters could have held the needed carbon. The earth's atmosphere and oceans, on the other hand, could not hold enough carbon without becoming toxic. Besides, today they hold only 5.6×10^{14} grams and 3.5×10^{18} grams, respectively. If the surface rocks, oceans, and atmosphere did not hold the vast carbon now locked in limestone, what was its source? Apparently, it was the highly compressed, subterranean waters.

Rapid Chemical Reaction. With both calcium ions and CO_2 in the escaping flood waters, the following chemical reactions would occur.[4,5]

$$H_3O^{1+}(aq) + HCO_3^{1-}(aq) \longrightarrow CO_2(aq) + 2H_2O(l)$$

$$Ca^{2+}(aq) + HCO_3^{1-}(aq) + H_2O(l) \longleftarrow CaCO_3(s) + H_3O^{1+}(aq)$$

The net reaction is

$$Ca^{2+}(aq) + 2HCO_3^{1-}(aq) \rightleftharpoons CaCO_3(s) + CO_2(aq) + H_2O(l)$$

The right side of this equation shows that for each mole of CO_2 gas that escaped from solution (as the high-pressure, subterranean water rose to the earth's surface), a mole of limestone would have precipitated. Later, during the flood phase, the precipitated particles would be sorted by liquefaction into more uniform layers of limestone. (See pages 134-145.)

CO_2 gas released from solution would redissolve if the surface waters were below their saturation level. If a surplus of calcium ions were in the flood waters and the waters did not become too acidic, any redissolved CO_2 would precipitate even more limestone.

The extremely tiny particles of precipitated limestone are excellent cementing agents when near-equilibrium conditions exist. The smaller and more irregular particles, having a larger surface-to-volume ratio, readily dissolve. Conversely, the larger particles grow. Cracks and gaps are easily sealed.[6] This explains why limestone rock is hard and plentiful. It was precipitated suddenly and massively over large areas while near equilibrium conditions were maintained. Many other rocks are cemented by limestone for the same reasons.

Today, limestone precipitates along the coasts of some eastern Caribbean islands. Sometimes the clear coastal waters suddenly become cloudy white. Studies of this phenomenon concluded that limestone precipitates when dissolved CO_2 suddenly degasses from water rich in calcium ions.[7] The above chemical reaction also occurs slowly on a small scale when limy water vents some CO_2 in caves, forming stalactites and stalagmites. (See **Corals and Caves** on page 22.) After the flood, such reactions in caves could have been many orders of magnitude faster. Conversely, CO_2-rich water flowing through limestone deposits will dissolve limestone and form caves and hollow underground pockets called ***karsts***.

The released CO_2 would be important for reestablishing the earth's flora. Table 8 shows that even after the flood much CO_2 would temporarily reside in the oceans. As plants removed CO_2 from the atmosphere, the oceans would release a similar amount into the atmosphere. This slow degassing of the ocean's CO_2 would result in continual precipitation of $CaCO_3$, some of it occurring between sedimentary particles, cementing the particles into rock.

This appears to explain the origin of limestone sediments on the earth, how the earth's vegetation was reestablished, and how sediments were cemented into rock. The abundance of calcium ions in the oceans after the flood may also explain the rapid growth of corals.

References and Notes

1. The generic term "limestone" is used instead of specific varieties of $CaCO_3$: calcite, aragonite, vaterite, oolites, travertine, marble, etc. The issues discussed here may also be applicable for dolomite and other carbonates.

2. *Van Nostrand's Scientific Encyclopedia*, 5th edition (New York: Van Nostrand Reinhold Company, 1976), p. 429.

3. Bert Bolin, *The Global Carbon Cycle* (New York: John Wiley & Sons, 1979), p. 5.

4. These chemical reactions are strictly correct under equilibrium conditions. While this would not be the case in the catastrophic events described here, the equilibrium reactions indicate what generally happened.

5. C. S. Patterson et al., "Carbonate Equilibria in Hydrothermal Systems: First Ionization of Carbonic Acid in NaCl Media to 300°C," *Geochimica et Cosmochimica Acta*, Vol. 46, 1982, pp. 1653-1663.

• C. S. Patterson et al., "Second Ionization of Carbonic Acid in NaCl Media to 250°C," *Journal of Solution Chemistry*, Vol. 13, No. 9, 1984, pp. 647-661.

• C. S. Patterson, personal communication, 18 November 1993.

6. C. S. Patterson, personal communication, 31 May 1995.

7. Jeffrey S. Hanor, "Precipitation of Beachrock Cements: Mixing of Marine and Meteoric Waters vs. CO_2-Degassing," *Journal of Sedimentary Petrology*, Vol. 48, No. 2, June 1978, pp. 489-501.

Illustration Credits

Figure 1: composition by Bradley W. Anderson using pictures by NASA and pictures copyright Aris Multimedia Entertainment, Inc. vi
Figure 2: design by Bradley W. Anderson using Corel Professional Photos by Jeanne White 2
Figure 3: Bradley W. Anderson 4
Figure 4: Australian Tourist Commission 5
Figure 5: NASA 6
Figure 6: used with permission of the Creation Research Society, P.O. Box 969, Ashland, OH 44805 7
Figure 7: Steve Daniels 7
Figure 8: D. L. Cramer 8
Figure 9: G. Elliot Smith, *Illustrated London News*, 24 June 1922, p. 944 9
Figure 10: Corel Professional Photos 12
Figure 11: copyright Boehringer Ingelheim International GmbH, photo by Lennart Nilsson, *The Incredible Machine*, National Geographic Society 13
Figure 12: arctic tern migration route by Bradley W. Anderson/cockpit photo by Walt Brown 14
Figure 13: drawing of microphotograph by Bradley W. Anderson 14
Figure 14: from "Learning How Bacteria Swim Could Set New Gears in Motion," by Tom Koppel, figure by Johnny Johnson. Copyright © September 1991 by Scientific American, Inc. All rights reserved 14
Figure 15: NASA 16
Figure 16: NASA 17
Figure 17: NASA 19
Figure 18: U. S. Naval Observatory 21
Figure 19: Walt Brown 21
Figure 20: used with permission of the Creation Research Society, P.O. Box 969, Ashland, OH 44805/composition by Bradley W. Anderson 23
Figure 21: composition by Bradley W. Anderson using photos by NASA 26
Figure 22: NASA 27
Figure 23: L. A. Frank, The University of Iowa 27
Figure 24: composition by Bradley W. Anderson using pictures by NASA 28
Figure 25: composition by Bradley W. Anderson using pictures copyright by Aris Multimedia Entertainment, Inc. 30
Figure 26: Steve Daniels 68
Figure 27: copyright-LANDISCOR INC. 70
Figure 28: World Ocean Floor, Bruce C. Heezen and Marie Tharp, 1977, copyright by Marie Tharp 1977, Reproduced with permission of Marie Tharp, 1 Washington Ave., South Nyack, NY 10960 72
Figure 29: U. S. Navy SEASAT satellite photo 73
Figure 30: Bradley W. Anderson 74
Figure 31: Walt Brown 74
Figure 32: Bradley W. Anderson 75
Figure 33: courtesy of the Geological Survey of Canada (photo no. GSC180345) 77
Figure 34: from "The Confirmation of Continental Drift," by Patrick M. Hurley, figure by Allen Beechel. Copyright © April 1968 by Scientific American, Inc. All rights reserved. 80
Figure 35: Bradley W. Anderson 80
Figure 36: Bradley W. Anderson 81
Figure 37: Bradley W. Anderson 83
Figure 38: Bradley W. Anderson 83
Figure 39: Steve Daniels 84
Figure 40: Steve Daniels/Bradley W. Anderson 84
Figure 41: Bradley W. Anderson 85
Figure 42: Bradley W. Anderson 85
Figure 43: Bradley W. Anderson 86
Figure 44: Steve Daniels 86
Figure 45: computer animation by Bradley W. Anderson 87
Figure 46: Bradley W. Anderson 88
Figure 47: Bradley W. Anderson 89

Figure 48: Bradley W. Anderson 89
Figure 49: Walt Brown 90
Figure 50: Walt Brown 91
Figure 51: Walt Brown 94
Figure 52: Bradley W. Anderson 95
Figure 53: Bradley W. Anderson 95
Figure 54: Bradley W. Anderson 96
Figure 55: Walt Brown 96
Figure 56: computer generated map by Bradley W. Anderson 98
Figure 57: computer generated illustration by Bradley W. Anderson 99
Figure 58: computer generated illustration by Bradley W. Anderson 99
Figure 59: courtesy of Zoological Museum of St. Petersburg 102
Figure 60: map drawn by Bradley W. Anderson 104
Figure 61: N. A. Transehe, "The Siberian Sea Road," *The Geographical Review*, Vol. 15, 1925, p. 375. 107
Figure 62: N. A. Transehe, "The Siberian Sea Road," *The Geographical Review*, Vol. 15, 1925, p. 375. 108
Figure 63: Steve Daniels 108
Figure 64: B. Willis et al., Research in China, Vol. 1 (Washington, D.C.: Carnegie Institution, 1907) 113
Figure 65: Steve Daniels 114
Figure 66: Steve Daniels 115
Figure 67: courtesy of Adrei Sher 116
Figure 68: George W. Housner 134
Figure 69: George W. Housner 134
Figure 70: Bradley W. Anderson 137
Figure 71: Walt Brown and Bradley W. Anderson 138
Figure 72: used with permission/anonymous 140
Figure 73: Walt Brown 141
Figure 74: Walt Brown 141
Figure 75: Walt Brown 142
Figure 76: Bradley W. Anderson 142
Figure 77: Australia's Northern Territory Tourist Commission 142
Figure 78: Australia's Northern Territory Tourist Commission 142
Figure 79: Bradley W. Anderson 143
Figure 80: Walt Brown 143
Figure 81: Walt Brown 143
Figure 82: Bradley W. Anderson 146
Figure 83: Gerhard Heilmann from *The Origin of Birds*, p. 168 148
Figure 84: courtesy of N. Chandra Wickramasinghe from *Archaeopteryx: The Primordial Bird*/design by Bradley W. Anderson 148
Figure 85: courtesy of N. Chandra Wickramasinghe from *Archaeopteryx: The Primordial Bird* 149
Figure 86: courtesy of N. Chandra Wickramasinghe from *Archaeopteryx: The Primordial Bird* 149
Figure 87: National Institute of Standards and Technology, Boulder, CO 154
Figure 88: National Optical Astronomy Observatories a) W. Schoening/N. Sharp b) NOAO c) T. Boroson d) NOAO e) NOAO f) N. A. Sharp/composition by Bradley W. Anderson 155
Figure 89: NASA 158
Figure 90: design by Peggy Brown and Bradley W. Anderson using Corel Professional Photos and photo by Bradley W. Anderson 163
Figure 91: Michihimo Yano 165
Figure 92: Michihimo Yano 165
Figure 93: Ian Taylor 165
Figure 94: photograph of a drawing of a plesiosaur from the Fraas Stuttgart Museum by Ian Taylor 165
Figure 95: Bradley W. Anderson 172
Figure 96: Walt Brown 177
Figure 97: Walt Brown 178
Figure 98: Bradley W. Anderson 182
Figure 99: Walt Brown 185
Figure 100: Bradley W. Anderson 186

Index

marine 120
material 151
meteorite 63
missing trunk 9
out-of-place 9, 45
plants 44
polystrate 8
Precambrian 141
rapid burial 7–8, 139
record 8, 41–44, 53, 81, 110, 131, 174
sea life on mountains 81
sequence 22
sorted 135, 138, 140–141, 144
Steinheim 10
superposition 138
termite 61
transitional 40–43, 148, 174
        See also *fossil inter-mediate*
tree trunks 76
Vertesszöllos 10
vertical sequence 9
with frozen mammoths 120, 123, 127
wood 107
fossil gaps 8, 40
fossil man 10, 47
  Calaveras skull 10, 47
  Castenedolo skeleton 10, 48
  Reck's skeleton 10
  Steinheim fossil 10
  Swanscombe skull 10
  Vertesszöllos fossil 10
fossil museum 4
fossilized cocoons 9
fossilized nests 9
fountain 84
fountains of the great deep 69, 84–85, 88, 115, 119
Fox, P. J. 93
Fraas Stuttgart museum 165
fracture zone 73–74, 76, 85–86, 95–97
Franks, Louis A. 64
Freedman, David H. 53
Freedman, Wendy L. 57
frequency-modulated radar 13
frictional
  drag 95
  heat generation 75, 87–88, 92, 100
  resistance 75–77, 92
Frings, Hubert 39
Frings, Marie 39
frog 37, 39
Frohlich, Cliff 100
frozen mammoths 31, 71, 76, 93, 103–132
frozen rhinoceroses 76
fruit flies 5, 34
fully-developed organs 5, 36
furcula 149

▲────────────

G

Galapagos Islands 4, 89
galaxies 19–21, 29, 155–156
galaxy 29, 56–59, 66, 153, 155–156, 158–159
  cluster 19, 29, 56–57, 66
  clusters 56
  distribution 56
  elliptical 57
  formation 59
  Milky Way 15, 21, 29, 56, 66, 156–158, 160
  observable 20
  spiral 21, 29, 155–156
  unstable 29, 66
galaxy clusters 29, 66
gallup poll 168
Gamwell, Thomas P. 63
Ganges Canyon 76
Gasbang, Walter 40
Geikie, Archibald 62
Geller, Margaret J. 56, 59
gene 161, 163
generation 158, 161, 163
genes 3–5, 7, 34, 36–37, 39, 51, 53
genetic 161
genetic characteristic 161, 163
genetic distances 11, 50
genetic information 11, 13, 50–51
genetic material 4, 6, 11
genetic potential 161
genetics 3, 32–35, 42, 163, 174
Gentry, Robert V. 59, 63
geocentric theory 93
geologic column 22, 60–61, 63
geologic record 40–41
geologist 78
George, T. Neville 44
geothermal gradient 94
geothermal heat 31, 71, 78, 88
Germany 7, 78, 88, 150
Ghosh, A. K. 44–45
gibbon 9
gigantic explosions 159
Gillespie, C. M. Jr. 65
Gilmore, Gerard 56
giraffe 3
Gish, Duane T. 46, 49, 170–171, 174
glacial retreat 92
glacier
  advance 120
  compared to rock ice 112, 121
  formation of 76, 92
  frozen mammoths 121–122
  in Siberia 122
  retreat 92
glaciers and the ice ages 31, 71, 76
Glaessner, Martin F. 40, 44
Glish, Gary L. 63
globular cluster 158–159
Glock, W. S. 153
goat 37
Gold, Thomas 64
Goldberger, Robert F. 49
Golden Gate bridge 91

Goldschmidt, Richard B. 34–35, 42
Golenberg, Edward M. 61
gorilla 43, 46
gosling 161
Goulay, Marcel 52
Gould, Meredith 52
Gould, Stephen Jay 37, 40, 42, 44, 46, 163
gradual development 9
grammar 5–6, 38
Grand Canyon 8–9, 22, 44–45, 97, 141–142
  compared to ocean trenches 75
  compared to submarine canyons 76
  consequence of 83
  cross-section 142
  formation of 70, 90, 97, 99
  inner gorge 87, 91
Grand Canyon and other canyons 31, 71
Grand Lake 90, 97–99
  elevation of 90
  location 98
  location of 90
  map 98
  map of 98
granite 78–79, 86–88, 94–95, 97, 186
  crushed 78
Grassé, Pierre-Paul 34–35
gravitational acceleration 186
gravitational attraction
  forming galaxies 21, 56, 59
  forming planets 18
  of binary stars 20
  of planets 26
  of sun & moon 136
  on sea floor 73
gravitational forces 159
gravity
  and Colorado plateau 79
  anomaly beneath mountains 97
  effect on hydroplates 74, 97
  effect on ice 112
  effects on light 20
  effects on subduction 185
  of black holes 20
  of Mercury 25
  of singularity 20
  of Venus 18, 25
Gray, Asa 36
Gray, Ginny 50
Grayloise, Presse 40
Great Salt Lake 79, 90
Greece 163
Green, David E. 49
Gregory, Stephen A. 56
Gribbin, John 65
Guatemala 163
Gunnison River 91
Guste, William J. Jr. 37
Guth, Alan H. 57
Guthrie, R. Dale 127–129, 132
Guyana 9
guyot
  See also *tablemount*

▲────────────

H

Häberlein, Ernst 149
Häberlein, Karl 149
Haeckel, Ernst 7, 39–40
Haldane, J. B. S. 53
half-life 151, 152
Hammond, Allen L. 46
handedness, left and right 11, 51
Hanor, Jeffrey S. 189
Hapgood, Charles H. 128–132
Hardy, A. C. 47
Harwit, Martin 58
Hasiotis, Stephen T. 45
Hasofer, Michael 156
Haymes, Robert C. 55
heat conduction 78
heavy elements 158
Hecht, Max K. 61
Heezen, Bruce C. 144
Heide, Fritz 63
Heidelberg man 10
Heisler, Julia 64
helium 17–20, 24, 56, 62–63, 65, 158
Helmick, Larry S. 59
hemophilia 34
Herz, O. F. 110, 128–131
hidden assumptions 21, 82, 153, 167, 171
Hill, William Charles Osman 43
Himalayan Mountains 88, 90
Himmelfarb, Gertrude 37
His, Wilhelm 40
Hitching, Francis 32, 35, 39, 41, 46, 48, 51, 171
Hitler, Adolf 161
Hodapp, Klaus-Werner 55
Hodge, Paul W. 59
Hodgkin's disease 7
Holland 163
Holm, Richard W. 39
Holmes, Francis S. 45
Holmes, William H. 47
Homo erectus 9, 46
Homo habilis 9, 46
homologous structures 39
honeybee 12
hoofprints 9, 166
Hopi Lake 91, 97–98
  elevation of 91
  location of 91
Hoppe, Kathryn 61
horizon 138–139
Hornaday, William T. 128
Hornbacher, Dwight 145
horse 9, 37–38
host 7
hot moon 26, 64
hot planets 27, 65
Hotton, Nicholas 170
Housner, George 144
Howe, George F. 39, 45, 64, 174
Howell, F. C. 170
Howorth, Henry H. 126–130, 132
Hoyle, Fred 36, 50, 52, 54, 57–58, 66, 131–132, 149–151, 171
Hsu, Kenneth J. 94

newt 39
Newton, Isaac 35, 83
Nicholson, Thomas D. 64
Nilsson, Lennart 13
Nilsson, N. Heribert 34–35, 38, 43, 52
nitrogen 10, 48, 111, 151
Noé, A. C. 45
Nolan, Edward J. 45
nonliving matter 3
Noorbergen, Rene 62
Nordenskiold, A. E. 126, 130
Norman, J. R. 44
Norman, Trevor 156
North America 41, 45, 71, 74–75, 79–80, 87, 106, 111, 132, 165
Novotny, Eva 58
nuclear fusion 27, 29
nuclear reaction 157
nuclear winter 92
nucleotide 11, 38, 51

O

O stars 21, 58
O'Connell, Patrick 46
O'Rourke, J. E. 60
Obolensky, Alexis Guy 157
observatory
  Royal Greenwich 28
  U.S. Naval 28, 154
ocean floor 15, 24, 71–76, 78, 80, 87, 89, 92–93, 97, 188
ocean floor map 72–73
ocean trench 71, 75, 91
offspring 3–4, 11–12
Okinawa 163
old DNA 22, 61
olivine 92, 100
Olsen, Roger L. 175
Ommanney, Francis Downes 43
ontogeny recapitulates phylogeny 39–40
Ontong-Java Plateau 78
Oort cloud 64
open invitation to a written debate 176
orbit
  backward 17
  binary stars 20–21
  circular 18
  cometary 26, 28
  inclined 17
  Moon 18
  Phoebe 17
  rings 27
orbital time 154, 157
organic evolution 3, 15, 32, 40–41, 44, 50, 131
Orgel, Leslie E. 51
origin of the moon 18, 55
origins research project 167, 168–173
Osborn, Henry Fairfield 36
OSCs 74, 95–96
Ostrom, John H. 150

outer space 156, 159–160
out-of-place fossils 9, 45
ovaries 7
Ovcharov, V. 45, 166
overlapping spreading center 74, 93, 95
overthrust 31, 45, 71, 77, **186**
Oxnard, Charles E. 46–47
oxygen 10, 22, 48, 111, 119, 132, 151
ozone 10

P

Pääbo, Svante 61
Pacific Ocean 74–75, 78, 88, 91
Page, Don N. 55
paleontologist 15, 33, 40–42, 60
paleontology 38, 41–42, 60–61
Paley, William 36
Palmer, Ralph S. 128
Paluxy River 166
Paneth, F. A. 63
Pappas, T. 157
parallel layers 8, 23, 62
parallel strata 8
parasite 7, 12
Parker, Gary E. 170–171, 175
parsimony 81
Patrusky, Ben 56
Patterson, C. S. 189
Patterson, Colin 41, 49–50
Peebles, P. J. E. 59
Peking man 9
Penniston, John B. 130
personal involvement 167–168
pesticide 4
Peter the Great 127
Peterson, Ivars 36, 56, 58–59, 144
Petit, Charles 55
petrified forest 9
Pettersson, Hans 63
Péwé, Troy L. 130, 132
Pfizenmayer, E. W. 110, 127–130
phase transformation 92
phenotype 39
Phillips, W. D. 157
phosphate beds 9
photosynthesis 15, 82
Pierce, Michael J. 57
pig's tooth 9
Piltdown 46
Piltdown man 9
Pithecanthropus erectus 46
Pitman, Michael 34, 40, 43, 49, 53
Pixie, N. W. 52
placebo 59
Planck's constant 154
planet 16, 32, 48–49, 51, 53–55, 59, 65, 154, 156, 159
  angular momentum 17
  backward orbit 17
  backward-spinning 17
  composition 17
  Earth 16–25, 27–29
  evolution 18
  evolving 18

formation 17–18, 20
  gaseous 18
  giant 18
  gravitational attraction 26–27
  hot 27
  inclined orbit 17
  Jupiter 16–18, 27, 55, 65
  Mars 5, 16–17, 27, 54, 154
  Mercury 16–17, 25, 54, 154
  Neptune 16–18, 27, 54–55, 65
  nonspinning 18
  Pluto 16–17
  rocky 18
  Saturn 16–18, 27, 55, 65
  spin 18
  strange 17
  unique 16
  Uranus 16–18, 27, 52, 55, 65
  Venus 16–19, 25, 27, 54–55, 65, 154
planetesimal 54
plant 44, 52, 61
  amino acids in 11–12
  buried in flood 8
  buried in Siberia 107, 109, 121, 124
  carbon-14 in 151–152
  distinct types 5
  DNA 22
  extinct 42
  flowering 9, 81
  fossil gaps 8
  fossil record 42
  fossilization of 81, 85
  found in mammoth's stomach 110–111
  immune system 13
  in rock ice 111–112
  in yedoma soil 112
  index fossil 22
  left and right handedness 12
  marine 15
  missing trunk 9
  mutations 33
  origin 43
  patchwork 5
  poisonous 12
  pollen-bearing 12
  radiocarbon dating 151
  sexual reproduction in 12
  symbiotic relationships 12
  transitional 41
  vascular 9, 15
  yucca 12
plate tectonic theory 73–75, 93–94, 96
plate tectonics 44, 93
  coal in Antarctica 76
  crashing plates 94
  earthquake explanation 100
  fracture zones 74, 96
  lacking explanations 71, 74, 93
  magnetic anomalies 76
  overlapping spreading centers 74
  plate movement 75, 93
  subduction 75
  trench formation 75
plateau 71, 79

Colorado 79, 90
Columbia 88, 90
Deccan 78, 88
definition of 79
formation of 89–90
Kaibab 98
problems of forming 79
Tibetan 79, 90
plateaus 31
platypus 5
plesiosaur 15, **164–166**
plume 141, 143–144
Pluto 16–17
  backward spinning 17
Poinar, George O., Jr. 61
Poinar, Hendrick N. 61
poisonous gases 159
pollen 9, 12, 45
polls 168
polystrate trees 7
pooled water 97
Popov, A. I. 130
Popov, Y. N. 130
population 161, 163
porpoise 13, 15
postflood lake 90
Powell, Corey S. 58
Powell, Jerry A. 52
Poynting-Robertson effect 27, 65
Precambrian 44, 140–142
Precambrian rock 9
precipitation 92
precision 153–154, 157
  definition 157
predator 37, 44
prediction
  binary stars 156
  bubbles in rock ice 119
  fracture zones 96
  fracture zones and magnetic intensity 97
  genetic distances 50
  loess in Antarctica 119
  made by evolution 131
  magnetic intensity and black smokers 97
  moon dust 64
  muck and rock ice 119
  muck on Siberian plateaus 119
  pooled water under mountains 97
  radiocarbon dating mammoths 120
  rock ice is salty 119
  salty water trapped in granite 97
  stopping earthquakes 92
  test of scientific theory 82
  undisturbed rock ice 120
  unwillingness to make 131
  V-shaped canyons 91
  young radiocarbon dates 152
preflood
  Earth 83
  forests 151
  hilltops 119
  mantle 100

In the Beginning: Compelling Evidence for Creation and the Flood (Sixth Edition) is meticulously documented and 240 pages of full color. It is sure to captivate readers of all backgrounds. This edition contains many Biblical questions and insights in addition to the scientific case for creation. Order this expanded edition from bookstores or directly from CSC.

The *In The Beginning Seminar* is a 6-7 hour program that examines Genesis and science. Over 140 of these popular programs, conducted by Dr. Walt Brown, have been held throughout the U.S. and Canada. For more information about how to schedule a seminar in your area, write to CSC at the address below. Please indicate the size of the auditorium where the seminar would be held and the full name and address of the potential seminar host.

To obtain additional copies of this book, order from your local bookstore or directly from CSC. You may pay with a check, money order, or credit card.

Name	Date
Address	Telephone
City/State/Zip	
Credit Card: Visa / Master Card	Exp. Date:
Card Number:	Signature:

Quantity	Item	Price Each	Total
	In the Beginning (sixth edition, softcover)	$17.95	
	In the Beginning (sixth edition, hardcover)	$24.95	
	In the Beginning (special edition softcover)	$17.95	
	In the Beginning (special edition hardcover)	$24.95	
		Sub-Total	
		Postage	
		TOTAL	

Book Rate Postage & Handling Charges:

For orders up to $25.00	$2.50
$25.00 to $50.00	$3.50
$50.00 to $95.00	$4.50
Postage to Canada add:	$2.00
Allow 2-3 weeks for delivery.	

Please send order to:

CSC
5612 North 20th Place
Phoenix, AZ 85016

Prices subject to change without notice.

Bulk order inquiries welcome.